A CONCISE HISTORY OF SCOTTISH WORDS, THEIR MEANING AND ORIGINS

The Auld Scots Dictionary

by
CHARLES MACKAY

LANG SYNE PUBLISHERS LTD.

The Auld Scots Dictionary, a facsimile reprint of A Dictionary of Lowland Scotch. (Whittaker & Co. 1888)

Published by Lang Syne Publishers Ltd
Strathclyde Business Centre.
120 Carstairs Street, Glasgow G40 4DJ.
Tel: 0141 554 9944
Printed by JSB Print
107 Coltness Lane, Queenslie Industrial Estate.
Glasgow G33 4DR
Tel: 0141 766 3355

First Published 1992 Reprinted 1995, 2002 and 2003.

DICTIONARY OF LOWLAND SCOTCH.

A

Ae, the indefinite article *a*, or one, and far more emphatic in poetical composition than *ane* or *one*, as in Burns's beautiful song "*Ae* fond kiss and then we sever." Some of the many half-English editors of the Scottish poet have altered *ae* into "one," which to a Scottish ear is the reverse of an improvement. *Ae* does not merely signify one, but *only one*, and is definite and particular, not indefinite and general, in its meaning.

Aboon, above.

Aiblins, perhaps, possibly; from *able*, conjoined with *lin* or *lins*, inclining to, as in the "westlin wind"—wind inclining to the west; hence *aiblins* means inclining to be possible.

> There's mony waur been o' the race,
> And *aiblins* ane been better.
>
> —BURNS: *The Dream.*
> *To George III.*

Aidle, ditchwater; derivation unknown, but possibly from the Gaelic *adhall*, dull, heavy, stagnant.

> Then lug out your ladle,
> Deal brimstone like *aidle*,
> And roar every note of the damned.
> —BURNS: *Orthodox, Orthodox.*

Ail at. *What ails ye at?* is a peculiarly Scottish synonym for What is your objection to her, him, or it?

An old servant who took a charge of everything that went on in the family, having observed that his master had taken wine with every lady at the table except one who wore a green dress, jogged his memory with the question, "*What ails ye at her in the green gown?*"—DEAN RAMSAY.

Air, early, from the Gaelic *ear*, the east, where the sun rises. "An air winter makes a sair winter;" which may be Englished, "An early winter makes a surly winter."

Airt, a point of the compass; also to direct or show the way. This excellent word ought to be adopted into English. It comes from the Gaelic *ard*, *aird*, a height. "Of a' the *airts* from which the wind can blaw," is better than "of all the *quar-*

ters from which the wind can blow."

> O' a' the *airts* the wind can blaw,
> I dearly lo'e the west,
> For there the bonnie lassie lives,
> The lassie I lo'e best.—BURNS.

> But yon green graff (grave), now huskie green,
> Wad *airt* me to my treasure.—BURNS.

Aizle, a live coal that flies out of the fire. It is a superstition in England to call the live coals violently ejected from the fire by the gas generated in them by the names of "purses" or "coffins," according to the fanciful resemblance which they bear to these articles, and which are supposed to be prophetic of money, or of a death in the family. Some such superstition seems to lie at the root of the Scottish word *aizle.*

> She noticed that an *aizle* brunt
> Her braw new worset apron.
> —BURNS : *Hallowe'en.*

Jamieson says the word was used metaphorically by the poet Douglas to describe the appearance of a country that has been desolated by fire and sword. In the Gaelic, *aisleine* signifies a death-shroud. The derivation, which has been suggested from hazel or hazel-nut, from the shape of the coal when ejected, seems untenable. The Gaelic *aiseal,* meaning joy, merriment, has also been suggested, as having been given by children to the flying embers shot out from the fire; but the derivation from *aisleine* seems preferable.

Anent, concerning, relating to. This word has only recently been admitted into the English dictionaries published in England. In Worcester's and Webster's Dictionaries, published in the United States, it is inserted as a Scotticism. Mr. Stormonth, in his Etymological Dictionary (1871), derives it from the Anglo-Saxon *ongean* and the Swedish *on gent,* opposite ; but the etymology seems doubtful.

> The anxiety *anent* them was too intense to admit of the poor people remaining quietly at home.—*The Dream Numbers, by* T. A. TROLLOPE.

Arl-penny, a deposit paid to seal a bargain ; earnest-money ; French *arrhes.* From the Gaelic *earlas* or *iarlas,* earnest-money, a pledge to complete a bargain.

> Here, tak' this gowd, and never want
> Enough to gar ye drink and rant,
> And this is but an *arl-penny*
> To what I afterwards design ye.
> —ALLAN RAMSAY.

Asse, the fireplace ; the hearth ; the place where the ashes or cinders fall. Asse-hole or ash-pit is supposed by some philologists to be derivable from the Gaelic *aisir,* a receptacle ; *ais,* the back part of anything, or backwards.

> Do ye no see Rob, Jock, and Hab,
> As they are girded gallantlie,
> While I am hurklin i' the *asse* ?
> I'll hae a new cloak about me.
> —*Ancient Ballad : Tak' your Auld Cloak about ye.*

Athol brose, whisky with honey, taken as a morning drop ; a powerful and indigestive mixture, that no one but a Highlander out in the open air and in active exercise during the whole day can safely indulge in. Why it is named from the district of Athol in preference to any other part of the Highlands is neither known nor perhaps discoverable.

An' aye since he wore tartan trews
He dearly lo'ed the *Athole brose*,
And wae was he, you may suppose,
To play farewell to whisky.
　　　　　　—NEIL GOW.

Auld lang syne. This phrase, so peculiarly tender and beautiful, and so wholly Scotch, has no exact synonym in any language, and is untranslatable except by a weak periphrasis. The most recent English dictionaries have adopted it, and the expression is now almost as common in England as in Scotland. Allan Ramsay included in "The Tea-Table Miscellany" a song entitled "Old Long Syne," a very poor production. It remained for Robert Burns to make "Auld lang syne" immortal, and fix it for ever in the language of Great Britain, America, and the Antipodes. *Lang sin syne* is a kindred, and almost as beautiful a phrase, which has not yet been adopted into English.

A wee, a short time ; contraction of a "*wee* while," or a little while. *Bide-a-wee*, wait a little.

Upon a summer afternoon,
A *wee* before the sun gaed doun.
　　　　　　—*The Lass o' Gowrie.*

Awmrie, a chest, a cabinet, a secretaire ; from the French *armoire.*

Close the *awmrie*, steek the kist,
Or else some gear will soon be missed.
—SIR WALTER SCOTT : *Donald Caird.*

Ayont, beyond or on the other side. A Northumbrian as well as a Scottish word. In the English Border "*ayont* the Tweed" is Scotland, and on the Scottish side of the Border it is England.

B

Bab. Any personal adornment worn by young lovers, either a bunch of flowers on the bosom, or a tassel or bow of ribbons. *Lug-bab*, an ear-ring ; *wooer-babs*, a knot of ribbons tied at the knee by the young peasant lads when they went courting. The word also signifies a cockade or other badge in the hat or bonnet.

Bauble is possibly of similar or the same origin. The word is derived from the Gaelic *babag* or *baban*, a tassel, a fringe, a knot, a cluster ; and *babach*, innocent pleasure, applied to the *bab* as a symbol.

A cockit hat with a *bab* o' blue ribbons at it.
　—SIR WALTER SCOTT : *Old Mortality.*

Bairn-time, a whole family of children, or all the children that a woman bears. This peculiarly Scottish word is a corruption of a *bairn-teem ;* from the Gaelic *taom*, the English *teem*, to bear, to produce, to pour out.

Your Majesty, most excellent !
  While nobles strive to please ye,
Will ye accept a compliment
  A simple Bardie gi'es ye ?
Thae bonny *bairn-time* Heaven has lent,
  Still higher may they heeze ye !
    —BURNS : *A Dream, Addressed to George III.*

The following lines, from "The Auld Farmer's New Year's Salutation to his Auld Mare, Maggie," show that Burns understood the word in its correct sense, though he adopted the erroneous spelling of *time* instead of *teem :*—

My pleugh is now thy *bairn-time* a',
Four gallant brutes as e'er did draw,
Forbye sax mae I sellt awa',
    That thou has nurst ;
They drew me thretteen pounds an' twa,
    The very warst.

Balow ! An old lullaby in the Highlands, sung by nurses to young children, as in the pathetic ballad entitled "Lady Anne Bothwell's Lament : "—

Balow ! my babe, lie still and sleep,
It grieves me sair to see thee weep !

Burns has "*Hee, baloo !*" to the tune of "The Highland *Balow :*"—

Hee, *baloo*, my sweet wee Donald,
Picture of the great Clanronald.

The phrase is derived from the Gaelic *bà*, the equivalent of *bye*

in the common English phrase "Bye ! bye ! " an adjuration to sleep—"Go to bye-bye ; " and *laogh*, darling, whence, by the abbreviation of *laogh* into *lao*, *bà-lao* or *balow*—"Sleep, darling." Jamieson has adopted a ludicrous derivation from the French—"*bas là le loup*," which he mis-translates " Be still ; the wolf is coming."

Bandster, one who makes a band or binds sheaves after the reapers in the harvest-field.

In hairst at the shearing, nae youths now
    are jeering,
  The *bandsters* are lyart and wrinkled
    and grey ;
At fair or at preaching, nae wooing or
    fleeching,
  The flowers o' the forest are a' weed
    away.
    —ELLIOT : *The Flowers of the Forest.*

In this pathetic lament for "the flowers" of Ettrick Forest —the young men slain at the doleful battle of Flodden—the maidens mourn in artless language for the loss of their lovers, and grieve, as in this touching stanza, that their fellow-labourers in the harvest-field are old men, wrinkled and grey, with their sparse locks, instead of the lusty youths who have died fighting for their country. The air of this melancholy but very beautiful song is pure Gaelic.

Bane-dry, dry as a bone ; *bane-idle*, thoroughly idle ; not only idle in the flesh, but in the bone and marrow.

Bang, to beat, to subdue; *bangie* or *bangsome*, quarrelsome, irritable, apt to take offence; *bang-beggar*, a constable or a constable's staff, and *bangree*, a scolding, irritable, and contentious woman. The etymology of these words is uncertain. The last seems to be derivable from the Gaelic *ban*, a woman; *banag*, a busy little woman; *ban cheaird*, a female tramp or gipsy.

Bannock, an oatmeal cake, originally compounded with milk instead of water.

Hale breeks, saxpence, and a *bannock*.
—Burns: *To James Tait, Glenconner.*

Bannocks o' bear-meal, bannocks o' barley.
—*Jacobite Song.*

From the Gaelic *bainne*, milk.

Bap, a small wheaten cake or roll, sold in Scotland for breakfast when porridge is not used. The grandfather of a late Prime Minister of Great Britain kept a small shop in Leith Walk, Edinburgh, where he sold "baps," flour, oatmeal, peas, &c., and where he was popularly known to the boys of the neighbourhood as "Sma' Baps," because his baps were reputed to be smaller than those of his brother tradesmen.

Barken, to clot, to harden on the surface, as some viscous and semi-liquid mixtures do on exposure to the air. The word is derived from the bark or outward covering of trees.

Barm, yeast; old English; not yet obsolete in the rural districts.

Barmkin, a corruption of *barbican*, a watch-tower on a castle or fortress. The derivation of *barbican* (the name of a street in old London, still retained) is from the Gaelic *bar*, a pinnacle or high place; and *beachan*, a place of watching or observation. From *beachan* is derived *beacon*, a watch-fire, a signal light.

And broad and bloody rose the sun,
And on the *barmkin* shone.
.   .   .   .   .
And he called a page who was witty
and sage
To go to the *barmkin* high.
—*Border Minstrelsy: Lord Soulis.*

Bauch, insipid, tasteless, without flavour, as in the alliterative proverb:—

Beauty but bounty's but *bauch*.
—Allan Ramsay.

(Beauty without goodness is without flavour.)

The etymology of this peculiarly Scottish word is uncertain, unless it be allied to the English *baulk*, to hinder, to impede, to frustrate; or from the Gaelic *bac*, which has the same meaning.

Baudrons, a pet name for a cat, for which no etymology has yet been found. The word remains as unaccountable as "Tybert," used by Shakspeare for the same animal.

Auld *baudrons* by the ingle sits,
Wi' her loof her face a washin'.
—Burns: *Sic a Wife as Willie had.*

Bauk, the cross-beam in the roof of a cottage; *baukie-bird,* a name given to the bat, that haunts the roof. *Bauk* is from the English *baulk,* of which the primary meaning was from the Gaelic *bac,* to hinder, to frustrate, and was applied to the cross-beam of the roof because it prevented the roof from giving way, and to other wooden partitions necessary for division. It also came to signify to disappoint, because disappointment was the prevention or *hindering* of the fulfilment and realisation of hope.

When lyart leaves bestrew the yird,
Or, waverin' like the *baukie-bird,*
      Bedim cauld Boreas' blast,
An' hailstanes drive wi' bitter skyte.
      —BURNS : *The Jolly Beggars.*

Bawbie, a halfpenny—metaphorically used for a fortune by Sir Alexander Boswell, the son of the more famous James Boswell, the biographer of Dr. Johnson. It occurs in the song of "Jennie's Bawbie:"—

Quoth he, " My goddess, nymph, and queen,
Your beauty dazzles baith my e'en,"
But deil a beauty had he seen
      But Jennie's *bawbee.*

Sir Alexander took the hint of his song from a much older one :—

A' that e'er my Jeanie had,
My Jeanie had, my Jeanie had,
A' that e'er my Jeanie had
      Was ae *bawbie.*
There's your plack, and my plack,
And your plack, and my plack,
      And Jeanie's *bawbie.*

Bawsont or **bawsins,** marked with white on the face, as in cattle ; of uncertain etymology, but possibly connected with *bash,* the forehead.

The stirk stands i' the tether,
   And our braw *bawsint* yade
Will carry ye hame your corn ;
   What wad ye be at, ye jade ?
      —*Woo'd and Married and a'.*

Bawtie, a watch-dog ; apparently from the Gaelic *beachd,* watch, observe, and *tigh* (pronounced *tee*), a house. A favourite name in Scotland for a faithful dog. The English word *Towser,* which is equally common, is also from the Celtic *tuisle,* to struggle or contend with.

Bourd na' in *Bawtie,* lest he bite (*i.e.,* do not play tricks or jest with the watchdog, lest he bite you).

Bazil, a sot, a fool ; of unknown etymology, but possibly connected with the Gaelic *peasanach,* an impertinent person.

He scorned to sock mang weirdless fellows,
Wi' menseless *bazils* in an alehouse.
      —GEORGE BEATTIE : *John o' Arnha'.*

Beak or **beek**—common in Ayrshire and Mearns—to sit by a fire and exposed to the full heat of it.

                           A lion,
To recreate his limbs and take his rest,
Beakand his breast and bellie at the sun,
Under a tree lay in the fair forest.
—ROBERT HENRYSON *in The Evergreen :
      The Lion and the Mouse.*

Beastie, an affectionate diminutive of *beast,* applied to any small and favourite animal.

Wee, sleekit, cowerin', timorous *beastie,*
Oh, what a panic's in thy breastie !
Thou needna start awa sae hastie,
　　Wi' bickerin' brattle.
　　　　　—BURNS : *To a Mouse.*

Beck, to curtsey.

" It's aye gude to be ceevil," as the auld wife said when she *beckit* to the deevil.— ALLAN RAMSAY'S *Scots Proverbs.*

Bed-fast, confined to bed or bed- ridden. In English, *fast* as a suffix is scarcely used except in *steadfast, i.e.,* fast fixed to the *stead* place or purpose.

For these eight or ten months I have been ailing, sometimes *bed-fast* and some- times not.—BURNS : *Letter to Cunning- ham.*

　　An earth-fast or *yird-fast* stane is a large stone firmly fixed in the earth. *Faith-fast, truth-fast,* and *hope-fast* are beau- tiful phrases, unused by English writers. If *faithful* and *truth- ful, faithless* and *truthless,* are permissible, why not *faith-fast, truth-fast,* and *hope-fast ?*

Beet, to feed or add fuel to a fire or flame ; from the Gaelic *beatha,* life, food, and *beathaich,* to feed, to nourish.

May Kennedy's far-honoured name
Lang *beet* his hymeneal flame.
　　　　　—BURNS : *To Gavin Hamilton.*

　It warms me, it charms me,
　　To mention but her name ;
　It heats me, it *beets* me,
　　And sets me a' aflame.
　　　　　—BURNS : *Epistle to Davie.*

I wonderin' gaze on her stately steps,
　And *beet* my hopeless flame.
　　　—ALLAN CUNNINGHAM : *Bonny Lady Ann.*

Beltain, the fire of Bel or Baal, kindled by the Druids annually on the first morning of May direct from the rays of the sun. Ben Ledi, in Perthshire—the hill of God, as the name signi- fies in Gaelic—was the most sacred of all the hills, on the summit of which this imposing ceremony was performed. The name of Bel or Baal is derived from the Gaelic *beatha* or *bea* (*th* silent), life, and *uile,* all ; whence Bel, Beul, or Baal, the life of all, and *tain,* a corrup- tion of *teine,* the fire. The cere- mony was also performed in Ire- land in pre-Christian times on the 21st of June. The word "Beltane" is of frequent occur- rence in the ballad poetry of Scotland, and in conjunction with " Yule " or Christmas is by no means obsolete ; as in the phrase, " The love that is hot at Beltane may grow cauld ere Yule."

Belyve, by-and-bye, immediately. This word occurs in Chaucer and in many old English ro- mances.
　　　Hie we *belyve*
　And look whether Ogie be alive.
　　　　　—*Romance of Sir Otuel.*

Belyve the elder bairns come droppin' in.
　　—BURNS : *Cotter's Saturday Night.*

Bicker, a drinking-cup, a beaker, a turn ; also a quarrel.

　Fill high the foaming *bicker !*
Body and soul are mine, quoth he,
　I'll have them both for liquor.
　　　—*The Gin Fiend and his Three Houses.*

Setting my staff wi' a' my skill
 To keep me sicker;
Though leeward whiles, against my will,
 I took a *bicker.*
—BURNS: *Death and Doctor Hornbook.*

Bicker means rapid motion, and, in a secondary and very common sense, quarrelling, fighting, a battle. Sir Walter Scott refers to the *bickers* or battles between the boys of Edinburgh High School and the Gutterbluids of the streets. In "Hallowe'en" Burns applies *bickering* to the motion of running water :—

Whiles glistened to the nightly rays,
 Wi' *bickerin'*, dancin' dazzle.
—R. DRENNAN.

Bide, to stop, to delay, to wait, to dwell or abide.

Bield, a shelter. Of uncertain etymology, perhaps from *build.*

Better a wee bush than nae *bield.*
Every man bends to the bush he gets *bield* frae.
 —ALLAN RAMSAY'S *Scots Proverbs.*

Beneath the random *bield* of clod or stane.
 —BURNS: *To a Mountain Daisy.*

Bien, comfortable, agreeable, snug, pleasant; from the French *bien*, well. Lord Neaves was of opinion that this derivation was doubtful, but suggested no other. If the French etymology be inadmissible, the Gaelic can supply *binn*, which means harmonious, pleasant, in good order; which is perhaps the true root of the word.

While frosty winds blaw in the drift
 Ben to the chimla lug,
I grudge a wee the great folk's gift
 That live sae *bien* and snug.
 —BURNS: *Epistle to Davie.*

 Bien's the but and ben.
 —JAMES BALLANTINE: *The Father's Knee.*

Bier or **beir**, a lament, a moan.

As I went forth to take the air
 Intil an evening clear,
I spied a lady in a wood
 Making a heavy *bier;*
Making a heavy *bier*, I wot,
 While the tears dropped frae her e'en,
And aye she sighed and said Alas!
 For Jock o' Hazelgreen.
 —*Old Ballad, on which* SIR WALTER SCOTT *modelled his "Jock o' Hazeldean."*

Jamieson says that *beir* (not *bier*) is allied to the Icelandic *byre*, a tempest, and to old English *bri, byre, bine*, force; but it is of more probable origin in the Gaelic *buir*, to lament, to whine; whence probably the prevalence of the custom among the Celtic nations of moaning over the dead body, and chanting the doleful coronach or death-wail, came afterwards to be applied to the *bier*, or table, board, or plank, on which the corpse was extended, or the coffin in which it was placed.

Bigly, beautiful; origin unknown.

Will ye come to my *bigly* bower,
 An' drink the wine wi' me?
—BUCHAN'S *Ancient Scottish Ballads.*

Billies, fellows, comrades, young men; a term of familiarity and affection.

When chapman *billies* leave the street,
And drouthy neebors neebors meet.
 —BURNS: *Tam o' Shanter.*

Rise up! rise up now, *billie* dear,
 Rise up! I speak these words to see
Whether thou'st gotten thy deadly wound,
 Or if God and good leaching may succour thee.—*Border Minstrelsy.*

"This word," says Jamieson,

"is probably allied to German *billig*, the Belgian *billiks*, equals, as denoting those that are on a footing as to age, rank, relation, affection, or employment."

This is an error. In German, *billig* means moderate in price, fair, just, equitable, reasonable. The Lowland Scotch *billie* is the same as the English *fellow ;* and both are derived from the Gaelic *ba-laoch*, a shepherd, a cowherd, a husbandman ; from *ba*, cows, plural of *bo*, a cow, and *laoch*, a lad, a young man.

Bink or **bunker**, a bench ; called in America a *bunk.*

> I set him in beside the *bink*,
> And gied him bread and ale to drink.
> —HERD'S *Collection : The Brisk Young Lad.*

A winnock (window) *bunker* in the east,
Where sat Auld Nick in shape o' beast.
> —BURNS : *Tam o' Shanter.*

Bird or **burd**, a term of endearment, applied to a young woman or child.

> And by my word, the bonnie *bird*
> In danger shall not tarry,
> And though the storm is raging wild,
> I'll row ye o'er the ferry.
> —THOMAS CAMPBELL.

Birdalane or **burdalane.** A term of sorrowful endearment, applied to an only child, especially to a girl, to signify that she is without household comrades or companions.

> And Newton Gordon, *birdalane*,
> And Dalgetie both stout and keen.
> —SCOTT'S *Minstrelsy.*

Birkie, a young and conceited person ; from the Gaelic *biorach*,

a two-year-old heifer ; *bioraiche*, a colt ; applied in derision to a very young man who is lively but not over-wise.

> Ye see yon *birkie* ca'd a lord,
> Wha struts and stares and a' that.
> —BURNS : *A Man's a Man.*

" And besides, ye donnard carle ! " continued Sharpitlaw, " the minister did say that he thought he knew something of the features of the *birkie* that spoke to him in the Park."—SCOTT : *Heart of Midlothian.*

" Weel, Janet, ye ken when I preach you're almost always fast asleep before I've well given out my text ; but when any of these young men from St. Andrews preach for me, I see you never sleep a wink. Now that's what I call no using me as you should do." " Hoot, sir," was the reply, " is that a' ? I'll soon tell you the reason o' that. When you preach, we a' ken the Word o' God is safe in your hands ; but when thae young *birkies* tak it in hand, ma certie ! but it tak's us a' to look after them."—DEAN RAMSAY.

Birl, to pour out liquor ; probably from the same root as the English *purl*, as in the phrase " a purling stream," probably derived from the ancient but now obsolete Gaelic *bior*, a well ; *bioral*, pertaining to a well or like a well.

There were three lords *birling* at the wine
On the dowie dens o' Yarrow.
> —MOTHERWELL'S *Ancient Minstrelsy.*

Oh, she has *birled* these merry young men
With the ale, but and the wine.
—Border Minstrelsy : Fause Foodrage.

Birs, the thick hair or *bristles* on the back of swine.

> The souter gave the sow a kiss.
> Humph ! quo' she, it's a' for my *birs* !
> —ALLAN RAMSAY'S *Scots Proverbs.*

Bismeres or **bismar**, the keeper of a brothel, a bawd ; from the

Gaelic *baois*, lust, lewdness, and *mathair* (pronounced *ma-air*), mother; also a prostitute. Jamieson derives the word from the Anglo-Saxon, and quotes Rudd —" *Bismer*, contumelia, aut *bismerian*, illudere, dehonnorare polluere." The Gaelic derivation is more satisfactory than that from the hybrid language called Anglo-Saxon, which is but inchoate and primitive old English based upon corrupted Celtic, with superadded Dutch and Flemish.

Bit and brat. To earn " bit and brat " is to earn food and raiment ; from the Gaelic *biadh*, food, and *brat*, a rag, a garment, or clothing.

Bittock, a small bit or piece. When a wayfarer on the road asks of a chance passer-by at what distance is the place to which he is bound, the probable reply is, that it is two, three, or any other number of miles " and a *bittock*," signifying that the respondent will not pledge himself to the exactitude of his reply, adding, with the proverbial cautiousness popularly ascribed in England to his countrymen, that there may be a *bittock* added to his computation ; though the qualifying *bittock* has often been found to exceed the primary estimate.

Black - mail. The word *mail* is derived from the Gaelic *màl*,

rent, tax, or tribute ; and *màla*, a bag, a sack, a purse, a budget to contain the tribute. Why the particular exaction called *black - mail*, levied by many Highland chieftains in former times to ensure the protection of the herds of cattle passing through their territories to southern markets, received the epithet of *black* has never been clearly explained. The word has been supposed by some to designate the moral turpitude and blackness of character of those who exacted such a tax, and by others it has been conjectured that *black*-mail derived its name from the *black* cattle of the Highlands, for whose protection against thieves and caterans the tribute was levied ; while yet another set of etymologists have set forth the opinion that *plack*-mail, not *black*-mail, was the proper word, derived from the small Scottish coin— the *plaque* or *plack*—in which the tribute was supposed to be collected. But as *mail* is undoubtedly from the Gaelic, and as *black-mail* was a purely Highland extortion, and so called at a time when few resident Highland chiefs and none of their people spoke English, it is possible that *black* is not to be taken in the English sense, but that it had, like its associated word, *mail*, a Gaelic origin. In that language, *blathaich*—pronounced (the *th* silent) *blá-aich*— signifies to protect, to cherish. Thus *black-mail* meant the tribute or tax of protection. If *black*, the colour, were really intended, the Highlanders would have used their own word and called the tribute *màl-dubh*. The Gaelic *blathaich* has the secondary meaning of to heat. In the same sense, the Flemish has *blaken*, to warm, to animate, to burn. In connection with the idea of warming, the Scottish language has several words which can scarcely be explained by *black* in the English sense. The first is *black-burning*, which Jamieson says is " used in reference to shame when it is so great as to produce deep blushing, or to *crimson* the countenance." This phrase is equivalent to the English, *a burning shame*, when the cheeks burn or glow, not with black, but with red. The second is *black-fishing*, which Jamieson defines as fishing for salmon by night by means of *torches*. He explains the epithet *black* in this instance by suggesting that "the fish" are *black* or foul when they come up the streams to deposit their spawn, an explanation which is wholly inadmissible. The third and fourth phrases are *black-foot* and *black-sole*, which both mean " a confidant in love affairs, or one who goes between a lover and his mistress endeavouring to bring the cold or coy fair one to compliance." In these instances, *black* is certainly more related to the idea of warming, inciting, animating, than to that

of blackness. *Black-foot* and *black-sole* in reality mean *hot*-foot and *hot*-sole, as in the corresponding phrase, *hot-haste*, applied to the constant running to-and-fro of the go-between. *Black-winter*, which signifies, according to Jamieson, " the last cart-load of grain brought home from the harvest-field," is as difficult as either of the phrases previously-cited to associate with the idea of *blackness*, either moral or physical; but rather with that of comfort, warmth—or provision for the winter months. The winter itself may be metaphorically black, but not by any extension of meaning or of fancy can the epithet *black*, in colour, be associated with a *cart-load of grain*. There are two other equivalent phrases in Scottish use in which *black* is an epithet, namely, *black victual*, meaning pulse, beans and peas, and *black crop*, which has the same signification. Jamieson says these crops are so called because they are always *green*, and extends the meaning to turnips, |potatoes, &c., for the same reason ! But *black* cannot be accepted as equivalent to *green*.

Of all the derivations ever suggested for *black-mail*, the word on which this disquisition concerning *black* started, the most unfortunate is that of Jamieson, who traces it to " the German *blakmal*, and to the Flemish *blaken*, to rob." It is sufficient for the refutation of

Jamieson to state that there is no such word as *blakmal* in the German language, and that *blaken*, as already observed, does not signify to rob, but to burn. In conclusion, it may be stated that the English *black* has long been a puzzle to the compilers of dictionaries. There is no trace of it to be found in the sense of colour in any of the Teutonic languages. *Black* in German is *schwarz;* in Dutch, Flemish, and Swedish, *swart;* in Danish, *svaerte;* and in old English, *swarth* and *swarthy.*

Worcester's Dictionary derives *black* from *bleak.* Mr. Wedgwood, who is one of the latest authorities, says "the original meaning of *black* seems to have been exactly the reverse of the present sense, viz., shining white. It is, in fact," he adds, "radically identical with the French *blanc,* from which it differs only in the absence of the nasal."

Perhaps it may be possible, *ex fumo dare lucem*, to kindle a light out of all this smoke. May not the real root of the English *black* (as a colour) be the Gaelic *blàaich*, or the Flemish *blaken*, to burn? That which is *burned* is *blackened.* A *black* man, or negro, is one whose skin has been tanned or burned by the sun; and *sun-burnt* in this case means *blackened.* It may be said of this explanation, whether correct or not, that it is at all events entitled to as much consideration as those from *bleak*

and *blanc,* and that it is far more probable than either.

Black saxpence, supposed in Scottish superstition to be a magical sixpence given by the Devil in payment for the soul of the person who accepted it. The virtue of this "black" sixpence consisted in its having always a bright sixpence alongside of it; that as soon as it was taken away and spent, it was replaced by another, and so on to the "crack of doom." Jamieson supposed that the infernal sixpence was so named from its colour; but possibly, and more probably, it was thus designated from the Gaelic *blathaich*, protection, as being a protection against absolute poverty as long as the unholy compact existed. See *Black-mail* and *Black-Watch* for this sense of the word *black.*

Black-Watch, a name given to the Highland regiment, the brave and very distinguished Forty-Second, which has fought, bled, and conquered in many a hard-won field in every part of the world, where its services were required to vindicate the right and uphold the honour of Great Britain. It is generally supposed that the name was given to them on account of the dark colour of the tartan which they wear; but the tartan is not black, but very dark green, like the tartans of many Highland clans, in which green is the predominant hue, varied by black, blue, red, or yellow stripes in some of them. It is possible, however, that *black* in this instance, as in *blackmail*, &c. (which see), signifies protection, and that the popular name of the illustrious regiment in question signifies the "*protecting* watch."

Blae, of a livid blue colour, sickly blue.

Blaeberries, bilberries.

> The morning *blae* and wan.
> —DOUGLAS : *Translation of the Æneid.*

> How dow you this *blae* eastlin' wind,
> That's like to blaw a body blind ?
> —BURNS.

> Be in dread, O sirs ! Some of you will stand with *blae* countenances before the tribunal of God.
> —BRUCE : *The Soul's Confirmation.*

Blash, a gust of wind.

> Amidst a glint o' sunshine comes a *blash* o' cauld sleet.—*Noctes Ambrosianæ.*

Blate, shy, modest, bashful; of unknown derivation. *Bleid* in Gaelic is the reverse of *blate* in Lowland Scotch, and means impertinent, troublesome, forward, presuming.

> Says Lord Frank Ker, Ye are na' *blate*
> To bring us the news o' yer ain defeat.
> —*Jacobite Ballad : Johnnie Cope.*

> A *blate* cat makes a proud mouse.
> —ALLAN RAMSAY.

Blaud, to lay anything flat with violence, as the wind or a storm of rain does the corn.

Curst common sense, that imp o' hell,

> . . . . .
> This day M'Kinlay takes the flail,
> And he's the boy will *blaud* her.
> —BURNS : *The Ordination.*

> Ochon ! ochon ! cries Haughton,
> That ever I was born
> To see the Buckie burn rin bluid,
> And *blauding* a' the corn.
> —*Aberdeenshire Ballad.*

Blavers. The blue cornflower.

> Blavers that grow amid white land.
> —BUCHAN'S *Ancient Ballads : The Gardener Lad.*

Blaw-i'-my-lug, a flatterer, a cajoler, a wheedler ; one who *blows* fair words into the ear of a ready listener for a selfish or sinister purpose.

Bledoch, skim-milk ; from the Gaelic *bleodhach* or *bleoghann*, to milk.

> She kirned the kirn and scummed it clean,
> Left the gudeman but *bledoch* bare.
> —ALLAN RAMSAY'S *Evergreen: The Wife of Auchtermuchty.*

Blether, to talk nonsense, to be full of wind like a bladder, *Bletherskite*, nonsense.

Blethers, nonsense, impertinence. *Blaidry*, foolish talk, from the Gaelic *blaidaireachd*, and *bleidir*, impertinence. *Bletherum-skate* or *bletherum-skite*, sometimes corrupted into *bladderskate*, are derivatives of this word, " ' Ye *blethrin loon* ' and ' ye *skyte*,' " says Cromek, the editor of the " Remains of Nithsdale and Galloway Song, " are terms of familiar reproach still in use, and are applied to those satiric rogues who have the art of mingling falsehood with truth with admirable art."

Stringing *blethers* up in rhyme
For fools to sing.
—BURNS: *The Vision.*

Fame
Gathers but wind to *blether* up a name.
—BEAUMONT AND FLETCHER.

Some are busy *bletherin*
Right loud that day.
—BURNS: *The Holy Fair.*

Right scornfully she answered him,
Jog on your gate, you *bladderṣkate*—
My name is Maggie Lauder.
—SEMPLE: *Maggie Lauder.*

"She's better to-night," said one nurse to another. "Night's come, but it's not gone," replied her helpmate, in the full hearing of the patient, "and it's the small hours'll try her." "The small hours'll not try me as much as you do with your *blethering* tongues," remarked the patient with perfect *sang-froid.—A Visit to the London Hospitals,* March 23, 1870.

I knew Burns's "Blethering Bitch," who in his later years lived in Tarbolton, and earned a scanty living by breaking stones on the road. In taking a walk round the hill mentioned in "Death and Dr. Hornbook," I came upon Jamie Humphrey (such was his name) busy at work, and after talking with him a short time, I ventured to ask him, "Is it true, Jamie, that you are Burns's *blethering bitch* ?" "Aye, deed am I, and mony a guid gill I hae gotten by it !" This was a broad hint ; but I did not take it.—R. DRENNAN.

Blinter, to flicker like a flame about to expire for want of nourishment.

Blirt, a sudden burst of grief or anger, also to weep, sob, and lament simultaneously. A "blirt of greeting" signifies an outburst of tears. The English

blurt is akin to the Scottish *blirt,* though not exactly synonymous, and is principally used to signify a sudden and unpremeditated disclosure of what ought to have been kept secret, as in the phrase "He blurted out the truth," or "He blurted out an oath." The root both of *blirt* and *blurt* is the Gaelic *blaor,* to cry out or roar, and *blaorte,* cried out or roared.

Blob, a large round drop of water or other liquid. A similar word, *bleb,* now obsolete, was once used in England to signify an air-bubble, and, in its form of *blebster,* is the root of *blister.*

We look on this troubled stream of the generations of men to as little purpose almost as idle boys do on dancing *blebs* or bubbles on the water. — SIR THOMAS MORE : *Consolations of the Soul.*

Her e'en the clearest *blob* o' dew out-shining.—ALLAN RAMSAY.

The bonnie red rose,
Wet wi' the *blobs* o' dew.
—ALLAN CUNNINGHAM.

Blouter, to bluster or talk idly ; Gaelic *bladair,* to talk idly.

Cacklin' aboutl Coleridge or *blouterin'* about Byron.—*Noctes Ambrosianæ.*

Blunk, to mismanage or spoil anything by clumsy, inexpert, or stupid handling ; also a dull, stolid, and foolishly inert person. Jamieson thinks it is derived from the Icelandic *blunda,* sleepy-headed. It is more probably from the Gaelic *blonach* or *blonag,* fat, greasy ; whence fat-headed and stupid.

Bluntie. In the Dictionary of the Scottish Language by an anonymous author (Edinburgh, 1818), *bluntie* is described as a stupid fellow. Jamieson has "*blunt,* stupid, bare, naked," and "*bluntie,* a sniveller," which he derives from the Teutonic *blutten,* homo stolidus.

> They mool me sair, and haud me doun,
> And gar me look like *bluntie,* Tam ;
> But three short years will soon wheel roun',
> And then comes ane-and-twenty, Tam.
> —BURNS.

The etymology of the English word *blunt* is uncertain, but as it signifies the opposite of sharp, the Scottish *bluntie* may be accepted as a designation of one who is not sharp or clever. No English dictionary suggests any etymology that can reasonably be accepted, the nearest being *plump,* round, or rounded without a point. "*Blunt,*" the slang word for money, is supposed by some to be derived from the name of Sir John *Blunt,* a rich director of the South Sea Company in the year 1720.

Bob, to make a curtsey, to bend, to bow down.

> Sweet was the smell of flowers, blue, white, and red,
> The noise of birds was maist melodious,
> The *bobbing* boughs bloom'd broad abune my head.
> —R. HENRYSON : *The Lion and the Mouse.*

> When she cam' ben she *bobbit.*
> —CHAMBERS'S *Scottish Songs.*

> Weel done, quo' he ; play up, quo' she ;
> Weel *bobb'd,* quo' Rob the Ranter,
> It's worth my while to play indeed
> When I hae sic a dancer.
> . —*Maggie Lauder.*

> When she came ben she *bobbit.*—BURNS.

> Out came the auld maidens a' *bobbin'* discreetly.
> —JAMES BALLANTINE : *The Auld Beggar Man.*

> When she came ben she *bobbit* fu' low,
> And what was his errand he soon let her know.
> Surprised was the laird when the lady said Na !
> As wi' a laigh curtsie she turned her a wa.
> —*The Laird o' Cockpen.*

Bodle, a small Scottish coin, of less value than a *bawbee,* the sixth part of an English penny.

> Black Madge, she is prudent, has sense in her noddle,
> Is douce and respectit ; I care na' a *bodle.*
> —JOANNA BAILLIE.

Bonailie, a parting drink, a stirrup-cup ; a *deoch an dorus,* offered to and partaken with a departing guest, with wishes for a good and pleasant journey ; a *bon voyage.* The word, sometimes written *bonalais* or *bonally,* is a corrupt spelling of the French *bonne allée,* or *bon aller.*

Bonnie, beautiful, good-natured, and cheerful—the three qualities in combination—as applied to a woman ; applied to natural objects, it simply signifies beautiful, as in "Ye banks and braes o' *bonnie* Doon." This is an old English word, used by Shakespeare and Ben Jonson, and still current in the Northern English counties, as well as in Scotland.

Bonnieness, a word that conveys the sense of both prettiness and goodness, that are sometimes, but ought never, to dwell apart.

Bonnieness gaed to the water to wash,
And prettiness gaed to the barn to thrash ;
Gae tell my maister to pay me my fee,
For *bonnieness* winna let prettiness be.
—CHAMBERS's *Scottish Songs.*

Bonspiel, sport or play.

I hae been at mony a bonspiel, but I ne'er saw such a congregation on the ice before.—*Noctes Ambrosianæ.*

Boodie, a ghost, a sprite, a hobgoblin ; by some derived from *bode*, a message, the German *bote*, a messenger, and by others, with more probability, from the Gaelic *bodach*, a spectre—a word which is also applied irreverently to an ill-favoured and churlish old man.

Borrow, to ransom, and not, as in English, to effect a loan.

And in cam' her brother dear,
  A waeful man was he.
I'd gie a' the lands I hae,
  Bonnie Jean, to *borrow* thee.
Oh, *borrow* me, brother, *borrow* me,
  Or *borrowed* I'll never be,
For I gar'd kill my ain dear lord,
  An' life's nae pleasure to me.
    —*The Laird o' Warristoun.*

Bourack or **bourock**, a name given by children to the little mounds of sand or earth that they raise on the sea-shore or in their playgrounds in imitation of castles or houses ;—a diminutive, apparently, of the word *bower*, a lady's chamber. The word is sometimes used for a shepherd's hut or shieling. In

some parts of Scotland it signifies a heap or mound of any kind, and also metaphorically a heap or crowd of people.

We'll ne'er big *bourocks* i' the sand together (*Old Proverb*), *i.e.*, we'll never be familiar or closely allied in sentiment or purpose.

Bourd, a jest, a joke ; also to jest, to play tricks with. In old English, *bord*. From the Gaelic *burt*, mockery.

The wizard could no longer bear her *bord*,
But, bursting forth in laughter, to her said.
    —SPENSER : *Faerie Queene.*

I'll tell the *bourd*, but nae the body.
A sooth *bourd* is nae *bourd*.
They that *bourd* wi' cats may count upon scarts.
    —ALLAN RAMSAY's *Scots Proverbs.*

Bouse, to drink deeply, to revel ; whence the colloquial English word "boozy."

Then let him *bouse* and deep carouse
  Wi' bumpers flowing o'er,
Till he forgets his loves and debts,
  And minds his griefs no more.—BURNS.

And though bold Robin Hood
Would with his Maid Marian
Sup and *bouse* from horn and can.
    —KEATS.

Brae, the brow or side of a hill ; from the Gaelic *bruaich*, a hill side, a steep.

We twa hae run about the *braes*,
  And pu'd the gowans fine,
But mony a weary foot we've trod
  Sin auld lang syne.—BURNS.

Brander, a gridiron, also a toasting-fork ; from the Teutonic *brennen*, to burn ; *gebrannt*, burned.

Brander, a gridiron, *i.e.*, a burner, on which to submit food to the direct action of the fire without the intervention of water; from the Teutonic *brennen*, to burn, and *gelvannt*, burnt.

Brander-bannock, a cake heated on a gridiron; a common mode of preparing oaten cakes in Scotland.

Brankie, gaudy, showy. *Brankit*, vain, conceited, proud of one's fine clothes. *Brankin'* a great show of finery.

Where hae ye been sae braw, lad?
    Where hae ye been sae *brankie*, O?
Where hae ye been sae braw, lad?
    Cam' ye by Killicrankie, O?
        —JOHNSON'S *Musical Museum.*

Branne, the calf of the leg; whence the English *brawny*, muscular.

Your stocking shall be like the cabbage leaf,
    That is baith braid and lang,
Narrow, narrow at the cute (the instep or ankle),
    And braid, braid at the *branne.*
        —*Ballad of the Gardener, from Kinloch's Collection.*

Brash, a sickness, a rash, an eruption.

The lady's gane to her chamber,
    A moanful woman was she,
As gin she had taken a sudden *brash*,
    An' were about to dee.
        —*The Gay Gosshawk.*

Brash, a sudden gust of wind, also a tuzzle or fight; *brashy* or *braushie*, stormy.

Brat, a rag or clothes; from the Gaelic *brat*, a covering, a mantle,

a rag; also *bratach*, a flag, a banner; whence perhaps the contemptuous English term of *brat*, for a beggar's child, in allusion to the rags in which it is clad.

We've aye had *bit* and *brat*, John,
    Great blessings here below;
And that helped to keep peace at home,
    John Anderson my jo.
—*From the old version of* " *John Anderson my Jo," abridged, amended, and purified by* ROBERT BURNS.

Bratchet, a contemptuous or angry term for a troublesome or mischievous child; a diminutive of *brat*, a child, so called from the Gaelic *brat*, a rag; synonymous with another Scottish phrase for a poor man's child, as used by Burns, "a smytrie o' wee *duddie* (ragged) weans."

Brattle, clatter, or any noise made by the rapid collision of hard substances; possibly from *be-rattle*, the augmentative of the English word *rattle*.

List'ning the doors an' windows rattle,
I thought me on the ourie cattle,
Or silly sheep, that tide the *brattle*
    O' winter war.
        —BURNS: *A Winter Night.*

Breathin'. "I'll do't in a *breathin'*," instanter, in the time which it would take to draw a breath. This phrase is far superior to the vulgar English "in a jiffy," or to the still more intolerable slang "the twinkling of a bedpost."

Bree, the juice, the essence, the spirit. Barley-*bree*, the juice of the barley, *i.e.*, whisky or ale.

B

Brew is to extract the spirit or essence of barley, malt, hops, &c. Both *bree* and *brew* are directly derived from the Gaelic *brigh*, spirit, juice, &c. The Italians have *brio*, spirit, energy, life, animation. From this source is derived the English slang word a "*brick*," applied to a fine, high-spirited, good fellow. Various absurd attempts have been made to trace the expression to a Greek source in a spurious anecdote borrowed from Aristotle, who speaks of a *tetragonos aner* or "four-cornered man," supposed in the slang of the Universities to signify a *brick*.

Breeks, the nether garments of a man, trousers, trews, breeches. The vulgar English word *breeches* is derived from the *breech*, the part of the body which they cover. The Scottish word has a more dignified origin in the Gaelic *breaghad*, attire, dress, or-nament, and *breaghaid*, adorn, embellish, "from which Celtic word," says Ainsworth in his Latin Dictionary, "the Romans derived *bracca* and *braccatus*, wearing trews, like the Gauls."

> Thir *breeks* o' mine, my only pair,
> I wad hae gien them aff my hurdies
> For ae blink o' the bonnie burdies.
> —BURNS: *Tam o' Shanter.*

Brent or **brant**, high, steep; also smooth.

> Her fair *brent* brow,
> Smooth as the unwrinkled deep.
> —ALLAN RAMSAY.

> John Anderson my jo, John,
>   When we were first acquaint,
> Your locks were like the raven,
>   Your bonnie brow was *brent.*
> —BURNS: *John Anderson my Jo.*

In " John Anderson my Jo," the auld wife means that her husband's brow was smooth. I believe that *brent* in this pas-sage is the past-participle of *burn.* Shin-ing is one of the effects of burning. I think the word is always used to mean smooth, unwrinkled—as in the Scottish phrase *brent* new, the English' *bran* new, shining with all the gloss of newness.— R. DRENNAN.

Brim, fierce, disastrous, fatal, furious; from the Gaelic *brea-mas*, mischief, mischance.

> The *brim* battle of the Harlaw.
> —ALLAN RAMSAY: *The Evergreen.*

Bring home, to be delivered of a child.

> Now when nine months were past and gone,
> The lady she *brought home* a son.
> —BUCHAN'S *Ballads: Lord Dingwall.*

Brook, to spot, or soil, or blacken with soot ; *brookit*, having a dirty face; and *brookie*, a nick-name either for a sweep or a blacksmith. *Bruckit* is tanned by the sun or freckled. The root is the Gaelic *brucach*, spotted, freckled, speckled, par-ticularly in the face.

Broostle, to perspire profusely; also to be in a great hurry, bustle, or confusion. From the Teutonic *braus*, bustle, noise, or tumult ; *brausen*, to ferment, to rush, to roar, to snort with anger or impatience.

Brownie, a household sprite in the ancient and not yet extinct superstition of Scotland, who, if conciliated, performed domestic duties, and made himself useful and agreeable, similar in his character to Puck or Robin Good-fellow in England. From the Gaelic *bronn*, a gift, a favour.

Brown study. This phrase, to signify deep, sad, or melancholy meditation, was originally Scotch, but has long become familiar in English. It has puzzled all the philologists, who persist in deriving almost every English word and phrase from the Teutonic, the Greek, or the Latin, to the exclusion of the Celtic, from which even these three languages are largely derived. But they have made no guesses superior to that which would trace it to a *brow* study, because those who fall into brown studies often knit their brows in deep thought! The real source of the word is the Gaelic *bron*, sorrow, grief, sadness, melancholy, mourning; *bronag*, a sorrowful woman; *bron bhrat*, a mourning cloth, a cerement or mortcloth; *bronach*, sorrowful, and *bronadh*, lamentation. This explanation ought to satisfy even the Keltophobists, and teach them to "rest and be thankful" in their study of this particular colloquialism.

B r u i k, to enjoy, to possess; from the Teutonic *brauchen*, to make use of. *Was braucht es?* What is the use of it?

Weel *bruik* ye o' yon broun, broun bride,
  Between ye and the wa',
And sae will I o' my winding-sheet,
  That suits me best of a'.
    —JAMIESON'S *Collection : Ballad of
      Lammikin.*

Brulzie or **brulyie**, a disturbance, a commotion, a quarrel. This word seems to be the root of the English *brawl, broil, embroil,* and *embroilment,* and the French *embrouiller ;* all derivable from the Gaelic *bruill,* to crush, to beat, to fight, to thrash.

Bannocks o' bear-meal, bannocks o' barley !
Wha' in a *brulzie* will first cry a parley?
Never the lads wi' the bannocks o' barley ;
Here's to the Highlandman's bannocks o'
  barley !
    —JOHNSON'S *Musical Museum.*

Brumble, to make a rumbling noise. The English *rumble* and the Lowland Scotch *brumble* are synonymous, and both appear to be derived from the Teutonic *brummen,* to rush audibly like a rapid stream ; to gurgle, to growl.

Bryttle, to cut up venison.

And Johnnie has *bryttled* the deer sae weel,
And has feasted his gude blude-hounds.
    —*Border Minstrelsy : Johnnie of
      Braidislie.*

Bubbly-jock, a turkey-cock.

Some of the idiot's friends coming to visit him at a farmhouse where he resided, reminded him how comfortable he was, and how grateful he ought to be for the care taken of him. He admitted the fact, but he had his sorrows and troubles like wiser men. He stood in awe of the great turkey-cock of the farm, which used to run and gobble at him. "Aye! aye!" he said, unburthening his heart, " I'm very weel aff, nae doubt ; but eh ! man, I'm sair hadden doun by the *Bubbly-jock !* " DEAN RAMSAY.

Buckie, a whelk or periwinkle.

An' there'll be partans [crabs] an' *buckies*.
      —*The Blithesome Bridal.*

Buckle-to, to marry ; derived from the idea of fastening or joining together. The word occurs in a vulgar English song to a very beautiful Scottish air, which was written in imitation of the Scottish manner by Tom D'Urfey in the reign of Charles II. It has been long popular under the title of " Within a Mile of Edinburgh Town."

Buckle-beggar signified what was once called a *hedge-priest*, who pretended to perform the ceremony of marriage. To " *buckle* with a person " was to be engaged in argument with another.

" **Buff nor stye**," a common colloquialism. To say of any one that " he would neither buff nor stye," means that he would neither do one thing or another, that he did not know his own mind, or that he was so obstinately wedded to his own purpose that nothing could make him deviate from it. It is probably a corruption of " he would neither *be off* nor *stay*." Jamieson, however, derives *buff* from the Teutonic *bof*, a cheer made by mariners ; and thinks that *stye* may refer to the act of mounting the shrouds, from the Swedish

stiga, to ascend ! He has thus had recourse to two languages to help him out of a difficulty, when one, and that his own, would have been sufficient.

He would neither *buff nor stye* for father or mother, friend or foe.—GALT : ⌊*The Entail.*

Buirdly, strong and stalwart, hearty, well-built.

Buirdly chiels [fellows]
Are bred in sic a way as this is.
      —BURNS : *The Twa Dogs.*

Burnewin, a contraction of " Burn-the wind," the popular and familiar name for a blacksmith.

Busk, to adorn, to dress ; from the Gaelic *busgadh*, a head-dress, an adornment for the person ; *busgainnich*, to dress, to adorn, to prepare.

A bonnie bride is soon *buskit*.
      —ALLAN RAMSAY'S *Scots Proverbs.*

Busk ye, busk ye, my bonnie bride,
Busk ye, busk ye, my winsome marrow.
      —HAMILTON *of Bangor.*

But. This word in Scotland long preserved the meaning it once had in England of "without," and was derived etymologically from "be out," of which it is an abbreviation. It remains in the heraldic motto of the Clan Chattan, " Touch not the cat *but* the glove ! " It does duty in the humorous Jacobite song, in ridicule of George I., the Elector of Hanover :—

Wha the deil hae we gotten for a king,
  But a wee, wee German lairdie ;
And when we gaed to bring him hame,
  He was delvin' in his yairdie,
Sheughin kail and layin' leeks,
But the hose, and *but* the breeks,
And up his beggar duds he cleeks,
  The wee, wee German lairdie.

But and ben, the out and in, the
  front and back rooms of a
  cotter's hut.

Toddlin *but* and toddlin *ben*,
I'm nae sooner slockened, than drouthy
  again.
      —SIR ALEXANDER BOSWELL : *A
            Matrimonial Duet.*

Had siller been made in the kist to lock by,
It wadna been round, but square as a dye,
Whereas by its shape ilka body may see
It aye was designed it should circulate free.
Then we'll toddle *but*, and we'll toddle *ben*,
An' aye when we get it, we'll part wi't
  again.—*Ibid.*

Byspel, an accidental piece of
  good fortune; a wonderful
  stroke of luck or dexterity. An
  epithet applied, generally in a
  half-hearted spirit of laudation,
  to any person of rare good
qualities or successful rise in
the world; as in the phrase
" He's just a *byspel*." The word
is from the Teutonic *beispiel*, an
example; literally a *by-play*. In
this sense it is sometimes held
to signify an illegitimate or
a love-child, a " by-blow," a
bastard.

Byssim, a monster, also a
worthless and shameless woman.
Supposed to be from the Icelandic *bysn*, a monster, a pro-
digy. The German *böse*, wicked,
and the Gaelic *baois*, lust, libi-
dinousness, and also madness,
have been suggested as the
root of this word. A third
derivation is worthy of study,
that from *baoth* (*bao*), wicked,
and *smuain*, thoughts, whence
bao - smuain, quasi bissim or
byssom, a wicked thought, or
a person with wicked thoughts.
The word *Bezonian*, which has
puzzled Shakespearian commentators to explain, may be allied.

C

Ca', to drive, or drive in, to smite ;
  also to contend or fight; from
  the Gaelic *cath*, pronounced *ca'*,
  to smite, to fight.

I'll cause a man put up the fire,
  Anither *ca'* in the stake,
And on the head o' yon high hill
  I'll burn you for his sake.
BUCHAN'S *Ballads : Young Prince James.*

Every naig was *ca'd* a shoe on,
The smith and thee got roaring fu' on.
      —BURNS : *Tam o' Shanter.*

Ca' cannie ! an exhortation to beware, to take heed or care as to
  what you are doing or saying;
  ca', to drive, and *cannie*, cautious or cautiously.

Cadgie—sometimes written *caigie*
  — cheerful, sportive, wanton,
  friendly ; possibly from the old
  Gaelic *cad*, a friend, whence,
  according to some philologists,

cadie, a lad (used in the sense of kindness and familiarity); but, according to others, from the French *cadet,* a younger born.

> A cock-laird fu' *cadgie*
> Wi' Jeanie did meet;
> He haused her, he kissed her,
> And ca'd her his sweet.
> —CHAMBERS'S *Scottish Songs.*

> Yon ill-tongued tinkler, Charlie Fox,
> May taunt you wi' his jeers and shocks;
> But gie't him het, my hearty cocks,
> E'en cowe the *cadie!*
> And send him to his dicing-box
> And sportin' lady.
> —BURNS: *Author's Earnest Cry and Prayer.*

Cair, to strain through. "This word," says Jamieson, "is used in Clydesdale, and signifies to extract the thickest part of broth or hotch-potch while dining or supping." It is probably from the Gaelic *cir,* a comb; whence also the English word to *curry* a horse, and *curry-*comb, the comb used for the purpose.

Caird, a tinker.

> Close the awmrie, steek the kist,
> Or else some gear will soon be miss'd;
> Tell the news in brugh and glen,
> Donald *Caird's* come again.
> —SIR WALTER SCOTT.

From the Gaelic *ceard,* a smith, a wright, a workman; with the prefix *teine,* fire, is derived the English *tin-caird* or *tinker,* a fire-smith. Johnson, ignorant of Celtic, traced *tinker* from *tink,* because tinkers struck a kettle and produced a tinkling noise to announce their arrival.

Caller, fresh, cool. There is no exact English synonym for this word. " *Caller* herrin," " *Caller* haddie," and " *Caller* ow" are familiar cries to Edinburgh people, and to all strangers who visit that beautiful city.

> Sae sweet his voice, sae smooth his tongue,
> His breath's like *caller* air;
> His very foot has music in't
> When he comes up the stair.
> —MICKLE: *There's nae Luck about the House.*

> Upon a simmer Sunday morn,
> When Nature's face is fair,
> I walked forth to view the corn
> And snuff the *caller* air.
> —BURNS: *The Holy Fair.*

Camsteerie, crooked, confused, unmanageable; from the Gaelic *cam,* crooked, and *stiuir,* to steer or lead.

> The phalanx broken into pieces like *camsteerie* clouds.—*Noctes Ambrosianæ.*

Cannie, knowing, but gentle; not to be easily deceived, yet not sly or cunning. A very expressive word, often used by Englishmen to describe the Scotch, as in the phrase, "a canny Scotsman," one who knows what he is about. The word also means dexterous, clever at a bargain, and also fortunate. It is possibly derived from the Gaelic *ceannaich,* to buy; and is common in the North of England as well as in Scotland.

> Bonny lass, *canny* lass, wilt thou be mine?
> —*The Cumberland Courtship.*

> He mounted his mare and he rode *can-nilie.*
> —*The Laird o' Cockpen.*

Hae naething to do wi' him ; he's no *canny.*

They have need of a *canny* cook who have but one egg for dinner.
—ALLAN RAMSAY's *Scots Proverbs.*

Cantie, joyous, merry, talkative from excess of good spirits ; from the Gaelic *cainnt*, speech, or *can*, to sing.

Contented wi' little and *cantie* wi' mair.
—BURNS.

Some cannie wee bodie may be my lot,
An' I'll be *cantie* in thinking o't.
—BROCKETT's *North Country Glossary: Newcastle Song.*

The *cantie* auld folks.
—BURNS : *The Twa Dogs.*

The clachan yill had made me *cantie.*
—BURNS : *Death and Dr. Hornbook.*

Cantrip, a charm, a spell, a trick, a mischievous trick. The word is a corruption of the Gaelic word *ceann*, head, chief, principal, and *drip*, a trick.

Coffins stood roun' like open presses,
That showed the dead in their last dresses ;
And by some devilish *cantrip* slight,
Each in its cauld hand held a light.
—BURNS : *Tam o' Shanter.*

Burns, in the "Address to the Deil," has another example of this word, in which the humour is great and the indecency greater.
—LORD NEAVES.

Capernoity, peevish, crabbed, apt to take offence, of singular and uncertain humour.

"Me forward !" answered Mrs. Patt ; "the *capernoity*, old, girning ale-wife may wait long enough ere I forward it !"—
SCOTT : *St. Ronan's Well.*

Gaelic, *cabair*, a gabbler, a tattler ; *naitheas*, mischief.

Cappernoytit, slightly deranged.

D'ye hear what auld Dominie Napier says about the mirk Monday? He says it's an eclipse—the sun and the moon fechting for the upper hand ! But, Lord ! he's a poor *capernoytit* creature.— *Laird of Logan.*

Carfuffle, agitation of mind, perplexity ; from the Gaelic *cearn*, a twist or wrong turn, and *baob*, *baobach*, and *baobhail*, an alarm, a fright, a perplexity ; and with the aspirate, the *b* pronounced as *f*, *bhaobail*, fuffle.

Troth, my lord may be turned fule outright an' he puts himsell into a *carfuffle* for ony thing ye could bring him, Edie.—
SCOTT : *The Antiquary.*

Carkin', grinding, oppressively wearying, vexatious. The root of this word is the Gaelic *garg*, rough, from whence also *gargle*, the rough noise produced by a liquor to foment the throat, but not to be swallowed.

The lisping infant prattlin' on his knee
Does a' his weary *carkin'* cares beguile,
An' makes him quite forget his labour and his toil.
—BURNS : *Cotter's Saturday Night.*

Carle, a man, a fellow ; from the Teutonic *kerl*. This word, which was used by Chaucer, has been corrupted into the English *churl*, which means a rude fellow. In Scotland it still preserves its original and pleasanter signification.

The miller was a stout *carle* for the nones ;
Full big he was of braune, and eke of bones.
—CHAUCER.

The pawky auld *carle* cam' ower the lea,
Wi' mony guid e'ens and guid days to me,
Saying, Kind sirs, for your courtesy,
Will you lodge a silly poor man ?
—RITSON's *Caledonian Songs.*

Oh ! wha's that at my chamber door ?
    Fair widow, are ye waukin'?
Auld *carle*, your suit give o'er,
    Your love lies a' in talkin'.
                            —ALLAN RAMSAY.

When lairds break, *carles* get land.
        —ALLAN RAMSAY's *Scots Proverbs.*

Up starts a *carle*, and gains good,
And thence comes a' our gentle blood.
                            —*Idem.*

My daddie is a cankered *carle*,
    He'll no twine wi' his gear;
But let them say or let them dae,
    It's a' ane to me;
For he's low doun, he's in the broom,
    That's waiting for me.
            —JAMES CARNEGIE, 1765.

Carle, a man, or fellow, is also used adjectively for male, manly, strong, vigorous : as in *carle-hemp*, the largest seed-bearing stalk of hemp ; *carle-dodder*, the largest stalk of dodder-grass ; *carle-heather* or *carlin-heather*, the largest species of heather or *erica ; carle-tangle*, the largest species of tangle or sea-weed ; *carle-wife*, a man who does women's work ; *carle-cat*, a tom-cat, a male cat, &c.

Ye have a stalk o' *carle-hemp* in you.
    —ALLAN RAMSAY's *Scots Proverbs.*

The *carle-stalk* of hemp in man—
Resolve.—BURNS.

Carle-wife, a husband who meddles too much with the household duties and privileges of the wife ; a much better word than its English equivalent—a "molly-coddle."

Carline or **carlin**, an old woman.

Cats and *carlines* love to sleep i' the sun.
            —ALLAN RAMSAY.

That auld capricious *carlin* Nature.
    —BURNS : *To James Smith.*

The Rev. Mr. Monro of Westray, preaching on the flight of Lot from Sodom, said : "The honest man and his family were ordered out of the town, and charged not to look back ; but the auld *carlin*, Lot's wife, looked owre her shouther, for which she was smote into a lump of sawt." And he added, with great unction : "Oh, ye people of Westray, if ye had had her, mony a day since ye wad hae putten her in the parritch-pat !"—DEAN RAMSAY.

Carp, by some commentators considered to signify to sing, by others to rehearse, from the oft-recurring phrase in old ballads recording the performances of bards and minstrels—" he *harpit* and he *carpit.*"

And ay he *harpit*, and ay he *carpit*,
    Till a' the nobles ga'ed o'er the floor ;
But and the music was sae sweet,
    The groom forgot the stable door.
        —SCOTT's *Border Minstrelsy : The
            Lochmaben Harper.*

To this passage **Mr. Robert Chambers**, in his " Collection of Scottish Ballads," appended the note :—" In the 'Minstrelsy of the Scottish Border' *carpit* is explained as meaning sung, but I suggest, with great deference, that it appears, from the use made of it in Barbour's 'Bruce,' that it refers to the *narrative* which the ancient minstrels accompanied on their instruments." But Mr. Chambers has left the doubt exactly where he found it, for the old minstrels sometimes sang and sometimes merely recited or declaimed their stories. The etymology and meaning are both as doubtful as ever. The English to *carp*, to cavil or find fault, is probably connected.

Carry, the driving clouds.

> Mirk and rainy is the night,
> No a starn (star) in a' the *carry.*
> —TANNAHILL.

The word is derived from the Gaelic *caraich*, to move, to stir ; *caraidh*, movement.

Castock, sometimes written **custock**, a cabbage-stalk.

> There's cauld kail in Aberdeen,
> An' *castocks* in Stra'bogie.
> —DUKE OF GORDON.

Every day's no Yule-day ;—cast the cat a *castock.*—ALLAN RAMSAY'S *Scots Proverbs.*

In their hearts they're as callous as *custocks.*—*Noctes Ambrosianæ.*

Cateran. A Highland *cateran* was a term formerly applied in the Lowlands to a Highland marauder or cattle-stealer, and generally to the Highlanders, who were all supposed to be lawless depredators on the wealth of the Lowlands. The word is probably from the Gaelic *cath*, a battle, a fight ; *cathach*, a fighter or warrior ; and *ran*, to shout, to roar ; whence, by emphatic denunciation, a roaring, a violent warrior or depredator.

> My love he was as brave a man
> As ever Scotland bred,
> Descended from a Highland clan,
> A *cateran* to his trade.
> —*Gilderoy.*

Cauld bark. To live in "the cauld bark," is to be dead and buried. *Bark*, in this metaphorical euphemism, is evidently not traceable to *bark*, a boat or ship, or to the *bark* of an animal ; but is possibly from *bark*, skin (which see), or from *berg* or *burg* or *burrow*, a hill or hillock, or slight mound raised over a grave.

Cauld coal. "He has a *cauld coal* to blaw," *i.e.*, he is engaged in a hopeless undertaking ; there is no spark of fire in it which can be blown into a flame.

Cauldrife, cold-hearted, cool in love or friendship, indifferent-minded.

> Gae, get you gone, you *cauldrife* wooer,
> Ye sour-looking *cauldrife* wooer.
> I straightway showed him to the door,
> Sayin', Come nae mair to me, oh !
> —HERD'S *Collection : The Brisk Young Lad.*

Cavée. According to Jamieson, this is an Aberdeenshire word, signifying a state of commotion or perturbation of mind. He suggests its derivation from the French *cas vif*, a matter that gives or requires activity (of mind). Is it not rather the Gaelic *cabhag (ca-vag)*, hurry, haste, dispatch, trouble, difficulty ? whence *cabhagach*, hasty, impetuous, hurried. *Cave* is used in the "Noctes Ambrosianæ" as synonymous with toss. "Gallopin' on a grey horse that *caves* the foam from its fiery nostrils."

Chandlers, candlesticks ; the English chandeliers.

> Hae ye ony pots or pans,
> Or ony broken *chandlers ;*
> I am a tinker to my trade,
> An' newly come frae Flanders.

As scant of siller as of grace,
    Disbanded, I'd a bad run ;
Gae tell the lady o' the place
    I've come to clout the cauldron.
—*The Tinker, or Clout the Cauldron.*

Channer, to contend, to complain, to grumble, to chide, to remonstrate ; from the Gaelic *canran*, a contentious murmuring, chiding ; *canranach*, querulous murmuring, contentions ; and *canranacha*, petulance, illhumour.

The cock doth craw, the day doth daw,
The *channerin'* worm doth chide.
        —*Border Minstrelsy : The Clerk's
        Twa Sons o' Ourenford.*

How the worm could *channer* or chide in the grave is incomprehensible, unless one of the meanings of the word is to fret or cause to fret with vexation. This interpretation has led to the supposition that "fret," in the sense of its former signification of "gnaw" or "eat," from the German *fressen*, Flemish *freten*, as in the Scripture phrase "The moth *fretteth* the garment," is synonymous with *channer*. This, however, is not the case, as the Gaelic etymology suffices to prove. But neither *channering* nor *fretting* supplies an intelligible or satisfactory explanation of the ballad-writer's meaning.

Chap, to knock ; *chaup*, a blow.

I dreamed I was deed, and carried far,
far, far up, till I came to Heaven's yett—
when I *chappit*, and *chappit*, and *chappit*,
till at last an angel keekit out and said,
" Wha are ye?"—DEAN RAMSAY.

The chiel was stout, the chiel was stark,
    And wadna bide to *chap* nor ca',
And Girzie, faint wi' holy wark,
    Had na the power to say him *na !*
            —*Holy Girzie.*

The Burnewin comes on like death at
    every *chaup.*
            —BURNS : *Scotch Drink.*

Chark, to make a grinding or grunting noise, also to complain petulantly and obstinately. A form of *cark*, with the substitution of *ch* for *c* or *k*, as in *church* for *kirk*, &c.

Cheep, to chirp or chirrup like a bird.

Ye're nae chicken for a your *cheepin'*.—
Proverb.

Chiel, a fellow, a youth ; the same as the ancient English *childe*, as used by Byron in " *Childe* Harold*." From the Gaelic *gille*, a youth.

The brawny, bainie ploughman *chiel.*
        —BURNS : *Scotch Drink.*
    A *chiel's* amang ye takin' notes.
            —BURNS.

Clachan, a village ; from the Gaelic *clach*, a stone, and *clachan*, the stones or houses.

The *clachan* yill (ale) had made me cantie.
    —BURNS : *Death and Dr. Hornbook.*
Ye ken Jock Hornbook o' the *clachan.*
            —*Idem.*
    The *clachan* of Aberfoyle.
    —SIR WALTER SCOTT : *Rob Roy.*

Many English and American tourists in Scotland, and other readers of the works of Sir Walter Scott, imagine that the " clachan of Aberfoyle " means the *mill* of Aberfoyle.

They derive the word from the English *clack*, the noise of the mill-wheel, and knowing nothing of *clachan*, the village, are disappointed when they find neither windmill nor watermill on the classic spot.

Clart, to defile, to make dirty.

Clarty, dirty; from the Gaelic *clabar* or *clabhar*, filth, mud, mire.

Searching auld wives' barrels;
    Ochon the day!
That *clarty* barm [dirty yeast] should stain
    my laurels!
    But—what'll ye say?
Those movin' things ca'd wives and weans
Wad move the very hearts o' stanes.
      —BURNS: *On being Appointed
      to the Excise.*

Clatch, to daub, to do any kind of work carelessly, awkwardly, recklessly, or ignorantly; *claught*, snatched.

Claur or **glaur**, mud, dirt, mire; "a gowpen o' *glaur*," a handful of mud; "a humplock of *glaur*," a heap of mud.

The wee laddie, greetin', said his brither Jock had coost a gowpen o' *glaur* at him and knockit him on the neb.—JAMES BALLANTINE.

Claut, to snatch, to lay hold of eagerly; something that has been got together by greed; a large heap.

Ken ye what Meg o' the Mill has gotten?
She's gotten a coof wi' a *claut* o' siller,
And broken the heart o' the barley miller.
      —BURNS: *Meg o' the Mill.*

   Claut is undoubtedly from the English

word *claw*, which had the sense in olden time of to scratch, to gather together, and is in that sense still in use in some parts of England. *Claut*, in Scotch, is most frequently used as a noun, and is the name given to a hoe used to gather mud, &c., together; to *claut* the roads, to gather the mud. I don't think the world itself contains the idea of getting together a large heap by *greed*. I don't recognise the other meanings, "to snatch," "to lay hold of eagerly." I would use a different word to express these meanings,—*to glaum, to play glaum*, would fit them exactly.— R. DRENNAN.

Clavers, idle stories, silly calumnies.

Hail Poesie! thou nymph reserved;
In chase o' thee what crowds hae swerv'd
Frae common sense, or sunk unnerv'd
    'Mong heaps o' *clavers*.
      —BURNS: *On Pastoral Poets.*

Claw, to flatter; from the Gaelic *cliù*, praise, and not, as ignorantly supposed, from the English *claw*, to scratch with the nails, in allusion to the itch.

Claw me and I'll *claw* you.—*Scottish Proverbs.*

I laugh when I am merry, and *claw* no man in his humour.
      —SHAKESPEARE: *Much Ado about Nothing.*

Claymore, the Highland broadsword; from the Gaelic *claidheamh*, or *glaive*, a sword, and *mor*, great.

Wha on the moor a gallant clan
  From boastin' foes their banners bore,
Who showed himself a better man
  Or fiercer waved the broad claymore?
      —SIR ALEXANDER BOSWELL.

Clepie, deceitful; from the Gaelic *clibe*, deceit.

Clishmaclaver, idle talk, foolish gossip, incessant gabble.

What further *clish-ma-claver* might been said.—Burns: *The Brigs o' Ayr.*

From the Gaelic *clis* (*clish*), nimble, rapid, and *clab* (*clabh*), an open mouth; *clabach*, garrulous; *clabairê*, a babbler, a loud disagreeable talker; *clabar*, the clapper of a mill.

Clocking-hen, a hen engaged in the act of incubation; from *clock* or *cluck*, the cry or cackle of the hen when hatching. The word is sometimes used jocularly or contemptuously for an elderly woman or nurse.

Clocksie, lively, sprightly, vivacious, talkative; possibly from *clack*, talk; and that, again, from the Gaelic *clach* or *cloch*, a bell; applied derisively to the tongue of a garrulous person, likened to the clapper of a bell.

The *clocksie* auld laird o' the Warlock Glen,
Wha stood without, half cowed, half cheerie,
Raised up the latch and cam' crousely ben.
—Joanna Baillie.

Cloot, a cloven foot; *Clootie*, one who is hoofed or cloven-footed, *i.e.*, the devil.

O thou, whatever title suit thee,
Auld Hornie, Satan, Nick, or *Clootie*.
—Burns: *Address to the Deil.*

Cloot (pronounced *clute*, long French *u*) is not a hoof, but the half of a hoof. We speak of a horse's hoof, and of a cow's cloots, and apply this latter word only to the feet of those animals that divide the hoof.—R. Drennan.

Clour, a lump on the flesh caused by a heavy blow.

That cane o' yours would gie a *clour* on a man's head eneuch to produce a phrenological faculty. — Professor Wilson: *Noctes Ambrosianæ.*

Clour is a heavy blow—the lump is only the *result* of a *clour*.—R. Drennan.

Clout, a rag; **cloutie**, a little rag, baby-clouts, baby-clothes. *Clout* also signifies a patch, or to patch, to mend, as in the old song of "Clout the Cauldron" (mend the kettle).

Wha my *baby-clouts* will buy?
—*Old Song.*

A countryman in a remote part of Aberdeenshire got a newly coined sovereign in the days when such a thing was seldom seen, and went about showing it to his friends and neighbours for the charge of a penny each sight. Evil days unfortunately overtook him, and he was obliged to part with his beloved coin. A neighbour one day called upon him and asked for a sight of his sovereign. "Ah! man," said he, "it's gane; but I'll let ye see the *cloutie* it was rowed (wrapped) in for a *bawbee!*"—Dean Ramsay.

Cluff, to strike with the fist, to slap; "a *cluff* i' the lug," a box on the ear. The word is akin to the English *fisticuff* and to *cuff.*

Clunk, the gurgling, confused sound of liquor in a bottle or cask when it is poured out; equivalent to the English *glug* in the song of "Gluggity Glug." It is derived by Jamieson from the Danish *glunk* and the Swedish *klunka*, which have the same meaning.

Sir Violino, with an air
That showed a man o' spunk,
Wished unison between the pair,
And made the bottle *clunk.*
—Burns: *The Jolly Beggars.*

An old English song has "and let the cannikin *clink*," which is obviously from the same root, though *clunk* is more expressive of a dull sound than *clink* is.

Clyte, a fall; to stop in the midst of a set speech for want of words or ideas, and sit down suddenly. "I couldna find words to continue my speech," said a Glasgow bailie, "and sae I *clyted.*"

I fairly *clyted*
On the cauld earth.
—Allan Ramsay.

Clyte, a heavy, sudden kind of fall. I have generally heard the word as a verb used in connection with the word *played* —"It played *clyte* at my heels," "He got as far as the road, and then played *clyte.*" —R. Drennan.

Clytie-lass, a servant girl whose duty is to carry out of the house all filth or ordure, and to deposit it on the midden or elsewhere. The first word is apparently from the Gaelic *cuil-aite*, the back place or latrine, from *cuil* or *cul*, back, and *aite*, a place, whence by abbreviation *clyte* and *clytie.*

Cock. This syllable, which enters into the composition of many words and phrases both in Lowland Scotch and modern English, has generally been associated with its supposed derivation from *cock*, the name given to the male of birds, and especially to the familiar gallinaceous barn-door fowl that "crows in the morning." Its true derivation, however, is from the Gaelic *coc*, which means to elevate, to erect, to stand up, to throw high, to lift, as in such phrases as a "*cocked-hat*," a "*cockade*," "*cock* up your beaver," "*cock-sure*" (manifestly or presumedly sure, or pretending to be so), "*cock-a-hoop*," and many others. It is more common in Lowland Scotch than in English. To *cock*, signifies to mount one boy on the back of another for punishment on the posteriors ; to *cock-shy*, to throw a stone or other missile high in the air ; *cock-a-penny* or *cock-a-pentie*, to live beyond one's income for pride or ostentation, or the disinclination to appear as poor as one is in reality by expending more pennies than one has honestly got ; *cockie-vain*, conceited, arrogant, stuck up ; *cockie-ridie*, a game among children, when one rides on the shoulders of another ; a *cock-horse*, a wooden horse, on which children mount for amusement ; *cock-laird*, a small landed proprietor, who affects the dignity and gives himself the airs of a great one ; *cock-headed* or *cockle-headed*, vain, conceited, whimsical, stuck up ; *cockernonie* (which see) ; *cock-raw*, manifestly or plainly raw, underdone ; *cock-up* nose, a turned-up nose, "tip-tilted," as Lord Tennyson more elegantly describes it, and *cock-eye*, a squint-eye, that cocks up or awry when it should look straight.

None of these words have any connection with the male bird of the Gallinaceæ, but all are traceable etymologically to the Gaelic root of *coc*. Philologists, if so disposed, may trace to this same source the vulgar and indecent English and Scottish words which may be found in Juvenal and Horace as *Mentula*.

Cockernonie, a gathering up of the hair of women, after a fashion similar to that of the modern " chignon," and sometimes called a " cock-up." Mr. Kirkton, of Edinburgh, preaching against " cock-ups "—of which chignons were the representatives a quarter of a century ago — said : " I have been all this year preaching against the vanity of women, yet I see my own daughter in the kirk even now with as high a ' cock-up ' as any one of you all."

Jamieson was of the opinion, that *cockernonie* signified a snood, or the gathering of the hair in a band or fillet, and derived the word from the Teutonic *koker*, a cape, and *nonne*, a nun, *i.e.*, such a sheath for fixing the hair as nuns were accustomed to use ! The word was a contemptuous one for false hair—a contrivance to make a little hair

appear to be a good deal—and seems to have been compounded of the Gaelic *coc*, to stand erect, and *neoni*, nothing.

> I saw my Meg come linkin' ower the lea,
> I saw my Meg, but Meggie saw na me,
> Her *cockernonie* snooded up fu' sleek.
>   —ALLAN RAMSAY.

> But I doubt the daughter's a silly thing : an unco *cockernony* she had busked on her head at the kirk last Sunday.—SCOTT : *Old Mortality.*

> My gude name ! If ony body touched my gude name I wad neither fash council nor commissary. I would be down upon them like a sea-falcon amang a wheen wild geese, and the best o' them that dared to say onything o' Meg Dods but what was honest and civil, I wad soon see if her *cockernonie* was made o' her ain hair or other folks' !—SCOTT : *St. Ronans' Well.*

Cod, from the Gaelic, *cod*, a cushion, a pillow, a bag, a receptacle ; *peas-cod*, the shell in which the peas are formed and retained. The word is retained in English in an indelicate sense for the *scrotum*.

> I hae guid fire for winter weather,
>   A *cod* o' caff (chaff) wud fill a cradle,
> A halter an' a guid hay tether,
>   A deuk about the dub to paidle.
>   —*The Wooin' o' Jenny and Jock.*

Cod-crune or **cod-crooning**, a curtain lecture ; from the Gaelic *cod*, a pillow, and *croon*, to murmur, to lament, to moan. Jamieson derives the word from the Teutonic *kreunen*, and says it is sometimes called a "bowster (bolster) lecture." No such word, however, as *kreunen* or *krunen* is to be found in the German dictionaries.

Codroch, miserable, ugly, detestable. These are the meanings assigned to the word by Allan Ramsay, though Jamieson, who cites it as used in Fifeshire and the Lothians, explains it as a rustic, or one who is dirty and slovenly.

> A *codroch coffe*, he is sure sich,
> And lives like ony wareit wretch.
> —*Pedder Coffe: The Evergreen.*

The final syllable seems to be the Gaelic *droch*, bad, evil, wicked, mischievous. *Co* is doubtless the Gaelic *comh* (pronounced *co*), a prefix equivalent to the Latin *co* and *con*. Jamieson derives it from the Irish Gaelic *cudar*, the rabble, a word that does not appear in O'Reilly's excellent Irish Dictionary, though *cudarman* and *cudarmanta* appear in it as synonymous with " vulgar and rustic."

Coffe, a fellow; in vulgar English, a *chap*. From the German *kaufen*, to buy; and *kaufmann*, a merchant, a tradesman.

Coft, bought, purchased. *Cooft*, to buy, from *kaufen*, has become obsolete; but *cooper*, a buyer or seller, survives in horse-cooper or horse-dealer.

> Then he has *coft* for that ladye
> A fine silk riding-gown ;
> Likewise he *coft* for that ladye
> A steed, and set her on.
> —Buchan's *Ancient Ballads: Jock o' Hazelgreen (old version).*

Cog and **cogie**, a bowl or cup, also a basin. From the Gaelic *cuach*, a cup, used either for broth, ale, or stronger drink.

> I canna want my *cogie*, sir,
> I canna want my *cogie;*
> I winna want my three-girred *cog*
> For a' the wives in Bogie.
> —Duke of Gordon.

It's good to have our *cog* out when it rains kail !—Allan Ramsay's *Scots Proverbs.*

Coggle, to shake, to waggle ; from the Gaelic *gog* or *cog*, to shake ; *gogail*, wavering, unsteady. Whence probably the French *coquette*, a flirt, or one who wavers or is unsteady in the bestowal of her favours to male admirers.

> It *coggled* thrice, but at the last
> It rested on his shoulders fast.
> —George Beattie : *John o' Arnha'.*

Collie-shangie, a loud dispute, a quarrel, an uproar, a noise of angry tongues.

> How the *collie-shangie* works
> Betwixt the Russians and the Turks.
> —Burns : *To a Gentleman who Sent him a Newspaper.*

" It has been supposed," says Jamieson, " that from *collie*, a shepherd's dog, and *shangie*, a chain, comes the word *collie-shangie*, a quarrel between two dogs fastened with the same chain." Under the word " collie," he explains it to mean a quarrel, as well as a dog of that species ; as if he believed that the gentle and sagacious shepherd's dog was more quarrelsome than the rest of the canine species. In Gaelic, *coileid* means noise, confusion, uproar; and *coileideach,* noisy, confused, angry; which is no doubt the etymology of *collie* in the compound word *collie-shangie.* The meaning of *shangie* is difficult to trace, unless it be from the Gaelic *seang* (pronounced *shang*), slender, lean, hungry.

Conundrum, a kind of riddle suggestive of resemblances where no resemblances exist; a wordy puzzle. The word is of comparatively recent introduction into English, and has been supposed by some etymologists to be derivable from the German *kennen,* to know. Stormonth was content to trace it to the Anglo-Saxon *cunnan;* but on its being pointed out to him by the present writer, in a private note, after the issue of the first edition of his Dictionary, that the derivation was so far unsatisfactory that it did not account for the final syllable, and that it was an ancient Scottish word, of which the components were the Gaelic *conn,* sense or meaning, and *antrom,* heavy or difficult, he abandoned the Anglo-Saxon derivation, and expressed his resolve to adopt the Gaelic etymology if his Dictionary ever reached a second edition. He died, unfortunately, before preparing a second edition for the press.

Coof, cuif, gowk, a fool, a simpleton, a cuckoo.

Ye see yon birkie ca'd a lord,
  Wha struts an' stares an' a' that;
Though hundreds worship at his word,
  He's but a *cuif* for a' that.
      —BURNS: *A Man's a Man.*

Coof and *gowk,* though apparently unlike each other in sound, are probably corruptions of the same Gaelic words, *cuabhag* (*cuaf ag*) and *cuach,* a cuckoo:—

Ye breed of the *gowk* (cuckoo), ye hae but ae note in your voice, and ye're aye singing it.—ALLAN RAMSAY'S *Scots Proverbs.*

In England, a "fool" and a "goose" are synonymous; but in Scotland the cuckoo is the bird that symbolises stupidity.

Cuif, fool, and blockhead, are not exact synonyms,—rather a useless fellow, a sort of male tawpie. A man may be a *cuif,* and yet the reverse of a fool or blockhead. —R. DRENNAN.

Coo-me-doo, a term of endearment for a turtle-dove, wood pigeon, or cushat.

O *coo-me-doo,* my love sae true,
  If ye'll come doun to me,
Ye'se hae a cage o' guid red gowd
  Instead o' simple tree.
    —BUCHAN'S *Ballads: The Earl o' Mar's Daughter.*

Corbie, the hooded-crow; also the raven; from the French *corbeau.*

Corbies will no pick out *corbies'* e'en (*Old Proverb*). [Signifying that two of a trade ought not to divulge the tricks of the trade; also applied among thieves to a confederate who informs against them, or *peaches.*]

The adder lies i' the *corbie's* nest,
  Beneath the *corbie's* wing;
And the blast that rives the *corbie's* nest
  Will soon bring hame the king.
    —*Jacobite Song,* 1745.

Cosh, quiet, snug. (*See* COZIE.)

> And sang fu' sweet the notes o' love,
> Till a' was *cosh* within.
> > —*Border Minstrelsy: The Gay Gosshawk.*

Cosie, cozie, comfortable, snug, warm.

> While some are *cozie* in the neuk,
> And forming assignations
> > To meet some day.
> > —BURNS: *The Holy Fair.*

Jamieson says that *cosie*, snug, warm, comfortable, seems to be of the same derivation as *cosh*, a comfortable situation, and comfortable as implying a defence from the cold. It is evidently from the Gaelic *coiseag*, a little, snug, or warm corner, a derivation from *cos* and *cois*, a hollow, a recess, a corner.

Couthie, well - known, familiar, handsome, and agreeable — in contradistinction to the English word *uncouth*.

> Some kindle, *couthie*, side by side,
> And burn together trimly.
> > —BURNS: *Hallowe'en.*
> My ain *couthie* dame,
> O my ain *couthie* dame ;
> Wi' my bonny bits o' bairns,
> And my ain *couthie* dame.
> > —*Ingleside Lilts.*

Cowp, to tumble over; akin to the French *coup*, a blow; whence to suffer a blow in falling.

> I drew my scythe in sic a fury,
> I near had *cowpit* in my hurry.
> —BURNS: *Death and Dr. Hornbook.*

Crabb, to find fault, to be angry, to complain for slight cause, or without real necessity. This word is traceable in the English *crabbed*, ill-tempered.

He that *crabbs* without cause should mease (apologise) without mends (making amends).—*Scottish Proverb.*

Crack, talk, gossip, conversation, confidential discourse, a story ; from the Gaelic *crac*, to talk ; *cracaire*, a talker, a gossip, and *cracaireachd*, idle talk or chat. To "*crack* a thing up" in English is to talk it into repute by praise. A *crack* article is a thing highly praised. Jamieson derives the word from the German *kraken*, to make a noise, though there is no such word in that language.

> But raise your arm, and tell your *crack*
> > Before them a'.
> > —BURNS: *Earnest Cry and Prayer.*

> They're a' in famous tune
> > For *cracks* that day.
> > —BURNS: *The Holy Fair.*

The cantie auld folk *crackin'* crouse,
The young anes rantin' through the house ;
My heart has been sae fain to see them,
That I for joy hae barkit wi' them.
> —BURNS: *The Twa Dogs.*

A lady on hiring a servant girl in the country, told her, as a great indulgence, that she should have the liberty of attending the kirk every Sunday, but that she would be expected to return home immediately after the conclusion of the service. The lady, however, rather unexpectedly found a positive objection raised against this apparently reasonable arrangement. "Then I canna engage wi' ye, mem, for indeed I wadna gie the *crack* i' the kirkyard for a' the sermon."—DEAN RAMSAY.

Craig, the neck.

> Ane got a twist o' the *craig*,
> Ane got a punch o' the wame ;
> > C

Symy Hair got lamed o' a leg,
And syne ran wabblin' hame.
  —*Border Minstrelsy : The Death of*
      Featherstonehaugh.

Crambo-clink or **crambo-jingle**, a
contemptuous name for dog-
gerel verse, and bad or medi-
ocre attempts at poetry, which
Douglas Jerrold, with wit as
well as wisdom—and they are
closely allied — described as
" verse and *worse*."

A' ye wha live by *crambo-clink*,
A' ye wha write and never think,
    Come mourn wi' me.
      —BURNS : *On a Scotch Bard.*

Amaist as soon as I could spell,
I to the *crambo-jingle* fell,
    Tho' rude and rough ;
But crooning to a body's sel'
    Does weel enough.
      —BURNS : *Epistle to Lapraik.*

Crambo seems to be derived
from the Gaelic *crom*, crooked,
or perhaps from " cramp "
or " cramped." " Clink " and
" jingle," assonance, conson-
ance, or rhyme, are from the
English.

Creel or **creil**, a fish-basket ; from
the French *creille*, with the same
meaning.

The boatie rows, the boatie rows,
The boatie rows fu' weel,
And muckle luck attend the boat,
The merlin, and the *creel.*—*Old Song.*

Creepie, a low stool ; from the
Gaelic *crub*, to bend low.

I sit on my *creepie* and spin at my wheel,
An' think on the laddie that lo'es me sae
weel.—*Logie o' Buchan.*

Creeshie, greasy.

Kamesters (wool-combers) are aye *creeshie* (*Old Proverb*), *i.e.*, people are ever
tainted with their trade, as in the phrase,
" Millers are aye mealy."

Crone, an old woman, a witch.
Worcester, in his Dictionary,
derives this word from the
Scottish " croon " " the hollow
muttering sound with which old
witches uttered their incanta-
tions." (*See* CROON.)

Crony, a comrade, a dear friend,
a boon companion ; derived in
a favourable sense from *crone.*
This Scottish word seems to
have been introduced to English
notice by James I. It was used
by Swift and other writers of
his period, and was admitted
into Johnson's Dictionary, who
described it as a " cant word."

To oblige your *crony* Swift,
Bring our dame a New Year's gift.
      —SWIFT.

My name is Fun, your *crony* dear,
The nearest friend ye ha'e.
      —BURNS : *The Holy Fair.*

And at his elbow Souter Johnny,
His ancient, trusty, drouthy *crony.*
      —BURNS : *Tam o' Shanter.*

Croodle, to coo like a dove : " a
wee *croodlin*' doo," a term of
endearment to an infant.

Far ben thy dark green plantin' shade
The cushat (wood-pigeon) *croodles* amor-
ouslie.—TANNAHILL.

There's ae thing keeps my heart light,
Whate'er the world may do ;
A bonnie, bonnie, bonnie, bonnie,
Wee *croodlin'* doo.—*Old Song.*

Croon, to hum over a tune, to
prelude on an instrument. The

word seems derivable from the Gaelic *cronan*, a dull, murmuring sound, a mournful and monotonous tune.

The sisters grey before the day
Did *croon* within their cloister.
—ALLAN RAMSAY.

Whiles holding fast his guid blue bonnet,
Whiles *croonin* o'er some auld Scots sonnet.
—BURNS : *Tam o' Shanter.*

Where auld ruined castles grey
Nod to the moon,
To fright the nightly wanderer's way
Wi' eldritch *croon.*
—BURNS : *Address to the Deil.*

Plaintive tunes,
Such as corpse-watching beldam *croons.*
—*Studies from the Antique.*

Crouse, merry, lively, brisk, bold, from the Gaelic *craos*, greedy, sensual, gluttonous, eager for any pleasure of the senses.

A cock's aye *crouse* on his ain midden.—
ALLAN RAMSAY'S *Scots Proverbs.*

The cantie auld folk crackin' *crouse,*
The young anes rantin' through the house.
—BURNS : *The Twa Dogs.*

Crowdie, oatmeal boiled to a thick consistency ; *crowdie-time,* breakfast-time or meal-time.

Jamieson goes to the Icelandic for the origin of the word *crowdie,* once the favourite and general food of the Scottish people, in the days before the less nutritious potato was introduced into the country. But the name of *crowdie* is not so likely to be derived from the Icelandic *graut-ur,* gruel made of groats, as from the Gaelic *cruaidh,* thick, firm, of hard consistency. Gruel is thin, but porridge or

crowdie is thick and firm, and in that quality its great merit consists, as distinguished from its watery competitor, the nourishment of the sick-room, and not to be compared to the strong wholesome "parritch," which Burns designated "the chief of Scotland's food."

Oh, that I had never been married,
I'd never had nae care ;
Now I've gotten wife and bairns,
An' they cry *crowdie* evermair !
Once *crowdie,* twice *crowdie,*
Three times *crowdie* in a day !
—BURNS.

Then I gaed hame at *crowdie-time,*
And soon I made me ready.
—BURNS : *The Holy Fair.*

My sister Kate came up the gate
Wi' *crowdie* unto me, man ;
She swore she saw the rebels run
Frae Perth unto Dundee, man.
—*The Battle of Sheriffmuir.*

Crowdie, properly, is oatmeal mixed with cold water ; but it is also used for food in general, as in the expression, " I'll be hame about *crowdie-*time."—R. DRENNAN.

Crummie, a familiar name for a favourite cow ; from the crooked horn. Gaelic *crom,* crooked. In the ancient ballad of " Tak' your auld cloak about ye," quoted by Shakespeare in " Othello," the word appears as *Crumbock.*

Bell, my wife, who loves no strife,
She said unto me quietlie,
Rise up and save cow *Crumbock's* life,
And put thine auld cloak about thee.

The word appears as *Crummock* in Burns's " Epistle to Major Logan."

Hale be your heart, hale be your fiddle,
Lang may your elbuck jouk and diddle,
To cheer you through the weary widdle
    O' this wide warl',
Until you on a *crummock* driddle,
    A grey-hair'd carl.

Crunt, a smart blow with a cudgel or fist on the crown of the head.

And mony a fellow got his licks
    Wi' hearty *crunt*.
    —Burns : *To Willie Simpson.*

This word seems to come either from the English *crown*, the head (hence a blow on the head), or from the Gaelic *crun*, which has the same meaning. The crown of the head, the very top of the head, is a common phrase ; the *croon* of the causeway—the top ridge of the road, or the middle of the road—is a well-known Scotticism. In slang English, a *crunt* is called a *nopper*, or one for his " *nob*."

Cuddie, a donkey; supposed by some to be derived from the Gaelic *cutach*, bob-tailed, or from *ceutach*, grace, elegance, beauty, applied to the animal by its owner either in affection or derision.

One day my grandfather saw Andrew Leslie's donkey up to the knees in a field of clover. " Hallo, Andrew ! " said he, " I thought your *cuddie* wad eat nothing but thistles and nettles." " Ay," said he, " but he misbehaved himself, and I put him in there just to punish him."—Dean Ramsay.

Cuddle. This word, which in the English vernacular means to embrace, to fondle, to press to the bosom, simply signifies in Scottish parlance to *sleep*, and is derived from the Gaelic *cadail*, sleep.

An auld beddin' o' claes
  Was left me by my mither ;
They're jet black o'er wi' flaes ;
  Ye may *cuddle* in them thegither.
   .   .   .   .

The bride she gaed to her bed,
  The bridegroom he came till her,
The fiddler crept in at the foot,
  An' they a' *cuddled* together.
      —*Maggie's Tocher: The Tea-*
         Table Miscellany.

Where shall I *cuddle* the night ?
    —Galt : *Mansie Wauch.*

Cuif or **coof**, a fool, a blockhead. (*See* Coof, *ante.*)

Cupar.

He that will to Cupar, maun to Cupar.

This proverb, applied to an obstinate man who will have his own way, has puzzled many commentators. Dean Ramsay asks, "Why Cupar? and whether is it the Cupar of Angus or the Cupar of Fife ? "

It has been suggested that the origin of " Cupar," in the sense employed in the proverb, is the Gaelic *comhar* (*covar*), a mark, a sign, a proof, and that the phrase is equivalent to " he who *will* be a marked man (by his folly or perversity) *must* be a marked man." It has also been suggested that " Cupar " is from *comharra* (*covarra*), shelter or protection of the sanctuary, to which a man resorted when hard pressed by justice for a crime which he had committed.

Curn, a grain of corn; whence *kernel,* the fruit in the nut; curny-gutty.

Mind to splice high with Latin—a *curn* or two of Greek would not be amiss: and if ye can bring in anything about the judgment of Solomon in the original Hebrew, and season with a merry jest or so, the dish will be the more palatable.—SCOTT: *Fortunes of Nigel.*

Allied words to *curn* are "kern" and "churn," a hand-mill for grinding corn, and "churn," a mill for stirring the milk so as to make butter.

Cushat, a turtle-dove, a wood-pigeon.

O'er lofty aiks the *cushats* wail,
And echo coos the dolefu' tale.
　　—BURNS: *Bess and her Spinning Wheel.*

Custock or **castock,** the edible stalk of cabbage; a kail-runt.

There's cauld kail in Aberdeen,
An' *custocks* in Stra'bogie,
An' ilka lad maun hae his lass,
An' I maun hae my cogie.
　　—HERD's *Collection: The Three-Girred Cog.*

Cutty or **cuttie,** short; from the Gaelic *cutach,* that has been cut, abridged, or shortened; whence *cutty*-pipe, a short pipe.

I'm no sae scant o' clean pipes as to blaw wi' a burnt *cutty.*—ALLAN RAMSAY'S *Scots Proverbs.*

Till first ae caper, then anither,
Tam tint his reason a' thegither,
And roared out "Weel done, *cutty* sark!"
And in an instant a' was dark.
　　—BURNS: *Tam o' Shanter.*

Her *cutty* sark, o' Paisley harn,
That when a lassie she had worn,

In longitude though sorely scanty,
It was her best, and she was vaunty.
　　　　　　　　—*Ibid.*

Cuttie-stool, a three-legged stool; a short stool, such as Jennie Geddes is reported to have thrown from the pulpit stairs at the head of the heretical minister.

A circumstance connected with Scottish church discipline has undergone a great change in my time—I mean the public censure from the pulpit of persons convicted of a breach of the seventh commandment. . . . This was performed by the guilty person standing up before the whole congregation on a raised platform called the *cutty-stool.*—DEAN RAMSAY.

The culprits did not always take the admonition patiently. It is recorded of one of them in Ayrshire, that when accused of adultery by the minister, he interrupted and corrected his reverend monitor by denying the imputation, and calling out, "Na! na! minister; it was simple *fornie* (fornication), and no *adultery* ava."—*Ibid.*

Cutty-mun and **tree-ladle.** These words, according to Jamieson, were the names of old tunes once popular in Scotland. No trace of them, however, has hitherto been discovered, and the interpretation given to them by Jamieson remains a mere supposition on his part. *Cutty-mun,* he says, means a spoon with a short handle. *Cutty* no doubt signifies short or small, as in *cutty-stool* and in *cutty-pipe;* but Jamieson should have been aware that in no known language does *mun* signify a spoon. Investigation would have shown him that the same language from which *cutty* is derived supplied the true etymology of *mun*, from *mainne*, delay, and that *cutty-mun* signified short delay. In like manner *tree-ladle* has no reference to a wooden spoon or ladle, as he supposed, but is derived from the Gaelic *triall*, departure on a journey, and *luathaich*, speed; *luathailteach*, swift, speedy. Thus the old tune mentioned by Jamieson resolves itself into a Lowland rendering of the Gaelic,

and signified "a short shrift and speedy exit." This would be an appropriate phrase applied to the hanging of a Highland criminal by a feudal chief, or to the more formal but equally efficacious justice as administered in the Lowlands, and is, there can be little or no doubt, the real meaning of the name of the old song on which Jamieson relied for his interpretation.

D

Daff, to make merry, to be sportive ; **daffin',** merriment.

> Wi' *daffin'* weary grown,
> Upon a knowe they sat them down.
> —BURNS : *The Twa Dogs.*

Dr. Adam, Rector of the High School of Edinburgh, rendered the Horatian expression "desipere in loco" by the Scottish phrase "weel-timed *daffin'*"—a translation which no one but a Scot could properly appreciate.—DEAN RAMSAY.

Daff has long ceased to be current English, though it was used by Shakespeare in the sense of to befool. In the scene between Leonato and Claudio in "Much Ado About Nothing," when Claudio refuses to fight with an old man, Leonato replies :

Canst thou so *daff* me—thou who killed my child ?

The Shakespearean commentators all agree that this word should be *doff* me, or put me off.

They interpret in the same way the line in King Lear :—

> The madcap Prince of Wales, that
> *daff'd* the world aside !

It would appear, however, that in both instances, *daff* was used in the sense which it retains in Scotch, that of fool or befool.

Daft, crazy, wild, mad.

> Or maybe in a frolic *daft*
> To Hague or Calais take a waft.
> —BURNS : *The Twa Dogs.*

Daidle, to trifle, to dawdle.

> *Daidlin'* in the mock-turtle ! I hate a' things mock.—*Noctes Ambrosianæ.*

Daiker or **daker,** to saunter, to stroll lazily or idly, or without defined purpose or object.

Dambrod, draught - board or chess-board ; from the Flemish *dambord ;* the first syllable from the French *dame,* or *jeu aux dames,* draughts.

Mrs. Chisholm entered the shop of a linen-draper, and asked to be shown some table-cloths of a *dambrod* pattern. The shopman was taken aback at such apparently strong language as "damned broad," used by a respectable lady. The lady, on her part, was surprised at the stupidity of the London shopman, who did not understand so common a phrase.—DEAN RAMSAY.

Dapperpye, brilliant with many colours; from *dapper,* neat and smart, the German *tapfer,* brave, English, *bravery* in attire, and *pied,* variegated.

Oh, he has pu'd off his *dapperpye* coat,
The silver buttons glanced bonny.
  —*Border Minstrelsy: Annan Water.*

Darg or **daurk,** a job of work; from the Gaelic *dearg,* a plough.

You will spoil the *darg* if you stop the plough to kill a mouse.—*Northumbrian Proverb.*

He never did a good *darg* that gaed grumbling about it.—ALLAN RAMSAY'S *Scots Proverbs.*

Monie a sair *daurk* we hae wrought.
  —BURNS: *To his Auld Mare Maggie.*

Darger, a day-labourer, one who works by the piece or job; also a ploughman.

The croonin kye the byre drew nigh,
The *darger* left his thrift.
  —*Border Minstrelsy: The Water Kelpie.*

Daud, to pelt; also a large piece.

I'm busy too, an' skelpin' at it,
But bitter *daudin'* showers ha'e wat it.
  —BURNS: *To J. Lapraik.*

He'll clap a shangan on her tail,
An' set the bairns to *daud* her
  Wi' dirt this day.
  —BURNS: *The Ordination.*

A *daud* o' bannock
Wad mak' him blithe as a body could.
  —ALLAN RAMSAY.

Daud and *blaud* or *blad* are synonymous in the sense of a large piece of anything, and also of pelting or driving, as applied to rain or wind.

I got a great *blad* o' Virgil by heart.
  —JAMIESON.

Dauner or **daunder,** to saunter, to stroll leisurely, without a purpose.

Some idle and mischievous youths waited for the minister on a dark night, and one of them, dressed as a ghost, came up to him in hopes of putting him in a fright. The minister's cool reply upset the plan. "Weel, Maister Ghaist, is this a general rising, or are ye jist taking a *dauner* frae your grave by yoursel'?" — DEAN RAMSAY'S *Reminiscences.*

Daunton, to subdue, to tame, to daunt, to dominate, to break in (applied to horses); from the Gaelic *dan,* bold, daring, and *danaich,* to exert boldness, to dare, to challenge, to defy.

To *daunton* me, and me sae young,
Wi' his fause heart an' flatterin' tongue,
That is the thing ye ne'er shall see,
For an auld man shall never *daunton* me.
  —*Old Song, altered by* BURNS.

Daut, to fondle, to caress.

Dautie, a darling, one who is fondled and affectionately treated; allied to the English *doat, doat upon,* and *dotage.*

> Whae'er shall say I wanted Jean,
> When I did kiss and *daut* her.
> —Burns : *Had I the wyte.*

> My *dautie* and my doo (dove).
> —Allan Ramsay.

To some it may appear that *dawtie* may have had its origin from the Gaelic *dalt*, a foster-child.—Jamieson.

> Yestreen ye were your daddie's doo,
> But an your mither's *dautie.*
> —Buchan's *Ancient Ballads : The Trooper and Fair Maid.*

Daw, a slut, akin to the colloquial English *dowdy*, an ill-dressed woman or sloven.

> See-saw, Margery *Daw,*
> Sold her bed and lay in the straw.
> —*Nursery Rhyme.*

Dawds and blawds is a phrase that denotes the greatest abundance.—Jamieson.

Dawk, a drizzling rain; *dawky*, moist, rainy, not exactly a downpour of steady rain, but of intermittent drizzle.

Day-daw, abbreviation of day-dawn, or dawn of day.

Dead is often used in the sense of *very*, extremely, or entirely, as in the English word *dead-beat*. It occurs in Scottish parlance as *dead-loun*, very calm and still; *dead-cauld*, extremely cold; *dead-ripe*, very ripe, or ripe to rottenness; *dead-sweir*, extremely lazy or tired out.

Dear me ! Oh dear me ! Deary me ! These colloquial exclamations are peculiar to the English and Scottish languages, and are indicative either of surprise,

pain, or pity. If the word "dear" be accepted as correct, and not a corruption of some other word with a different meaning, the explanation, if literally translated into any other language, would be nonsensical ; in French, for instance, it would be *O cher moi !* and in German, *Ach theuer mich !* The original word, as used by our British ancestors, and misunderstood by the Danes, Flemings, and Dutch, who succeeded them in part possession of the country, appears to have been the Gaelic *Dia (dee-a)*, God. *Oh Dia !* or *Oh dear !* and *Oh dear me !* would signify, God! Oh God ! or Oh my God ! synonymous with the French *Mon Dieu !* or *Oh mon Dieu !* and the German *Mein Gott !* or *Ach mein Gott !*

Deas, a stone seat in the porch, or at the porch of a church, probably so named from its usual position at the right hand side ; from the Gaelic *deas*, the right side, on the right hand.

> An' when she came to Marie's kirk,
> An' sat down in the *deas,*
> The licht that came frae fair Annie
> Enlichten't a' the place.
> Percy's *Reliques : Sweet William and Fair Annie.*

The etymology of the English and French word *dais* has given rise to much diference of opinion. Stormonth's English Dictionary defines *dais* as "a canopy over a throne, afterwards the whole seat," and suggests a derivation from the "old French *dais*, a table, from Latin *discus*, a quoit—the raised floor at the upper end of a dining-room ; a raised seat, often canopied." Brachet's Etymological Dictionary, in which the compiler follows Littré, says that "*dais* in old French *always* meant a dinner-table, but especially a state table with a canopy ; that gradually the sense of table has been lost, and that of canopy prevails ; whereas in England the sense of canopy is lost, while that of the platform on which the table stands has taken its place."

May not all these apparent discrepancies between canopy, platform, table, seat, and disk or discus, be explained by the Gaelic *deas*, as the real origin of dais ? The right-hand side of the host was the place of honour, reserved for the most distinguished guest ; and the canopy was raised, as a matter of course, at the upper end of the banqueting hall, where kings and great nobles held their festivals. The suggestion will be taken by philologists *quantum valeat*. It is certainly as well deserving of consideration as the derivation from *discus* is, which has hitherto found favour with philologists who are ignorant of the Gaelic.

Deave, to deafen.

Last May a braw wooer came down the lang glen,
An' sair wi' his love he did *deave* me ;

I said there was naethin' I hated like men,
The deil gae wi'm to believe me.
—BURNS.

A drunken wife I hae at hame,
Her noisome din aye *deaves* me ;
The ale-wife, the ale-wife,
The ale-wife she grieves me ;
The ale-wife an' her barrelie
They ruin me an' *deave* me.
—BUCHAN'S *Scots Songs and Ballads.*

Deil's-buckie or **Deevil's-buckie**, an angry epithet applied to any mischievous lad or small boy. Jamieson says *buckie* signifies a spiral shell of any kind, and adds that a refractory urchin is not only designated by irate persons as a *deil's buckie*, but as a *thrawn* or twisted *buckie*. It may be questioned, however, whether *buckie* is not derived from the Gaelic *buachaille*, a cowherd, and not from a shell, as far more likely to be in use among a pastoral and agricultural peasantry than a shell, that is not in any way suggestive of either a good boy or a bad one.

Deray, disorder, disarray. The word is also applied to any amusement of a boisterous character.

Sic dancin' and *deray.*
—*Christ's Kirk on the Green.*

The word is used by the old poets Barbour and Douglas, but seldom or never by those of the seventeenth and eighteenth centuries, and is all but obsolete.

Dern, dismal, gloomy.

> Auld Dourie never saw a blink,
> The lodging was so dark and *dern*.
> —*Border Minstrelsy: Chirstie's Will.*

Deuch, a drink, a draught; a corruption of the Gaelic *deoch*, which has the same meaning. Jamieson has *deuch-an-dorach* and *deuch-an-doris*, both corruptions of the Gaelic *deoch-an-dorus*, a drink at the door, the parting cup, the stirrup-cup. The alehouse sign, once common in England as well as in Scotland, "The Dog and Duck," appears to have had no relation to aquatic sports, but to have been a corruption of the Gaelic *deoch an diagh*, a drink to-day. In the same manner, "Mad Dog" —once set up as a sign at a place called Odell, as recorded in Hotten's "History of Signboards"—is merely the Gaelic of *math deoch* or *maith deoch*, good drink. In the London slang of the present day, *duke* is a word used among footmen and grooms for gin.

Deuk. A vulgar old song, which Burns altered and sent to "Johnson's Museum," without much improvement on the coarse original, commences with the lines:—

> The bairns gat out wi' an unco shout,
> The *deuk's* dang o'er my daddie, oh!
> The fient may care, quo' the ferlie auld wife,
> He was but a paidlin' body, oh!

The glossaries that accompany the editions of Burns issued by Allan Cunningham, Alexander Smith, and others, all agree in stating that *deuk* signifies the aquatic fowl the duck. But "the *duck* has come over, or beaten over, or flown over my father," does not make sense of the passage, or convey any meaning whatever. It is probable— though no editor of Burns has hitherto hinted it—that the word *deuk* should be *deuch*, from the Gaelic *deoch*, drink, a deep potation, which appears in Jamieson without other allusion to its Gaelic origin than the well-known phrase the *deoch-an-dorus*, the stirrup-cup or drink at the door. (*See* DEUCH, *ante.*) Seen in this light, the line "the *deuch's* dang o'er my daddie" would signify "the *drink* or drunkenness has beaten or come over my daddie," and there can be little doubt that this is the true reading.

Dew-piece, a slight refreshment, a piece of bread, a scone, or oatcake, given out to farm-servants in the early morning before proceeding to out-of-door work.

Dight, to wipe, or wipe off.

> *Dight* your mou' ere I kiss you.
> —*Old Song.*

Just as I *dight* frae the table the wine drops in ma sleeve.—*Noctes Ambrosianæ.*

Dilly castle. This, according to Jamieson, is a name given by boys to a mound of sand which they erect on the sea shore, and stand upon until the advancing tide surrounds it and washes it away. He thinks the name comes from the Teutonic "*digle* or *digel*, secretus, or from the Swedish *doelja* or *dylga*, occultare suus, a hiding-place." The etymology was not so far to seek or so difficult to find as Dr. Jamieson supposed, but is of purely home origin in the Gaelic *dile* (in two syllables), a flood, an inundation, an overflow of water.

Ding, to beat, or beat out; from the Gaelic *dinn*, to trample, to tread down.

If ye've the deil in ye, *ding* him out wi' his brither. Ae deil *dings* anither.

It's a sair *dung* (beaten) bairn that manna greet.—ALLAN RAMSAY, *Scots Proverbs.*

Ding only survives in English in the phrase *ding*, dong, bell; and is the slang of working people out on the strike for an advance of wages, who call a comrade who has left the confederacy, and yielded to the terms of the employer, a *dung*, *i.e.*, one who is beaten in the conflict.

The following ludicrous example of the use of *dung* as the past tense of *ding*, to beat, is given by Dean Ramsay in an anecdote of two *bethrels* or *beadles*, who were severally boasting of the fervour of their two ministers in preaching :—

" I think," said one, " our minister did weel. Ay! he gart the stour fly out o' the cushion." To which the other replied with a calm feeling of superiority, " Stour out o' the cushion! Hoot! our minister, sin' he cam' till us, has *dung* the guts out o' twa Bibles!"

Dink, from the Gaelic *diong*, worthy, highly esteemed, proud, is suggested by Jamieson to mean neat, prim, saucy. The word occurs in the song, " My lady's gown there's gairs upon't," in which a lover draws a contrast between the great lady of his neighbourhood and the humble lass that he is in love with, to the disadvantage of the former. To " *dink* up " is to dress gorgeously or ostentatiously. *Gair*, in the title of the song, signifies an ornamental fold in the dress.

My lady's *dink*, my lady's dressed,
The flower and fancy o' the West ;
But the lassie that a man lo'es best,
That's the lass to make him blest.

Dinsome, noisy, full of din.

Till block an' studdie (stithy or anvil) ring and reel
Wi' *dinsome* clamour.
—BURNS : *Scotch Drink.*

Dirdum, noise, uproar ; supposed to be a corruption of the Gaelic *torman*, noise, uproar, confusion.

Humph ! it's juist because—juist that the *dirdum's* a' about yon man's pockmanty.—SCOTT : *Rob Roy.*

Sic a *dirdum* about naething.
—*Laird of Logan.*

What wi' the *dirdum* and confusion, and the lowpin here and there of the skeigh brute of a horse.—SCOTT : *Fortunes of Nigel.*

Dirl, a quivering blow on a hard substance.

> I threw a noble throw at ane,
> . . . . . .
> It jist played *dirl* upon the bane,
> But did nae mair.
> —BURNS: *Death and Dr. Hornbook.*

Divot, a piece of turf ready cut and dried for burning.

> The deil sat girnin' in the neuk,
> Rivin' sticks to roast the Duke,
> And aye they kept it hot below,
> Bonnie laddie ! Highland laddie !
> Wi' peats and *divots* frae Glencoe,
> Bonnie laddie ! Highland laddie !
> —*Jacobite Ballad.*

Doited, confused, bewildered, stupid ; hopelessly perplexed ; of a darkened or hazy intellect.

> Thou clears the head o' *doited* lear,
> Thou cheers the heart o' droopin' care,
> Thou even brightens dark despair
> Wi' gloomy smile.
> —BURNS: *Scotch Drink.*

> Ye auld, blind, *doited* bodie,
> And blinder may ye be—
> 'Tis but a bonnie milking cow
> My minnie gied to me.
> —*Our Gudeman cam' Hame at E'en.*

This word seems to be derivable from the Gaelic *doite*, dark-coloured, obscure.

Doited evidently has some connection with the modern English word *dotage*, which again comes from *dote*, which anciently had, in addition to its modern meaning, that of to grow dull, senseless, or stupid.—R. DRENNAN.

Do-nae-guid and **Ne'er-do-weel.** These words are synonymous, and signify what the French call a *vaurien*, one who is good for nothing. *Ne'er-do-weel* has lately become much more common in English than "never-do-well."

Donnart, stupefied.

> "Has he learning?" "Just dung *donnart* wi' learnin'."
> —SCOTT: *St. Ronan's Well.*

Jamieson traces this word to the German *donner*, thunder ; but it comes most likely from the Gaelic *donas*, ill-fortune, or *donadh*, mischief, hurt, evil—corrupted by the Lowland Scotch by the insertion of the letter *r*. The English word *dunce* appears to be from the same source, and signifies an unhappy person, who is too stupid to learn.

Donnot or **donot**, a ne'er-do-weel, usually applied to an idle or worthless girl or woman ; a corruption of *do-nought*, or do-nothing.

> Janet, thou *donot*,
> I'll lay my best bonnet
> Thou gets a new gudeman afore it be night.
> —*Minstrelsy of the Scottish Border.*

Donsie, unlucky ; from the Gaelic *donas*, misfortune ; the reverse of *sonas*, sonsie or lucky.

> Their *donsie* tricks, their black mistakes,
> Their failings and mischances.
> —BURNS: *Address to the Unco Guid.*

Jamieson admits that the word may be derived from the Gaelic *donas*, and says that it means not only unlucky, but pettish, peevish, ill-natured, dull, dreary. But all these epithets resolve themselves more or less intimately into the idea of unluckiness.

Doo, a dove, a pigeon ; *doo*-tart or tert, a pigeon-pie. " My bonnie *doo* " is a familiar and tender salutation to a lover. *Doo-cot*, a dove-cot.

Oh, lay me doun, my *doo*, my *doo*,
  Oh, lay me doun, my ain kind dearie ;
For dinna ye mind upo' the time
  We met in the wood at the well sae wearie.
     —BUCHAN'S *Ancient Ballads.*

Dook or **douk**, to dive under water. Colloquial English, to duck or dive.

Gae *douk*, gae *douk*, the king he cried,
Gae *douk* for gold and fee,
Oh, wha will *douk* for Hunter's sake.
    —HERD'S *Collection ; Young Hunter.*

Dool or **dule**, pain, grief, dolefulness ; from the Gaelic *dolas*, the French *deuil*, mourning.

Of a' the numerous human *dools*,
  Thou bear'st the gree.
  —BURNS : *Address to the Toothache.*

Though dark and swift the waters pour,
  Yet here I wait in *dool* and sorrow ;
For bitter fate must I endure,
  Unless I pass the stream ere morrow.
     —*Legends of the Isles.*

Oh, *dule* on the order
  Sent our lads to the Border—
The English for once by guile won the day.
    —*The Flowers of the Forest.*

Dorty, haughty, stubborn, austere, supercilious ; from *dour*, hard (q.v.)

Let *dorty* dames say na !
  As lang as e'er they please,
Seem caulder than the snaw
  While inwardly they bleeze.
  —ALLAN RAMSAY : *Polwarth on the Green.*

Then though a minister grow *dorty*,
  Ye'll snap your fingers
    Before his face.
  —BURNS : *Earnest Cry and Prayer.*

Douce, of a gentle or courteous disposition ; from the French *doux*, sweet.

Ye dainty deacons and ye *douce* conveners.
    —BURNS : *The Brigs of Ayr.*

Ye Irish lords, ye knights and squires,
Who represent our brughs and shires,
An' *doucely* manage our affairs
    In Parliament.
  —BURNS : *The Author's Earnest Cry and Prayer.*

Doun - draught. A pull - down, draw-down, or drag-down.

Twa men upon ae dog's a sair *doun-draught.—Noctes Ambrosianæ.*

Dour, hard, bitter, disagreeable, close-fisted, severe, stern ; from the French and Latin, *dur* and *durus.*

When biting Boreas, fell and *dour*,
Sharp shivers through the leafless bower.
    —BURNS : *A Winter Night.*

I've been harsh-tempered and *dour* enough, I know ; and it's only fitting as they should be hard and *dour* to me where I'm going.—A. TROLLOPE : *Vicar of Bullhampton.*

Dous or **Doos**, *i.e.*, doves. To " shoot amang the *dous* " is a metaphorical phrase for making an assertion at random or without knowledge. It is sometimes applied to any wilfully false assertion. The true meaning is merely that of an indiscriminate shot, in the hope of hitting or killing something — as in the barbarous practice, miscalled *sport*, which was the fashion under royal patronage at Hurlingham, of firing into a cloud of pigeons with the chance or the certainty of killing some of them.

Dow, to be able, of which the synonym in the infinitive mood *to can*, from the Teutonic *kannen*, has long been obsolete. The misuse and perversion of this word in English in the customary greeting "How do you do?" is a remarkable instance of the corruption of the popular speech by the illiterate multitude, and its adoption after long currency by the literate, until it acquires an apparent authenticity and a real vitality which no correction however authoritative can rectify. "How do you *do?*" originally meant, and still means, how do you *dow?* *i.e.*, how is your strength or ability? how do you thrive or prosper or get on? as in the German phrase *Wie geht's?* or *Wie befinden sie sich?* the Italian *Come state?* or *Come sta?* in the French *Comment vous portez vous?* or *Comment vous va-t-il?* or the Gaelic *Cia mar tha sibh an diugh*, pronounced *ca-mar-a shee an dew*, equivalent to the English *How are you?* The ancient word *doughty*, strong, is a derivative of *dow*, able. *Dow* is provincial in England, but common in Lowland Scotch.

Facts are chiels that winna ding,
And *downa* be disputed.—BURNS.

And now he goes daundrin' about the dykes,
An' a' he *dow* do is to hund the tykes.
—LADY GRIZZEL BAILLIE.

Dowd, stale, flat; from the Gaelic *daoidh*, weak, feeble, worthless.

Cast na out the *dowd* water till ye get the fresh.—ALLAN RAMSAY'S *Scots Proverbs.*

Dowf, doof, doofing, doofart. All these words are applied to a stupid, inactive, dull person, and appear to be the originals of the modern English slang a *duffer*, which has a similar meaning.

Her *dowff* excuses pat me mad.
—BURNS: *Epistle to Lapraik.*

They're *dowf* and *dowie* at the best,
Dowf and *dowie, dowf* and *dowie,*
Wi' a' their variorum;
They canna please a Highland taste
Compared wi' Tullochgorum.
—Rev. JOHN SKINNER.

Dowie, gloomy, melancholy, forlorn, low-spirited; from the Gaelic *duibhe*, blackness.

It's no the loss o' warl's gear
That could sae bitter draw the tear,
Or mak' our bardie, *dowie*, wear
The mourning weed.
—BURNS: *Poor Mailie's Elegy.*

Come listen, cronies, ane and a',
While on my *dowie* reed I blaw,
And mourn the sad untimely fa'
O' our auld town.
—JAMES BALLANTINE.

Down. The Scottish language contains many more compounds of *down* than the English, such as *down-drag* and *down-draw*, that which drags or draws a man down in his fortunes, an incumbrance ; *down-throw*, of which the English synonym is *overthrow ; down-way*, a declivity or downward path ; *down-put* or *down-putting*, a rebuff ; *down-coming*, abandonment of the sick-room on convalescence ; *down-look*, a dejected look or expression of countenance ; all of which are really English, although not admitted into the dictionaries.

Downa-do, impotency, powerlessness, inability.

> I've seen the day ye buttered my brose,
> And cuddled me late and early, O !
> But *downa-do's* come o'er me now,
> And oh I feel it sairly, O !
> —BURNS : *The Deuk's Dang o'er my Daddie.*

Dowp, the posterior, sometimes written *dolp*. This word applies not only to the human frame, but to the bottom or end of anything, and is used in such phrases as the " *dowp* of a candle," "the *dowp* of an egg," as well as in the threats of an angry mother to a young child, " I'll skelp your *dowp*." " Where's your grannie, my wee man ? " was a question asked of a child. The child replied, " Oh, she's ben the house, burning her *dowp*," *i.e.*, her candle-end.

Deil a wig has a provost o' Fairport worn sin auld Provost Jervie's time, and he had a quean o' a servant lass that dressed it hersel' wi' the *dowp o' a candle* and a dredging-box.—SCOTT : *The Antiquary.*

Dowp-skelper. A humorous word applied to a schoolmaster ; from *skelp*, to smite with the palm of the hand. A similar idea enters into the composition of the English phrase " a bum-brusher," with the difference that *brusher* refers to the rod, and not to the palm of the hand. Burns applies the epithet to the Emperor Joseph of Austria, with what allusion it is now difficult to trace :—

> To ken what French mischief was brewin'
> Or what the drumlie Dutch were doin'—
> That vile *dowp-skelper* Emperor Joseph,
> If Venus yet had got his nose off.
> —BURNS : *To a Gentleman who had Promised to send him a Newspaper.*

This word is not to be mistaken for *dub*-skelper—from *dub*, a pool, a pond, a puddle—and applied to one who rushes on his way recklessly, through thick and thin, heedless of dirt or obstruction.

Draibles or **drabbles**, drops of liquor or crumbs of food allowed to fall from the hand upon the clothes in the act of drinking or eating ; akin to the English *driblets*, signifying small quantities of anything.

Draidgie. A funeral entertainment ; from the French *dragée*, a comfit, a sweetmeat. This word does not appear in Jamieson, but is to be found in a small and excellent handbook of the Scottish vernacular, published in Edinburgh, 1818.

Dram. This ancient Scottish word for a small glass or "nip" of whisky or any other alcoholic liquor has long been adopted into English, but has no synonym of any allied sound in any other European language. The French call it a "*petit verre*," and the Germans a "*schnapps*," while the Americans have recently taken to calling it a "*smile*," or "*an eye-opener*." Philologists have been contented to derive it from the Greek *drachma*, though, if this be the fact, it is curious that the word has not found its way into the vernacular of any other people than those of the British Isles. But though the classic etymology be too firmly rooted in popular estimation to be readily abandoned, it may be interesting to note that in Lowland Scotch *dram* originally signified melancholy, heaviness of mind, from the Gaelic *truime*, heaviness, and that the *dram* was resorted to in order to raise the spirits and drive out melancholy —an idea which seems to have suggested the current American slang of a "*smile.*"

ᵣ A story is told in Scotland of an old farmer too much addicted to his "dram" and his toddy, who was strictly forbidden by his medical attendant to indulge in more than an *ounce* of whisky per *diem*, if he hoped to escape a serious illness. The old man was puzzled at the word "ounce," and asked his son, who had studied at the University of St. Andrews and was qualifying for the Scottish ministry, what the doctor meant by an *ounce*. " An ounce," said his son, "why, every one knows that an ounce is sixteen *drams* (drachms)." " Ah! weel," said his sire, "if I may tak' saxteen drams i' the day, it's a' *richt*, an' I'll dae weel eneuch. The doctor, nae doot, kens his business. I've already had twa the day, and I've still fourteen to the fore!" Tradition does not record the ultimate fate of the old farmer.

Dreder, terror, apprehension, dread of impending evil; sometimes written *dredour.*

What aileth you, my daughter Janet,
 You look so pale and wan?
There is a *dreder* in your heart,
 Or else you love a man.
 —BUCHAN'S *Ancient Ballads: Lord
 Thomas and the King's Daughter.*

Dree, to endure, to suffer; probably from the Teutonic *trüben*, to trouble, to sadden, and thence to endure trouble or suffering; or from *tragen*, to bear, to carry, to draw.

Sae that no danger do thee deir
 What dule in dern thou *dree*
(What soon thou mayst suffer in secret).
 —*Robyn and Makyn: The Evergreen.*
Oh wae, wae by his wanton sides,
 Sae brawlie he could flatter,
Till for his sake I'm slighted sair,
 And *dree* the kintra clatter.
 —BURNS: *Here's his Health in Water.*

In the dialects of the North of England, to *dree* is used in the sense of to draw or journey towards a place.

In the summer-time, when leaves grow green,
 And birds sing on the tree,
Robin Hood went to Nottingham
 As fast as he could *dree.*
 —*Robin Hood and the Jolly Tinker.*

Dreigh, difficult, hard to travel, tedious, prolix, dry.

Hech, sirs! but the sermon was sair *dreigh!*
 —GALT.
Dreich at the thought and dour at the delivery.—*Noctes Ambrosianæ.*

Driddle. This is a word of several meanings, all more or less significant of anything done by small quantities at a time, such as to urinate often, to move with slow steps, to spill a liquid by unsteady handling of the vessel which contains it. It appears to be traceable to the Gaelic *drudh* or *druidh*, to ooze, to drip, to penetrate, and *drudhag*, a small drop.

Droddum, a jocular name for the breech, the posteriors, but more popularly known as the *hurdies* or *dowp* (which see).

My sooth ! right bauld ye set your nose out,
As plump and grey as ony grozet ;
Oh, for some rank mercurial rozet,
    Or fell red smeddum,
I'd gie ye sic a hearty dose o't,
    Wad dress your *droddum*.

  —BURNS : *To a Louse, on seeing one on
    a Lady's Bonnet at Church.*

The word seems to be of kin to *drod*, thick, squat, fleshy. The derivation is uncertain.

Droich, a dwarf ; from the Gaelic *troid* or *troich*, with the same meaning.

Only look at the pictures (of the aristocracy) in their auld castles. What beautiful and brave faces ! Though now and then, to be sure, a dowdy or a *droich.—Noctes Ambrosianæ.*

Drook, to wet ; **drookit**, wet through, thoroughly saturated with moisture ; from the Gaelic *druchd*, dew, moisture, a tear, a drop ; *drudhag (dru-ag)*, a drop of water ; and *drughadh*, penetrating, oozing through. The

resemblance to the Greek δακρυ, a tear, is noteworthy.

There were twa doos sat in a dookit,
The rain cam' doun and they were *drookit*.
        —Nursery Song.

The last Hallowe'en I was waukin'
  My *drookit* sark sleeve, as ye ken,
His likeness cam ben the house stalkin',
  And the vera grey breeks o' Tam Glen.
        —BURNS : *Tam Glen.*

My friends, you come to the kirk every Sabbath, and I lave you a' ower wi' the Gospel till ye're fairly *drookit* wi't.—*Extract from a sermon by a minister in Arran :* ROGERS'S *Illustrations of Scottish Life.*

Drouth, thirst ; **drouthie**, thirsty ; from *dry, dryeth.*

Tell him o' mine and Scotland's *drouth*.
      —BURNS : *Cry and Prayer.*

Folks talk o' my drink, but never talk o' my *drouth.*—ALLAN RAMSAY'S *Scots Proverbs.*

When *drouthie* neebors neebors meet.
      —BURNS : *Tam o' Shanter.*

Drumlie, turbid or muddy (applied to water), confused, not clear ; applied metaphorically to thoughts or expression. This word would be a great acquisition to the English language if it could be adopted, and lends a peculiar charm to many choice passages of Scottish poetry. All its English synonyms are greatly inferior to it, both in logical and poetical expression. It is derived from the Gaelic *trom* or *truim*, heavy (and applied to water), turbid. The word appears at one time to have been good English.

Draw me some water out of this spring. Madam, it is all foul, *drumly*, black, muddy !—*French and English Grammar,* 1623.

D

Haste, boatman, haste ! put off your boat,
    Put off your boat for golden monie ;
I'll cross the *drumlie* stream to-night,
    Or never mair I'll see my Annie.
        —*Minstrelsy of the Scottish Border.*

When blue diseases fill the *drumlie* air.
                —ALLAN RAMSAY.

    Drink *drumly* German water
To make himself look fair and fatter.
                —BURNS : *The Twa Dogs.*

They had na sailed a league, a league,
    A league but barely three,
When dismal grew his countenance,
    And *drumlie* grew his e'e.
        —LAIDLAW : *The Demon Lover.*

    There's good fishing in *drumlie* waters.
ALLAN RAMSAY'S *Scots Proverbs.*

I heard once a lady in Edinburgh ob-
jecting to a preacher that she did not
understand him. Another lady, his great
admirer, insinuated that probably he was
too deep for her to follow. But her ready
answer was, " Na, na !—he's no just deep,
ut he's *drumly*."—DEAN RAMSAY.

Drummock, cold porridge.—*Noctes
Ambrosianæ.*

Drunt, draunt, to drawl, to whine,
to grumble; a fit of ill-humour,
pettishness. Both of these words
are from the Gaelic *dranndan,*
grumbling, growling, mourning,
complaining ; *dranndanach,* peevish, morose, though erroneously derived by Jamieson from
the Flemish *drinten,* tumescere.

        May nae doot took the *drunt,*
        To be compared to Willie.
                —BURNS : *Hallowe'en.*

Nae weel-tocher'd aunts to wait on their
        drunts,
And wish them in hell for it a', man.
        —BURNS : *The Tarbolton Lasses.*

But lest he think I am uncivil,
To plague you with this *draunting* drivel.
                —BURNS.

Dub, a small pool of dirty water.
The *Goose-dubs* is the name of a
street in Glasgow.   *Deuk-dub,* a
duck-pond.

        O'er *dub* and dyke
        She'll run the fields all through.
                —*Leader Haughs and Yarrow.*

There lay a *deuk-dub* afore the door,
    And there fell he, I trow.
        —HERD'S *Collection : The Brisk
            Young Lad.*

Dud, a rag ; **duddies,** little rags.

    Then he took out his little knife,
        Let a' his *duddies* fa',
    An' he was the brawest gentleman
        That stood amang them a'.
            —*We'll Gang nae Mair a Rovin'.*

A smytrie o' wee *duddie* weans.
                —BURNS.

    The *duddie* wee laddie may grow a braw
man.—DAVID HUTCHESON.

Dunnie-wassal, a Highland gentleman.

There are wild *dunnie-wassals* three
        thousand times three
Will cry *oich* for the bonnets o' Bonnie
        Dundee.—SIR WALTER SCOTT.

    This word, generally mis-
printed in the Lowlands, and
by Sir Walter Scott in his excellent ballad of "Bonnie Dundee," is from the Gaelic *duine,* a
man, and *uasal,* gentle, noble, of
good birth.

Dunsh, to sit down hastily and
heavily.

His dowp *dunshin'* down.—*Noctes Ambrosianæ.*

Dunt, a blow, a knock ; from *dint,*
to deal a heavy blow that leaves
a mark on a hard substance.

I am naebody's lord,
I am slave to naebody;
I hae a gude broad sword,
I'll tak' *dunts* frae naebody.
—BURNS : *Naebody.*

Dush or **dish,** to push with the head or horns like animals, to butt, to ram ; also to give a hard blow, to destroy or discomfit.

Ye needna doubt I held my whisht,
The infant aith, half-formed, was crusht ;
I glower'd as eerie's I'd been *dusht*
  In some wild glen ;
Then sweet, like modest worth, she blusht,
  And steppit ben.
          —BURNS : *The Vision.*

The English slang *dish,* to defeat or conquer, seems to be of similar origin ; as when the late Lord Derby made use of the expression " *Dish* the Whigs," he meant to discomfit, circumvent them, or defeat them as a party. The root seems to be the Gaelic *dith (di),* to press, to squeeze, and *disne,* a die or press.

Duxy, ugly, mischievous ; from the Gaelic *duaich* and *duaich-nidh,* ugly.

You *duxy* lubber, brace your lyre ;
Still higher yet ! you fiend, play higher.
  .   .   .   .   .
Sic themes were never made to suit
Your dozen o' lugs, ye *duxy* brute.
  —GEORGE BEATTIE : *John o' Arnha'.*

Dwam, a swoon, a fainting fit.

Fast congealin' into a sort of *dwam* and stupefaction.—*Noctes Ambrosianæ.*

Dyke-louper, an immoral unmarried woman, or mother of an illegitimate child. The *dyke* in this phrase means the marriage tie, obligation, or sacramental wall that prohibits the illicit intercourse of the sexes ; and *louper,* one who treats the wall and its impediment as nonexistent, or who despises it by *louping,* jumping, or leaping over it.

Dyvor, a bankrupt ; from the Gaelic *dith (di),* to destroy, to break ; and *fear,* a man—a broken man or bankrupt. Jamieson derives the word from the French *devoir,* duty, or to serve.

Smash them, crash them a' to spails,
And rot the *dyvors* in the jails.
  —BURNS : *Address of Beelzebub.*

E

Eastie - wastie, a person who does not know his own mind, who veers round in his purpose from one side to the other, *i.e.,* from *east* to *west.*

Eee-bree, an eyebrow.

There's no a bird in a' this forest
  Will do as muckle for me

As dip its wing in the warm water
An' straik it on my *ee-bree.*
  —*Johnnie o' Braidislee (when dying
      alone in the forest).*

Eerie, gloomy, wearisome, full of fear.

In mirkiest glen at midnight hour
  I'd rove and ne'er be *eerie,* O !
If thro' that glen I gaed to thee,
  My ain kind dearie, O.—BURNS.

It was an *eerie* walk through the still chestnut woods at that still hour of the night.—*The Dream Numbers, by* T. A. TROLLOPE.

Aft yont the dyke she's heard you bummin'
  Wi' *eerie* drone.
   —BURNS: *Address to the Deil.*

Eerie is a most difficult word to explain. I don't know any English word that comes near it in meaning. The feeling induced by eerieness is that sort of superstitious fear that creeps over one in darkness,—that sort of awe we feel in the presence of the unseen and unknown. Anything unusual or incongruous might produce the feeling. "The cry of howlets mak's me *eerie*," says Tannahill. The following anecdote illustrates the feeling when a thing unusual or incongruous is presented : —An Ayrshire farmer, who had visited Ireland, among other *uncos* he had seen, related that he went to the Episcopal church there, and this being the first time he had ever heard the English service, he was startled by seeing a falla' come in with a long white sark on, down to his heels. "Lord, sir, the sicht o' him made me feel quite *eerie.*"—R. DRENNAN.

Eith, easy; etymology uncertain, but neither Gaelic, Flemish, nor German.

It's *eith* defending a castle that's no besieged.
It's *eith* learning the cat the way to the kirn.
Eith learned, soon forgotten.
It's *eith* working when the will's at hame.
 —ALLAN RAMSAY'S *Scots Proverbs.*

Eke, to add to, an addition ; "*eik* to a testament," a codicil to a will. This English word has acquired a convivial meaning in Scotland among toddy-drinkers. When a guest is about to depart, after having had a fair allowance of whisky, the host presses him to "tak an eke"—*i.e.*, another glass, to eke out the quantity. "I hate intemperance," said a northern magistrate, who was reproached by an ultra-temperance advocate for the iniquity of his trade as a distiller, "but I like to see a cannie, respectable, honest man tak' his sax tumblers and an *eke* in the bosom o' his family. But I canna thole intemperance!"

Eldritch, fearful, terrible. Jamieson has this word *elrische*, and thinks it is related to *elves* or evil spirits, and that it is derived from two Anglo-Saxon words signifying *elf* and *rich*, or rich in elves or fairies! The true derivation is from the Gaelic *oillt*, terror, dread, horror, which, combined with *droch*, bad, wicked, formed the word as Burns and other Scottish writers use it.

On the *eldritch* hill there grows a thorn.
  —PERCY'S *Reliques: Sir Carline.*

   The witches follow
Wi' mony an *eldritch* screech and hollow.
  —BURNS: *Tam o' Shanter.*

 I've heard my reverend grannie say,
 In lonely glens ye like to stray,
 Or where auld ruined castles gray
  Nod to the moon,
 To fright the nightly wanderer's way
  Wi' *eldritch* croon.
  —BURNS: *Address to the Deil.*

Eme, an uncle ; from the Teutonic *oheim.*

 The pummel o' a guid auld saddle,
 And Rob my *eme* bocht me a sack,
 'Twa lovely lips to lick a ladle,
 Gin Jenny and I agree, quo' Jock.
  —*The Wooin' o' Jenny and Jock.*

Ettle, to try, to attempt, to endeavour.

For Nannie, far before the rest,
Hard upon noble Maggie prest,
And flew at Tam wi' furious *ettle*,
But little wist she Maggie's metal.
—BURNS : *Tam o' Shanter.*

I *ettled* wi' kindness to soften her pride.
—JAMES BALLANTINE : *The Way to Woo.*

They that *ettle* to get to the top of the ladder will at least get up some rounds.— They that *mint* at a gown of gold will always get a sleeve of it.—SCOTT : *The Monastery.*

Ettle.—The correct synonyms are to intend, to expect, to aim at. Intention is the essential element in the meaning of this word.—R. DRENNAN.

Everly, continually, always, for ever.

To be set doun to a wheelie (spinning wheel),
An' at it for ever to ca',
An' syne to hae't reel by a chielie (fellow)
That *everly* cryed to draw.
—*Woo'd an' Married an' a.*

Ewe-bucht, a sheepfold ; **buchtin'**, or **buchtin'-time**, the evening time or gloaming, when the cattle are driven into the fold.

When o'er the hill the eastern star
Tells *bughtin'-time* is near, my jo,
And owsen frae the furrow'd field,
Return sae dowf and wearie, O.
—BURNS : *My Ain Kind Dearie, O.*

Oh, the broom, the bonnie, bonnie broom,
The broom o' the Cowden knowes !
And aye sae sweet as the lassie sang,
In the *ewe-bucht*, milking her ewes.
—*The Broom o' the Cowden Knowes.*

The word *bught* seems to be an abbreviation of the Gaelic

buaigheal, a cow-stall, and *buai-chaille*, a cowherd, a shepherd ; *buaile*, a fold ; *buailte*, folded, or driven into the fold. Jamieson goes to Germany for the root of the word and does not find it.

Eydent, diligent, earnest, zealous ; from the Gaelic *eud*, zeal.

My fair child,
Persuade the kirkmen *eydently* to pray.
—HENRYSONE : *The Lion and the Mouse : The Evergreen.*

Their master's and their mistress's command
The youngsters a' were warned to obey,
An' mind their labours wi' an *eydent* hand.
—BURNS : *Cotter's Saturday Night.*

Eyrie, an eagle's nest ; from the Gaelic *eirich*, to rise, and *eirigh*, a rising.

The eagle and the stork
On cliffs and cedar tops their *eyries* build.
—MILTON.

'Tis the fire shower of ruin all dreadfully driven
From his *eyrie* that beacons the darkness of heaven.
—CAMPBELL : *Lochiel's Warning.*

Eytyn, Etyn, Etaine, Aiten, Red-Aiten. This word, with its different but not unsimilar spellings, appears to be a corruption of the Norse *Jotun*, a giant. It was formerly used in England as well as in Scotland. *Hynde Etyn*, or the gentle giant, is the title of a Scottish ballad in Kinloch's Collection.

They say the King of Portugal cannot sit at his meat, but the giants and *etyns* will come and snatch it from him.—BEAUMONT AND FLETCHER : *Burning Pestle.*

F

Fa', the Scottish abbrevation of *fall*. The word is used by Burns in the immortal song of "A man's a man for a' that," in a sense which has given rise to much doubt as to its meaning:—

A king can mak' a belted knight,
  A marquis, duke, and a' that ;
But an honest man's aboon his might,
  Gude faith, he mauna *fa'* that.

The context would seem to imply that *fa'* means to try, to attempt. No author except Burns uses the word in this sense ; and none of the varieties of words in which *fall* or the act of *falling*, either physically or metaphorically, is the primary meaning, meets the necessities of Burns's stanza. Halliwell has *fay* as an archaic English word, with five different meanings, of which the fourth is to succeed, to act, to work. The *fa'* of Burns may possibly be a variety of the English word, current in Ayrshire in his time. It finds no place in Jamieson.

Burns did not originate the idea, so well expressed, and to which he has given such wide currency. It is to be found in an anecdote recorded of King James VI. and his faithful old nurse, who came uninvited from Edinburgh to pay him a visit. It is told that the King was delighted to see her, and asked her kindly what he could do for her. After some hesitation, she replied that she desired nothing for herself, only that she wanted his Majesty to make her son a gentleman. "Ah, Jeanie, Jeanie!" said the King, "I can mak' him a duke, if ye like ; but I canna mak' him a gentleman unless he mak's himsel' ane!"

Faird, a journey, a course. Jamieson thinks it signifies a hasty and noted effort, and quotes a Mid-Lothian phrase, "Let them alane ; it's but a *faird*, it'll no last lang ; they'll no win (arrive) far afore us." The word is evidently from the same source as *fare*, to travel, as in way-*farer ;* the Teutonic *fahren*, to go, to travel ; and *fähre*, a ferry, a passage over the water, and *gefährlich*, dangerous ; as originally applied to travelling in primitive and unsettled times.

Fairdy, clever, tight, handy ; fair to do.

With ane ev'n keel before the wind,
  She is right *fairdy* with a sail. .
    The Fleming Bark—belonging to Edinburgh.
  —ALLAN RAMSAY : *The Evergreen.*

Fairin' signifies either reward or punishment; one's deserts. *Fair fa'!* may good or fair things befall you! is equivalent to a benison or benediction.

Jamieson derives the word from *fair* or market, and thinks it means a present bought at a fair. But this is guess-work, and does not meet the sense of the passage in "Tam o' Shanter." Possibly it has some connection with the Teutonic *gefahr*, danger, also a doom or punishment ; supposed, in its favourable term, to be derived from a present purchased at a fair to be bestowed as a gift on one who was not at it.

Fair fa' your honest, sonsie face,
Great chieftain o' the puddin' race.
—BURNS : *To a Haggis.*

Ah, Tam ! ah, Tam ! thou'lt get thy
fairin';
In hell they'll roast thee like a herrin'.
—BURNS : *Tam o' Shanter.*

Fank, a coil, a tangle, a noose ; possibly from *fang*, to take hold of. To *fank* a horse in a field, to catch him with a rope noose or lasso ; *fankit*, entangled ; *a fank o' tows*, a coil of ropes. It may also be the root of the English *funk*, *i.e.*, to be in a coil of perplexity or dread. The common derivation of *funk*, from the German *funk*, a sparkle of light, is not tenable. The Gaelic *fainnich* signifies to curl, from *fainne*, a ring.

Farle, a small oaten or wheaten cake, the fourth part of a bannock ; from *farthel*, or fourth part ; the Flemish *viertel* and German *fiertel*.

An' there'll be gude lapper-milk kebbucks,
An' sowens, an' *farles*, an' baps.
—*The Blithesome Bridal.*

F a s h, to bother, to worry, to distress one's self ; from the French *se fâcher*, to be angry.

Fashious, troublesome.

Speak out, and never *fash* your thumb.
—BURNS : *Earnest Cry and Prayer.*

The Rev. John Brown of Whitburn was riding out one day on an old pony, when he was accosted by a rude youth. " I say, Mr. Brown, what gars your horse's tail wag that way ? " " Oh ! " replied Brown, "just what gars your tongue wag ; it's *fashed* wi' a weakness."—DEAN RAMSAY.

Fazard, dastard, coward.

They are mair fashious nor of feck ;
Yon *fazards* durst not, for their neck,
  Climb up the crag with us.
    —MONTGOMERY : *The Cherry and
      the Slae.*

The root of this word would appear to be the Gaelic *fas*, vacant, hollow, good-for-nothing, with the addition of *ard*, as in dast*ard*, cow*ard*, wiz*ard*, a suffix which signifies eminent, or in a high degree. Thus, *fazard* or *fasard* means worthless in the extreme.

Feck, power, activity, vigour. *Feck* seems to be derivable from the Gaelic *fiach*, worth, value. *Feckful*, full of power. *Feckless*, without power or vigour of body or mind. Worcester, in his dictionary, derives this word from *effectless*.

Many a *feckful* chield this day was slain.
—BLIND HARRY'S *Wallace.*

The lazy luxury which *feckless* loons indulge in.—SCOTT.

Feckless folk are aye fain o' ane anither.
—ALLAN RAMSAY's *Scots Proverbs.*

Poor devil! see him o'er his trash,
As *feckless* as a withered rash.
—BURNS : *To a Haggis.*

That *feckless* fouter !— *Noctes Ambrosianæ.*

Fell, to kill.

The sister of a lady, who had died of a surfeit from eating too bountifully of strawberries and cream, was consoled with by a friend, who said to her, "I had hoped your sister would have lived many years." "Leeve!" she replied, "how could she leeve, when she just *felled* hersel' at Craigo wi' strawberries an' cream?"—DEAN RAMSAY.

Fend, to ward off — probably a contraction from defend. *Fend* also means to prosper or do well, to provide, to live comfortably—possibly from the idea of warding off want or poverty.

Can she mak' nae better *fend* for them than that ?—SCOTT : *The Monastery.*

But gie them guid coo-milk their fill,
Till they be fit to *fend* themsel'.
— BURNS : *Dying Words of Poor Mailie.*

Here stands a shed to *fend* the showers,
And screen our countra gentry.
—BURNS : *The Holy Fair.*

How is he *fendin'*, John Tod, John Tod?
He is scouring the land wi' a song in his hand.
—CHAMBERS's *Scots Songs : John Tod.*

Fendy, clever at contrivances in difficulty, good at making a shift.

"Alice," he said, "was both canny and *fendy*."—SCOTT : *Waverley.*

Ferlie, a wonder, to wonder, wonderful.

Who harkened ever slike a *ferlie* thing.
—CHAUCER : *The Reeve's Tale.*

On Malvern hills
Me befel a *ferly.*
—*Piers Ploughman.*

Never breathe out of kin and make your friends *ferly* at you.

The longer we live the more *ferlies* we see.
—ALLAN RAMSAY's *Scots Proverbs.*

And tell what new taxation's comin',
And *ferlie* at the folk in Lunnon.
—BURNS : *The Twa Dogs.*

Ferlie and wonner. In this phrase *wonner* is a corruption of the English *wonder ;* a contemptuous and ludicrous term to designate a person or thing that is strangely, wondrously ugly, ill - favoured, or mean ; almost synonymous with the modern English slang a *guy* or a *cure.* Burns uses both words in the same poem :—

Ha! where ye gaun, ye crawlin' *ferlie!*
. . . .
Ye ugly, creepin', blastit *wonner,*
Detested, shunned by saint and sinner ?
—*To a Certain Insect, on seeing one
on a Lady's Bonnet at Church.*

Ferrikie. Jamieson cites this as an Upper Clydesdale word for "strong, robust." He derives it from the German *ferig,* which he translates *expeditus, alacer ;* but there is no such word as *ferig* in the German language. It is more probably from the Gaelic *fear,* a man, *fearachas,* manhood, and *fearail,* manly, virile, strong, lusty. The Welsh has *ffer,* solid, strong.

Feu, to let land for building ; a possession held on payment of a certain rent to the feudal proprietor, heritor, or owner of the soil. Where the English advertise "land to let for building purposes," the Scotch more tersely say "land to *feu*."

There is, or was lately, a space of unoccupied ground on the "Corran" at Oban, contiguous to Dunolly Castle, in the midst of which on a pole was a board inscribed "This land to *feu*." An English bishop on his holiday tour having observed the announcement, and wondering what it meant, turned to his wife and asked her if she knew. She did not, and the bishop thereupon hazarded the conjecture that it meant to "fire," from the French *feu*. "Very likely," replied the lady, "to burn the grass." Before the bishop left Oban his ignorance on the subject was dispelled by a guest at the *table-d'hôte* of the hotel to whom he applied for information. "Curious language, the Scotch!" was his lordship's rejoinder.—C. M.

Fey, fated, bewitched, unlucky, doomed ; one whose fate is foreknown or prophesied ; from the Gaelic *faidh*, a prophet, the Latin *vates*.

Let the fate fall upon the *feyest*.
Take care of the man that God has marked, for he's no *fey*.
—ALLAN RAMSAY'S *Scots Proverbs*.

We'll turn again, said good Lord John,
  But no, said Rothiemay,
My steed's trepanned, my bridle's broke,
  I fear this day I'm *fey*.
—*Minstrelsy of the Scottish Border*.

They hacked and hashed, while broadswords clashed,
And through they dashed, and hewed, and smashed,
Till *fey* men died awa, man.
—*The Battle of Sheriffmuir*.

Fidgin'-fain, extremely anxious ; from *fidge*, the English *fidget*, to be restless or anxious, and *fain*, willing or desirous.

It pat me *fidgin'-fain* to hear it.
—BURNS : *Epistle to Lapraik.*

Fiel. The glossaries to Burns explain this word to mean "smooth and comfortable," apparently from the context :—

Oh, leeze me on my spinnin'-wheel,
And leeze me on my rock and reel,
Frae tap to tae that cleeds me bien,
And haps me *fiel* and warm at e'en !
—*Bess and her Spinning-Wheel.*

Jamieson, who has *feil* and *fiel*, defines the words to mean " soft and smooth like velvet, silky to the touch, and also clean, neat, comfortable." The word must not be confounded with *feil, feill, fele*, which signify much, many, and very, and are clearly derivable from the Teutonic *viel*, which has the same meaning ; as *viel gelt*, much money. Jamieson derives the word used by Burns from the Icelandic *felldr*, habitis idorem ; but this is exceedingly doubtful. The Gaelic has *fial*, generous, liberal, bountiful, good, hospitable ; and possibly it is in this sense that Bess applies the word to the spinnin'-wheel that provides her with raiment.

Fient, none, not a particle of ; equivalent to "the devil a bit," from *fiend*, the devil ; *fient-hait*, not an iota, the devil a bit.

But though he was o' high degree,
The *fient* o' pride—nae pride had he.
—BURNS : *The Twa Dogs.*

The queerest shape that e'er I saw,
For *fient* a wame it had ava !
—BURNS : *Death and Dr. Hornbook.*

Fient-haet o't wad hae pierced the heart
O' a kail runt.—BURNS : *Idem.*

Fiere, a friend, a comrade. This word is supposed by some to be a misprint for *frere*, a brother.

> And here's a hand, my trusty *fiere*,
> And gie's a hand o' thine.
> —BURNS: *Auld Langsyne.*

This word may either be a synonym for the Latin *vir* and the Gaelic *fear*, a man, or may be derived from *fior*, true, or a true man. The Scottish poet Douglas has *fior* for sound and healthy. It is sometimes spelt *feer*.

First-foot, the first person who is met by lad or lass in the morning.

> Early morning she drest up
> And all her maides fair,
> The ploughman chiel was her *first-foot*
> As she went to take the air.
> —BUCHAN'S *Ancient Ballads.*

Flaff, a momentary display.

> Ga' I ever for a *flaff* in the Park forget my ain cosie bield.—*Noctes Ambrosianæ.*

Flamfoo. According to Jamieson this word signifies a gaudily-dressed woman, or any gaudy ornament of female dress. He derives it from an alleged old English word meaning "moonshine in the water!" It seems, however, to come from the Gaelic *flann*, corrupted into *flam*, red, the showy colour so much admired by people of uneducated taste; conjoined with the Scottish *fu'* for full. The English word *flaunting*, and the phrase *flaunts*, fiery red ribbons, are from the same root.

Flannen, the Scottish as well as the English vernacular *flannen* for *flannel*, seems to be preferable to *flannel* as the correct pronunciation of the word. Both are correct if the etymology be correct, which traces the word to the Gaelic *flann*, red, and *olann*, wool. In the early ages of civilisation, when wool was first woven for garments to clothe mankind, the favourite colours were red and yellow. In Hakluyt's Voyages it is said—"By chance they met a canoe of Dominicans, to the people whereof he gave a waistcoat of *yellow* flannel." Probably red was the first dye used, whence *flann-olann*, red wool. At an after time, when gaudy colours were not so much in request, the wool was bleached, whence *blanket* or *blanquette*, whitened.

> I wadna be surprised to spy
> You on an auld wife's *flannen* toy (cap),
> Or aiblins some bit duddie boy,
> On's wylie-coat;
> But Miss's fine Lunardi, fy!
> How daur ye do't?
> —BURNS: *To a Louse, on seeing one on a Lady's Bonnet at Church.*

Flaucht or **flaught**, a flash of lightning, a sudden blaze in the sky; from the Flemish *flakkeren* and *flikkerin*, to flicker, to shine out quickly or instantaneously.

> The thunder crack'd, and *flauchts* did rift
> Frae the black vizard o' the lift.
> —ALLAN RAMSAY: *The Vision.*
> Fierce as ony *fire-flaught* fell.
> —*Christ's Kirk on the Green.*

Flaw, a burst of bad weather, from the Gaelic *fliuch*, a rainstorm.

> Like an auld scart (cormorant) before a *flaw.*—*The Antiquary.*

Fleech or **fleich**, to pet, to wheedle, to cajole; also, to entreat or supplicate with fair words. *A fleeching day* is a day that promises to be fine, but that possibly may not turn out so. Possibly from the French *flechir*, to give way, to ask humbly, instead of demanding loudly.

Duncan *fleeched* and Duncan prayed—
Ha ! ha ! the wooin' o't.—Burns.

Expect na, sir, in this narration,
A *fleechin'*, flatterin' dedication.
—Burns : *Epistle to Gavin Hamilton.*

Hoot ! toot ! man—keep a calm sough.
Better to *fleech* a fool than fight wi' him.
—Scott : *The Monastery.*

Fleer, a gibe, a taunt—etymology doubtful. The Flemish has *fleers*, a box on the ear.

Oh, dinna ye mind o' this very *fleer*,
When we were a' riggit out to gang to Sherramuir,
Wi' stanes in our aprons ?
—Chambers's *Scottish Ballads : The Threatened Invasion.*

Fley, to scare, to frighten. Etymology unknown, but possibly from *flee*, to run away for fear, whence *fley*, to cause to run away for fear, to frighten.

A wee thing *fleys* cowards.—Allan Ramsay's *Scots Proverbs.*

It spak' right howe, My name is Death,
But he na' *fley'd*.
—Burns : *Death and Dr. Hornbook.*

Flichter, to flutter, to fly feebly ; a great number of small objects flying in the air, as " a *flichter* of birds ; " a multitude of small objects flying, floating, or fluttering in the air, as a *flichter* or flight of birds ; a *flichter* of motes in the sunbeams ; a *flichter* of heavy or large snowflakes. To *flichter* is to flutter, to quiver with joyous excitement, and also to startle or alarm. The word is evidently akin to the English *flight* and the Teutonic *flucht.*

The bird maun *flichter* that has but ae wing.—Allan Ramsay's *Scots Proverbs.*

The expectant wee things, toddlin', sprachle through,
To meet their dad, wi' *flichterin'* noise and glee.
—Burns : *Cotter's Saturday Night.*

Flinders, fragments, splinters.

He put his fingers to the lock,
I wat he handled them sickerlie ;
And doors of deal and bands of steel
He gart them all in *flinders flee.*
—Buchan's *Ancient Ballads : The Three Brothers.*

Flinging-tree, a flail, the pole of a carriage, a bar of wood in any agricultural implement.

The thresher's weary *flingin'-tree*
The lee-lang day had tirèd me,
And when the day had closed his e'e
Far i' the west,
Ben i' the spence, right pensivelie,
I gaed to rest.
—Burns : *The Vision.*

Flit, to remove from one residence to another ; a *flittin'*, a removal.

As doun the burnside she gaed slow in the *flittin'*,
Fare ye weel, Lucy, was ilka bird's sang ;
She gaed by the stable where Jamie was stannin',
Richt sair was his kind heart the *flittin'* to see.
—*Lucy's Flittin'*, by William Laidlaw (*the steward, amanuensis, and trusted friend of Sir Walter Scott*).

Flite or **flyte**, to reproach, to blame, to animadvert, to find fault with.

They *flyte* me wi' Jamie because he is poor ;
But summer is comin', cauld winter's awa,
An' he'll come back an' see me in spite
  o' them a'
—GEORGE HALKET : *Logie o' Buchan.*

Hed ! gude-wife ! ye're a *flytin'* body ;
Ye hae the will, but ye want the wit.
—SIR ALEXANDER BOSWELL : *A Matrimonial Duel.*

Floan, to flirt. Jamieson says that "*floan* means to show attachment, or court regard in an indiscreet way," and derives the word from the Icelandic *flon,* stolidus. Is it not rather from the old English *flone,* arrows (Halliwell and Wright), whence metaphorically to dart glances from the eye, and consequently to flirt or cast amorous looks ? The Kymric Celtic has *ffloyn,* a splinter, a thin wand, an arrow.

And for yon giglet hussies i' the glen,
That night and day are *floaning* at the
  men.—Ross's *Helenore.*

Flunkey, a servant in livery ; metaphorically applied to a person who abjectly flatters the great. The word was unknown to literature until the time of Burns. Thackeray and Carlyle in our own day have made it classical English, although the most recent lexicographers have not admitted it or its derivative, *flunkeyism,* to the honours of the dictionary.

Our laird gets in his rackèd rents,
  .   .   .   .

He rises when he likes himsel',
His *flunkeys* answer to his bell.
—BURNS : *The Twa Dogs.*

The word is supposed to be derived from the Gaelic *flann,* red, and *cas,* a leg or foot—red-legs, applied to the red or crimson plush breeches of footmen. The word red-shanks was applied to the kilted Highlanders by the English, and hence the Highland retort of flunkey to the English.

I think this derivation wrong ; *vlonk* in Danish signifies proud, haughty.—LORD NEAVES.

Fodgel, sometimes written and pronounced *fodyell* plump, short, corpulent, and good-tempered. A man in Scottish parlance may be stout and plump without being *fodgel,* as *fodgel* implies good nature, urbanity, and cheerfulness, as well as plumpness.

If in your bounds ye chance to light
Upon a fine, fat *fodgel* wight,
Of stature short, but genius bright,
    That's he, mark weel.
—BURNS : *On the Peregrinations of Captain Grose Collecting Antiquities throughout the Kingdom.*

Fog, moss ; from the Gaelic *bog* or *bhog,* moist, soft.

"And so, John," said the minister, " I understand you have gone over to the Independents ? " " Deed, sir," said John, " that's true." " Oh, John," rejoined the minister, " I'm sure ye ken that a rowin' stone gathers nae *fog.*" " Aye," said John, " that's true, too ; but can ye tell me what gude the *fog* does to the stone ? "—DEAN RAMSAY.

Fogie, a dull, slow man, unable or unwilling to reconcile himself to the ideas and manners of the new generation. The derivation of this word, which Thackeray did much to popularise in England, is uncertain, though it seems most probable that it comes from "foggy," for a foggy, misty, hazy intellect, unable to see the things that are obvious to clearer minds; or it may be from the Gaelic *fogaire*, an exile, a banished man. In the United States the word is generally applied to an ultra-Conservative in politics.

Ay, though we be
    Old *fogies* three,
We're not so dulled as not to dine;
    And not so old
    As to be cold
To wit, to beauty, and to wine.
            —*All the Year Round.*

Fog-moss, foggage, tall grass used for fodder. The etymology is uncertain. The English *fodder* is from the Gaelic *fodar;* but this scarcely affords a clue to *fog* or *foggage.* Though possibly *foggage* may be a corruption of the old and not yet obsolete *fodderage.*

Thy wee bit housie too in ruin!
Its silly wa's the winds are strewin',
An' naething left to big a new ane,
        O' *foggage* green,
An' bleak December's winds ensuin',
        Baith snell and keen.
            —BURNS: *To a Mouse.*

Forbears, ancestors.

Forbye, besides, in addition to, over and above.

> *Forbye* sax mae I sell't awa.
>   —BURNS: *Auld Farmer.*

Forbye some new uncommon weapons.
    —BURNS: *Death and Dr. Hornbook.*

Foreanent, directly opposite.

Foremost. In English this word signifies first as regards place. In Scottish parlance it also signifies first as regards time.

They made a paction 'twixt them twa,
    They made it firm and sure,
That whoe'er should speak the *foremost* word
    Should get up an' bar the door.
            —*The Barrin' o' oor Door.*

Forfoughten, sometimes written and pronounced *forfoughen,* worn out with struggling or fatigue.

And though *forfoughten* sair eneugh,
    Yet unco proud to leave.—BURNS.

I am but like a *forfoughen* hound,
Has been fighting in a syke (ditch).
    —*Border Minstrelsy: Hobbie Noble.*

Forgather, to meet.

Twa dogs
Forgathered ance upon a time.
    —BURNS: *The Twa Dogs.*

Forjeskit, wearied out, jaded, exhausted; derivation uncertain, but probably from the Flemish or Dutch patois.

The fiend, *forjeskit,* tried to escape
Thro' frequent changing o' his shape.
    —BEATTIE: *John o' Arnha'.*

Fou, drunk, is generally supposed to be a corruption of *full (i.e.,* of liquor); but if such were the fact the word ought to be contracted into *fu',* as wae*fu',* sorrow*fu',* which cannot be written wae*fou* or sorrow*fou. Fou,* in French, signifies insane, a word that might be applied to an intoxicated person; but if the Scottish phrase be not derived from the French, it ought to be written *fu'*, and not *fou*. Possibly the root of the word is the Gaelic *fuath* (pronounced *fuà*), which signifies hatred, abhorrence, aversion, whence it may have been applied to a person in a hateful and abhorrent state of drunkenness. This, however, is a mere suggestion. Jamieson has *fowsom*, filthy, impure, obscene.

> We are na' *fou*, we're na' that *fou*,
> We've just a wee drap in our e'e.
> —BURNS: *Willie Brewed a Peck o' Maut.*

Fouter, an expression of extreme contempt for a hateful person. The French *foutre* has the same, and even a worse meaning. Both the Lowland Scotch and the French are from the Gaelic and Celtic *fuath*, hatred.

Fouth or **rowth**, abundance. *Fouth* is from *full*, on the same principle as the English words *tilth* from *till*, *spilth* from *spill*, *youth* from *youngeth*, *growth* from *grow*, *drouth* from *dryeth*. *Rowth* has the same signification, and is from *row* or *roll*, to flow on like a stream.

> He has a *fowth* o' auld knick-nackets,
> Rusty airn and jinglin' jackets.
> —BURNS: *To Captain Grose.*

They that hae *rowth* o' butter may lay it thick on their scones.—ALLAN RAMSAY'S *Scots Proverbs.*

Fremit, **frammit**, strange, unrelated, unfamiliar; from the Teutonic *fremd*, foreign.

> Ye ha'e lien a' wrang, lassie,
> In an unco bed,
> Wi' a *fremit* man.—BURNS.

> And mony a friend that kissed his caup
> Is now a *frammit* wight,
> But it's ne'er sae wi' Whisky Jean.
> —BURNS: *The Five Carlins.*

Frist, to delay, to give credit; from the Teutonic *fristen*, to spare, to respite.

> The thing that's *fristed* is nae forgi'en.
> —ALLAN RAMSAY'S *Scots Proverbs.*

Frush, brittle.

> Oh, woe betide the *frush* saugh wand (willow wand),
> And woe betide the bush o' briar,
> It brak into my true love's hand.
> —*Border Minstrelsy: Annan Water.*

Fulzie, surfeited with gluttony and over-eating; full of meat and food.

> Enough to sicken a *fulzie* man.—*Noctes Ambrosianæ.*

Furth, out of doors, to go forth, to go out. The *muckle furth*, is the full, free open air. *Furthy*, forward, frank, free, affable, open in behaviour. *Furth-setter*, one who sets forth or puts forth; a publisher, an author.

> Sir Penny is of a noble spreit,
> A *furthy* man, and a far seeand;
> There is no matter ends compleit
> Till he set to his seil and hand.
> —*A Panegyrick on Sir Penny: The Evergreen.*

Fusionless, pithless, silly, sapless, senseless; corrupted from "foison," the old English word for plenty; the opposite of "geason," scarce.

For seven lang years I ha'e lain by his side,
And he's but a *fusionless* bodie, O !
 —BURNS : *The Deuks Dang o'er my
 Daddy.*

The mouths of fasting multitudes are
crammed wi' *fizzenless* bran, instead of the
sweet word in season.—SCOTT : *Old Mortality.*

Fusionless.—In Bailey's Dictionary the
word *foison* means "the natural juice or
moisture of the grass or other herbs, the
heart and strength of it :" used in Suffolk.—R. DRENNAN.

Fy ! or **fye !** This exclamation is
not to be confounded with the
English *fye!* or *O fye !* or the
Teutonic *pfui !* which are used
as mild reproofs of any act of
shame or impropriety.

Fy ! let us a' to the bridal,
 For there will be lilting there ;
 For Jock's to be married to Jeanie,
 The lass wi' the gowden hair.
 —*Old Song.*

In this old song, all the in-
cidents and allusions are expressive of joy and hilarity.
Jamieson suggests that *fy* means
"make haste ! " " *Fye-gae-to,*"
he says, "means much ado, a
great hurry ; and *fye haste,* a
very great bustle, a hurry." He
gives no derivation. As the
Teutonic cannot supply one, it
is possible that the root is the
Gaelic *faich,* look ! behold ! lo !
in which sense " *Fye !* let us a'
to the bridal," might be translated " Look ye ! let us all go
to the bridal."

Fyke, to be ludicrously and fussily
busy about trifles, to be restless without adequate reason,
akin to *fidget,* which is possibly
from the same root. The word
is also used as a noun. *Fiddle-
fyke* and *fiddle-ma-fike* are inten-
sifications of the meaning, and
imply contempt for the petty
trifling of the person who
fykes.

Some drowsy bummle,
Wha can do nought but *fyke* and fumble.
 —BURNS : *On a Scotch Bard.*

Gin he 'bout Norrie lesser *fyke* had made.
 —Ross's *Helenore.*

Weening that ane sae braw and gentle-like
For nae guid ends was makin' sic a *fyke.*
 —Ross's *Helenore.*

Fytte, the subdivision of a long
poem, now called a canto. Percy,
in a note in his " Ancient Reliques," considers the word to
signify no more than a division,
a part to " fit " on to another.
As the bards of the Druids, who
sung in their religious festivals,
and who delivered their precepts
to the people in short verses of
couplets or triads—better for
committal to memory than long
prose homilies would have been
—were called *fiadhs* or prophets,
it is possible that that word, and
not the English *fit,* as Dr. Percy
says, was the origin of *fytte* as
applied to the subdivision of a
sacred song.

G

Gabbock, a hunk, a large piece or slice.

> And there'll be
> Fouth o' gude *gabbocks* o' skate.
> —*The Blithesome Bridal.*

Gaberlunzie, a wallet or bag carried by beggars for collecting in kind the gifts of the charitable; whence *gaberlunzie-man*, a beggar.

> Oh, blithe be the auld *gaberlunzie-man*,
> Wi' his wallet o' wit he fills the lan';
> He's a warm Scotch heart an' a braid Scotch tongue,
> An' kens a' the auld sangs that ever were sung !—JAMES BALLANTINE.

> To love her for aye he gied her his aith,
> Quo' she, To leave thee I will be laith,
>   My winsome *gaberlunzie-man.*
>   —*The Gaberlunzie-Man (a ballad attributed to King James V.)*

Much research and ingenuity have been exercised to find the etymological origin of this peculiarly Scottish word. Jamieson says that *gaberlunzie* or *gaberlunyie* means a beggar's bag or wallet, and implies that the word has been transferred from the bag to the bearer of it.

Gae-through-land, a wanderer, a vagrant, a pilgrim, an exile, a gangrel.

> Oh, God forbid, said fair Annie,
> That e'er the like fa' in my hand ;
> Should I forsake my ain gude lord,
>   And follow you, a *gae-through-land.*
>   —BUCHAN'S *Ancient Scottish Ballads*, 1828.

Gair, the English *gore*, an insertion in a skirt, robe, or other article of dress; also a strip of a different colour inserted as a plait or ornament, sometimes signifying a coloured belt from which the sword or other weapon was suspended; *gaired* or *gairy*, streaked with many colours; piebald, as a *gairy* cow or horse.

> Young Johnston had a nut-brown sword
>   Hung low down by his *gair*,
> And he ritted it through the young colonel,
>   That word he never spak' mair.
>   —HERD'S *Collection: Young Johnston.*

Gale, to sing, whence *nightingale*, the bird that sings by night. The word is usually derived from the Teutonic, in which language, however, it only exists in the single word *nachtigall*. Jamieson refers it to the Swedish *gäll* (gale), a sharp, penetrating, or piercing sound. Probably, however, it is akin to the Gaelic *guil*, to lament, and *guileag*, that which sings or warbles; and a *gale* of wind is referable to the Kymric or Welsh *galar*, mourning, lamentation; *galw*, (galu), to call, to invoke; and *galaries*, mournful, sad, so called because of the whistling, piping sound of a storm.

> In May the gowk (cuckoo) begins to *gale*,
> In May deer draw to down and dale,
>   In May men mell with feminie,
> And ladies meet their lovers leal,
>   When Phebus is in Gemini.
>   —ALLAN RAMSAY : *The Evergreen*.

Gallie - hooin', making a loud noise, blustering, talking violently without sense or reason. *Gullie-hoolie*, a loud, blustering, talkative, and conceited fool. These two words seem to be derivable from the Gaelic *gal* or *guil*, to cry out, and *uille*, all; whence *gal-uille*, all outcry or bluster, or nothing but outcry and noise. *Gilhooly*, a well-known Irish patronymic, is possibly of the same Gaelic origin, applied to a noisy orator.

Gang, gae, gaed, gate. These words, that are scarcely retained even in colloquial English, do constant duty in the Lowland Scotch; they are all derived from the Flemish. *Gang* and *gae* are the English *go; gaed* is the English *went*, and *gate* is the road or way by which one goes. "*Gang* your ain *gate*," means go your own road, or have your own way. The English *gate*, signifying a doorway, a barred or defended entrance, is a relic of the older and more extended meaning of the Scotch.

I gaed a waefu' *gate* yestreen,
  A *gate* I fear I'll dearly rue.
          —BURNS.

Gangrel, vagrant, vagabond wandering ; from *gang*, to go.

Ae night at e'en, a merry core
  Of randie *gangrel* bodies
At Posie Nansie's held the splore.
    —BURNS: *The Jolly Beggars.*

This word is sometimes employed to designate a young child who is first beginning to walk.

Gardies, defensive weapons ; from the Gaelic *gairdein*, an arm or armour, and the French *garde ;* as in the phrase *prenez-garde*, take care, or defend yourself.

He wields his *gardies*,
Or at the worst his *aiken rung* (oaken staff).
—GEORGE BEATTIE : *John o' Arnha'.*

Garraivery. This curious word signifies, according to Jamieson, "folly and revelling of a frolicsome kind." He thinks it is evidently corrupted from *gilravery* and *gilravage*, which are words of a similar meaning. *Gilravage* he defines as "to hold a merry meeting with noise and riot." He attempts no etymology. It seems, however, that *garraivery* is akin to the French *charivari*, or the loud, discordant uproar of what in England is called "marrow bones and cleavers," when a gang of rough people show their displeasure by serenading an unpopular person—such, for instance, as a very old man who has married a very young wife—by beating bones against butchers' axes and cleavers, or by rattling pokers and shovels against iron pots and pans under his windows, so as to create a painful and discordant noise. The word and the custom are both of Celtic origin, and are derived from the Gaelic *garbh*, rough, and *bairich* or *bhairich*, any obstreperous and disagreeable noise ; also the lowing, roaring, or routing of cattle. The initial *g* or *c* of the Gaelic is usually softened into

E

the English and French *ch*, as the *k* in *k*irk becomes *ch* in the English *church*, and as the Latin *carus* and the Italian *caro* become *cher* in French.

Gash, sagacious, talkative. Jamieson defines the word, as a verb, "to talk much in a confident way, to talk freely and fluently;" and as an adjective, "shrewd, sagacious." It seems derivable from the Gaelic *gais* (pronounced *gash*), a torrent, an overflow; the English *gush*, *i.e.*, an overflow or torrent of words, and hence by extension of meaning applied to one who has much to say on every subject; eloquent, or, in an inferior sense, loquacious.

> He was a *gash* and faithful tyke.
> —Burns : *The Twa Dogs.*

> Here farmers *gash* in ridin' graith.
> —Burns : *The Holy Fair.*

> In comes a gaucie *gash* good-wife,
> And sits down by the fire.—*Idem.*

Gaucie, jolly, brisk, lively.

> His *gaucie* tail in upward curl.
> —Burns : *The Twa Dogs.*

> In comes a *gaucie* gash good-wife,
> And sits down by the fire.
> —Burns : *The Holy Fair.*

Gaucie, big, of large dimensions; jolly, perhaps. It has almost the same meaning as *gash*, with the additional idea of size; very like the English use of the word "jolly"—a jolly lot—a jolly pudding, &c. The Scotch use *gaucie* in precisely the same way.—R. D.

Gaud, a bar, the shaft of a plough; **gaudsman**, a plough-boy. The English *goad* signifies a bar or rod, and to *goad* is to incite or drive

with a stick or prong. The word is derived from the Gaelic *gat*, a prong, a bar of wood or iron, and *gath*, a sting.

> Young Jockie was the blithest lad
> In a' our town or here awa';
> Fu' blithe he whistled at the *gaud*,
> Fu' lightly danced he in the ha'.
> —Burns : *Young Jockie.*

> I've three mischievous boys,
> Rum deils for rantin' and for noise—
> A *gaudsman* ane, a thrasher t'other.
> —Burns : *The Inventory.*

> They'll turn me in your arms, Janet,
> A red-hot *gaud* o' airn.
> —*Ballad of the Young Tamlane.*

Gauf or **gawf**, a loud, discordant laugh; the English slang *guffaw.* According to Jamieson, it was used by John Knox. *Gawp*, a kindred word, signifies a large mouth wide opened; whence, possibly, the origin of the Flemish *gapen*, and the English *gape*, which, according to the late John Kemble, the tragedian, ought to be pronounced with the broad *a*, as in *ah*. *Gauffin*, a giggling, light-headed person, seems to be a word of the same parentage. *Gawpie* is a silly person who laughs without reason.

> Tehee, quo' she, and gied a *gawf.*
> —Allan Ramsay : *A Brash of Wooing: The Evergreen.*

Gauner, to bark, to scold vociferously.

Gaunt, to yawn. *Gaunt-at-the-door*, an indolent, useless person, who sits at the door and yawns; an idler, one without mental resources.

This mony a day I've groaned and *gaunted*
To ken what French mischief was brewing.
—BURNS.

Auld gude-man, ye're a drunken carle,
And a' the day ye *gape* and *gaunt*.
—SIR ALEXANDER BOSWELL.

Gaupie, a silly fellow, from *gaup*, to yawn or gape; one who yawns, from weariness, indifference, or stupidity, when he is expected to pay intelligent attention to what is said of him. A word of similar import, founded upon the same idea of listless and foolish yawning, is found in the English phrase to go *mooning* about, a word that has no reference to the moon, but that is derived from the Gaelic *meunan*, a yawn; *meunanach*, yawning; and *dean-meunan*, to yawn or make a yawn.

Gawk, to romp, applied to girls who are too fond of the society of men, and who either play roughly themselves or suffer men to play roughly in their company. The word is probably a variety of *geck*, to sport or mock (*see* that word).

Gawkie, a clumsy or inexpert person, from the French *gauche*, the left hand, and *gaucherie*, clumsiness. The word is colloquial in England as well as in Scotland.

Gear, money, wealth, property, appurtenance; from the Teutonic *gehörig*, belonging to, appertaining to.

He'll poind (seize) their *gear*.
—BURNS : *The Twa Dogs.*

And gather *gear* by every wile
That's justified by honour.
—BURNS : *Epistle to a Young Friend.*

Geck, to bear one's self haughtily, to toss the head in glee or scorn, to mock; possibly from the Flemish *gek*, a vain fool.

Adieu, my liege ! may freedom *geck*
Beneath your high protection.
—BURNS : *The Dream. To George III.*

Gee. To *take the gee*, is an old colloquialism, signifying to take umbrage or offence, to give way to a sudden start of petulance and ill-humour. Jamieson derives it from the Icelandic *geig*, offence, in default of tracing it to another origin. But the derivation is doubtful.

On Tuesday, to the bridal feast,
  Came fiddlers flocking free ;
But hey ! play up the rinaway bride,
  For she has ta'en the *gee*.
Woman's love a wilfu' thing,
  An' fancy flies fu' free ;
Then hey ! play up the rinaway bride
  For she has ta'en the *gee*.
     —HERD'S *Collection.*

"My wife has ta'en the *gee*," is the title of an old and once extremely popular song.

Gell, brisk, keen, sharp, active ; from the Gaelic *geall*, ardour, desire, love ; *geallmhor*, greatly desirous ; and *geallmhorachd*, high desire and aspiration.

Gell, intense, as applied to the weather ; a *gell* frost is a keen frost. "There's a gey *gell* in the market to-day," *i.e.*, a pretty quick sale ; "in great *gell*," in great spirits and activity ; "on the *gell*," a phrase applied to one who is bent on making merry.—JAMIESON.

Gerss. "This term," says Jamieson, " is well known in the councils of boroughs. When a member becomes refractory, the ruling party vote him out at the next election. This they call *gerssing* him, or turning him out to *gerss.* The phrase," he adds, " is evidently borrowed from the custom of turning out a horse to *graze* when there is no immediate use for his service." Perhaps, however, the etymology is not quite so evident as Jamieson supposed. The Gaelic *geur* or *gearr* signifies to cut, to cut off, to shear ; *gearraich* or *geurraich*, to shorten, and *geariadh*, a cutting ; *gearran*, a gelding ; *gearrta*, cut. To cut or shorten, rather than to graze or turn out to graze, appears, *pace* Jamieson, to be the real root of the word. Jamieson has the same word differently spelled as *girse*, to turn out of office ; *girse-folk*, cotters at will, liable to be ejected at short notice, to which the Gaelic etymology of *geurr* and its derivatives applies with more force than that which he suggests from *grass.*

Gey, a humorous synonym for *very.* This word in Jamieson's Dictionary is rendered "tolerable, considerable, worthy of notice." "A *gey* wheen," he says, means "a great number." It is doubtful whether the derivation be from the English *gay* or the Gaelic *gu.* In vulgar English, when " jolly" is sometimes used for "gay," "a jolly lot" would be equivalent to the Scottish "a *gey* wheen." In Gaelic *gu* is an adverbial prefix, as in *gu leoir*, plentiful or plentifully, whence the phrase, "whisky *galore*," plenty of whisky ; *gu fior*, with truth or truly.

A miller laughing at him (the fool of the parish) for his witlessness, the fool said, " There are some things I ken and some things I dinna ken." On being asked what he knew, he said, " I ken a miller has aye a *gey* fat sow !" " And what do ye no ken ?" said the miller. "I dinna ken at wha's expense she's fed."—DEAN RAMSAY'S *Reminiscences.*

The word is sometimes followed by *an'*, as in the phrase "*gey an* toom," very empty ; "*gey an* fou," very drunk. The word *gaylies*, meaning tolerably well in health, is probably from the same source as *gey*, as in the common salutation in Glasgow and Edinburgh, " How's a' wi' ye the day ?" " Oh, gailies, gailies !" The editor of *Noctes Ambrosianæ*, Edinburgh, 1866, erroneously explains *gey an* to mean *rather.*

Your factors, grieves, trustees, and bailies,
I canna say but they do *gailies.*
    —BURNS : *Address of Beelzebub.*

Mr. Clark, of Dalreach, whose head was vastly disproportioned to his body, met Mr. Dunlop one day. " Weel, Mr. Clark, that's a great head of yours." " Indeed, it is, Mr. Dunlop ; it could contain yours inside of it." " Just sae," replied Mr. Dunlop, " I was e'en thinking it was *gey an* toom (very empty)."—DEAN RAMSAY.

Gielanger, one who is slow to pay his debts ; etymology unknown. It has been thought that this word is an abbreviation of the request to *give longer* or *gie langer* time to pay a debt, but this is doubtful. The Flemish and Dutch *gijzelen* signifies to arrest for debt, *gijzeling*, arrest for debt, and *gizzel kammer*, a debtor's prison; and this is most probably the origin of *gielanger*.

The greedy man and the *gielanger* are well met.—ALLAN RAMSAY'S *Scots Proverbs.*

Gillravage, to plunder, also to live riotously, uproariously, and violently; from the Gaelic *gille*, a young man, and *rabair*, litigious, troublesome; *rabach*, quarrelsome.

Ye had better stick to your auld trade o' blackmail and *gillravaging.* Better steal nowte than nations.—SCOTT : *Rob Roy.*

Gilpie or **gilpey**, a saucy young girl.

I was a *gilpey* then, I'm sure
I wasna past fifteen.
—BURNS : *Hallowe'en.*

I mind when I was a *gilpie* o' a lassock, seeing the Duke—him that lost his head in London.—SCOTT : *Old Mortality.*

Gin (*g* hard, as in *give*) signifies *if.*

Oh, *gin* my love were yon red rose
That grows upon the castle wa ;
And I myself a drap o' dew,
Into her bonnie breast to fa'.
—HERD'S *Collection,* 1776.

Gin a body meet a body
Comin' through the rye.
—*Old Song* (*rearranged by* BURNS).

Horne Tooke, in his letter to Dunning, Lord Ashburton, on the English particles, conjunctions, and prepositions, derives

if from *given;* "*if* you are there," *i.e., given* the fact that you are there. The more poetical Scottish word *gin* is strongly corroborative of Horne Tooke's inference.

Girdle, a gridiron or brander, a circular iron plate used for roasting oat-cakes over the fire.

Wi' quaffing and daffing,
They ranted and they sang,
Wi' jumping and thumping
The very *girdle* rang.
—BURNS : *The Jolly Beggars.*

The carline brocht her kebbuck ben,
Wi' *girdle-cakes* weel toasted broon.
—*Tea-Table Miscellany : Andro and his Cutty Gun.*

On reading the passage in the Bible to a child where the words occur, " He took Paul's *girdle*," the child said with much confidence, " I ken what he took that for." On being asked to explain, she replied at once, " To bake his bannocks on !"—DEAN RAMSAY.

Girnagain, from *girn* or *grin;* a derisive epithet applied to a person who was always on the *grin*, with or without reason.

An' there'll be *girnagain* Gibbie
An' his *glaikit* wife, Jeannie Bell.
—*The Blithesome Bridal.*

Girnel, a meal-chest; from *corn, kern,* and *kernel.*

Amaist as roomy as a minister's *girnel.*
—*Noctes Ambrosianæ.*

Glack, a ravine, a cleft in the ground.

Deep i' the *glack* and round the well,
Their mystic rites I canna tell.
—*John o' Arnha'.*

Glaik, glaikit, giddy-headed, thoughtless, dazed, silly, foolish, giddy, volatile. From the Gaelic *gleog*, a silly look ; *gleogach*, silly, stupid ; *gleogair*, a stupid fellow ; *gleosgach*, a vain, silly woman.

That frequent pass douce Wisdom's door
  For *glaikit* Folly's portals.
    —Burns : *Address to the Unco Guid.*
Wi' his *glaikit* wife, Jeannie Bell.
        — *The Blithesome Bridal.*

Glamour, enchantment, witchcraft, fascination ; once supposed to be from the Gaelic *glac*, to seize, to lay hold of, to fascinate ; and *mor*, great ; whence great fascination, or magic not to be resisted. Lord Neaves thought the word was a corruption of *grammar*, in which magic was once supposed to reside. This word, once peculiar to the Scotch, has within the present century been adopted by English writers both of prose and verse, and has become familiar in the conversation of educated people. It signifies the kind of halo, fascination, and magical charm that a person or thing receives from the imagination ; the high and fanciful reputation which the French language expresses by *prestige*, a word which has also striven to naturalise itself in English. Its etymology has scarcely been attempted by English philologists, some few of whom, however, have discovered, as they think, a kindred origin for it in *clamor*, from the Latin *clamare*, to cry out, or make a great noise. It is possible that this idea lies in reality at the root of the poetical word

glamour, in its signification of a glorified repute ; repute itself being the outward manifestation of the popular belief in the excellence of the person or thing spoken of, and which would not be known unless for the spoken opinion or voice of the multitude, which gives and extends fame and glory. In the Gaelic and British languages, *fuaim* signifies noise, sound, recalling the classical embodying of Fame as an angel blowing a trumpet, making a loud sound ; and *gloir* signifies praise loudly expressed, and therefore *glory*. In like manner, *glamour* may resolve itself into the two Gaelic words, *glaodh*, pronounced *glao*, a shout, and *mor*, great, whence *glao-mor* or *glamour*, a great or loud cry or shout, attesting the applause and approbation of those who raise it. Stormonth, the latest etymologist who has attempted to explain the word, adopts the etymology that found favour with Jamieson, and derives it from *glimmer* or *glitter*, "a false lustre, a charm on the eyes, making them see things different from what they are." This etymology is plausible, and will possibly be accepted by all to whom the Gaelic derivation has not been offered for consideration ; but the Gaelic, supported as it is by the primitive but highly philosophic ideas that gave rise to the simple but now grandiose words of " fame " and " glory," merits the attention and study of all students who love to trace words to their origin, and endeavour by their means to sound the depths of human intelligence in the infancy of society and of language.

> And one short spell therein he read,
> It had much of *glamour* might,
> Could make a lady seem a knight,
> The cobweb on a dungeon wall
> Seem tapestry in a lordly hall.
> —SCOTT : *The Lay of the Last Minstrel.*

As soon as they saw her weel-faur'd face,
They cast their *glamour* o'er her.
> —*Johnnie Faa, the Gipsie Laddie.*

Ye gipsy gang that deal in *glamour,*
And you, deep read in Hell's black grammar,
> Warlocks and witches.
> —BURNS : *On Captain Grose.*

This Scottish word has been admitted into some recent English dictionaries. Mr. Wedgwood seems to think it is akin to *glimmer.* The fascination of the eye is exemplified in Coleridge's *Ancient Mariner :—*

> *He holds him with his glittering eye,*
> The wedding-guest stood still,
> And listens like a three-year child—
> The mariner hath his will.

Glamp, to clutch at, to seize greedily or violently ; from the Gaelic *glaim,* to seize voraciously.

> Some glower'd wi' open jaws,
> Syne *glampit* on the vacant air.
> GEORGE BEATTIE : *John o' Arnha'.*
>
> *Glampin* round, he kent nae whither.
> —*Ibid.*

Glaum, to grasp at, to clutch, to endeavour to seize, without strength to hold ; from the

Gaelic *glam,* to devour greedily ; *glamair,* a glutton.

> Clans frae wuds in tartan duds,
> Wha *glaumed* at kingdoms three, man.
> —BURNS : *The Battle of Sheriffmuir.*

Gled or **glaid**, a kite, a hawk, a vulture ; etymology uncertain.

> And aye as ye gang furth and in,
> Keep well the gaislings frae the *gled.*

> He ca'd the gaislings forth to feed,
> There was but sevensone o' them a',
> And by them cam' the greedy *gled,*
> And lickit up five—left him but twa.
> —*The Wife of Auchtermuchty.*

The name of Gladstone is derived from *gled-stane,* the hawk or vulture stone, and synonymous with the German *Geir-stein,* the title of one of the novels of Sir Walter Scott.

Gleed or **gleid**, a burning coal, a temporary blaze, a sparkle, a splinter that starts from the fire.

> And cheerily blinks the ingle *gleed*
> Of honest Lucky.—BURNS.

> Mend up the fire to me, brother,
> Mend up the *gleed* to me ;
> For I see him coming hard and fast
> Will mend it up for thee.
> —*Ballad of Lady Maisry.*

Gleg, sharp, acute, quick-witted ; *gleg-tongued,* voluble ; *gleg-lugg'd,* sharp of hearing; *gleg-ee'd,* sharp-sighted.

> Sae for my part I'm willing to submit
> To what your *glegger* wisdom shall think
> fit.—ROSS's *Helenore.*

> Unskaithed by Death's *gleg* gullie.
> —BURNS : *Tam Samson's Livin'.*

> He'll shape you aff fu' *gleg*
> The cut of Adam's philibeg.
> —BURNS : *Captain Grose.*

Jamieson derives *gleg* from the Icelandic and Swedish, unaware of the Gaelic etymology from *glac*, to seize, to snatch, to lay hold of quickly.

Glent, glint, a moment, a glance, a twinkling; also to glance, to shine forth, to peep out. From the same root as the English *glance*, the Teutonic *glänzen*, and Flemish *glinster*.

And in a *glent*, my child, ye'll find it sae.
—Ross's *Helenore.*
Yet cheerfully thou *glinted* forth
Amid the storm.
—Burns : *To a Mountain Daisy.*
The risin' sun owre Galston muir
Wi' glowing light was *glintin'*.
—Burns : *Hallowe'en.*

Gley, to squint; *aglee* or *agley*, crooked, aslant, in the wrong direction; probably from the Gaelic *gli*, the left hand, awkward.

There's a time to *gley* and a time to look even.—Allan Ramsay's *Scots Proverbs.*

Gleyed Sandy he came here yestreen,
And speired when I saw Pate.
—James Carnegie, 1765.
The best-laid schemes of mice and men
Gang aft *aglee*.
—Burns : *To a Mouse.*

Glib-gabbet, having "the gift of the gab," speaking glibly with voluble ease; apparently derived from the Gaelic *glib* or *gliob*, slippery, and *gab*, a mouth.

And that *glib-gabbet* Highland baron,
The Laird o' Graham.
—Burns : *Cry and Prayer.*

Gliff, a moment, a short slumber, a nap.

I'll win out a *gliff* the night for a' that,
to dance in the moonlight.—Scott : *The Heart of Midlothian.*

"Laid down on her bed for a *gliff*,"
said her grandmother.—Scott : *The Antiquary.*

Gloaming, the twilight; from the English *gloom* or darkness. This word has been adopted by the best English writers.

When ance life's day draws near its *gloaming*.
—Burns : *To James Smith.*
'Twixt the *gloaming* and the mirk,
When the kye come hame.
—Hogg, *the Ettrick Shepherd.*

Glower, to look stupidly or intently, to glare, to stare.

Ye *glowered* at the moon and fell in the midden.—Allan Ramsay's *Scots Proverbs.*

I am a bard of no regard,
Wi' gentle folks and a' that ;
But Homer-like, the *glowrin'* byke (swarm)
Frae town to town I draw that.
—Burns : *The Jolly Beggars.*

He only *glowered* at her, taking no notice whatever of her hints.—A. Trollope : *Vicar of Bullhampton.*

Glunch, an angry frown, a sulky or forbidding expression of countenance. "To *glunch* and gloom," to look angry, discontented, sulky, and gloomy. *Glunschoch,* one who has a frowning or morose countenance ; from the Gaelic *glonn,* a qualm, a feeling of nausea ; *glonnach,* one who has a disagreeable or stupid expression on his face :—

A *glunch*
O' sour disdain.
—Burns : *Scotch Drink.*
Does ony great man *glunch* and gloom ?
—Burns : *Cry and Prayer.*

Glunch and gloom.—Glunch, giving audible expression to discontent in a series of interjectional *humphs ; gloom,* a frowning, silent expression of displeasure.— R. DRENNAN.

Gomeril, a fool, a loud-talking fool; from the Gaelic *geum,* to bellow. The English and Cockney slang "Give us none of your *gum,*" *i.e.,* of your impudence or loud bellowing, is from the root of *geum.*

He's naught but a *gomeril,* never tired of talking.—*Noctes Ambrosianæ.*

Gowan, a daisy ; *gowany,* sprinkled with gowans or daisies. Chaucer was partial to the word daisy, which he derived from "day's eye;" though it is more probably to be traced to the Gaelic *deise,* pretty, a pretty flower. The word *gowan,* to a Scottish ear, is far more beautiful.

Where the blue-bell and *gowan* lurk
  lowly unseen.—BURNS.

The night was fair, the moon was up,
The wind blew low among the *gowans.*
  —*Legends of the Isles.*

Her eyes shown bright amid her tears,
Her lips were fresh as *gowans* growing.
  —*Idem.*

In *gowany* glens the burnie strays.
  —BURNS.

I'd not be buried in the Atlantic wave,
But in brown earth with *gowans* on my
  grave,
Fresh *gowans* gathered on Lochaber's
  braes.—*All the Year Round.*

Gowdspink, the goldfinch.

Nancy's to the greenwood gane,
  To hear the *gowdspink* chattering ;
And Willie he has followed her,
  To win her love by flattering.
  —*Scornful Nancy.*

Gowff or **gouff,** to pull violently.

She broke the bicker, spilt the drink,
And tightly *gouff'd* his haffets (long hair).
  —HERD'S *Collection: The Three-
  Girred Cog.*

Gowk, the cuckoo ; also a fool, or a person who has but one idea and is always repeating it ; from the Gaelic *cuach,* with the same meaning.

Ye breed o' the *gowk,* ye hae never a song but ane.—ALLAN RAMSAY'S *Scots Proverbs.*

Conceited *gowk,* puffed up wi' windy pride.
  —BURNS : *The Brigs of Ayr.*

Gowl, to weep loudly, to whine and blubber ; from the Gaelic *gul,* with the same meaning. The French has *gueule,* a mouth that is very wide open. *Gowl* also signifies large and empty, as "a *gowl* or *gowlsome* house," and "a *gowl* (a hollow) between the hills;" possibly allied in idea to the French *gueule.*

Ne'er may Misfortune's *gowling* bark
Howl through the dwelling o' the clerk.
  —BURNS : *To Gavin Hamilton.*

Gowl means to bawl, to howl, but has the additional idea of threatening or terrifying. To *gowl* at a person is to speak in a loud threatening tone—"He gied me a *gowl,*" "What mak's ye *gowl* that way at the weans ?" I have an idea that this is one of the words that have crept into the Scotch through the French.—R. DRENNAN.

Gowpen, two handfuls ; from the Flemish *gaps,* which has the same meaning.

Those who carried meal seldom failed to add a *gowpen* to the alms-bag of the deformed cripple.—SCOTT : *The Black Dwarf.*

Gowpen means placing the two palms together, and the hollow formed thereby is a *gowpen.* The miller would have had but a scanty "mouter" if his *gowpen* had been only a handful. An ordinary beggar would get a nievefu' o' meal, but a weel kent ane and a favourite would get a *gowpen.* Hence, you never heard the crucial test of an Englishman's knowledge of Scotch when he was asked "What's a *gowpen* o' glaur?" and his acquaintance with the tongue failing him, he was enlightened by the explanation that it was "twa neivefu' o' clairts."—R. DRENNAN.

Gracie, well-behaved, graceful, of pleasant manners and behaviour.

"A wife's ae dochter is never *gracie.*"
--*Proverb.*

Signifying that an only daughter is likely to be spoiled by over-indulgence, and therefore not likely to be as agreeable in manners as if she had sisters to compete with her for favour.

Gradden, the coarse meal that is ground in the quern by hand.

Grind the *gradden*, grind it ;
We'll a' get crowdie when it's done,
An' bannocks steeve to bind it.

Whisky gars the bark of life
Drive merrily and rarely,
But *gradden* is the ballast gars
It steady gang and fairly.
—R. JAMIESON : *The Queen Lily.*

Graith, tools, requisites, implements, appurtenances of a business or work, harness ; *graithing-clothes*, accoutrements.

Then he in wrath put up his *graith*—
"The deevil's in the hizzie."
—*Jacob and Rachel : attributed to* BURNS, 1825.

And ploughmen gather wi' their *graith.*
—BURNS : *Scotch Drink.*

Ye'll bid her shoe her steed before
An' a gowd *graithing* was behind.
—BUCHAN'S *Ancient Ballads.*

Gramarye, magic ; French *grimoire*, a magic-book. Attempts have been made to derive this word from *grammar*. It is more likely, considering the gloomy ideas attached to the French *grimoire* (the immediate root of the word), that it comes originally from the Gaelic *gruaim*, gloom, melancholy, wrath, intense sadness or indignation ; and *gruamach*, sullen, surly, morose, gloomy, grim, frowning.

Whate'er he did of *gramarye*,
Was always done maliciously.
—SCOTT : *Lay of the Last Minstrel.*
The wild yell and visage strange,
And the dark woods of *gramarye*,
—*Idem.*

Grandgore, sometimes written **glengore** and **glandgore**, the venereal disease. Jamieson suggests its origin from the French *grand*, great, and *gorre;* but does not explain the meaning of *gorre*, which does not appear in French dictionaries.

The word appears to be rightly *grandgore*, and not *glen* or *gland gore*, and to be derived from the Gaelic *grain*, horrid, disgusting, and *gaorr*, filth.

Gree, to bear the *gree*, to excel, to be acknowledged to excel. The origin of this phrase is uncertain, though supposed to be connected with *degree*, *i.e.*, a degree of excellence and superiority.

Then let us pray that come it may,
    As come it will for a' that,
That sense and worth, o'er a' the earth,
    Shall bear the *gree* and a' that.
                            —BURNS.

I wad hae nane o' them, though they wad
    fancy me,
For my bonnie mason laddie he bears
    awa' the *gree*.
        —CHAMBERS'S *Scottish Songs : The
                Mason Laddie.*

Greetie, the affectionate diminutive of *greet*, to weep or cry ;
not to be rendered into English
except by a weak paraphrase
and dilution of the touching
Scottish phrase, such as a small,
faint, or little cry or lament,
The same remark applies to the
diminutive of *feet* in the sub-
joined verse.

We'll hap an' row, we'll hap an' row,
    We'll hap an' row the *feetie* o't ;
It is a wee bit wearie thing,
    I downa bide the *greetie* o't.
—WILLIAM CREECH, *Lord Provost of
    Edinburgh, and publisher of the
    Poems of Robert Burns.*

Gregorian, a popular name for a
wig in the seventeenth century,
introduced into England by the
Scottish followers of James VI.
when he succeeded to the English throne. Blount, in his
" Glossographia," says : " Wigs
were so called from one Gregorie, a barber in the Strand,
who was a famous perruque-
maker."

He cannot be a cuckold that wears a
gregorian, for a periwig will never fit
such a head.—NARES.

Yet, though one Gregorie, a
wig-maker, may have lived and
flourished in London in the
early part of the seventeenth
century, it does not follow that
the word *gregorian* was derived
from his name, any more than
that of the designation of a
tailor by trade had its origin in
the patronymic of *taylor*. At
all events, it is worthy of note
that in Gaelic *gruaig* signifies a
wig ; *gruagach*, hairy ; *gruagag*,
a little wig, or a bunch of hair ;
and *gruagair*, a wig-maker and
hairdresser.

Grien or **grene,** to covet, to long
for, to desire ardently and unreasonably ; *grening*, longing,
akin to the English *yearn*, " a
yearning desire," German *gern*,
Flemish *gearne*, willingly, desirous of. From this comes probably "*green* sickness," a malady
that afflicts growing girls when
they long for unwholesome and
unnatural food, and would eat
chalk, charcoal, unripe fruit, and
any kind of trash. The medical
name of this malady is *chlorosis*,
a Greek translation of " *green*
sickness," arising from the fact
that English physicians understood the popular word *green*,
the colour, but not *grien* or
grene, to covet, which is the
main symptom of the dis-
ease.

Teuch Johnnie, staunch Geordie an' Walie,
    That *griens* for the fishes an' loaves.
                —BURNS : *The Election.*

They came there justice for to gett,
    They'll never *grene* to come again.
    —*Border Minstrelsy : The Raid of the
            Redswire.*

Grip, tenacity, moral or physical ; to hold fast.

Will Shore couldna conceive how it was that when he was drunk his feet wadna haud the *grip.—Laird of Logan.*

But where you feel your honour *grip*,
Let that be aye your border.
—Burns : *Epistle to a Young Friend.*

I like the Scotch ; they have more *grip* than any people I know.—Sam Slick.

Grog, a mixture of spirits and water ; usually applied to hot gin and water, as distinguished from rum-punch and whisky-toddy. The word is now common in England, and is supposed by careless philologists, who follow blindly where their predecessors lead them, to have been first used by the sailors in a ship of war commanded by Captain, afterwards Admiral Vernon, commonly called " Old Grog," from the grogram jacket or coat which he usually wore. But *grog* was known and named long before the days of Admiral Vernon, and was in common use in Scotland, as well as in England, as *croc*, afterwards corrupted into *grog*. The word *croc* in Gaelic signifies a horn, used in districts and in houses where glass was too expensive for purchase. A horn or *croc* of liquor was synonymous with a glass of liquor, and to offer a guest a *croc* or *grog* of spirit of any kind was the same as to invite him to take a social glass ; and in time *croc* came to signify the liquor in the horn, as well as the horn itself. To invite a man to take a friendly glass is not to invite him to take the glass itself, but the drink that is in it. Hence the word *grog*, which has no more connection with the grogram suit of Admiral Vernon than it has with " the man in the moon." The French have the phrase " cric et *croc* " in the slang vernacular.

Groof, the belly, so called from its rumbling when deprived of food ; from the Gaelic *gromhan (grovan)*, to growl.

Rowin' yoursel' on the floor on your *groof*, wi' your hair on end and your e'en on fire.—*Noctes Ambrosianæ.*

Grue or **grew**, a greyhound.

I dreamed a weary dream yestre'en,
I wish it may come to gude :
I dreamed that ye slew my best *grew-hound*,
And gied me his lapper'd blude.
—*Ballad of Sir Roland.*

What has come ower ye, Muirland Tam ?
Your leg's now grown like a wheelbarrow tram ;
Ye'd the strength o' a stot, the weight o' a cow,
Now, Tammy, my man, ye have grown like a *grew.*
—Hew Ainslie : *Tam o' the Balloch.*

A *grew* is a female *greyhound* in the South of England, according to Mr. Halliwell Phillips, while in the eastern counties the word is a *grewin*, and in Shropshire *groun.* In old French *grous* signifies any kind of hunting-dog—a greyhound among the rest.

The modern French do not

call the animal a "chien *gris*," but a *limier*, which means a dog which leaps or springs, from the Celtic *leum*, to leap, or a *levrier*, because it courses the *lièvre* or hare. In "Anglo-Saxon," which is merely Teutonic with a large substratum of Gaelic, it appears that this word is *grig-hound*. The pure Teutonic calls it a *windel spiel*, a grotesque term, for which it is difficult to account. The Dutch and Flemish call it a *speurhond*, or tracking-hound. The Italians call the animal a *véltro*. It is evident from all these examples that the dog was not named from *grey*, which is not its invariable colour. *Grey* is not adopted as its designation by any other nation than the English. Philology is thus justified in seeking elsewhere for the root of *grue*, which the Teutonic nations do not afford. The old grammarian Minshew thought he had found it in *græcus*, and that the hound was so called because the Greeks hunted with it; but this derivation is manifestly inadmissible, as is that from *grip*, the hound which grips or snatches. Possibly the Scottish hound came from the Highlands and not from the Lowlands, or may be derived from *gaoth*, wind or breath, and *gaothar* (pronounced *gao-ar*), long-winded, strong-winded, provided with wind for rapid motion. *Gaothar* is rendered in the Gaelic dictionaries as a *lurcher*, half foxhound and half greyhound, and anciently

as greyhound only. As *gaor* is easy of corruption, first into *grao*, and afterwards into *grew* or *grue*, it is extremely probable that this is the true derivation of a word that has long been the despair of all lexicographers who were not so confident as Minshew and Dr. Johnson.

Gruesome, highly ill-favoured, disagreeable, horrible, cruel. *Grue*, to shudder, to be horrified. From the Teutonic *grau*, horror; *grausam*, horrible, cruel; and *grausamkeit*, cruelty. This word has been recently used by some of the best English writers, though not yet admitted to the honours of the dictionaries.

> Ae day as Death, that *gruesome* carle,
> Was driving to the ither warl (world).
> —Burns: *Verses to J. Rankine.*

> And now, let us change the discourse.
> These stories make one's very blood *grew*.
> —Scott: *Fortunes of Nigel.*

> "They're the Hieland hills," said the Bailie; "ye'll see and hear eneuch about them before ye see Glasgow Green again. I downa look at them, I never see them, but they gar me *grew*."—Scott: *Rob Roy.*

Grugous or **allagrugous**, grim, ghastly, disagreeable, morose, ill-natured; from the Gaelic *grug*, morose, ill-conditioned and surly, and *uille*, all.

> Whilk added horror to his mien,
> A *grugous* sight he was, I ween.
> —George Beattie: *John o' Arnha'.*

> An *allagrugous*, gruesome spectre,
> A' gored and bored like Trojan Hector.
> —*Ibid.*

Gruntle, a word of contempt for a snub nose or snout; erro-

neously rendered by " countenance " in some of the glossaries to Burns ; *gruntle-thrawn*,
crooked in the nose.

May gouts torment him, inch by inch,
Wha twists his *gruntle* wi' a glunch
    O' sour disdain,
Out owre a glass o' whisky-punch
    Wi' honest men.
      —Burns : *Scotch Drink*.

Akin to the Gaelic *graineil*,
ugly, loathsome ; *graineilachd*,
ugliness.

Grunzie, a ludicrous name for the
nose or mouth ; possibly applied
originally to the snout of a hog,
in reference to the grunting of
the animal. (*See* Gruntle.)

But Willie's wife is nae sae trig,
  She dights her *grunzie* wi' a hushon
(*i.e.*, she wipes her nose with a cushion).
    —Burns : *Sic a Wife as Willie had*.

Grushie, of rapid growth, thickly
sown.

The dearest comfort o' their lives,
Their *grushie* weans and faithful wives.
    —Burns : *The Twa Dogs*.

Gryce, a young pig.

A yeld (barren) sow was ne'er good to
gryces. — Allan Ramsay's *Scots Proverbs*.

My bairn has tocher o' her ain,
  Although her friends do nane her len',
A stirk, a staig, an acre sawn,
    A goose, a *gryce*, a clocking-hen.
      —*The Wooing o' Jenny and Jock*.

Gryme, to sprinkle ; **gryming**, a
sprinkling. The English word
grimy signifies foul with dirt.
The Scottish *gryme* has a wider
meaning, and is applied both
to pure and impure substances
when out of place.

The sun wasna up, but the moon was
  down,
It was the *griming* of new fa'n snaw.
    —*Border Minstrelsy : Jamie Telfer*.

Guller, an indistinct noise in the
throat. (*See* Gowl.)

Between a grunt, a groan, and a *guller*
—*Noctes Ambrosianæ*.

Gullie or **gully** (sometimes written
goolie), a large pocket-knife ;
gullie-gaw, a broil in which
knives are likely to be drawn
and used. *Gullie-willie*, according to Jamieson, is a noisy,
blustering fool—possibly from
his threatening the knife, but
not using it.

I rede ye weel, tak' care o' skaith—
  See, there's a *gullie*.—Burns.

The carles of Kilmarnock had spits and
  had spears,
And lang-hafted *gullies* to kill Cavaliers.
—Sir Walter Scott : *Bonnie Dundee*.

Stickin' gangs nae by strength, but by
right guidin' o' the *gully*.—Allan Ramsay's *Scots Proverbs*.

" To guide the *gullie*," is a
proverbial phrase, signifying to
have the management of an
affair. The derivation is uncertain, but is perhaps from the
Gaelic *guaillich*, to go hand in
hand, to accompany ; applied
to the weapon from its ready
conveniency to the hand in case
of need.

Gumlie, muddy, turbid, synonymous with *drumlie* (*q.v.*). Etymology obscure.

O ye wha leave the springs o' Calvin,
For *gumlie* dubs [pools] o' your ain delvin'.
    —Burns : *To Gavin Hamilton*.

Gump, a stupid old woman, of the kind so well portrayed in the Mrs. Gamp of Dickens, and which possibly may have suggested the name to the brilliant novelist, who married a Scotswoman, the grand-daughter of George Thompson, the celebrated correspondent of Robert Burns. **Gumphie**, a fool; **gommeril**, a foolish or stupid person; **gomf** or **gomph**, an idiot. The root is possibly the Gaelic *geum*, to low or bellow like a cow or a bull, and which finds its equivalent in the English slang, " Give us none of your *gum*."

Gump not only signifies an old woman not over-wise, but a fat and chubby infant, so that the Gaelic etymology for *geum*, if correct, can only be accepted in the case of the child, on the supposition that the child is a noisy one, and bellows or lows in expression of its wants or its ill-temper. To take the *gumps* is to indulge in a fit of ill-temper. Jamieson defines *gomeril* or *gomrell* as a stupid fellow, so called, he intimates, from the French *goimpre*, " one who minds nothing but his belly." The word, however, is not to be found in the " Dictionnaire Etymologique" of Noel and Carpentier (1857), nor in the comprehensive dictionary of " argot," or French slang, by the erudite and industrious Professor Barrère, published in 1887, nor in that of M. Brachet, published by the Clarendon Press in 1882, or in the volumi-nous work of M. Littré, the last recognised exponent of the French language. Professor Barrère, however, has *goinfre*—slang of thieves—from a pie-eater, " an allusion to his opening his mouth like a glutton," which may possibly be the word which Jamieson adopts as *goimfre*. But neither *goinfre* nor *goimfre* throws any light upon *gump* or the closely-related words that spring out of it, unless it be in support of the Gaelic derivation from *geum*, to low or bellow, and consequently to open the mouth widely.

Gumption, wit, sense, knowledge. This word is akin to the Gaelic *cuimse* (*cumshe*), moderation, adaptation, and *cuimsichte*, well-aimed, that hits the mark.

Nor a' the quacks with all their *gumption*
  Will ever mend her.
    —Burns : *Letter to John Goudie.*

Gurl, to growl; **gurly**, boisterous, stormy, savage, growly ; from the German and Flemish *grollen*, the English *growl*, to express displeasure or anger by murmurs, and low, inarticulate sounds.

The lift grew dark and the wind blew sair,
  And *gurly* grew the sea.
    —*Sir Patrick Spens.*

Waesome wailed the snow-white sprites,
  Upon the *gurly* sea.
    —Laidlaw : *The Demon Lover.*

There's a strong *gurly* blast blawing snell frae the south.—James Ballantine : *The Spunk Splitters.*

Gurr, to snarl, to growl like an angry dog ; **gurrie**, a loud and angry disputation, and also the growling, yelping, and barking of dogs in a fight. Allied in meaning and derivation, though spelled with *i* instead of *u*, are *girnie*, peevish; *girnigoe* and *girnigoe-gibbie*, a snarling and ill-natured person; and *girnin' gyte*, a fractious child.

Gurthie, corpulent, obese, large round the waist or *girth*.

Applied especially to what burdens the stomach. Roquefort renders it *pesant*, ponderous, burdensome.—JAMIESON.

Gutcher, a grandfather. This ungainly word seems to be a corruption of *gude-sire*, *gude-sir*, *gudsir*, or *good sir*, a title of reverence for a grandfather.

God bless auld lang syne, when our *gutchers* ate their trenchers.—ALLAN RAMSAY'S *Scots Proverbs.*

This was a reproach directed against over-dainty people who objected to their food.

Gae 'wa wi' your plaidie, auld Donald, gae 'wa;
I fear na the cauld blast, the drift, nor the sna',
Gae 'wa wi' your plaidie—I'll no sit beside ye;
Ye might be my *gutcher!* auld Donald, gae 'wa!
—HECTOR MACNEIL: *Come under my Plaidie.*

The derivation from *good-sire* is rendered the more probable by the common use of the word *good* in Scotland to express degrees of relationship, as *good*-mother, a mother-in-law; *good*-brother, a brother-in-law; *good*-sister, a sister-in-law; *good*-son, a son-in-law, &c., as also in the familiarly affectionate phrases of *good*-wife for wife, and *good*-

man for husband. The French use *beau* or *belle* in a similar sense, as *beau*-père, a father-in-law; *belle*-fille, a daughter-in-law; *belle*-mère, a mother-in-law. Possibly the English words *god*-father and *god*-mother, applied to the sponsors at the baptism of a child, were originally *good*, and not *god*.

Gyre - carline. This is in some parts of Scotland the name given to a woman suspected of witchcraft, and is from *gyre*, the Teutonic *geier*, a vulture, and *carline*, an old woman. The harpies in Grecian mythology are represented as having the beaks and claws of vultures, and are fabled to devour the bodies of warriors left unburied on the battle-field. The name of "Harpy," given in the ancient mythology to these supposed malevolent creatures, has been conclusively shown to be derived from the Gaelic, and to be traceable to *ar*, a battle-field, and *pighe* (pronounced *pee*), a bird, whence *ar pighe*, a harpy, the bird of the battlefield, the great carrion hawk or vulture.

I wad like ill to see a secret house haunted wi' ghaists and *gyre-carlines.*—SCOTT: *The Monastery.*

Gyte, deranged, mad; from the Flemish *guit*, mischievous, roguish; *guitenstuk*, a piece of mischief.

Surprised at once out of decorum, philosophy, and phlegm, he skimmed his cocked-hat in the air. "Lord sake," said Edie, "he's gaun *gyte*."—SCOTT: *The Antiquary.*

H

Hadden and dung, a phrase that signifies "held down and beaten," *i.e.*, held in bondage and ill-used; from *hadden*, preterite of *hold*, and *dung*, preterite of *ding*, to beat or strike. (*See* DING.)

Haddin, furniture, plenishment, household stuff.

Oh, Sandie has owsen an' siller an' kye,
A house an' a *haddin*, an' a' things forbye ;
But I'd rather ha'e Jamie wi 's bonnet in hand,
Than I wad ha'e Sandie wi' houses an' land.
—*Logie o' Buchan.*

Haet, a whit, an iota ; *deil a haet*, the devil a bit.

But gentlemen, an' ladies warst,
Wi' evendoun want o' wark are curst ;
They loiter, lounging, lank and lazy,
Though *de'il haet* ails them, yet uneasy.
—BURNS : *The Twa Dogs.*

In Bartlett's "Dictionary of Americanisms" the word occurs as *hate*.

I don't care a *hate*—I didn't eat a *hate*.

Haffets or **haffits**, the long hair of men, also applied to the long hair of women when old, but never when they are young.

Jamieson says that *haffits* means the cheeks, but as used by Burns in "The Cotter's Saturday Night" it clearly signifies the front hair on the venerable cotter—"His lyart *haffits* wearin' thin an' bare." His lyart (grey) *haffits* are evidently

not meant for grey cheeks, and cheeks, though they may grow thin, do not necessarily grow *bare*. The etymology of *haffits* as long hair is unknown ; but supposing it to be cheeks, Jamieson derives it from the Anglo-Saxon *healf heafod*, half head, a semi-cranium.

His lyart *haffits* wearin' thin an' bare.
—BURNS : *Cotter's Saturday Night.*

Lyart signifies *grey*, from the Gaelic *liath*, grey, and *liathach*, grey-headed.

Hafflins, almost or nearly one-half, formed from *half* and *lins*, pertaining to or approaching towards half, as in *aiblins* (which see).

While Jeanie *hafflins* is afraid to speak,
Weel pleased the mother hears he's nae wild worthless rake.
—BURNS : *Cotter's Saturday Night.*

When it's cardit, row'd and spun,
Then the work is *hafflins* done.
—*Tea-Table Miscellany : Tarry Woo.*

Haggis, the national dish *par excellence* of Scotland, which shares with cock-a-leekie and hotch-potch the particular favour of Scotsmen all over the world. Sir Walter Scott describes it in the introduction to "Johnnie Armstrong," in the "Minstrelsy of the Scottish Border," as "an olio composed of the liver, head, &c., of a sheep, minced down with oat-

F

meal, onions, and spices, and boiled in the *stomach* of the animal by way of bag." In Tim Bobbin's Glossary *hag* and *haggus* are defined as meaning the *belly*.

> Fair fa' your honest, sonsie face,
> Great chieftain o' the puddin' race;
> Aboon them a' you tak' your place,
>   Painch, tripe, or thairm;
> Weel are ye worthy o' a grace
>   As lang's my arm.
>   —BURNS: *To a Haggis.*

Even a *haggis*, God bless her! could charge down the hill.—SCOTT: *Rob Roy.*

An illustrious American, travelling in Scotland, was entertained at a public dinner, when towards the end of the repast a very large haggis was brought in on a gigantic dish, carried by four waiters, to the tune of "See the Conquering Hero Comes," played by the band. He was very much amused at the incident, and having heard much of the national dish, but never having tasted it, was easily induced to partake of it. He did not appear to ike its flavour very much, and being asked his opinion of it, replied that "the *haggis* must have been invented to give Scotsmen an excuse for a dram of whisky after it, to take the taste out of the mouth," adding, "But if I were a Scotsman, I should make it a patriotic duty to love it, with or without the dram—but especially with it!" —C. M.

The word, formerly spelled *haggass*, is usually derived from the French *hachis*, a hash of viands cut into small pieces, from *hacher*, to mince, the English *hack*, to cut. The dish is quite unknown to the French, though the etymology is possibly correct. The allusion of Burns to the "sonsie face" of the pudding which he praised so highly, renders it possible

that he knew the Gaelic words *aogas*, a face, and *aogasach*, seemly, comely, sonsie. Anyhow, the coincidence is curious.

Haimert, homely, home-like, or tending *homewards*, of which latter word it is a variety or corruption.

> Quoth John, They're late; but, by jingo,
> Ye'se get the rest in *haimert* lingo.
>   —GEORGE BEATTIE: *John o' Arnha'.*

Hain, to preserve, to economise, so as to prevent waste and extravagance; to protect with a hedge or fence; to spare for future use. *Hain* seems to be derived from the German *hagen*, to enclose with a hedge or fence; the Danish *hegne*, with the same meaning; and the Dutch and Flemish *heenen;* *omheenen*, to fence around, and *onheining*, an enclosure. From the practical idea of enclosing anything to protect it came the metaphorical use of this word in Scotland, in the sense of preservation of a thing by means of care, economy, and frugality.

> The weel-*hained* kebbock (cheese).
>   —BURNS: *Cotter's Saturday Night.*
> Wha waste your weel-*hained* gear on
>   damned new brigs and harbours.
>   —BURNS: *The Brigs of Ayr.*

Kail *hains* bread.—ALLAN RAMSAY'S *Scots Proverbs.*

> We've won to crazy years thegither,
> We'll toyte about wi' ane anither;
> Wi' tentie care I'll flit thy tether
>   To some *hain'd* rig.
>   —BURNS: *The Auld Farmer.*

Hain, to preserve, does not seem to me

to be a correct synonym; the word rather means to use economically. "Her weel-*hain'd* kebbuck" does not mean that the cheese had been preserved from danger, from mites, or the cheese-fly and maggots, but that it had not been used wastefully; *haining clothes*, means a second goodish suit to save your best one. The English expression "eke it out" comes very near the meaning of *hain*. In Fifeshire the word used instead of *hain* is *tape—tape* it, make it last a good while, don't gobble up a nice thing all at once; in fact, *hain* it.— R. DRENNAN.

Haiver, to talk in a desultory manner, foolishly, or idly, to drivel.

> Wi' clavers and *haivers*
> Wearin' the day awa'.
> —BURNS.

Haiver or *haver* seems to be a corruption of the Gaelic *abair*, to talk, to say.

Hale-scart, without *scratch* or damage; from *scart*, to scratch, and *hale*, well or intact.

Hale-scart frae the wars without skaith-ing,
Gaed bannin' the French awa' hame.
—ANDREW SCOTT : *Symon and Janet.*

Hallan-shaker, a sturdy, importunate beggar. Jamieson derives the word from *hallan*, a partition in a cottage between the "but" and the "ben;" and *shaker*, one who shakes the *hallan* by the noise he makes. If he had sought in the Gaelic, he might have found a better derivation in *alla, allan, allanta*, wild, ferocious, savage; and *seachran* (the Irish *shaughraun*), a vagrant, a wanderer, a beggar.

Right scornfully she answered him,
Begone, you *hallan-shaker!*
Jog on your gate, you *bladderskate*,
My name is Maggie Lauder.
—FRANCIS SEMPLE.

Hantle, a good deal, a quantity; from the Flemish *hand*, a hand, and *tel*, to count or number; a quantity that may be reckoned by the handful.

A Scottish clergyman related as his experience after killing his first pig, that "nae doot there was a *hantle* o' miscellaneous eating about a swine."—DEAN RAMSAY.

Some hae a *hantle* o' fauts; ye are only a ne'er-do-weel.—ALLAN RAMSAY'S *Scots Proverbs.*

Are we better now than before? In a few things better; in a *hantle* waur.— *Noctes Ambrosianæ.*

Hap, to cover, to wrap up.

I digged a grave and laid him in,
And *happ'd* him wi' the sod sae green.
—*Lament of the Border Widow.*

Hap and rowe, *hap* and rowe the feetie o't,
It is a wee bit ourie thing,
I downa bide the greetie o't.
—CHAMBERS'S *Scottish Songs.*

Happer, thin, lank, shrunken; *happer*-lipped, having thin lips; *happer*-hipped, having small or shrunken hips.

An' there'll be *happer*-hipped Nannie,
An' fairy-faced Flora by name;
Muck Maudie, and fat-luggit Girzie,
The lass wi' the gowden wame.
—*The Blithesome Bridal.*

Harns, brains; from the German *hirn* or *gehirn*, the brain; *hirn-schale*, the brain-pan; Dutch and Flemish, *hersens.*

A wheen midden-cocks pike ilk others' *harns* out (a lot of dunghill cocks pick each others' brains out).—SCOTT : *Rob Roy.*

Lastly, Bailie, because if I saw a sign o'
your betraying me, I would plaster that
wa' wi' your *harns*, ere the hand o' man
could rescue ye.—SCOTT : *Rob Roy.*

Hatter (sometimes written **hotter**)
signifies, according to Jamieson,
to bubble, to boil up and also a
crowd in motion or in confusion.
The English slang expression
" Mad as a hatter " does not
apply—though commonly supposed to do so—to a hat-maker,
— any more than it does to a tailor
or a shoemaker. It seems to
have been borrowed by the Lowland Scotch from the Gaelic
at, to swell like boiling water,
and *ataircachd*, the swelling
and foaming of waters as in
a cataract, and, by extension
of the image, to the tumultuous action of a noisy crowd.
In Tim Bobbin's Lancashire
Glossary *hotter* signifies to vex,
and *hottering*, mad, very mad,
very vexed.

Haugh, low ground or meadows
by the river-side; from the
Gaelic *ac*, *ach*, and *auch ;* the
Teutonic *aue*, a meadow. *Holm*
and *hagg* have the same meaning. The word *acre* is from the
same etymological root.

> By Leader *haughs* and Yarrow.

> Let husky wheat the *haughs* adorn,
> And aits set up their awnie horn.
> —BURNS : *Scotch Drink.*

Haur, an easterly wind; and **hoar**,
frost produced by an easterly
wind.

> The sleet and the *haur*—misty, easterly
> *kaur.*—*Noctes Ambrosianæ.*

Hause-bane, the neck-bone; from
the Flemish and German *hals*,
the neck.

> Ye shall sit on his white *hause-bane*,
> And I'll pike out his bonny blue een ;
> Wi' ae lock o' his yellow hair
> We'll theek our nest when it grows bare.
> —*The Twa Corbies.*

To *hause* or *hals* signifies to
embrace, *i.e.*, to put the arms
round the neck.

Haveril, a half-witted person, a
silly talker ; from *haiver*, to talk
nonsense ; the Gaelic *abair*, to
talk.

> Poor *haveril* Will fell aff the drift,
>   And wandered through the bow-kail,
> And pu'd, for want o' better shift,
>   A runt was like a sow-tail.
>   —BURNS : *Hallowe'en.*

Havers, oats ; **haver-meal**, oatmeal ; from the French *avoine*.

> Oh, where did ye get that *haver-meal*
>   bannock ?
>   Oh, silly auld body, dinna ye see ?
> I got it frae a sodger laddie
>   Betwixt St. Johnstoun and Bonnie
>   Dundee.
>   —HERD'S *Collection: altered and
>   amended by* BURNS.

Havins, good manners and behaviour, courteous and kindly de-
meanour, personal accomplishments which one *has ;* thence
havings or acquirements.

> Awa, ye selfish warldly race,
> Wha think that *havins*, sense, and grace,
> E'en love and friendship, should give place
>   To catch-the-plack (the money) ;
> I dinna like to see your face
>   Or hear you crack (talk).
>   —BURNS : *Epistle to Lapraik.*

H a w k i e, a pet name for a favourite cow or one who is a good milker.

> Dawtit twal-pint *Hawkie's* gaen
> As yell's the bull.
>   ---BURNS : *Address to the De'il.*

> I'd rather sell my petticoat,
> Though it were made o' silk,
> Than sell my bonnie broun *Hawkie,*
> That gies the sup o' milk.
>   —CHAMBERS'S *Scottish Songs.*

"Brown hawkie," says Jamieson, "is a cant name for a barrel of ale"—*i.e.*, the milk of drunkards and topers. The word is traceable to the Gaelic *adhach* (pronounced *awk* or *hawk*), lucky, fortunate.

Heartsome, cordial, hearty; full of heartiness.

Farewell to Lochaber, fareweel to my Jean,
Where *heartsome* wi' her I ha'e mony a
   day been.—*Lochaber no More.*

Hech, an exclamation of surprise, of joy, or of pain; softened from the Gaelic *oich.* On the shore of Loch Ness, near the waterfall of *Abriachan,* where the road is steep and difficult, the rock near the summit of the ascent has received from the shepherds and drovers the name of "Craig Oich," from their stopping to draw breath and exclaiming, "*Oich ! oich !*" (in the Lowland Scottish, *hech*). The English *heigho* is a kindred exclamation, and is possibly of the same etymology. *Hech-howe* signifies *heigh-ho !* "In the *auld hech-howe,*" *i.e.*, as in the old *heigho* condition, a mode of complaining that one is in the customary state of ill-health.

Hecht, to offer, to promise. This verb seems to have no present tense, no future, and no declensions or inflexions, and to be only used in the past, as :—

> Willie's rare, Willie's fair,
>   And Willie's wondrous bonny,]
> And Willie *hecht* to marry me,
>   Gin e'er he married ony.
>   —*Tea-Table Miscellany.*

The miller he *hecht* her a heart leal and
  loving,
The laird did address her wi' matter mair
  moving.—BURNS : *Meg o' the Mill.*

He *hecht* me baith rings and mony braw
  things,
And were na my heart light I wad die.
     —LADY GRIZZEL BAILLIE. ⸱

The word is of doubtful etymology : perhaps from the Teutonic *echt*, sincere, true, genuine —which a promise ought to be.

Heckle, a sort of rough comb used by hemp and flax dressers. Metaphorically the word signifies to worry a person by cross-questioning or impertinence. To *heckle* a parliamentary candidate at election time is a favourite amusement of voters, who think themselves much wiser than any candidate can possibly be ; and of insolent barristers in a court of law, who cross-examine a hostile witness with undue severity— an operation which is sometimes called "badgering." There was a well-known butcher in Tiverton who always made it a point to *heckle* the late Lord

Palmerston when he stood as candidate for that borough. Lord Palmerston bore the infliction with great good-humour, and always vanquished the impudent butcher in the wordy warfare.

Adown my beard the slavers trickle,
I throw the wee stools o'er the mickle,
As round the fire the giglets keckle
    To see me loup ;
While raving mad I wish a *heckle*
    Were in their doup !
—Burns : *Address to the Toothache.*

He was a hedge unto his friends,
  A *heckle* to his foes, lads,
And every one that did him wrang,
  He took him by the nose, lads.
    —Chambers's *Scottish Ballads :
         Rob Roy.*

This was the son of the famous Rob Roy, and was called Robin *Og.* Chambers translates Robin *Og,* " Robin the *Little.*" *Og,* in Gaelic, signifies not *little,* but *young.*

Heership, plunder ; from *herry* or *harry,* to rob, to pillage.

But wi' some hope he travels on while he
The way the *heership* had been driven
    could see.—Ross's *Helenore.*

Heft, the haft or handle of a knife. The *heft* of a sword is called the hilt. To give a thing " heft and blade," is to give it wholly and without restriction, " stock, lock, and barrel."

A knife, a father's throat had mangled,
  Whom his ain son o' life bereft—
The grey hairs yet stuck to the *heft ;*
Wi' mair o' horrible and awfu',
Which e'en to name would be unlawfu'.
    —Burns : *Tam o' Shanter.*

Hein-shinn'd, having large ankles. *Ain* or *an,* the augmentative prefix in Gaelic to nouns and adjectives, signifying size, or excess, is probably the root of *hein* in this word.

She's bough-houghed and *hein-shinn'd.*
         —Burns.

Her nain sel', " his own self," and " my own self." This phrase is supposed by the Lowland Scotch to be the usual mode of expression employed by the Highlanders, on account of the paucity of pronouns in the Gaelic language.

Oh, fie for shame, ye're three for ane,
Her nain sel's won the day, man.
    —*Battle of Killiecrankie.*

Mr. Robert Chambers, in a note on this passage, says : "*The Highlanders have only one pronoun,* and as it happens to resemble the English word *her,* it has caused the Lowlanders to have a general impression that they mistake the masculine for the feminine gender." Mr. Chambers, knowing nothing of Gaelic, was utterly wrong in this matter of the pronouns. The Gaelic has the same number of personal pronouns as the English, namely — *mi,* I ; *do,* thou ; *e,* he ; *i,* she ; *sinn,* we ; *sibh,* you or yours ; *iad,* they or theirs. They have also the possessive pronouns —*mo,* mine ; *ar,* ours ; *bhur* and *ur,* yours ; and all the rest of the series. It was doubtless the *ur* or the *ar* of the Gaelic which, by its resemblance to *her*, suggested to Mr. Chambers the error into which he fell.

Herryment, plague, devastation, ruin ; from *herry* or *harry*, to plunder and lay waste.

The *herryment* and ruin of the country.
—BURNS : *The Brigs of Ayr.*

Heuchs and haughs, hands, legs, or thigh. *Heuchs* is probably a corruption of *hooks*, as applied to the hands, or, as Shakespeare calls them, " pickers and stealers." *Haughs* is the Scottish form of the English *hocks*, the hind part of the knee.

The kelpie grinned an eldrich laugh,
And rubbed his *heuchs* upon his *haughs*.
—GEORGE BEATTIE : *John o' Arnha'.*

Hiddil, a hiding-place, the hole or refuge of a shy or wild animal.

The otter yap his prey let drap,
And to his *hiddil* flew.
—*Water Kelpie : Border Minstrelsy.*

Hinnie or **honey**, a term of endearment among the Scottish Highlanders, and more particularly among the Irish.

Oh, open the door, my *hinnie*, my heart,
Oh, open the door, my ain true love.
—CHAMBERS's *Scottish Songs :
Legend of the Padda.*

Honey, in the sense of *hinnie*, occurs in the nursery-rhymes of England :—

There was a lady loved a swine ;
" *Honey !* my dear," quoth she,
" My darling pig, wilt thou be mine ?"
" Hoogh, hoogh ! " grunted he.

The word *hinnie* is supposed to be a corruption of *honey*, though *honey* in the English may be a corruption of *hinnic*. They both express the idea of fondness ; and those who believe honey to be the correct term explain it by assuming that the beloved object is as " sweet as *honey*." But if this be really the fundamental idea, the Gaelic-speaking population of Ireland and the Highlands might be supposed to have used the native word *mil*, rather than the Teutonic *honey* or *honig*, which does not exist in their language. However this may be, it is at all events suggestive that the Gaelic *ion* signifies fitting ; and the compound *ion-amhuil* means like, equal, well-matched ; and *ion-mhuin*, dear, beloved, kind, loving. The Irish Gaelic has *ionadh* (pronounced *hinna*), admiration, or an object of admiration ; whence *ionadh-rhuigte*, adorable. The Scotch and old English *marrow* is a term of endearment to a lover, and signifies mate, one of a pair, as in the ballad :—

Busk ye, busk ye ! my bonnie bride,
Busk ye, busk ye ! my winsome *marrow*.
—HAMILTON *of Bangour.*

In Scotland *hinnie* and *joe* (Jamieson) signify a lass and her lover who are very fond of each other. This phrase is equivalent to the English " Darby and Joan," and describes a greatly-attached wedded pair. The opinions of philologists will doubtless differ between the Teutonic and the possible Gaelic derivation of *honey* or *hinnie*; but the fact that the Teutonic nations do not draw the similar expression of fondness, as applied to a woman, from *honey*, is worthy of consideration in attempting to decide the doubtful point.

Hirple, to limp, to run with a limping motion.

> The hares were *hirplin'* doun the furs.
> —BURNS: *The Holy Fair.*

> And when wi' age we're worn doun,
> An' *hirplin'* at the door.
> —*The Boatie Rows.*

> I'm a pair silly auld man,
> An' *hirplin'* at the door.
> —*Gin Kirk wad Let me be.*

Hirsel. a flock, a multitude; derived by Jamieson from the Teutonic *heer*, an army; but more probably from the Gaelic *carras*, wealth (in flocks and herds), and *earrasail*, wealthy. *Hirsel*, among shepherds, means to arrange or dispose the sheep in separate flocks, and *hirseling*, the separating into flocks or herds: sometimes written and pronounced *hissel.*

As scabbed sheep will smit the hale *hirsel.* —ALLAN RAMSAY'S *Scots Proverbs.*

"Jock, man," said he, "ye're just telling a *hirsel* o' e'endown [downright] lies." —HOGG: *Brownie of Bodsbeck.*

The herds and *hissels* were alarmed. —BURNS: *Epistle to W. Simpson.*

Hirsel or **hersel.** The primary idea of this word is to remove the body. when in a sitting position, to another or contiguous seat without absolutely rising. Jamieson suggests the derivation from the coarse word applied to the posteriors in all the Teutonic languages, including English. He is probably correct; though, as a verb, *aerselen*, which he cites, is not to be found in the Swedish, Danish, Dutch, Flemish, or German dictionaries.

An English gentleman once boasted to the Duchess of Gordon of his familiarity with the Scottish language. "*Hirsel* yont, my braw birkie," said she. To her great amusement, as well as triumph, he could not understand one word except "my."—DEAN RAMSAY.

Hizzie, a lass, a huzzy; a term of jocular endearment. Supposed to be a corruption of *housewife.*

> Buirdly chiels and clever *hizzies*
> Are bred in sic a way as this is.
> —BURNS: *The Twa Dogs.*

Hoast, a cough, or to cough.

Jamie Fraser, a poor half-witted person, who was accustomed to make inconvenient or unseemly noises in the kirk, was one day cautioned not to make fidgety movements during divine service, under the penalty of being turned out. The poor creature sat quite still and silent, till in a very important part of the sermon he felt an irresistible inclination to cough. Unable to restrain himself, he rose in his seat, and shouted out, "Minister, may not a pair body like me gie a *hoast?*"—DEAN RAMSAY.

Hodden-grey. In the glossary to the first edition of Allan Ramsay's "Tea-Table Miscellany," 1724, "*hodden*" is described as a coarse cloth. *Hodden* appears to be a corruption of the Gaelic *adhan*, warm; so that *hodden*-grey would signify warm grey. It was usually home - made by the Scottish peasantry of the Lowlands, and formed the material of their working-day clothes.

What though on homely fare we dine,
  Wear *hodden-grey*, and a' that ;
Gi'e fools their silks an' knaves their wine,
  A man's a man for a' that.—BURNS.

If a man did his best to murder me, I should not rest comfortably until I knew that he was safe in a well-ventilated cell, with the *hodden-grey* garment of the gaol upon him.—*Trial of Prince Pierre Bonaparte, Daily Telegraph*, March 26, 1870.

Hogmanay or **Hogmenay**. This is a peculiarly Scottish name for a festival by no means peculiar to Scotland—that of New Year's Day, or the last hours of the old year and the first of the new. On these occasions, before the world grew as prosaic as it is with regard to old customs and observances, the young men, and sometimes the old, paid visits of congratulation to the girls and women of their acquaintance, with words of goodwill or affection, and very commonly bore with them gifts of more or less value according to their means. It was a time of good-fellowship, conviviality, and kindly offices. Many attempts have been made to trace the word. Some have held it to be from the Greek *hagia* (αγια), holy, and *μηνε*, a month. But as the festival lasted for a few hours only, the etymology is unsatisfactory. Others have thought to find its source in

the French *gui*, the mistletoe, and *mener*, to lead—*au gui mener*, to lead to the mistletoe ; and others, again, to the Gaelic *oige*, youth ; and *madhuin*, the morning, because the celebration took place in the earliest hours of the daylight. It cannot be admitted that any one of these derivations is wholly satisfactory. Nobody has ever thought of looking to the Flemish— which has supplied so many words to the vocabulary of the Lowland Scotch—for a solution of the difficulty. In that language we find *hoog*, high or great ; *min*, love, affection, and *dag*, a day—*hoog-min-dag*, the high or great day of affection. The transition from *hoog-min-dag* to *hog-man-ay*, with the corruption of *dag* into *ay*, is easily accomplished. This etymology is offered with diffidence, not with dogmatic assertion, and solely with this plea on its behalf—that it meets the meaning better perhaps than any other, or, if not better, at least as well as the Greek, French, or Gaelic.

Holme, holm, sometimes written *houm*, a meadow.

Doun in a glen he spied nine armed men,
  On the dowie *holms* o' Yarrow.
  —*Border Minstrelsy: The Dowie Dens
    o' Yarrow.*

Hoodock, the hooded owl.

The harpy, *hoodock*, purse-proud race
Wha count a' poortith as disgrace,
    They've tuneless hearts.
    —BURNS : *Epistle to Major Logan.*

The glossaries to Burns explain this word as meaning "miserly," which is a mere conjecture from the context, to fit it into "purse-proud;" whereas it is but a continuation of the ornithological idea of harpy, a vulture. The origin is the French *duc*, an owl, of which in that language there are three varieties—*grand duc*, or great owl; *petit duc*, or little owl; and *haut duc*, large, great owl. Possibly, however, the first syllable in *hood*ock is the English *hood*. The idea in Burns is that of a greedy bird or harpy. Jamieson has "*hoodit* craw" for carrion crow; and *hoody*, the hooded crow.

Hool, the husk of grain, the integument, the case or covering.

> Ilk kind o' corn has its ain *hool;*
> I think the world is a' gane wrang
> When ilka wife her man wad rule.
> —*Tak' your Auld Cloak about ye.*

> Poor Leezie's heart maist lap the *hool*,
> Near laverock height she loupit.
> —Burns: *Hallowe'en.*

In Dutch, *hülle*, cover, integument, veil; Swedish, *holja*, cover, envelope, case, or hull; whence also the English *holster*, the case of a pistol; and *upholster*, to make cases or coverings for furniture, and *upholsterer*, one who *upholsters*. The unnecessary and corrupt prefix of *up* to this word has led philologists to derive it erroneously from *uphold.*

The English *hoils*, applied to the beard and husks of barley, and *hull*, a husk or shell of peas and beans, seems to be from the same source as the Scottish *hool*, and in like manner the *hull* or outer case of a ship.

> Sad was the chase that they ha'e gi'en to me,
> My heart's near out o' *hool* by getting free.
> —Ross's *Helenore.*

Hoolie or **hooly**. This word is commonly used in conjunction with "fairly," as in the phrase "*hooly* and fairly." Jamieson renders it "slowly and cautiously." It is derived from the Gaelic *ŭigheil, ui-eil*, heedful, cautious. The glossaries to Burns render it "stop!" There is an old Scottish song—"Oh, that my wife would drink *hooly* and fairly." In the glossary to Mr. Alexander Smith's edition of Burns, where "stop" would not convey the meaning, the explanation that the word means "stop" is a mere guess from the context, which proves that the editor did not really understand the word.

> Still the mair I'm that way bent,
> Something cries "*Hoolie!*"
> I rede you, honest man, tak' tent,
> You'll show your folly.
> —Burns: *Epistle to James Smith.*

> Sin' every pastime is a pleasure,
> I counsel you to sport with measure;
> And, namely now, May, June, and July,
> Delight not long in Lorea's leisure,
> But weit your lipps and labour *hooly*.
> —*On May:* Alex. Scott *in the Evergreen.*

> Oh, *hooly, hooly*, rose she up
> To the place where he was lyin',

And when she drew the curtain bye—
"Young man, I think ye're dyin'."
—*Ballad of Barbara Allan.*

Hooly and fair gangs far in a day.—
ALLAN RAMSAY'S *Scots Proverbs.*

In the North of England *hooly* means
tenderly, gently.—HALLIWELL.

Hootie, a ludicrous but expressive word, applied to a man
like Pococurante in Voltaire's
romance, who impresses the
ingenuous Candide with an
idea of the immensity of his
wisdom, because nothing could
please him. The word is derivable from *hoot !* or *hoots !* an
interjection expressive of contempt, or of more or less angry
dissent. *Hoot ! toot !* is an intensification of the same idea.
The English have *pshaw ! pish !*
and *tut !* The word in the form
of *ut ! ut !* is very common
among Highlanders.

Horn. Drinking vessels, before
glass was much used for the
purpose, were made of horn,
and are still to be found both
among the poor and the rich.
"To take a *horn* " ultimately
came to signify to take a drink
—just as the modern phrase,
" Take a glass," does not mean
to take the glass itself, but the
liquor contained in it. (*See*
GROG, *ante.*)

By the gods of the ancients ! Glenriddel
replies,
Before I surrender so glorious a prize,
I'll conjure the ghost of the great Rorie
More,
And *bumper his horn* with him twenty
times o'er.—BURNS : *The Whistle.*

Horn-dry, according to Jamieson,
means " dry as a horn ; eager
for drink ; an expression frequently used by reapers when
exhausted by the labours of the
harvest." But the obvious etymology—viewed in the light of
the other words that have been
cited—is not *dry* as a horn, but
dry for want of a *horn* of liquor.
(For further reference to horn
as signifying a drink, see GROG,
ante.) To take a *croc*, or *grog*
(the same as to take a *horn* or a
glass), meant simply to take a
drink. The French have *cric*
and *croc* for a glass of spirits, as
in the chorus of the old song :—

Cric, croc ! à ta santé !

Horn-mad is defined in the Dictionary of Lowland Scotch
(1818) as signifying quite mad ;
though the compiler did not
seem to be aware that the madness was that which came from
intoxication or the too frequent
emptying of the horn. *Horn-
daft* is of similar meaning and
origin, though expressive of a
minor degree of intoxication.
Jamieson renders it " outrage-
ous," and imagines it may be
an allusion to an animal that
pushes with its horns. *Horn-
idle* is defined by Jamieson to
mean " having nothing to do,
completely unemployed." He
derives the first syllable from
the Saxon, and the second from
the Gaelic. *Horn* is certainly
Teutonic or Flemish, but *idle* is as
certainly not Gaelic. The allusion in this case is obviously to

the sloth or drowsiness that in lethargic persons often results from intoxication.

Hornie is a word used in Ayrshire, according to Jamieson, to signify amorous, lecherous, libidinous. Still, with the notion in his head that *horn* is to be taken literally, and not metaphorically, he suggests that a *hornie* person is one who is apt to reduce another to the state of cuckoldom, or a *cornutus ;* and to confer upon him the imaginary horns that are supposed to grace the forehead of those ill-used and unfortunate persons. It is evident, however, that *hornie* meant nothing more than intoxicated to such an extent as to excite the intoxicated person to take improper liberties with women. Burns employs the word as one of the names popularly and jocularly bestowed upon the devil.

Host, to cough with effort or difficulty. The colloquial phrase, " It didna cost him a *hoast* to do it," signifies that the thing was done easily and without effort. From the German *husten*, the Flemish *hosten*, to cough. (*See* HOAST, *ante.*)

—— Joyless Eild (old age),
  Wi' wrinkled face,
Comes *hostin'*, hirplin' ow'r the field
  Wi' creepin' pace.
  —BURNS: *Epistle to James Smith.*

Houghmagandie, child-bearing; wrongly supposed to mean the illicit intercourse of the sexes. This word has not been found in any author before Burns, and is considered by some to have been coined by that poet. But this is not likely. It is usually translated by "fornication." No etymology of the word has hitherto been suggested. Nevertheless, its component parts seem to exist in the Flemish. In that language *hoog* signifies high or great, and *maag*, the stomach or belly ; *maagen*, bellies ; and *je*, a diminutive particle commonly added to Flemish and Dutch words, and equivalent to the Scottish *ie* in *bairnie, wifie, laddie, lassie,* &c. These words would form *hoog-maagan-je*—a very near approach to the *houghmagandie* of Burns. If this be the derivation, it would make better sense of the passage in which it occurs than that usually attributed to it. The context shows that it is not fornication which is meant— for that has already been committed—but the possible result of the sin which may appear "some other day," in the enlarged circumference of the female sinner.

There's some are fu' o' love divine,
  And some are fu' o' brandy ;
And mony a job that day begun
  May end in *houghmagandie*
    Some other day.
    —BURNS: *The Holy Fair.*

Ayrshire and Dumfriesshire retained for a longer time than the eastern counties of Scotland the words and phrases of the Gaelic language, though often greatly corrupted ; and in the poems and songs of Burns words from the Gaelic are of frequent occurrence. It is not likely that Burns ever took it upon himself to invent a word; and if he did, it is even more than unlikely that it should find acceptance. Whatever it may mean, *houghmagandie* does not mean fornication, for the whole spirit and contents of the "Holy Fair" show that fornication is what he stigmatises as the practice of the gatherings which he satirises; and that which he calls *houghmagandie* is, or is likely to be, the future result of the too promiscuous intercourse of the sexes, against which he jocosely declaims. The Gaelic *og* and *macan*, a little son, may possibly afford a clue to the word; but this is a suggestion merely.

I don't remember to have met with this word anywhere except in the "Holy Fair." It may have been a word in use in Burns's day, or it may have been a coinage of Burns, that would readily convey to the minds of his readers what he meant. It may have conveyed the idea of a "dyke-louper" appearing before the Session, the "snoovin' awa afore the Session" for a fault, the doing penance for "jobbing." *Gangdays* were the three days in Rogation week, on which priest and parishioners were accustomed to walk in procession about the parish; a remnant of the custom is still to be seen in London in the perambulations of boys about the bounds of the parish. *Gandie* would not be a very violent alteration of *gandeye*, the more especially that the spelling of Scotch words partook a good deal of the phonetic, and *gangday* was very probably pronounced *gandie*. Now, we know as a fact that, in the lapse of time, many of the ceremonies of the Church became corrupted from their original intention, and processions became in time a sort of penance for faults, and in this way it is just possible that *gandie* came itself to mean a penance, and *houghmagandie* conveyed the idea of doing penance for some wrong action that the *hough* or leg had something to do with.— R. DRENNAN.

Howdie or **howdie-wife,** a midwife, an accoucheuse. This word is preferable to the English and the foreign term borrowed from the French. *Howdie-fee,* the payment given to a midwife.

When skirlin' weanies see the light,
Thou makes the gossips clatter bright,
How funkin' cuifs their dearies slight—
    Wae worth the name!
Nae *howdie* gets a social night
    Or plack frae them.
        —BURNS : *Scotch Drink.*

No satisfactory clue to the etymology of this word has been made known. In Gaelic the midwife is called the "knee-woman," *beangloinne;* in French, the *sage femme,* or wise woman; in Teutonic, the *weh mutter;* in Spanish, *partera,* and in Italian, *comare,* the latter word signifying the French *commère*—the old English and Scotch *cummer* —or gossip. Possibly the true origin of the Scottish word is to be found in *houd* or *haud,* to hold, to sustain; and the midwife was the *holder,* helper, sustainer, and comforter of the woman who suffered the pains of labour; the *sage femme* of the French, who was wise and skilful enough to perform her delicate function.

Howff, a favourite public-house, where friends and acquaintances were accustomed to resort; from the Gaelic *uamh* (*uaf*), a cave. "Caves of harmony," as they were called, were formerly known in Paris, and one long existed in London under the name of the *Coalhole*. They were small places of convivial resort, which, in London, have grown into music-halls. Jamieson traces *howff* to the Teutonic *hof*, a court-yard, and *gast-hof*, an inn or yard. It is possible that he is right, though it is equally possible that the German *hof* is but a form of the Gaelic *uamh*.

This will be delivered to you by a Mrs. Hyslop, landlady of the Globe Tavern here, which for many years has been my *howff*, and where our friend Clarke and I have had many a merry squeeze.—Burns: *Letter to George Thompson.*

Burns's *howff* at Dumfries.—Chambers.

Where was't that Robertson and you were used to *howff* thegither?—Scott: *Heart of Midlothian.*

Howk, formerly spelled **holk**, to dig, to grub up, to root up, to form a hole in the ground.

Whiles mice and moudieworts (moles) they *howkit*.
            —Burns: *The Twa Dogs.*
And in kirkyards renew their leagues
            Owre *howkit* dead.
            —Burns: *Address to the De'il.*
He has *howkit* a grave that was lang and was deep,
And he has buried his sister wi' her baby at her feet.
            —Motherwell: *The Broom Blooms Bonnie.*

Howk the tow out o' your lug an' hear till a sang.—*Noctes Ambrosianæ.*

How-towdies, barndoor fowls; origin of the word unknown, though it has been suggested that it may be a corruption of the Gaelic *eun-doide*, a fowl to the hand, or a fowl ready to the hand if wanted.

Hunting the fox prevents him from growing ower fat on *how-towdies.*—*Noctes Ambrosianæ.*

Huggers, stockings or hose without feet.

But a' her skill lies in her buskin,
    And oh, if her braws were awa,
She soon would wear out o' the fashion,
    And knit up her *huggers* wi' straw.
            —*Woo'd and Married and a'.*

Hummel-corn, mean, shabby, of small account; a term applied to the lighter grain which falls from the rest when it is winnowed.

A lady returning from church expressed her low opinion of the sermon she had heard by calling it a *hummel-corn* discourse.—Dean Ramsay.

The derivation is unknown, though *humble-corn* has been suggested.

Hummel-doddie, dowdy, ill-fitting, in bad taste.

Whatna *hummel-doddie* o' a mutch [cap] hae ye gotten?—Dean Ramsay's *Reminiscences.*

Humple, to walk lamely and painfully, to hobble.

Then *humpled* he out in a hurry,
    While Janet his courage bewails.
            —Chambers's *Scottish Songs.*

Hunkers, the loins; to *hunker down*, to squat on the ground.

The word seems to be allied to the English *hunk*, a lump; whence to squat down on the earth in a lumpish fashion.

> Wi' ghastly ee, poor Tweedle Dee
> Upon his *hunkers* bended,
> And prayed for grace wi' cuthless face
> To see the quarrel ended.
> —BURNS: *The Jolly Beggars.*

Hurdies, the hips, the *podex* of the Romans, the *pyge* of the Greeks. From the Gaelic *aird*, a rounded muscle or swelling; plural *airde*, also *airdhe*, a wave, or of a wavy form.

> His tail
> Hung o'er his *hurdies* wi' a swirl.
> —BURNS: *The Twa Dogs.*

Ye godly brethren o' the sacred gown,
Wha meekly gie your *hurdies* to the smiters.—BURNS: *The Brigs of Ayr.*

> Thir breeks o' mine, my only pair,
> That ance were plush, o' guid blue hair,
> I wad ha'e gi'en them aff my *hurdies*,
> For ae blink o' the bonnie burdies!
> —BURNS: *Tam O'Shanter.*

Pendable? ye may say that; his craig wad ken the weight of his *hurdies* if they could get haud o' Rob.—SCOTT: *Rob Roy.*

The old French poet, François Villon, when condemned to be hung, wrote a stanza in which the above idea of Sir Walter Scott occurs in language about as forcible and not a whit more elegant:—

> Je suis Français (dont ce me poise),
> Né de Paris, emprês Ponthoise,
> Or d'une corde d'une toise
> Sçaura mon col que mon cul poise.

Burns also uses the word in the sense of "rounded or swell-ing," without reference to any portion of the human frame, as in the following:—

> The groaning trencher there ye fill;
> Your *hurdies* like a distant hill.
> —*To a Haggis.*

Hurkle, to yield obedience or deference.

> Grant, an' Mackenzie, an' Murray,
> An' Cameron will *hurkle* to nane.
> HOGG, *the Ettrick Shepherd.*

Hurl, to wheel; *hurl - barrow*, wheel-barrow; a corruption of *whirl*, to turn round; *hurley-hacket*, a contemptuous name for an ill-hung carriage or other vehicle.

It's *kittle* for the cheeks when the *hurl-barrow* gangs o'er the brig o' the nose. —ALLAN RAMSAY'S *Scots Proverbs.*

"I never thought to have entered ane o' these *hurley-hackets*," she said, as she seated herself, "and sic a thing as it is—scarce room for twa folk."—SCOTT: *St. Ronan's Well.*

Hynde, gentle, courteous. An illi-terate member of Parliament in the unruly session of 1887 ob-jected to the use of this word as applied to an agricultural labourer, believing that it signi-fied a deer or other quadruped, and never having suspected that it was a term of courtesy. The member himself, called honour-able by the courtesy of Parlia-ment, was ignorant of the fact that courtesy was extended even to farm-labourers by all gentle-men and men of good heart and good manners.

Then she is to yon *hynde* squire's yetts,
 And tirled at the pin,
And wha sae busy as the *hynde* squire
 To let the lady in.
  —BUCHAN'S *Ancient Ballads: Hynd
   Horn.*

Hyte, joyous; excited unduly or
 overmuch.

Ochone for poor Castalian drinkers!
The witchin', cursed, delicious blinkers
 Ha'e put me *hyte.*
  —BURNS: *Epistle to Major Logan.*

This word is derived from the
Gaelic *aite,* joy, gladness, fun,
and appears to be related to
the English *hoity-toity.*

I

Ier-oe, a great grandchild; erroneously spelled *jeroy* in the new
 editions of Jamieson, and cited
 as a "Shetland word."

May health and peace with mutual rays
Shine on the evening o' his days,
Till his wee curlie John's *ier oe,*
When ebbing life nae mair shall flow,
The last sad mournful rites bestow.
  —BURNS: *A Dedication to Gavin
   Hamilton.*

 The word is from the Gaelic
oghe, a grandchild, and *iar,*
after; whence an after grandchild, or great grandchild.

Igo and ago, iram, coram, dago.
 The chorus of ancient Gaelic
 boat-songs, or *Ramh-rans,* introduced by Burns in his song,
 "Ken ye aught o' Captain
 Grose?" The words resolve
 themselves into the Gaelic
 *aighe, aghach, iorram, corruig-
 heamh dachaidh,* which signify
 "Joyous and brave is the song
 of the boat that is rowing
 homewards."

Ilka, each, as "ilka ane," each
 one; *ilk,* that same. *Ilk* is used

for the designation of a person
whose patronymic is the same
as the name of his estate—such
as Mackintosh of Mackintosh—
i.e., Mackintosh of that *Ilk.*
This Scottish word has crept
into English, though with a
strange perversion of its meaning, as in the following:—

We know, however, that many bar-
barians of their *ilk,* and even of later
times, knowingly destroyed many a gold
and silver vessel that fell into their
hands.—*St. James's Gazette.*

Matilda lived in St. John's Villas,
Twickenham; Mr. Passmore in King
Street of the same *ilk.*—*Daily Telegraph.*

Ingine, genius, "the fire of
 genius" or "poetic fire," are
 common expressions. Burns, in
 an "Epistle to John Lapraik,"
 whose poetry he greatly admired, and thought equal to
 that of Alexander Pope or
 James Beattie, made inquiries
 concerning him, and was told
 that he was "an odd kind o'
 chiel about Muirkirk."

An' sae about him there I spier't,
Then a' that ken'd him round declar't
        He had *ingine*,
That nane excelled it—few cam near't,
        It was sae fine.

It would seem on first consideration that this peculiarly Scottish word was of the same Latin derivation as genius, ingenious, ingenuity, and the archaic English word cited in Halliwell, "ingene," which is translated "genius or wit." It is open to inquiry, however, whether the idea of *fire* does not underlie the word, and whether it is not in the form in which Burns employs it, traceable to the Gaelic *ain*, an intransitive prefix or particle signifying great, very, or intense; and *teine*, fire.

The late Samuel Rogers, author of the "Pleasures of Memory," in a controversy with me on the character of Lord Byron, spoke very unfavourably of his poetical genius, which I praised and defended to the best of my ability. Mr. Rogers, however, always returned to the attack with renewed vigour. Driven at last to extremity, I thought to clench all argument by saying —"At least you will admit, Mr. Rogers, that there was *fire* in Byron's poetry?" "Yes," he answered, "*hell-fire!*"—C. M.

Ingle, the fire; *ingle-side*, the fireside, the hearth; *ingle-neuk*, the chimney corner; *ingle-bred*, home-bred, or bred at the domestic hearth; *inglin*, fuel.

Better a wee *ingle* to warm you, than a muckle fire to burn you.—ALLAN RAMSAY's *Scots Proverbs.*

    His wee bit *ingle* blinkin' bonnilie.
                    —BURNS.

It's an auld story now, and everybody tells it, as we were doing, in their ain way by the *ingle-side*.—SCOTT : *Guy Mannering.*

The derivation of *ingle*, in the Scottish sense of the word, is either from the Gaelic *aingeal*, the Kymric *engyl*, heat, fire, or from *ion*, fit, becoming, comfortable; and *cuil*, a corner. That of the English *ingle*, meaning a favourite, a friend, or lover, is not easy to discover. The word occurs in a passage from an Elizabethan play, with a detestable title, quoted by Nares :—

Call me your love, your *ingle*, your cousin, or so ; but *sister* at no hand.

Also in Massinger's "City Madam" :—

His quondam patrons, his dear *ingils* now.

Ingle, from one signifying a lover in the legitimate use of that word, was corrupted into an epithet for the male lover of a male, in the most odious sense. In "Donne's Elegies," it is used as signifying amorous endearment of a child to its father :—

Thy little brother, which like fairy spirits,
Oft skipped into our chamber those sweet nights
And kissed and *ingled* on thy father's knee.

No satisfactory etymology for the English word has ever been suggested, and that from the Spanish *yngle*, the groin, which finds favour with Nares and other philologists, is manifestly inadmissible. It is possible, however, that the English *ingle* was originally the same as the Scottish, and that its first

G

meaning as "love" was derived from the idea still current, that calls a beloved object a *flame.* Hotten's Slang Dictionary has "*flame,* a sweetheart." *Ingle* was sometimes written *enghle,* which latter word, according to Mr. Halliwell, signifies, as used by Ben Jonson, a gull—also, to coax or to wheedle.

Intill, into; *till,* to. What's *in-till't?* What's in it?

An English traveller, staying at a great hotel in Edinburgh, was much pleased with the excellence of the hotch-potch at dinner, and asked the head-waiter how it was made, and of what it was made? The waiter replied that there were peas *intill't,* and beans *intill't,* and onions *intill't.* "But what's *intill't?*" asked the Englishman. "I'm just tellin' you that there's beans *intill't,* and peas *intill't,* and neeps *intill't,* and carrots *intill't*"——

"Yes! yes! I know—beans, peas, onions, turnips, and carrots," said the Englishman; "but what's *intill't?* Is it salt, pepper, or what? Please tell me what's *intill't?*"

"Eh, man!" replied the impatient waiter, "ye maun be unco' slow o' comprehension. I was tellin' ye owre and owre again that there are beans *intill't,* and peas *intill't*"——

"And *tult!* What the devil is *tult,* or *intill't,* or whatever the name is? Can you not give a plain answer to a plain question? Does *tult* mean barley, or mutton, or mustard, or some nameless ingredient that is a trade secret, or that you are afraid to mention?"

"Oh, man!" said the waiter, with a groan, "if I had your head in my keeping, I'd gie it sic a thumpin' as wad put some smeddum *intill't.*"

Tradition records that the Englishman has never yet ascertained what *intill't* means, but wanders through Scotland vainly seeking enlightenment.—*Knife and Fork,* edited by BLANCHARD JERROLD.

I wish ye were in Heckie-burnie.

"This," says Jamieson, "is a strange form of imprecation. The only account given of this place is that it is three miles beyond *hell.* In Aberdeen, if one says, 'go to the devil!' the other often replies, 'go you to *Heckie-burnie!*'" No etymology is given. Possibly it originated in the pulpit, when some Gaelic preacher had taken the story of Dives and Lazarus for his text; and the rich Dives, amid his torments in hell, asked in vain for a drop of water to cool his parched tongue. The intolerable thirst was his greatest punishment; and in Gaelic *Aicheadh* is refusal, and *buirne,* water from the burn or stream, whence the phrase would signify the refusal or denial of water. This is offered as a suggestion only, to account for an expression that has been hitherto given up as inexplicable.

J

Jamph, to trudge, to plod, to make way laboriously, to grow weary with toil; also, to endeavour to take liberties with an unwilling or angry woman; to pursue her under difficulty and obstruction.

" Oh bonnie lass ! " says he, " ye'll gie's a kiss,
And I shall set you right on, hit or miss."
" A hit or miss, I want na help of you,—
Kiss ye sklate stanes, they winna wat your mou."
And off she goes ;—the fellow loot a rin,
As gin he ween'd with speed to tak her in ;
But as luck was, a knibbloch took his tae,
And o'er fa's he, and tumbles down the brae ;
His neebor leugh, and said it was well wair'd—
" Let never *jamphers* yet be better sair'd."
    —Ross's *Helenore.*

The etymology of *jamph*— whether it means to plod or flirt, or both—is obscure. It is possibly, but not certainly, from the Gaelic *deanamh* (*de* pronounced as *je*), doing, acting, performing. Jamieson thinks that, in the sense of flirting, it may come from the Teutonic *schimpfen*, to mock ; and in the sense of plod or trudge, from *schampfen*, to slip aside.

Jauner, idle talk ; to wander listlessly about without any particular object.

Oh, haud your tongue now, Luckie Laing,
Oh, haud your tongue and *jauner*.
  —Burns : *The Lass of Ecclefechan.*
We'se had a good *jauner* this forenoon.
    —Jamieson.

In the sense of wandering idly, this word seems to be but a variety or corruption of *dauner.*

Jawp, to bespatter with mud or water. To "*jawp* the water" is a metaphor for spending time in any negotiation or transaction without coming to a definite conclusion, " I'll no *jawp* water wi' ye "—" I'll not enter into further discussions or wrangles with you." " To *jawp* waters with one," to play fast and loose, to strive to be off a bargain once made.

Then down ye'll hurl, deil nor ye never rise,
And dash the gumly *jawps* up to the skies.
    —Burns : *The Brigs of Ayr.*

Jawthers, quasi synonymous with the English slang " to *jaw*," to dispute or argue abusively, as in the phrase " let me have none of your *jaw*." *Jawthers*, idle wranglings, and also any frivolous discourse.

Jee, to move. This word survives in English as a command to a horse, in the phrase *jee-up* and *jee-wo.*

   I am sick an' very love sick,
   Ae foot I canna *jee*.
    —Buchan's *Ancient Ballads.*

Jimp, slender in the waist.

   She is as *jimp* i' the middle sae fou'
   As is a willow wand.
    —*The Laird o' Warriston.*

Jink, to play, to sport, to dodge in and out, from whence the phrase "high-jinks," sometimes used in England to describe the merriment and sport of servants in the kitchen when their masters and mistresses are out; a quick or sudden movement; also to escape, to trick, "to gie the *jink*," to give the slip, to elude.

And now, auld Cloots, I ken ye're thinkin'
A certain bardie, rantin', drinkin',
Some luckless hour will send him linkin'
    To your black pit;
But faith he'll turn a corner *jinkin'*,
    And cheat ye yet!
        —Burns: *Address to the Deil.*

¦ Lang may your elbuck *jink* and diddle.
      —Burns: *Second Epistle to Davie.*

Oh, thou, my muse! guid auld Scotch drink,
Whether through wimplin' worms thou *jink*,
Or, richly brown, ream o'er the brink
    In glorious faem.
        —Burns: *Scotch Drink.*

Jamieson derives the word from the Swedish *dwink-a*, and the German *schwinken*, to move quickly, but no such word appears in the German dictionaries, and the etymology is otherwise unsatisfactory. The Gaelic *dian* (pronounced *jian*) and *dianach* signifies brisk, nimble, which is probably the root of *jink* as used by Burns.

Jirble, jirgle. Both of these words signify to spill any liquid by making it move from side to side in the vessel that contains it; to empty any liquid from one vessel to another; also, the small quantity left in a glass or tea-cup.

The waur for themselves and for the country baith, St. Ronan's; it's the junketing and the *jirbling* in tea and sic trumpery that brings our nobles to ninepence, and mony a het ha' house to a hired lodging in the Abbey.—Scott: *St. Ronan's Well.*

Jock in Scottish, and in English *Jack*, are used as familiar substitutes for the Christian name John, and are supposed to be derived from the French *Jacques*. This word, however, means James, and not John. The use of the prefixes *Jack* and *Jock* in many English and Scottish compounds that have no obvious reference to the Christian names either of James or John, suggests that there may possibly be a different origin for the word. Among others that may be cited, are *Jack*-tar, *Jack*-priest, *Jack*-of-all-trades, and such implements in common use as boot-*jack*, roasting-*jack*, *jack*-knife, the *jacks* or hammers of a pianoforte, the *jack* or clapper of a bell, *jack*-boots, *jack*-chain, the Union-*jack* or flag, *jack*-staff, *jack*-towel, *jack*-block, and many others which are duly set forth in the dictionaries, without suggestion of any other etymology than that from John. Shakspeare in his sonnets uses the word *jack* for the hammers of the virginal, and in *Richard II.* employs it to signify a working-man :—

Since every *jack* became a gentleman,
There's many a gentle person made a *jack.*

Besides the Scottish term of familiarity or affection for a man, the word *Jock* occurs in two singular words cited by Jamieson—*Jock-te-leer*, which he says is a cant term for a pocket almanack, "derived from *Jock* the liar," from the loose or false predictions with regard to the weather which are contained in such publications; and *Jock-te-leg*, a folding or clasp-knife.

It is difficult to connect either the Scottish *Jock* or the English *Jack* in these words with the name of John, unless upon the supposition that John and Jack are synonymous with *man*, and that the terms are transferable to any and every implement that aids or serves the purpose of a man's work. Is it not possible that *Jock* and *Jack* are mere varieties of the Gaelic *deagh* (the *de* pronounced as *j*), which signifies good, excellent, useful, befitting? or the Kymric *iach*, whole, useful? and *deach*, a movement for a purpose? This derivation would meet the sense of all the compound words and phrases in which *jock* and *jack* enter, other than those in which it indubitably signifies a Christian name.

The word *jocteleer*—an almanack, in Jamieson—tried by this test, would signify, good to examine, to learn; from *deagh*, good, and *leir*, perception.

In like manner, the English words and phrases, *Jack*-tar, *Jack*-priest, *Jack*-of-all-trades, might signify good, able-bodied sailor, good priest, and good at all trades. Even jockey, a good rider, may be derivable from the same source. Thus, too, in Shakspeare's phrase, *Jack* may signify, not a John, as a generic name, but *deagh* (*jeack*), as applied in the common phrase "my good man," and in French *bon homme*—epithets which, although in one sense respectful, are only employed by superiors to inferiors, and infer somewhat of social depreciation.

In reference to *Jocteleg* or *Jocktelag*, it should be mentioned that Burns spells the word in the first manner, and Allan Ramsay in the second. Jamieson says that there was once a famous cutler of Liege, in Belgium, named Jacques, and that his cutlery being in repute, any article of his make was called a *Jacques de Liege*. As no mention of this man or his business has been found anywhere except in the pages of Jamieson, it has been suspected that the name was evolved from the imagination of that philologist. Whether that be so or not, it is curious that the Gaelic *dioghail* signifies to avenge, and *dioghail taiche* (pronounced *jog-al taiche*), an avenger. In early times it was customary to bestow names of affection upon swords, such as *Excalibur*, the sword of King Arthur, *Durandarte*, and many others, the swords of renowned knights of romance and chivalry; and if upon swords, probably upon daggers and knives; and no epithet in a barbarous age—when every man had to depend upon his own prowess for self-defence or revenge for injuries—could be more appropriate for a strong knife than the "avenger."

Joe or **Jo**, a lover, a friend, a dear companion; derived not from Joseph, as has been asserted, nor from the French *joie* or English *joy*, as Jamieson supposes, but more probably from the Gaelic *deo* (the *d* pronounced as *j*), the soul, the vital spark, the life; Greek ξῶη.

> John Anderson my *jo*, John.
> —BURNS.
>
> Kind sir, for your courtesy,
>   As ye gae by the Bass, then,
> For the love ye bear to me,
>   Buy me a keeking-glass, then.
> Keek into the clear draw-well,
>   Janet, Janet,
> There ye'll see your bonnie sel',
>   My *jo*, Janet.
> —*Old Song: remodelled by* BURNS.

Joram, a boat song; a rowing song, in which the singers keep time with their voices to the motion of the oars; from the modern Gaelic *iorram*. This word is often erroneously used in the phrase "push about the *jorum*," as if *jorum* signified a bowl of liquor which had to be passed round the table. An instance of this mistake occurs in Burns:—

> And here's to them that, like oursel',
>   Can push about the *jorum;*
> And here's to them that wish us weel—
>   May a' that's guid watch o'er 'em.
> —*Oh May, thy Morn.*

The ancient and correct Gaelic for a boat song is *oran iomraidh* or *iomramh ;* from *oran*, a song; *iom*, many, and *ramh*, an oar, of which *iorram*, or the song of many oars, is a corruption. The connection between *iorram*, a boat song, and *jorum*, a drinking vessel, is probably due to the circumstance that the chorus of the boat song was often sung by the guests at a convivial party, when the bottle or bowl was put in circulation.

Jouk, to stoop down; in the English vernacular to duck the head, or duck down; also to evade a question. *Jouker*, a dissembler, a deceiver.

> Neath the brae the burnie *jouks*.
> —TANNAHILL: *Gloomy Winter.*

Jouk and let the jaw go by (*Proverb*)—*i.e.*, evade replying to intemperate or abusive language.

Jow, the swing or boom of a large bell.

> Now Clinkumbell
>   Began to *jow*.
> —BURNS: *The Holy Fair.*

> And every *jow* the kirk bell gied.
> BUCHAN's *Ancient Ballads.*

Jow means to swing, and not the "clang or boom of a large bell."

> Now Clinkumbell, wi' rattling tone
> Began to *jow* and croon.

The bell-rope began to shake,—the bell began to swing (*jow*) and (croon) ring out.
—R. DRENNAN.

Jowler. This word is used by Burns in the "Address of Beelzebub to the President of the Highland Society," in which, speaking of gipsies, he says:—

An' if the wives an' dirty brats
E'en thigger at your doors an' yetts,
Get out a horsewhip or a *jowler,*

.   .   .   .   .   .

An' gar the tattered gipsies pack
Wi' a' their bastards on their back.

Jamieson does not include the word in his Dictionary, nor do the glossaries to Allan Ramsay or Burns contain it. By the context, it would seem to mean a cudgel. In this sense the word has support in the northern counties of England. *Jolle,* according to Mr. Halliwell Phillips, signifies to beat ; and *jowler* means thick and clumsy—epithets which describe a bludgeon and a cudgel.

" Did you give him a good drubbing?"
"I gave him a good tidy *jowling.*"—
WRIGHT's *Archaic Dictionary.*

In the sense of thick and clumsy, *jolle* and *jowl* are apparently the roots of English *jolter-head,* a thick-headed fellow. *Jowler,* as the name of an instrument of punishment, whether a cudgel or not, is probably from the Gaelic *diol* (*jole, d* pronounced as *j*), to punish, to avenge, to requite, to pay ; *diolair,* an avenger. In colloquial English the threat, "I'll pay you out," has a similar meaning.

Jundie, to jostle, to struggle, to contend and push in a crowd ; to *hog-shouther,* or push with the shoulders in order to force a way.

If a man's gaun down the brae, ilk ane gi'es him a *jundie.*—ALLAN RAMSAY's *Scots Proverbs.*

The warldly race may drudge and drive,
Hog-shouther, *jundie,* stretch, and strive.
—BURNS : *To William Simpson.*

Jute, a term of reproach applied to a weak, worthless, spiritless person, especially to a woman. It is also used in reference to sour or stale liquor, and to weak broth or tea. It seems to be derived from the Gaelic *diùid* (*diù* pronounced as *ju*), sneaking, mean-spirited, silly, weak ; and *diu,* the worst, the refuse of things.

K

Kail, cabbage, the German *kohl ;* a word that survives in English in the first syllable of *cauliflower.* By an extension of meaning *kail* sometimes signifies dinner, as in the familiar invitation once common, "Come an' tak' your *kail* wi' me," *i.e.,* come and dine with me.

Kail-runt, a cabbage stalk ; *kail-blade,* a cabbage leaf.

When I lookit to my dart,
It was sae blunt,
Fient haet it wad hae pierced the heart
O' a *kail-runt.*
—BURNS : *Death and Dr. Hornbook.*

Just —— in a *kail-blade* and send it,—
Baith the disease and what'll mend it,
At ance he'll tell't.—*Idem.*

Kain, tribute, tax, tithe; from the Gaelic *cain*, tribute; *cain-tach*, tributary.

> Our laird gets in his racked rents,
> His coal, his *kain*.
> —BURNS : *The Twa Dogs.*
>
> *Kain* to the King.
> —*Jacobite Song* (1715).

Kain-bairns, says a note in Sir Walter Scott's "Minstrelsy of the Scottish Border," were infants, according to Scottish superstition, that were seized in their cradles by warlocks and witches, and paid as a *kain*, or tax, to their master the devil. Jamieson is in error in deriving *kain* from the Gaelic *cean*, the head.

Kaur-handit, left-handed. In this combination, *kaur* does not signify the left as distinguished from the right, but is from the Gaelic *car*, signifying a twist or turn. The hand so designated implies that it is twisted or turned into a function that ought to be performed by the other.

Kaury-maury is used in the "Vision of Piers Ploughman."

> Clothed in a *kaury-maury*
> I couthe it nought descryve.

In the glossary to Mr. Thomas Wright's edition of this ancient poem, he suggests that *kaury-maury* only means care and trouble: a conjecture that is supported by the Gaelic *car*, and *mearachd*, an error, a mistake, a wrong, an injustice.

Kebar, a rafter, a beam in the roof of a house; from the Gaelic *cabar*, a pole, the trunk of a tree. "Putting" or throwing the *cabar* is a gymnastic feat still popular at Highland games in Scotland.

> He ended, and the *kebars* shook
> Above the chorus roar.
> —BURNS : *The Jolly Beggars.*

Kebbuck, a cheese; *kebbuck heel*, a remnant or hunk of cheese. From the Gaelic *cabag*, a cheese.

> The weel-hained *kebbuck*.
> —BURNS : *Cotter's Saturday Night.*
>
> In comes a gaucie, gash, gude wife,
> An' sits down by the fire ;
> Syne draws her *kebbuck* and her knife—
> The lasses they are shyer.
> —BURNS : *The Holy Fair.*

Keck or **keckle**, to draw back from a bargain, to change one's mind, to flinch ; from the Gaelic *caochail*, to change.

> "I have *keck'd*"—I decline adhering to the offer.—JAMIESON.

Keckle is also a form of the English *cackle*, and has no affinity or synonymity with *keck*.

Keek, to peep, to pry, to look cautiously about ; possibly from the Gaelic *cidh*, pronounced *kidh* or *kee*, to see ; a *cidhis*, a mask to cover the face all but the eyes, a vizor.

> The robin came to the wren's nest
> And *keekit* in.—*Nursery Rhyme.*
> Stars dinna *keek* in,
> And see me wi' Mary.—BURNS.

When the tod [fox] is in the wood, he cares na how many folk *keek* at his tail.—ALLAN RAMSAY'S *Scots Proverbs.*

A clergyman in the West of Scotland once concluded a prayer as follows :—" O Lord ! Thou art like a mouse in a drystane dyke, aye *keekin'* out at us frae holes and crannies, but we canna see Thee."— ROGERS' *Illustrations of Scottish Life.*

Keeking-glass, a looking-glass, a mirror.

She. Kind sir, for your courtesy,
　　As ye gang by the Bass, then,
　　For the love ye bear to me,
　　Buy me a *keeking-glass*, then.

He. *Keek* into the draw-well,
　　Janet, Janet !
　　There ye'll see your bonnie sel',
　　My jo, Janet.—BURNS.

Keel or keill, a small vessel or

skiff, a lighter, and not merely the *keel* of any ship or boat as in English. It is synonymous with *coracle*, or the Gaelic *cur-ach*, and is probably derived from the Gaelic *caol*, narrow, from its length as distinguished from its breadth.

Oh, merry may the *keel* row,
　The *keel* row, the *keel* row ;
Oh, merry may the *keel* row,
　The ship that my love's in.
　　— *Northern Ballad.*

Keelivine, a crayon pencil. Ori-

gin unknown.

Kell, a woman's cap ; from the

Gaelic *ceil*, a covering.

Then up and gat her seven sisters,
　And served to her a *kell*,
And every steek that they put in
　Sewed to a silver bell.
　　—*Border Minstrelsy : The Gay
　　Goss-hawk.*

Kelpie, a water-sprite. Etymo-

logy unknown ; that suggested by Jamieson from *calf* is not probable.

What is it ails my good bay mare ?
　What is it makes her start and shiver ?
She sees a *kelpie* in the stream,
　Or fears the rushing of the river.
　　　—*Legends of the Isles.*

The *kelpie* gallop'd o'er the green,
He seemed a knight of noble mien ;
And old and young stood up to see,
And wondered who this knight could be.
　　　—*Idem.*

The side was steep, the bottom deep,
　Frae bank to bank the water pouring ;
And the bonnie lass did quake for fear,
　She heard the water-*kelpie* roaring.
　　—*Ballad of Annan Water.*

Keltie, a large glass or bumper,

to drain which was imposed as a punishment upon those who were suspected of not drinking fairly. " Cleared *keltie* aff," according to Jamieson, was a phrase that signified that the glass was quite empty. The word seems to be derived from *kelter*, to tilt up, to tip up, to turn upside down, and to have been applied to the glasses used in the hard-drinking days of our great-grandfathers, that were made without stems, and rounded at the bottom like the Dutch dolls that roll from side to side, from inability to stand upright. With a glass of this kind in his hand, the toper had to empty it before he could re-place it on the table. Jamieson was probably ignorant of this etymology, though he refers to the German *kelter*, which signi-fies a wine-press. *Keltern*, in the same language, is to tread the grapes. But these words do not apply to either the Scottish *keltie* or *kelter*.

Kemmin, a champion, a corruption of *kemp* (*q.v.*).

> He works like a *kemmin*.
> He fechts like a *kemmin*.
> —JAMIESON.

The Kymric has *ceimmyn*, a striver in games; the Flemish *kampen;* and German *kämpfen*, to fight, to struggle, to contend.

Kemp, a warrior, a hero, a champion; also to fight, to strive, to contend for the superiority or the mastery. *Kemper* is one who *kemps* or contends; used in the harvest field to signify a reaper who excels his comrades in the quantity and quality of his work. *Kempion*, or *Kemp Owain*, is the name of the champion in two old Scottish ballads who "borrows," or ransoms, a fair lady from the spells cast upon her by demoniacal agency, by which she was turned into the shape of a wild beast. *Kempion*, or *Kemp Owain*, kisses her thrice, notwithstanding her hideousness and loathsomeness, and so restores her to her original beauty. *Kempion* is printed in Scott's "Border Minstrelsy," and *Kemp Owain* in Motherwell's "Minstrelsy, Ancient and Modern."

Kennawhat, a nondescript, a "je ne sais quoi," or know-not-what.

Kenspeckle, noticeable, conspicuous, noteworthy.

Kep, to catch, to receive; from the Gaelic *ceap*, to intercept, to stop, to receive.

> Ilka blade o' grass *keps* its ain drap o' dew.
> —JAMES BALLANTINE.

> Ilk cowslip cup shall *kep* a tear.
> —BURNS.

Ker haund or **ker-handed**, left-handed, awkward; from the Gaelic, *cer*, a twist; and *cearr*, wrong, awkward. See KAUR-HANDIT, *ante*.

> It maun be his left foot foremost, unless he was *ker-haund.*—*Noctes Ambrosianæ.*

Ket, a fleece; *tawted ket*, a matted or ropy fleece. From the Gaelic *ceath*, a sheep or sheep-skin.

> She was nae get o' moorland tips,
> Wi' *tawted ket* an' hairy hips.
> —BURNS.

Kevil, a lot; to cast *kevils*, to draw lots.

> Let every man be content with his ain *kevil.*—ALLAN RAMSAY'S *Scots Proverbs.*

> And they coost *kevils* them amang
> Wha should to the greenwood gang.
> —COSPATRICK : *Border Minstrelsy.*

Kidney. "Of the same *kidney*," of a like sort. The Slang Dictionary has, "Two of a *kidney*, or two of a sort—as like as two pears, or two *kidneys* in a bunch." Sir Richard Ayscough says that Shakspeare's phrase, which he put into the mouth of Falstaff, means "a man whose *kidneys* are as fat as mine—*i.e.*, a man as fat as I am." A little knowledge of the original language of the British people would show the true root of the word to be the Gaelic *ceudna*—pronounced *keudna*, sort, or of the same sort; *ceudnachd*, identity, similarity.

> Think of that ! a man of my *kidney*, that am as subject to heat as butter.—*Merry Wives of Windsor.*

Your poets, spendthrifts, and other fools
of that *kidney.*—BURNS : *Letter to Mr.
Robert Ainslie.*

Kill-cow, an expressive colloquialism which signifies a difficulty that may be surmounted by
resolution and energy. Jamieson translates it "a matter of
consequence, a serious affair;
as in the phrase, 'Ye needna
mind; I'm sure it's nae sic great
kill-cow ; '" and adds, "in reference, most probably, to a blow
that is sufficient to knock down
or *kill a cow !*" Jamieson forgot
the reference in his own Dictionary to *cow*, in which the
word signifies a ghost, spectre,
or goblin. The phrase might
be rendered, "a ghost that
might be laid without much
difficulty."

Killicoup, a somersault, head-
over-heels.

That gang tried to keep violent lease-
hold o' your ain fields, an' your ain ha',
till ye gied them a *killicoup.*—HOGG'S
Brownie of Bodsbeck.

Kilt, a garment worn by Highlanders, descending from the
waist to the middle of the knee;
to lift the petticoats up to the
knee, or wear them no lower
than the knee; to raise the
clothes in fording a stream.
"High kilted" is a metaphor
applied to conversation or
writing that savours of immodesty. From the Gaelic *ceil*, to
cover; *ceilte*, covered.

Her tartan petticoat she'll *kilt.*
—BURNS : *Cry and Prayer.*

She's *kilted* her coats o' green satin,
She's *kilted* them up to the knee,
And she's off wi' Lord Ronald M'Donald,
His bride and his darling to be.
—*Old Song : Lizzie Lindsay.*

Kimmer, a female friend, gossip,
or companion; from the French
commère ; synonymous with the
English *gammer.*

My *kimmer* and I gaed to the fair
Wi' twal punds Scots on sarkin' to wear;
But we drank the gude braw hawkie dry,
And sarkless cam hame, my *kimmer* and I.
—CROMEK'S *Remains.*

Kink, a knot, an entanglement,
an involution; the same in
Flemish; whence *kink-host*, or
kink-cough, the hooping-cough,
or generally a violent fit of
coughing, in which the paroxysm
seems to twist knots into each
other. The word *kink* is sometimes applied to a fit of irre-
pressible laughter. *Kink-cough*
has been corrupted in English
into *king*-cough. Mr. Robert
Chambers, on a note on *kink*,
which occurs in the "Ballad of
the Laird o' Logie," explains it
as meaning to wring the fingers
till the joints crack, which he
says is a very striking though a
simple delineation of grief.

And sae she tore her yellow hair,
Kinking her fingers ane by ane,
And cursed the day that she was born.

Kinnen, rabbits; corruption of
the English *coney.*

Make *kinnen* and caper ready, then,
And venison in greit plentie,
We'll welcome here our royal King.
—*Ballad of Johnnie Armstrong.*

Kinsh. According to Jamieson, this word signifies kindred.

The man may *eithly* tine a *stot* that canna count his *kinsh.*—ALLAN RAMSAY'S *Scots Proverbs.*

"The man may easily lose a young ox that cannot count his *kinsh.*" The meaning of *kinsh* in this passage is not clear. It has been suggested that it is a misprint for either *kine* or *kindred.* Perhaps, however, the true meaning is to be sought in the Gaelic *cinneas (kinneash)*, which means growth or natural increase. This interpretation renders the proverb intelligible—a man may afford to lose one stot who cannot count the increase of his flocks and herds.

Kintra cooser, one who runs about the country; a term sometimes applied to an entire horse, which is taken from place to place for the service of mares.

If that daft buckie, Geordie Wales,
Was threshin' still at hizzie's tails,
Or if he was grown oughtlins douser,
And no a perfect *kintra cooser.*

　　—BURNS : *To one who had sent him
　　　a newspaper.*

The word *cooser* appears in Shakspeare as *cosier* or *cozier*, and has puzzled all the commentators to explain it. *Cosier's catches* were songs sung by working men over their libations in roadside ale-houses. Johnson thought that *cosier* must mean a *tailor*, from *coudre*, to sew ; and *cousue*, that which is sewed ;

while others equally erudite were of opinion that *cosiers* were *cobblers* or *tinkers.* The *cosiers* who sang *catches* might have belonged to all or any of these trades ; but the word, now obsolete in English, and almost obsolete in Scotch, is the Gaelic *cosaire*, a pedestrian, a wayfarer, a tramp. Up to the time of Dr. Johnson's visit to the Hebrides, Highland gentlemen of wealth or importance used to keep servants or gillies to run before them, who were known as *cosiers*—misprinted by Boswell as *coshirs.* Jamieson, unaware of the simple origin of the word, as applied to a horse made to perambulate the country, states that *cooser* is a stallion, and derives it from the French *coursier*, a courser. But courser itself is from the same root, from *course*, a journey. The coarse allusion of Burns to the Prince of Wales expressed a hope that he had ceased to run about the country after women.

Kipper, to split, dry, and cure fish by salting them. Kippered herrings, haddocks, and salmon are largely prepared and consumed in Scotland, and to a much smaller extent in the large cities of England. The mode of *kippering* is scarcely known to the south of the Tweed, and where known, is not so successfully practised, or with such delicate and satisfactory results, as in Scotland. The derivation of the word is uncertain.

Kirk, is the original form of the word, which has been Anglicised into *church*. It is derived from the idea of, and is identical with, circle or *kirkle*, the form in which, in the primitive ages of the world, and still later, in the Druidical era, all places of worship — whether of the supreme God or of the Sun, supposed to be His visible representative—were always constructed. The great stone circle, or *kirkle*, of Stonehenge was one of the earliest kirks, or churches, erected in these islands. The traces of many smaller stone circles are still to be found in Scotland. The word is derived feom the Gaelic *coir*, a circle ; whence also *court*, and the French *cour*.

Kirnie, a forward boy who gives himself prematurely and offensively the airs and habits of a man. Shakspeare speaks of "kerns and gallowglasses," *kern* being a contraction of the Gaelicc *eathairneach* [*kearneach*], an armed peasant serving in the army, also a boor or sturdy fellow. Jamieson derives *kirnie* from the Kymric *coryn* or *cor*, a dwarf or pigmy ; but as the Lowland Scottish people were more conversant with their neighbours of the Highlands than with the distant Welsh, it is probable that the Gaelic and not the Kymric derivation of the word is the correct one.

Kist, a chest, a trunk, a box ; from the French *caisse*.

Steek the awmrie, shut the *kist*,
Or else some gear will soon be mist.
—Sir Walter Scott : *Donald Caird*.

A man who had had four wives, and who meditated a fifth time entering the marriage state, was conversing with a friend on the subject, who was rather disposed to barter upon his past matrimonial experience, as having made a good deal of money by his wives. " Na ! na ! " said he, " they came to me wi' auld *kists*, an' I sent them hame (to the grave) wi' new anes."—Dean Ramsay.

Kith, known to or acquainted with ; from *kythe*, to show, and the old English *couth*, to know or see ; a word that survives in *concouth*, with a somewhat different meaning, as strange, odd, or unfamiliar. *Kith* is generally in modern English used in combination with *kin*, as *kith* and *kin*, whence the word is erroneously supposed to mean relationship in blood and ancestry, and to be synonymous with *kin* and *kinship*.

Whether thousands of our own *kith* shall be sacrificed to an obsolete shibboleth and the bloodthirsty operations of an artificial competition.—*Letter on Large Weights*, *by* Arnold White—*Times, November* 30, 1887.

Kittle, difficult, ticklish, dangerous. From the Dutch and Flemish *kittelen*, to tickle.

It's *kittle* shooting at corbies and clergy.
It's *kittle* for the cheeks when the hurl-barrow gangs o'er the brig o' the nose.
Cats and maidens are *kittle* ware.
It's *kittle* to waken sleeping dogs.
—Allan Ramsay's *Scots Proverbs*.

As for your priesthood I shall say but little,
Corbies and clergy are a shot right *kittle*.
—Burns : *The Brigs of Ayr*.

Kivan, kivin. These words signify a covey, a bevy, a troop, a company, a flock, a crowd, or an assemblage. They are evidently from the Gaelic *coimh* (*coiv*), equivalent to the prefix *co* or *con*, and *feadhain* (*d* silent), a troop or band of people, or of living animals of any description.

Klem or **clem.** In Lancashire and other parts of England, *clem* signifies to become stupefied or worn out with hunger, to starve. In Scotland, *klem* sometimes means perverse, obstinate, insensible to reason and to argument; and, according to Jamieson, "means low, paltry, untrustworthy, unprincipled; and, as used by the boys of the High School of Edinburgh, curious, singular, odd, queer." He derives it from the Icelandic *kleima*, macula, a blot or stain—*i.e.*, having a character that lies under a stain. But the Icelandic does not convey either the Scottish or the English meaning of the word, which is in reality the Flemish *kleum*, lethargic, stupefied either from cold, hunger, or by defect of original vitality and force of mind or body. The Flemish *verkleumte* is translated in the French dictionaries as *engourdi*, benumbed, stupefied, stiffened. By a metaphorical extension of meaning, all these physical senses of the word apply to mental conditions, and thus account for all the varieties of the Scottish meaning.

The English *clem* may be possibly traced to the German *klemmen*, to pinch, to squeeze; from *klemme*, a narrow place, a strait, a difficulty, whence *clemmed*, pinched with hunger.

Knack, to taunt, to make a sharp answer; the same apparently as the English "nag," as applied to the *nagging* of a disagreeable woman. *Knacky*, or *knacksy*, quick at repartee.

Knappin-hammer. A hammer with a long handle used for breaking stones on the road, or in houses of detention for vagrants or criminals. From the English *knap* or *nap*, a smart blow on the head, as in the colloquial threat to an unruly boy, "you'll *nap* it."

> What's a' your jargon o' the schools—
> Your Latin names for books or stools;
> If honest Nature made you fools,
> What sairs your grammars?
> Ye'd better ta'en up spades or shools
> Or *knappin hammers*.
>   —BURNS : *Epistle to Lapraik.*

Kneef, active, alert; "ower *kneef*" or over active suggests, according to Jamieson, the charge of illicit intercourse. The derivation is probably from the Gaelic *gniomh* (gniof), a doer, to do, or a *deed.* The word is sometimes pronounced *griomh*, whence *grieve*, a factor, bailiff, or agent.

> Jenny sat jouking like a mouse,
> But Jock was *kneef* as ony cock,
> Says he to her, Haud up your brows,
> And fa' to your meet.
>   —*The Wooing o' Jenny and Jock.*

Knowe, a hillock, a knoll.

Ca' the yowes [ewes] to the *knowes*.
—ALLAN RAMSAY.

Upon a *knowe* they sat them down,
And there began a long digression,
About the lords of the creation.
—BURNS : *The Twa Dogs.*

Knowe-head, the hill top.

Yon sunny *knowe-head* clad wi' bonnie
wild flowers.—JAMES BALLANTINE.

Knurl, a dwarf ; *knurlin*, a dwarf-
ling, or very little dwarf.

The miller was ´strappin', the miller was
ruddy—
A heart like a lord, and a hue like a lady,
The laird was a widdiefu' fleerit *knurl*—
She's left the good fellow, and taken the
churl.—BURNS : *Meg o' the Mill.*

Wee Pope, the *knurlin*, rives Horatian
fame.—BURNS : *On Pastoral Poetry.*

These words are apparently
derived from the English *gnarl*,
twisted, knotted, as in the
phrase, " the *gnarled* oak," and
the Teutonic *knorren*, a knot,
a wart, a protuberance. They
were probably first applied in
derision to hunch-backed people,
not so much for their littleness
as for their deformity. Burns,
when speaking of Pope as a
knurlin, seems to have had in
memory the ill-natured comparison of that poet to a note
of interrogation, because " he
was a *little crooked thing* that
asked questions."

Through an English misconception of the meaning of " *a
knurl* " (pronounced exactly like
" *an earl* "), arose the vulgar slang
of the London streets used to
insult a hunchback.

" My Lord " is a nickname given with
mock humility to a hunchback.—HOT-
TEN'S *Slang Dictionary.*

Koff or **coff**, to buy ; from the
Teutonic *kaufen*, Flemish *koopen*,
to buy ; whence by corruption
horse-kooper, a dealer in horses.

Kindness comes wi' will ; it canna be
kofft.—ALLAN RAMSAY'S *Scots Proverbs.*

Kute, coot, or **queete**, the ankle.
Cutes or *kutes*, according to
Wright and Halliwell, is a
Northern word for the feet.
" To let one cool his *cutes* at the
door (or in the lobby)," is a
proverbial expression for letting
a man wait unduly long in ex-
pectation of an interview. *Cootie*
or *kutie* is a fowl whose legs are
feathered. *Cootikins*, spatter-
dashes or gaiters that go over
the shoe and cover the ankle.

Your stockings shall be
Narrow, narrow at the *kutes*,
And braid, braid at the braune
[the brawn or calf].
—CHAMBERS' *Scottish Ballads.*

The firsten step that she steppit in [the
water],
She steppit to the *kute.*
. . . . . .
The neisten step that she wade in,
She waded to the knee ;
Said she, " I wad wade further in,
Gin my true love I could see."
—*Willie and May Margaret.*

It is difficult to trace the
origin of this peculiarly Scottish
word. The French call the
ankle the " *cheville* du pied."
Bescherelle defines *cheville* as
" part of the two bones of the
leg which rise in a *boss* or *hump*
on each side of the foot." The

Germans call the ankle the "knuckle of the foot." Jamieson derives *cute* from the Teutonic *kyte*, "*sura;*" but the Latin *sura* means the calf of the leg and not the ankle; and *kyte* is not to be found in any German or Teutonic dictionary. *Kyte*, in the Scottish vernacular, has nothing to do with *kute*, and signifies a part of the body far removed from the ankle, viz., the belly. Possibly the Swedish *kut*, a round boss or rising, as suggested in the extract from Bescherelle, may be the root of *cute*. The Gaelic affords no assistance to the discovery of the etymology. The word does not appear in the glossaries to Ramsay or Burns.

Kyle, a narrow strait of water between islands, or between an island and the mainland, as the *Kyles* of Bute, and *Kyle* Akin, between Skye and the continent of Scotland. The word is derived from the Gaelic *caol*, a narrow passage, a strait, whence *Calais*, the French town on the *straits* of Dover.

Kyte, the belly. *Kytie*, corpulent, big-bellied. The Gaelic *cuid*, victuals, food, has been suggested as the origin of the word, on the principle that to "have

a long *purse*," signifies to have money, or much money, so that to have a *kyte* is to have food to put into it. But this etymology is not satisfactory, nor is that given by Jamieson from the Icelandic.

Then horn for horn, they stretch and strive—
Deil tak' the hindmost—on they drive,
Till a' their well-filled *kytes* belyve
    Are stretched like drums.
      —BURNS : *To a Haggis.*

But while the wifie flate and gloom'd,
The tither cake wi' butter thoomb'd,
    She forced us still to eat,
Till our wee *kites* were straughtit fou,
When wi' our hearties at our mou',
    We felt maist like to greet.
  —JAMES BALLANTINE : *The Pentland Hills.*

Kythe, to show or appear; and *kythesome*, of pleasant and prepossessing appearance. Jamieson has the phrase "*blythsome* and *kythsome*," used in Perthshire, and signifying, as he thinks, "happy in consequence of having abundance of property in *cows.*" If he had remembered his own correct definition of *kythe*, "show, to be manifest," he would not in this instance have connected it with cows or *kye*, but would have translated the phrase, "blythe and pleasant of appearance."

Kythe is your ain colours, that folk may ken ye.—ALLAN RAMSAY.

L

Laigh, low, or low-down, short.

The higher the hill, the *laigher* the grass.
—ALLAN RAMSAY'S *Scots Proverbs.*

> Dance aye *laigh* and late at e'en,
> —BURNS : *My Jo, Janet.*

Laired, overthrown, cast to the ground. From the Gaelic *lar*, the ground ; the English *lair*, as applied to the retreat of a wild animal ; or possibly from *lure*, to entice or inveigle.

> Laired by *spunkies* i' the mire.
> —GEORGE BEATTIE : *John o' Arnha'.*

Lammas, the first day of August ; supposed to be derived from the Anglo-Saxon *hlaf*, a loaf, but more probably from *lamb*, the Lamb of God. All the ancient festivals appropriated to particular days had an ecclesiastical origin—such as Mary-mass (now called Lady Day), from the Virgin Mary ; Michaelmas, Hallowmas, Candlemas, Christmas, &c.

Landart, rural, in the country ; from landward.

> There was a jolly beggar,
>   And a begging he was boun',
> And he took up his quarters
>   Into a *landart* town.
> —Song : *We'll Gang nae mair a Roving.*

> Then come away, and dinna stay,
>   What gars ye look sae *landart ?*
> I'd have ye run, and not delay,
>   To join my father's standard.
>   —COCKBURN : CHAMBERS'S *Scottish Songs.*

Landlash, a great fall of rain, accompanied by a high wind. Jamieson is of opinion that this word is suggested by the idea that such a storm *lashes* the land. It is more probably from the Gaelic *lan*, full ; and *laiste*, fury ; whence *lanlaiste* (pronounced *lanlashte*, and abbreviated into *lanlash*), the storm in full fury. A *lash* of water signifies a great, heavy, or furious fall of rain.

Landlord and **landlady**. These words, commonly pronounced *lanlord* and *lanlady*, do not solely imply the proprietorship of land, as their constant application to the owners of public-houses, and to house-owners generally, as well as to women who merely let lodgings, are sufficient to show. The Scottish *laird*, without the prefix *land*, conveys the idea of proprietorship. *Landlord* and *landlady*, in one of the senses in which the words are continually used, both in English and Scottish parlance, are traceable not to *land* in the Teutonic sense of the word, but to *lan*, the Gaelic for full, or an enclosure, and all that it contains or is full of. Thus the keeper of a public, or the owner of a private house, is lord or master of the *lan* or enclosure which he occupies or possesses.

H

Land-louper, a vagabond, a wanderer from place to place without settled habitation; sometimes called a *forloupin* or *forlopin*, as in Allan Ramsay's " Evergreen."

Lane, alone, lone, or lonely; this word, which in the English lone or lonely is an adjective, is a noun in the Scottish *lane*. " I was all alone," or " we were all alone," are in Scottish, " I was a' my lane," and " we were a' our lane." " I canna lie my lane," is, " I cannot sleep alone."

> I waited lang beside the wood,
> Sae wae and weary *a' my lane*,
> Och hey ! Johnnie lad,
> Ye're no so kind's ye should hae been.
> —TANNAHILL.

> " But oh, my master dear," he cried,
> " In a green wood, ye're gude *your lane*."
> —*Ballad of Gil Morrice.*

> I wander my *lane* like a night-troubled ghaist.—BURNS.

Lanrien (sometimes written **landrien**). Jamieson defines this word as meaning " in a straight course ; a direct, as opposed to a circuitous course," and quotes a phrase used in Selkirkshire— " He cam rinnin' *landrien*," or straight forward. It seems to be a corruption of the Gaelic *lan*, full, complete ; and *rian*, order, method, arrangement, regularity.

Laroch or **lerroch**, the site of a building which has been demolished, but of which there are remains to prove what it once was. From the Gaelic *lar*, the ground or earth ; and *larach*, the ground on which an edifice once stood.

Lave, the residue, the remainder, that which is left, or, as the Americans say in commercial fashion, the " balance."

> We'll get a blessing wi' the *lave*,
> And never miss't.
> —BURNS : *To a Mouse.*

> First when Maggie was my care,
> Whistle o'er the *lave* o't.—BURNS.

Laverock, the lark. This word, so pleasant to the Scottish ear, and so entirely obsolete in English speech and literature, was used by Gower and Chaucer:—

> She made many a wondrous soun',
> Sometimes like unto the cock,
> Sometimes like the *laverock*.
> —GOWER : *Quoted in* HALLIWELL'S
> *Archaic Dictionary.*

> Why should I sit and sigh,
> When the wild woods bloom sae briery,
> The *laverocks* sing, the flowerets spring,
> And a' but me are cheery.
> —BUCHAN'S *Songs of the North of Scotland.*

> Thou *laverock* that springs frae the dews o' the lawn.—BURNS.

Lark and the Teutonic *lerche* are doubtless abbreviations of the primitive word *laverock*, but whence *laverock ?* Possibly from the ancient Gaelic *labhra (lavra)*, and *labhraich*, eloquent, loud— two epithets that are highly appropriate to the skylark.

Law. This word is often used in Scotland to signify a hill or rock, especially to one standing alone, as Berwick *Law*, so familiar by sight to the Mid-Lothian people. It is derived from the Gaelic *leach*, a stone; and *leachach*, the bare summit of a hill. It sometimes signifies the stony or shingly ground by the side of a river, as in the Broomie-*law* in Glasgow. Possibly in this case also the word is of the same derivation as *leach*, and means not only a high stone, but a flat stone, a flag stone, whence *leachaig*, to pave or lay with flat stones.

Lawin. This eminently Scottish word is from the Gaelic *lachan*, the expense of an entertainment; the price of the drink consumed at a tavern; *lachag*, a very small reckoning. "Ye're *lawin-free*," i.e., you are not to pay your share of the bill. The root of the word seems to be *lagh*, law, order, method—the law of the tavern, that the guests should pay before they go. It was formerly written *lauch*.

> Aye as the gudewife brought in,
>   Ane scorit upon the *wauch* [wall],
> Ane bade pay, anither said " Nay,
> Bide while we reckon our *lauch.*"
>   —*Peblis to the Play.*

> Then, gudewife, count the *lawin*,
>   The *lawin!* the *lawin!*
> Then, gudewife, count the *lawin*,
>   And bring a cogie mair.
>   —BURNS : *Old Chorus.*

Lawin, the *reckoning* at an inn. Isn't reckoning a Scotticism? I doubt very much if you would be understood if you asked an English landlord for the reckoning, meaning an account of what you have had at his inn. I don't think reckoning is specially associated with an inn bill in

this country. In Scotland reckoning has almost entirely superseded the word *lawin*. In Sweden the regular word for a hotel bill is the "reckoning."—R. DRENNAN.

Leal, loyal, true, true-hearted. "The land o' the *leal*," i.e., Heaven.

A *leal* heart never lied.—*Scots Proverbs.*

> I'm wearin' awa', Jean,
>   Like snaw when it's thaw, Jean,
> I'm wearin' awa'
>   To the Land o' the *Leal.*
>   —LADY NAIRNE.

> Robin of Rothesay, bend thy bow,
> Thy arrows shoot so *leal.*
>   —*Hardyknute.*

Lear or **leer**, learning; from the German *lehren*.

> When Sandie, Jock, and Jeanitie,
>   Are up and gotten *lear*,
> They'll help to gar the boatie row
>   An' lighten a' our care.
>   —*The Boatie Rows.*

Lea-rig, a ridge in a corn or other field, left fallow between two ridges that are bearing grain.

> Will ye gang o'er the *lea-rig*,
>   My ain kind dearie O.
>   —FERGUSSON.

> Corn *rigs* and barley *rigs*,
>   And corn *rigs* are bonnie ;
> I'll ne'er forget that happy night,
>   Among the *rigs* wi' Annie.—BURNS.

Leed, a song or incantation, from the German *lied*, a lay or song.

> Thrice backward round about she tottered,
>   While to hersel the *leed* she muttered.
>   —GEORGE BEATTIE : *John o' Arnha'.*

Lee-lang, as long as it is light, as in the phrase "the *lee-lang* day," which has hitherto been supposed to mean the "life-long day." It is more probably from the Gaelic *li*, a colour, and especially a bright colour, the colour of daylight, and from the allied word *liath (lia)*, pale grey, as distinguished from dark or black.

> The thresher's weary flingin' tree
> The *lee-lang* day had tired me.
> BURNS : *The Vision.*

Leeshin, lazily, in a dilatory manner. From the Gaelic *leise*, lazy.

> And cam' *leeshin* up behind her.
> —GEORGE BEATTIE : *John o' Arnha'.*

Leesome, agreeable, pleasant, like the light. (*See* LEE-LANG.)

> Oh, gear will buy me rigs o' land,
> And gear will buy me sheep and kye ;
> But the tender heart o' *leesome* luve
> The gowd and siller canna buy.
> —BURNS : *The Countrie Lassie.*

> Fair and *leesome* blew the wind,
> Ships did sail and boats did row.
> —BUCHAN'S *Ancient Ballads.*

A fairy ballad in Buchan's collection is entitled "*Leesome Brand.*" Jamieson derives *lee-some* from the German *liebe*, love; perhaps, however, the root of the word is the Gaelic *leus*, light; *li*, colour; and *leusach*, bright, shining.

Leeze or **leeze me on** (a reflective verb), to be satisfied with, to be pleased or delighted with. A Gaelic periphrase for "I love." The Highlanders do not say "I love you," but "love is on me for you." Hence the

Scottish phrase—"*loes* (or *lees*) me" or "love is on me."

> *Leeze me on* my spinning-wheel.—BURNS.

> *Leeze me on* thee, John Barleycorn,
> Thou king o' grain.
> —BURNS : *Scotch Drink.*

> *Leeze me on* drink, it gies us mair,
> Than school or college.
> —BURNS : *The Holy Fair.*

Leglin or **leglan**, a milking-pail.

> At buchts, in the mornin', nae blithe lads
>   are scornin',
> The lasses are lanely, and dowie and
>   wae,
> Nae daffin', nae gabbin', but sighin' and
>   sabbin',—
> Ilk ane lifts her *leglin* and hies her
>   away.
> —ELLIOT : *The Flowers of the Forest.*

> Donald Caird can lilt and sing,
> Blithely dance the Highland fling,
> Hoop a *leglan*, clout a pan,
> Or crack a pow wi' ony man.
> —SIR WALTER SCOTT : *Donald Caird.*

Jamieson traces *leglin* to the Teutonic *leghel*. This word, however, has no place in German, Dutch, or Flemish dictionaries. The Gaelic has *leig*, to milk a cow, which, with *lion*, a receptacle (also a net), or *lion*, to fill, becomes *leglin* in Lowland Scotch.

Leister, a three-pronged instrument, or trident, for killing fish in the water ; commonly applied to illegal salmon fishing in the rivers of Scotland.

> I there wi' something did forgather
> That pat me in an eerie swither,
> An awfu' scythe out owre ae shouther
>   Clear dangling hang,
> A three-taed *leister* on the ither
>   Lay large and lang.
> —BURNS : *Death and Dr. Hornbook.*

Donald Caird can wire a maukin (a hare),
Leisters kipper, makes a shift
To shoot a moor-fowl i' the lift.
Water-bailiffs, rangers, keepers,
He can wake when they're sleepers;
Not for bountitt or reward,
Dare they mell wi' Donald Caird.
　　　　　　—Sir Walter Scott.

Jamieson traces the word to the Swedish *liustra*, to strike fish with a trident. But the derivation may be doubted. "To *leister*," says the Gaelic Etymology of the Languages of Western Europe, "is a mode of taking salmon at night, by attracting them towards the surface by torches held near the water, and then driving a spear, trident, or large fork into them. The word is derived from the light that is employed to lure the fish, rather than from the spear that impales them, and is traceable to the Gaelic *leasdair*, a light, or a lustre." It seems probable that the word is of home origin, rather than of Swedish. Halliwell and Wright claim it as a common word in the North of England. Burns evidently uses it in the sense of a trident, without any reference to the illegal practice of fishing.

Lemanry; from *leman*, a concubine; a poetical word for harlotry.

Oh, wed and marry, the knight did say,
　For your credit and fame,
Lay not your love on *lemanry*,
　Nor bring a good woman to shame.
　　—Buchan's *Ancient Ballads: Hynd Horn.*

Let on, to let appear; *loot*, appeared; *lutten*, the past-participle of *let*.

"Weel, Margaret," said a minister to an auld wife, who expressed her dissatisfaction with him for leaving the parish, "ye ken I'm the Lord's servant. If He have work for me in Stirling, ye'll admit that it's my duty to perform it." "Hech!" replied Margaret, "I've heard that Stirling has a great muckle stipend, and I'm thinking if the Lord had gi'en ye a ca' to Auchtertool [a very poor parish], ye wad ne'er hae *lutten on* that ye heard Him."—Rogers: *Anecdotes of Scottish Wit and Humour.*

Leure, a ray of light, a gleam; from the French *lueur*, a shining light; and the anterior Gaelic root *lur*, brightness, splendour, treasure. The Gipsy slang has *lowre*, money; and *gammy* [or crooked] *lowre*, bad money. The ideas of brightness and beauty go together in most languages. *Lurach*, in Gaelic, is a term of endearment for a beautiful—that is, a bright—young woman.

Levin, the lightning. This word, that has long been obsolete in English literature, is not yet obsolete in the Scottish vernacular. It was employed with fine effect, centuries ago, by Dunbar, the Scottish, and by Chaucer, the English poet. Attempts have recently been made to revive it, by Sir Walter Scott and others, not altogether ineffectually. Chaucer makes splendid use of it when he denounces one who habitually speaks ill of women:

With wild thunder-bolt and fiery *levin*
May his welked [wicked] neck be broke.
　　　　　—*Wife of Bath's Prologue.*

　To him as to the burning *levin*,
　Short, resistless course was given.
　　　　　　　—Scott : *Marmion.*

The clouds grew dark and the wind grew
　loud,
　And the *levin* filled her e'e,
And waesome wailed the snow-white sprites
　Upon the gurly sea.
　　　　　—Laidlaw : *The Demon Lover.*

　The etymology is obscure,
There is no trace of it in the
Teutonic or Latin sources of
the language. Spencer, in the
" Faerie Queene," has—

His burning *levin*-brand in hand he took.

　The etymology is probably to
be found in the Gaelic *liath*
(pronounced *lia, lee-a*) meaning
white or grey, and sometimes
vivid white, which may perhaps
account for the first syllable.
Buin, to shoot, to dart ; *buinne*,
or *bhuinne* (*vuin*), signifies a
rapid motion, which may account for the second—a derivation which is not insisted upon,
but which may lead philologists
to inquire further.

Lewder, lewdering, to flounder
　through bog and mire, to plod
　wearily and *heavily* on.

　　　Thus *lewdering* on
Through scrubs and crags wi' mony a
　heavy groan.
　　　　　　　—Ross's *Helenore.*

　Jamieson derives the word
from the Teutonic *leuteren,
morari,* a word which is not to
be found in the Teutonic Dic-

tionaries. It is probable that
the root is the Gaelic *laidir,*
strong, heavy. The English
slang, " To give one a good
leathering," is to give him a
strong or heavy beating.

Lib, to castrate, geld, *Libbet,* an
　animal on which that operation
　has been performed ; a eunuch.
　This word still remains current
　in the Northern Counties. In
　Flemish *lubbing* signifies cas-
　tration ; and *lubber,* he who
　performs the operation. Burns
　speaks contemptuously of Italian
　singers as *libbet :*—

How cut-throat Prussian blades were
　hinging,
How *libbet* Italy was singing.

Lichtly or **lightly**, to treat with
　neglect or scorn, or speak lightly
　of anybody.

I leaned my back unto an aik,
　And thought it was a trusty tree,
But first it bowed, and syne it brak,
　Sae my true love did *lichtly* me.
—*Ballad of the Marchioness of Douglas.*

Oh is my helmet a widow's cuid [cap],
　Or my lance a wand of the willow tree,
Or my arm a lady's lily hand
　That an English Lord should *lichtly* me.
　　　　　　　—*Kinmont Willie.*

Aye vow and protest that ye care na for me,
And whiles ye may *lichtly* my beauty a
　wee ;
But court na anither tho' daffin' ye be,
For fear that she wyle your fancy frae me.
　　　—Burns : *Whistle and I'll come to
　　　　　　　you, my Lad.*

Liddisdale drow, Liddisdale dew ;
　the fine rain that is said not
　to wet a Scotsman, but that
　drenches an Englishman to the
　skin. Jamieson defines *drow* to

mean a cold mist heavy with rain, also a squall or severe gust; and derives the word from the Gaelic *drog*, the motion of the sea, which, however, is not to be found in Gaelic dictionaries. *Drow* is from the Gaelic *druchd*, with the elision of the guttural, signifying *dew*, hence the Liddisdale joke.

Lift, the sky; from the Teutonic *luft*.

> When lightnings fire the stormy *lift*.
> —BURNS: *Epistle to Robert Graham.*

> Is yon the moon, I ken her horn,
>   She's glintin' i' the *lift* sae heigh,
> She smiles sae sweet to wile us hame,
>   But by my troth she'll bide a wee.
> —BURNS.

Lil for lal, an ancient Scottish synonym for the English *tit for tat*, that appears in Wynton, who wrote in the sixteenth century. It is supposed by Jamieson to be from the Anglo-Saxon " *lael with laele,*" or *stripe for stripe*, though it may be of Gaelic origin; from *li*, light or colour; and *là*, day, and *lathail* (*la-ail*) daily; or *li-la*, for day, or one light for another.

Lilt, to sing cheerfully, or in a lively manner. Also, according to Jamieson, a large pull in drinking frequently repeated.

> Nae mair *liltin'* at the ewe-milkin',
> The flowers of the forest are a' wede awa'.
> —*Lament for the Battle of Flodden.*

> Mak' haste an' turn King David owre,
> An' *lilt* wi' holy clangour.
> —BURNS: *The Ordination.*

The origin of this word seems to be the Gaelic *luailte*, speed, haste, rapid motion, and *luailtich*, to accelerate, to move merrily and rapidly forward. This derivation would explain the most common acceptation of the word, as applied to singing, as well as the secondary meaning attributed to it by Jamieson.

Limmer, a depreciatory epithet for a woman; from the Gaelic *leum*, to leap—one who leaps over the bounds of propriety or moderation, or breaks through the bounds of the seventh commandment.

Linder, a short linen jacket or vest worn next to the skin by both sexes, though Jamieson says only by old women and children.

> He'll sell his jerkin for a groat,
>   His *linder* for another o't,
> And ere he want to pay his shot
>   His *sark* will pay the t'other o't.
> —ALEXANDER ROSS: *The Bridal o't.*

Link, to trip, to leap, to skip, to jump; **linkin'**, tripping; from the Gaelic *leum*, to leap, *leumnach*, skipping, jumping, whence *leumanach*, a frog, a creature that jumps. The glossaries to Burns render this word by " trip." Jamieson says it means to walk smartly, or to do anything with cleverness and expedition.

> And coost her duddies to the wark,
> And *linkit* at it in her sark.
> —BURNS: *Tam O'Shanter.*

And now, auld Cloots, I ken ye're thinkin'
A certain Bardie's rantin', drinkin',
Some luckless hour will send him *linkin'*
　　To your black pit,
But faith! he'll turn a corner jinkin'
　　[dodging],
And cheat you yet.
　　—Burns: *Address to the Deil.*

Lin or **lins**. This termination to many Scottish words supplies a shade of meaning not to be expressed in English but by a periphrasis, as *westlins,* inclining towards the west. *Aiblins*— perhaps, for able-lins—inclining towards being able, or about to become possible (see Aiblins, *ante*). *Backlins*, inclining towards a retrograde movement.

The *westlin* winds blaw loud and shrill.
　　—Burns: *My Nannie, O.*

Now frae the east neuk o' Fife the dawn
Speel'd *westlins* up the lift.
　　—Allan Ramsay: *Christ's Kirk on
　　the Green.*

And if awakened fierce*lins,* aff night flee.
　　—Ross's *Helenore.*

This termination properly is *lings,* and is a very common termination in several Teutonic dialects, such as the Dutch, and still more, the German, though not common in English. See Grimm's Grammar. —Lord Neaves.

Lins corresponds nearly to the English affix *ly,* though not exactly. In Pitscottie's account of the apparition that appeared to James IV. in St. Catherine's Aisle of the Church at Linlithgow, the word *Grofflins* occurs. This has been interpreted to mean gruffly. "He leaned down *grofflins* on the desk before him (the king) and said," &c. *Grufe* or *groff* is a common Scotch word, meaning the belly, or rather the *front* of the body, as distinguished from the back; and Pitscottie's expression means nothing more than that the apparition leaned the fore part of his body, say his breast, upon the back of the desk at which the king was kneeling.—R. Drennan.

Linn, a waterfall; **Cora Linn,** the falls of the Clyde; properly, the pool at the bottom of a cataract, worn deep by the falling water; from the Gaelic *linne,* a pool.

Grat his e'en baith bleer't and blin',
Spak o' lowpin' o'er a *linn.*
　　—Burns: *Duncan Gray.*

Ye burnies, wimplin' down your glens,
Or foaming strang frae *linn* to *linn.*
　　—Burns: *Elegy on Captain Matthew
　　Henderson.*

Whiles owre a *linn* the burnie plays.
　　—Burns: *Hallowe'en.*

Lintie, a linnet.

Nae *linties* lilt on hedge or bush,
　　Poor things, they suffer sairly.
Up in the mornin's no for me,
　　Up in the mornin' early;
When a' the hills are covered wi' snaw,
　　I'm sure it's winter fairly.
　　—*Old Song, modernised by* John
　　Hamilton.

Dr. Norman Macleod mentioned a conversation he had with a Scottish emigrant in Canada, who in general terms spoke favourably of his position in his adopted country. "But oh! sir," he said, "there are no *linties* in the woods, and no braes like Yarrow." The word *lintie* conveys to my mind more of tenderness and endearment towards the little bird than linnet.— Dean Ramsay.

Lippen, to incline towards, to be favourable to any one, to rely upon, to trust. Apparently from the Flemish *liefde,* and the German *lieben,* love.

Lippen to me, but look to yoursell.
　　—Allan Ramsay's *Scots Proverbs.*

An ancient lady, when told by the minister that he had a call from his Lord and Master to go to another parish, replied, "Deed, sir, the Lord might ha' ca'd and ca'd to you lang eneuch, and ye'd ne'er hae *lippened* till Him if the steepen [stipend] had na been better."—DEAN RAMSAY.

Lippin' fu', full up to the lip or brim of a glass or goblet, brimful; *owre-lippin'*, full to overflow.

> A' the laughin' valleys round
> Are nursed and fed by me,
> And I'm aye *lippin' fu'*.
> —JAMES BALLANTINE : *Song of the Four Elements—the Water.*

See ye, wha hae aught in your bicker to spare,
And gie your poor neighbours your *owre-lippin'* share.
> —JAMES BALLANTINE : *Winter Promptings.*

Lire, sometimes written *lyre*, the complexion. Jamieson defines *lire* as " the part of the skin which is colourless," and " as the flesh or muscles as distinguished from the bones "—" the lean part of butchers' meat." He derives the word from the Anglo-Saxon *lire*, the fleshy part of the body. The word is traceable to the Gaelic *liath* (pronounced *lia*), pale grey, and *liathaich* (*lia-aich*), to become grey.

> As ony rose her *rude* was red,
> Her *lyre* was like the lilies.
> —*Christ's Kirk on the Green.*

Lirk, a crease, a plait, a fold, a hollow in a hill; from the Gaelic *laraich* (see *lar, ante*, p. 114).

> The hills were high on ilka side,
> An' the bricht i' the *lirk*.
> —*Border Minstrelsy—The Broom o' the Cowdenknowes.*

Lith, a joint, a hinge; and metaphorically, the point of an argument on which the whole question turns. To *lith*, to separate the joints; from the Gaelic *luth*, a joint; *luthach*, well-jointed, or having large joints.

> " Fye, thief, for shame ! " cries little Sym,
> " Wilt thou not fecht wi' me ;
> Thou art mair large of *lith* and limb
> Nor I am "——
> —ALLAN RAMSAY'S *Evergreen : Questioning and Debate betwixt Adamson and Sym.*

> And to the road again wi' a' her pith,
> And souple was she ilka limb and *lith*.
> —ROSS's *Helenore.*

Dr. Johnson and Lord Auchinleck were quarrelling over the character of the great Protector, and the sturdy old English Tory pressed the no less sturdy old Scottish Whig to say what good Cromwell had ever done to his country. His lordship replied, " He gart kings ken that they had a *lith* in their necks."—BOSWELL.

> Ye'll tak a *lith* o' my little fingerbane.
> —BUCHAN'S *Ancient Ballads—The Bonnie Bows o' London.*

Littit, coloured; from the Gaelic *liath*, grey.

> Weel dyed and *littit* through and through.
> —GEORGE BEATTIE : *John o' Arnha'.*

Loaning, a meadow, a pasture; a green lane.

> I've heard them lilting at the ewe-milking—
> Lasses a' lilting before dawn of day ;
> But now they are moaning in ilka green *loaning*,
> The flowers o' the forest are a' wede away.
> —*The Flowers o' the Forest.*

> Joy gaed down the *loaning* wi' her,
> Joy gaed down the *loaning* wi' her,
> She wadna hae me—but has ta'en another—
> And a' men's joy but mine ga'ed wi her !
> —CHAMBERS's *Scottish Songs.*

Loe-some, or **love-some**, pleasant and amiable, is sometimes wrongly written *leesome*, as in Burns's song of "The Countrie Lassie":—

> The tender heart o' *leesome* luve
> Gowd and siller canna buy.

Loof, the palm of the hand; from the Gaelic *lamh* (*lav*), the hand.

> Gie's yer *loof*, I'll ne'er beguile you.
> —*Scots Proverbs.*

> Wi' arm reposed on her chair back,
> He sweetly does compose him,
> Which by degrees slips round her neck,
> An's *loof* upon her bosom,
>   Unkenned that day.
> —BURNS: *The Holy Fair.*

Lofa is used by Ulphilas for the open hand; *slaps lofa*, a slap of the hand. The Gaelic *lam*, when the *m* gets aspirate, becomes *lamh — lav* or *laf.*—LORD NEAVES.

Losh, a ludicrous objurgation that does duty as a paltry oath; generally supposed to be a corruption of "Lord!"

> *Losh* me! hae mercy wi' your natch,
> Your bodkin's bauld.
> —BURNS: *Epistle to a Tailor.*

Losh me! that's beautiful.—*Noctes Ambrosianæ.*

The English corruptions of "Lord!" becomes O Lor'! Lawks! and O La'! The name of the Supreme Being, in like manner, is vulgarised into *Gosh*, as "By *Gosh!*" "*Gosh* guide us!" is a common expression in Scotland, with the object apparently of avoiding the breach of the Third Commandment in the letter, though not in the spirit.

Loup, to leap; to "*loup* the dyke," a proverbial expression, to leap over the dyke (of restraint), applied to unchaste unmarried women; *land-louper*, a vagrant.

> Spak o' *loupin*' o'er a linn.
> —BURNS: *Duncan Gray.*

> He's *loupen* on the bonnie black,
> He steer'd him wi' the spur right sairly;
> But ere he won to Gatehope slack
> I think the steed was wae and weary.
> —*Minstrelsy of the Scottish Border—
>   Annan Water.*

> I bade him *loup*, I bade him come,
> I bade him *loup* to me,
> An' I'd catch him in my armis twa.
> —*The Fire o' Frendraught.*

Loup-hunting. "The odd phrase, 'Hae ye been a *loup-hunting?*' is a query," says Jamieson, "addressed to one who has been very early abroad, and is an *evident* allusion to the hunting of the wolf (the French *loup* in former days)." The allusion is not so evident as Jamieson imagined. A wolf was not called *loup* either in the Highlands or in the Lowlands. In the Highlands the animal was either called *faol*, or (*madadh alluidh*), a wild dog; and in the Lowlands by its English, Flemish, and German name, "wolf." It is far more likely that "loup" in the phrase is derived from the Gaelic *lobhar*, the Irish Gaelic *lubhar*, a day's work; a hunt more imperative than that after an animal which has not been known in Scotland since 1680, when the last of the race, according to tradition, was killed by Sir Ewen Cameron of Lochiel. Another tradition, recorded in the third volume of Chambers's "Annals of Scotland," fixes in 1743 the date of the last wolf slain, and records the name of the slayer as Macqueen, a noted deer-stalker in the forest of Moray. *Lub* is an obsolete Gaelic word for a youth of either sex. It is therefore possible that *loup-hunting* may have had a still more familiar meaning.

Lout or **loute**, to jump, or leap.

> He has *louted* him o'er the dizzy crag
> And gien the monster kisses ane.
> —*Border Minstrelsy.*

Low, to stand still, to stop, to rest; *lowden*, to calm; applied to the cessation of a stormy wind; also, to silence, or cause to be silent.

Lowan drouth, burning thirst.

> With the cauld stream she quench'd her *lowan drouth.*—Ross's *Helenore.*

Lowe, a flame; *lowin'*, burning, to burn, to blaze. *Lò* is the ancient Gaelic word for day, or daylight; superseded partially by the modern *là*, or *làtha*, with the same meaning. The syllable *lò* appears in the compound word *lo-inn*, joy, gladness, beauty— derived from the idea of light— that which shines, as in the Teutonic *schön* or *schoen*, the old English *sheen*, beautiful.

> A vast unbottomed boundless pit,
> Filled fou o' *lowin'* brunstane.
> —Burns: *The Holy Fair.*

The sacred *lowe* o' weel-placed love
Luxuriantly indulge it.
> —Burns: *Epistle to a Young Friend.*

The bonnie, bonnie bairn sits poking in the ase,
Glowerin' in the fire wi' his wee round face,
Laughin' at the fuffin' *lowe*—what sees he there?
Ha! the young dreamer's biggin' castles in the air.
> —James Ballantine.

Lown, quiet, calm, sheltered from the wind. The *lown* o' the dyke, the sheltered side of the wall.

> "Unbuckle your belt, Sir Roland," she said,
> "And sit you safely down."
> "Oh, your bower is very dark, fair maid,
> An' the nicht is wondrous *lown*."
> —*Ballad of Sir Roland.*

Lown is used in relation to concealment, as when any ill report is to be hushed up. "Keep it *lown*," *i.e.*, say nothing about it.
—Jamieson.

> Blaw the wind ne'er sae fast,
> It will *lown* at the last.
> —Allan Ramsay's *Scots Proverbs.*

Come wi' the young bloom o' morn on thy brow,
Come wi' the *lown* star o' love in thine e'e.
> —James Ballantine: *Wifie, Come Hame.*

Lounder, to strike heavily right and left.

> I brak a branch off an ash, and ran in among them *lounderin'* awa' right and left.
> —*Noctes Ambrosianæ.*

Luckie, a term of familiarity applied to elderly women in the lower and middle ranks of society:—

> Oh, haud your tongue, now, *Luckie* Laing,
> Oh, haud your tongue and jaumer;

I held the gate till you I met,
Syne I began to wander.
—BURNS : *The Lass of Ecclefechan.*

Hear me, ye hills, and every glen,
And echo shrill, that a' may ken
The waefu' thud
O' reckless death wha came unseen
To *Luckie* Wood.
—BURNS.

Mrs. Helen Carnegie of Montrose died in 1818, at the advanced age of ninety-one. She was a Jacobite, and very aristocratic, but on social terms with many of the burghers of the city. She preserved a very nice distinction in her mode of addressing people according to their rank and station. She was fond of a game of quadrille (whist), and sent out her servant every morning to invite the ladies required to make up the game. " Nelly, ye'll gang to Lady Carnegie's, and mak' my compliments, and *ask the honour* of her ladyship's company, and that of the Miss Carnegies, to tea this evening. If they canna come, ye'll gang to the Miss Mudies, and ask the *pleasure* of their company. If they canna come, ye maun gang to Miss Hunter, and ask the *favour* of her company. If she canna come, ye maun gang to *Luckie* Spark, and *bid her come!*"—DEAN RAMSAY'S *Reminiscences.*

It is probable that this word, as a term of respect as well as of familiarity, to a middle-aged or elderly matron, is a corruption of the Gaelic *laoch*, brave. The French say, " une *brave* femme," meaning a good woman ; and the Lowland Scotch use the adjective *honest* in the same sense, as in the anecdote recorded in Dean Ramsay's " Reminiscences " of Lord Hermand, who, about to pass sentence on a woman, began remonstratively, " *Honest woman*, what garred ye steal your neighbour's tub ? "

Lug, the ear, a handle ; also to pull, to drag or haul. *Luggie*, a small wooden dish with handles. *Luggie*, the horned owl, so called from the length of its ears.

His hair, his size, his mouth, his *lugs*,
Showed he was nane o' Scotland's dogs.
—BURNS : *The Twa Dogs.*

Up they got and shook their *lugs*,
Rejoiced they were na men but dogs.
—*Idem.*

How would his Highland *lug* been nobler fired,
—His matchless hand with finer touch inspired.
—BURNS: *The Brigs of Ayr.*

Lug, to pull by the ear, or otherwise to haul a load, is still current in English ; but *lug*, the ear, is obsolete, except in the Northern Counties, though common in English literature in the Elizabethan era. Two derivations have been suggested for the word in its two divergences. The Gaelic *lag*, genitive *luig*, signifies a cavity, whence it is supposed that *lug* signifies the cavity of the ear. Coles, however, renders *lug* by the Latin, " auris lobus, auricula infinia," not the interior cavity, but the exterior substance of the ear. The derivation of *lug*, to pull, to drag a load, seems to be from another source altogether ; from the Gaelic *luchd*—the English for a load, a burden, or a ship's cargo, and for *lugger,* a kind of barge used for the transference of the cargo from the hold of a larger vessel. In this case the meaning is transferred from the load itself to the action of moving it.

Lum, the chimney, the vent by which the smoke escapes from the fireplace. The word is used in the north of England as well as in Scotland. The etymology is uncertain. The Kymric has *llumon,* a beacon, a chimney; the Irish Gaelic has *luaimh,* swift; and the Scottish Gaelic *luath* (*lua*), swift; and *ceum,* aspirated into *cheum* or *heum,* a way, a passage, whence *lua-heum,* the swift passage by which the smoke is carried off.

The most probable derivation is from the Gaelic *laom,* a blaze; whence, by extension of meaning, the place of the blaze or fire.

Lume, a tool, a spinning-machine, a loom.

Lunch, a piece, a slice, whence the modern English *lunch,* a slight meal in the middle of the day.

Cheese and bread frae women's laps
Was dealt about in *lunches*
    And dawds that day.
        —BURNS: *The Holy Fair.*

Lunt, the smoke of tobacco, to emit smoke; from the Flemish *lont,* a lighted wick.

The *luntin'* pipe.
    —BURNS: *The Twa Dogs.*

Lurder, an awkward, lazy, or worthless person; from the French *lourd,* heavy; *lourdaud,* a heavy and stupid man.

Let alane maks many a *lurder* (neglect makes many a one worthless).—DEAN RAMSAY.

Lyart, grey; from the Gaelic *liath* (*lia*), which has the same meaning.

His *lyart* haffets [locks of thin grey hair].
    —BURNS: *Cotter's Saturday Night.*

Twa had manteels o' doleful black,
But ane in *lyart* hung.
    —BURNS: *The Holy Fair.*

Lyke-wake, the ceremonial of the watching over a dead body. *Lyke* is from the German *leiche,* the Dutch and Flemish *lijk,* a corpse.

She has cut off her yellow locks
    A little aboon her e'e,
And she's awa' to Willie's *lyke,*
    As fast as gang could she.
        —BUCHAN'S *Ballads: Willie's Lyke-Wake.*

M

Machless, lazy, sluggish, indolent. Jamieson derives this word from the Teutonic *macht,* power, strength, might; whence *macht-los,* without might or strength; but the Scottish word is without the *t,* which somewhat detracts from the probability of the etymology. The Gaelic has *macleisg,* a lazy, indolent person, literally a "son of laziness," which is a nearer approach to *machless* than *machtlos*. *Machle* is defined by Jamieson as signifying to busy one's self about nothing, which would seem to be an abbreviation of *macleisg*. He says that *machless* is generally used in an unfavourable sense, as in the phrase, "get up, ye *machless* brute." This supports the Gaelic etymology.

Mad as a hatter. This is English as well as Scottish slang, to signify that a person is more or less deranged in his intellect. Why a hatter should be madder than a shoemaker, a tailor, or any other handicraftsman, has never been explained. The phrase most probably arises from a corruption and misconception of the Gaelic word *atadh*, a swelling, *aitearachd*, swelling, blustering, foaming like a cataract in motion, or the assembling of a noisy crowd. Jamieson, unaware of the Gaelic origin, defined the Scottish *hatter* as a numerous and irregular assemblage of any kind, a *hatter* of stanes, or a confused heap of stones; and *hattering*, as collecting in crowds. So that *mad as a hatter* merely signifies mad as a cataract or a crowd. In the old Langue Romane—the precursor of modern French—*hativeau* meant *un fou, un étourdi*, a madman.

Maggie-rab or **Maggie-rob**, an ancient popular term for a violent, quarrelsome, and disagreeable woman.

He's a very guid man, but I trow he's gotten a *Maggie-rob* o' a wife.—JAMIESON.

This strange phrase, though now so apparently inexplicable, must originally have had a meaning, or it would never have acquired the currency of a proverb. If the word *Maggie* for Margaret be accepted as the generic name for a woman, like Jill in the nursery rhyme of "Jack and Jill went up the hill;" or like Jenny in the old song of "Jock and Jenny;" and *Rob* or *Rab* be held to signify a man, the phrase may mean a virago, a woman with the behaviour and masculine manners of the other sex.

The *rab* or *rob* in the phrase is susceptible of another interpretation. The Gaelic *rab*, or *rabach*, means quarrelsome, litigious, violent, exasperating—while in the same language *rob* means dirty and slovenly. Either of these epithets would very aptly describe the kind of woman referred to in the extract from Jamieson.

But these are suggestions only for students of language, and are not offered as true derivations for the guidance of the unlearned. *Rabagas* was the name recently given by a popular French playwright to a very quarrelsome and litigious character.

Maigs or **mags**, a ludicrous term for the hands, from the Gaelic *mag* or *mog*, a paw.

Haud aff yer *maigs*, man!—JAMIESON.

Mailin', a farm-yard and farm-buildings ; a farm for which rent is paid—from *mail*, a tax. Gaelic *mal*, tax, tribute.

> A weel-stockit *mailin'*, himself o't the laird,
> And marriage off-hand, were his proffers.
> —BURNS : *Last May a Braw Wooer.*

> Quoth she, my grandsire left me gowd,
> A *mailin'* plenished fairly.
> —BURNS : *The Soldier's Return.*

Mairly, rather more.

> Argyle has raised a hundred men,
> A hundred men and *mairly*,
> And he's awa by the back o' Dunkeld,
> To plunder the house o' Airly.

> The lady look't o'er her window sae hie,
> She lookit lang and sairly,
> Till she espied the great Argyle
> Cam' to plunder the house o' Airly.
> —*The House of Airly.*

Maks na, or **it maks na**, it does not signify, it does not matter.

> Away his wretched spirit flew,
> It *maks na* where.
> —ALLAN RAMSAY : *The Last Speech of a Wretched Miser.*

> Tho' daft or wise, I'll ne'er demand,
> Or black or fair, it *maks na* whether.
> —ALLAN RAMSAY : *Gie me a Lass wi' a Lump o' Land.*

Malison, a curse. The twin word, *benison*, a blessing, has been admitted into English dictionaries, but *malison* is still excluded ; although it was a correct and recognised English word in the time of Langland, the author of Piers Ploughman, and Chaucer.

> Thus they serve Sathanas,
> Marchands of *malisons*.
> —LANGLAND : *Piers Ploughman.*

> And all-Hallowes, have ye, Sir Chanone,
> Said this priest, and I her *malison*.
> —CHAUCER : *The Chanones Yemanne's Tale.*

> I've won my mother's *malison*,
> Coming this night to thee.
> —*Border Minstrelsy.*

> That is a cuckold's *malison*,
> John Anderson, my joe.
> —*John Anderson*, old version.

Mansweir, to commit perjury. This word is almost peculiar to Scotland, though Halliwell has *mansworn*, perjured, long obsolete, but once used in England. The first syllable can have no relation to *man*, homo. The Flemish *meineed*, and the German *meineid*, signify perjury, and one who perjures himself is a *meineidiger*. The Scottish word seems to be derived from the Gaelic *mionn*, an oath, and *suarach*, worthless, valueless, mean, of no account—whence *mionn suarach*, corrupted into *man sweir*, signifying a valueless or false oath. Jamieson thinks it comes from the Anglo-Saxon *man*, perverse, mischievous, and *swerian*, to swear ; a derivation which, as regards the syllable *man*, he would have scarcely hazarded if he had been aware of the Gaelic *mionn*, or of the German *meineid*.

Mare's Nest. This originally Scottish phrase is no longer peculiar to Scotland, but has become part of the copious vocabulary of English slang. Hotten's Slang Dictionary defines it to mean " a supposed discovery of marvels, which turn out to be no marvels at all." The compiler accounts for the expression by an anec-dote of "three cockneys, who, out ruralising, determined to find out something about *nests*. Ultimately, when they came upon a dung-heap, they judged by the signs that it must be a *mare's nest*, especially as they could see the mare close by." This ridiculous story has hitherto passed muster. The words are a corruption of the Gaelic *mear-achd*, an error, and *nathaist* (*th* silent), a fool, whence a fool's error, *i.e.*, mare's nest. Some Gaelic scholars are of opinion that the word is compounded of *mearachd*, an error, and *sna-saichte*, or *snasta*, reduced into order or system, *i.e.*, systematic error.

Mark and burn. To say of a thing that it is lost, *mark and burn* signifies that it is totally lost, beyond trace and recogni-tion ; not that it is marked or burned in the sense of the English words, but in the sense of the Gaelic *marc*, a horse— from whence *march*, a boundary traced by the perambulations at stated periods of men on horseback—and *burn*, a stream of running water, the natural, and often the common boundary, between contiguous estates and territories. *March balk* signifies the narrow ridge which some-times serves as the boundary between lands of different pro-

prietors. *Marche dyke*, a wall separating one farm or estate from another.

When one loses anything and finds it not again, he is said never to see *mark nor burn* of it.—JAMIESON.

Marmor, an ancient title of nobility equivalent to an earl ; from the Gaelic *maor*, an officer, chieftain, and *mor*, great.

Lords of the Isles, and Thanes, and Jarls,
    Barons and *Marmors* grim,
With helm on head and glaive in hand,
    In rusty armour dim,
Responsive to some powerful call,
    Gathered obedient one and all.
                —Legends of the Isles.

Marrow, one of a pair, a mate, a companion, an equal, a sweet-heart — from the Gaelic *mar*, like, similar. This word is beautifully applied to a lover or wedded partner, as one whose mind is the exact counterpart of that of the object of his affection. It appears in early English literature, but now sur-vives only in the poetry and daily speech of the Scottish and northern English people.

One glove or shoe is *marrow* to an-other.—*Lansdowne MS., quoted in* HAL-LIWELL'S *Archaic Dictionary.*

And when we came to Clovenford,
    Then said my winsome *marrow*,
Whate'er betide, we'll turn aside,
    And see the braes o' Yarrow.
—WORDSWORTH : *Yarrow Unvisited.*

Thou took our sister to be thy wife,
    But ne'er thought her thy *marrow*.
        —The Dowie Dens o' Yarrow.

Mons Meg and her *marrow* three vol-leys let flee,
For love of the bonnets of bonnie Dundee.—SIR WALTER SCOTT.

Meddle with your *marrow* (*i.e.*, with your equal).—*Scottish Proverb.*

Your e'en are no *marrows* (*i.e.*, you squint).—ALLAN RAMSAY.

Marschal, a steward, an upper servant ; from the Gaelic *maor*, an officer, a superintendent, and *sgalag*, a farm-servant, a serf, a hired labourer.

Mart or **mairt**, cow-beef salted for winter provision. So called, says Jamieson, "from *Martin-mas*, the term at which beeves are usually killed for winter store." Perhaps the future editors of Jamieson will take note that *mart* in Gaelic signifies a cow ; *mart bainne*, a milch cow ; and *mart fheoil*, beef ; and that consequently the word has no relation to the Martinmas festival. In a note to "Noctes Ambrosianæ," Professor Ferrier says *mart* is an ox killed at Martinmas. *Mart* originally signified a market, where kine and horned cattle were sold, as distinguished from *market*, a horse fair ; from *mare*, a horse.

Mashlum, mixed corn, or rye and oats with the bran.

Twa *mashlum* bannocks (cakes).
—BURNS : *Cry and Prayer.*

Mask, to infuse ; usually employed in connection with the tea-table. To *mask* the tea is, in Scottish phrase, to make the tea, by pouring the boiling water upon it. The word is from the Gaelic *masg*, to mix, to infuse. Jamie-son erroneously derives it from the Swedish *mask*, a mash.

Maughts, power.

They had nae *maughts* for sic a toilsome task,
The barefaced robbers had put off the mask—
Among the herds that played a *maughty* part.
—Ross's *Helenore.*

She starts to foot, but has nae *maughts* to stand.—*Idem.*

The word is from the Teutonic *macht*, power, might, ability. The root seems to be the Gaelic *maith*, powerful, able, strong, and *maithich* or *maithaich*, to make strong.

Maukin, a hare ; from the Gaelic *maigheach*, and *maoidheach*, with the same meaning.

God help the day when royal heads
Are hunted like a *maukin*.
—BURNS : *Our Thistles flourished Fresh and Fair.*

Mauks, maggots.

I saw the cook carefully wi' the knife scrapin' out the *mauks*.—*Noctes Ambrosianæ.*

Maun, must. This Scottish verb, like its English synonym, has no inflections, no past or future tense, and no infinitive. The peculiarity of the Scottish word is that it sometimes signifies *may*, and sometimes *must*, as in the line of D'Urfey's clumsy imitation of a Scottish song, "Within a Mile of Edinburgh Town"—

I canna, *maunna*, winna buckle to (I cannot, *may* not [or *must* not], will not, be married).

I

Perhaps the use of *may* as *must*, and *vice versa*, was introduced into the Lowland Scotch by the Gaelic-speaking Highlanders. *Feud* in Gaelic signifies *may* or *can*, and *fheudar domh*, "obligation or necessity is to me, or upon me," *i.e.*, I must.

Mavis, the singing thrush. This word, once common in English poetry, is now seldom employed. Spenser, in the following passage from his "Epithalamium," seems to have considered the *mavis* and the thrush to be different birds :—

> The thrush replies ; the *mavis* descant plays.

In Scottish poetry the word is of constant occurrence.

> In vain to me in glen or shaw
> The *mavis* and the lintwhite sing.
> —BURNS.

> Oh, tell sweet Willie to come doun,
> And hear the *mavis* singing ;
> And see the birds on ilka bush,
> And green leaves round them hinging.
> —BUCHAN'S *Ancient Ballads.*

An eccentric divine discoursing on a class of persons who were obnoxious to him, concluded with this singular peroration, "Ma freens, it is as impossible for a *moderate* to enter into the kingdom of heaven as for a soo (sow) to sit on the tap o' a thistle, and sing like a *mavis*."— ROGERS'S *Illustrations of Scottish Life.*

Mawmet, an idol. This word is usually derived from Mahomet,

but as Mahomet was not an idol, but asserted himself to be the prophet of the true God, it is possible that the philologists of an earlier day accepted the plausible etymology, without caring to inquire further. It is, nevertheless, worthy of consideration whether the word does not come from the Gaelic *maoim*, horror, terror, fright ; and *maoimeadh*, a state of terror or awe, such as devotees feel before an idol.

Mawsie, a large, dirty, slovenly, unshapely woman ; a corruption and abbreviation of the Gaelic *maosganach*, a lump, a lumpish person.

May, a lass, a maid, a young girl.

> There was a May an' a weel-farèd May
> Lived high up in yon glen.
> —*Border Minstrelsy : Katharine Ganfarie.*

Meggy Monyfeet, the popular name for the centipede.

Mell, to be intimate with, to mingle or associate ; from the French *meler*, to mix. *Mell* also signifies a company, and *melling* an intermeddling.

Mellder, the quantity of grain sent at one time to the miller to be ground.

> Ae market-day thou wast na sober ;
> That ilka *mellder*, wi' the miller,
> Thou sat as lang as thou hadst siller ;
> That every naig was ca'd a shoe on
> The smith and thee gat roarin' fou' on.
> —BURNS : *Tam o'Shanter.*

Melvie, to soil with meal, as the miller's clothes and hair are soiled from the flying dust of the mill. Erroneously explained in the glossaries to Burns as "to soil with *mud.*" It is probably a corruption of *mealy.*

> *Mealie* was his sark,
> *Mealie* was his siller,
> *Mealie* was the kiss
> That I gat frae the miller.
> —*Old Song.*

> To *melvie* his braw claithing.
> —BURNS: *The Holy Fair.*

Mense, mind, good manners, dignity, decorum; *menseful*, dignified; *mensefully*, in a proper and respectable manner. From the Latin *mens*, whence mental.

> Auld Vandal, ye but show your little *mense*,
> Just much about it wi' your scanty sense.
> —BURNS: *The Brigs of Ayr.*

> I wat she was a sheep of sense,
> And could behave herself wi' *mense*;
> I'll say't, she never brak a fence
> Thro' thievish greed.
> Our Bardie lanely keeps the spence
> Since Mailie's dead.
> —BURNS: *Poor Mailie's Elegy.*

To *mense* a board, is to do the honours of the table.

> She has a' the *mense* o' the family.—
> JAMIESON.

Mensk, manly dignity; *menskful*, manly, becoming, dignified; *menskly*, worthily. Jamieson traces the word to the Icelandic *menska*, humanitas.

Merg or **mergh**, marrow pith; from the Flemish.

> There was *merg* in his fingers and fire in his eye.—*Jock o' Arnha'.*

> And the *mergh* o' his shin-bane,
> Has run down on his spur leather whang.
> —*Border Minstrelsy: Fray of Suport.*

Merle, the blackbird. The Scottish, which is also the French, name for this delightful songster is far more poetical and distinctive than the prosaic "blackbird" of modern English—a name which might with as much propriety be applied to the rook, the crow, the raven, and the jackdaw. The *merle* is as much noted for his clear, beautiful notes, as for the tribute he levies upon the fruits of the summer and autumn—a tribute which he well deserves to obtain, and amply pays for by his music. The name of *merle*, in Gaelic *meirle*, signifies theft; and *meirleach*, a thief. In the same language *meirneil*, the English *merlin*, signifies a hawk or other predatory bird. As regards the *merle*, it must be confessed that he is, in the matter of currants and strawberries, deserving of his name. The depredations of the *merle* have created several proverbial phrases in the French language, such as—*C'est un fin merle*, applied to a clever and unscrupulous man; *un beau merle*, a specious false pretender. The French call the hen-blackbird a *merlette*. The word *merle* was good English in the days of Chaucer, and considerably later.

> Where the sweet *merle* and warbling mavis be.—DRAYTON.

Merry Scotland. The epithet "merry" was applied to England as well as to Scotland, and was a common mode of address to a company or multitude of soldiers, hunters, or boon companions.

Old King Cole was a *merry* old soul,
  And a *merry* old soul was he,
And he called for his pipe, and he called
  for his bowl,
And he called for his fiddlers three.
.   .   .   .
Of all the girls in *merry Scotland,*
  There's none to compare to Marjorie.
          —Old King Cole.

Few words have puzzled philologists more completely than *mirth* and *merry.* Johnson suggested no etymology; Skinner derived *merry* from the German *mehren*, to magnify; and Junius from the Greek μυριζην, to anoint, because the Greeks anointed themselves with oil when they made *merry* in their public games! The word has no root in any of the Teutonic languages, German, Dutch, Flemish, Danish, or Swedish; and cannot be traced to either French, Latin, Italian, or Spanish. The Gaelic yields *mir*, sport; *mireach*, festive, sportive; *mear*, cheerful, joyous. It thus appears on the evidence of etymology that the pleasant epithet for these islands was given by the Celtic inhabitants, and not by the Saxon and other Teutonic invaders, though it was afterwards adopted by them.

Messan, or **messin**, a cur, a lap-dog, a pet dog.

But tho' he was o' high degree,
The fient o' pride, nae pride had he,
But wad hae spent an hour caressin'
E'en wi' a tinker gipsy's *messan.*
      —BURNS: *The Twa Dogs.*

The glossaries to Burns, judging from the context, and the gipsy, imagine *messin* to mean a mongrel, a dog of mixed breeds. Jamieson says it is a small dog, a country cur, so called from *Messina*, in Sicily, whence this species was brought; or from the French *maison*, a house, because such dogs were kept in the house! The word, however, is the Gaelic *measan*, a pet dog, a lap-dog; from *meas*, fancy, kindness, regard.

We hounds slew the hare, quoth the
  blind *messan.*
    —ALLAN RAMSAY'S *Scots Proverbs.*

Mess John, the old epithet in Scottish ballad poetry for a priest, derived from the celebration of the mass, so that *Mess John* signified in irreverent phrase, John, who celebrated the mass. The English has the kindred phrase, *Jack Priest.*

The auld folk soon gied their consent,
  Syne for *Mess John* they quickly sent,
Wha ty'd them to their heart's content,
  And now she's Lady Gowrie.
       —The Lass o' Gowrie.

Midden or **midden hole**, the dung-hill or dungpit, a receptacle for the refuse, filth, and manure of a farm, situated in the centre of the farmyard, an arrangement not yet wholly superseded:—

Ye glowered at the moon, and fell in the
  midden.
    —ALLAN RAMSAY's *Scots Proverbs.*

The tither's something dour o' treadin',
But better stuff ne'er claw'd a *midden.*
    —BURNS : *Elegy on the Year* 1788.

The word is still used in the Northern counties of England, and was derived by Ray from *mud.* The true derivation is from the Gaelic *meadhon,* the centre, the middle, or midst.

Therein lay three and thirty sows,
  Trundlin' in a *midden*
    Of draff.
      —*Peblis to the Play.*

Mim, meek, modest, prudish, prim, reticent, affected and shy of speech; applied only to young women, or contemptuously to effeminate young men. This word is usually derived from the English *mum,* which means silent or speechless. The Scottish *mim* means mealy mouthed, only speaking when spoken to, over-discreet in conversation, assertion, or reply :—

See ! up he's got the Word o' God,
And meek and *mim* he's view'd it.
    —BURNS : *The Holy Fair.*

Maidens should be *mim* till they're
married.—ALLAN RAMSAY.

Some *mim*-mou'd pouther'd priestie,
Fu' lifted up wi' Hebrew lore,
And hands upon his breastie.
    —BURNS : *To Willie Chalmers.*

Mim, as distinguished from *mum,* is an evident rendering of the Gaelic *min,* soft, delicate, smooth, mild, meek; *min bheŭl-ach* is from *min* and *beul,* a mouth, the same as the Scottish

mim-mouthed, used by Burns ; *min-bhriathar,* a soft word or expression, from *min* and *bria-thar,* a word. *Mim* is provincial and colloquial in England.

First go the ladies, *mim, mim, mim,*
Next come the gentlemen, prim, prim,
  prim ;
  Then comes the country clown,
    Gallop a-trot, trot, trot.
      —*Nursery Rhymes of England.*

Minikin, very small, applied in derision to a little affected person of either sex ; derived possibly from the Gaelic *min,* small; or from the Flemish *mannikin,* a little man.

Minnie, a term of endearment for a mother.

My daddie looks glum, and my *minnie*
  looks sour,
They flyte me wi' Jamie because he is
  poor.—*Logie o' Buchan.*

From the Flemish *min,* love, and the Gaelic *min,* sweet, soft, pleasant, kind, musical ; also little, used as a term of endearment.

Mint, to attempt, to try, to essay, to aim at. The resemblance in the idea of the Scottish *mint,* to attest, to try, to essay, and the *Mint,* where the precious metals are essayed, or tried as to their purity before they are coined into money, is curious, especially when it is remembered that the Mint was formerly and is still sometimes called the Assay Office. The English word *Mint,* for the Assay Office, is usually traced to the German *münze*, the Dutch *munte*, the Latin *moneta*, money. The etymology of the Scottish *mint*, to essay, or try, is unknown; though it is possibly to be found in the Allemanische or German patois *meinta*, to intend, to mean to do a thing.

Mintin's nae makin'.—ALLAN RAMSAY'S *Scots Proverbs.*

A man may *mint* and no' hit the mark. —ALLAN RAMSAY.

Mird, to ogle, to leer, to make amorous signs and advances to a woman.

Donald was smerkit wi' *mirds* and mockery.—JAMES HOGG: *Donald Mac-Gillvray.*

Mird wi' your makes (equals).—JAMIE-SON.

Mirk, dark. Of uncertain etymology, but probably derivable from the Gaelic *murcach*, sad, sorrowful, gloomy.

A man's mind is a *mirk* mirror.—ALLAN RAMSAY'S *Scots Proverbs.*

Oh *mirk ! mirk !* is the midnight hour,
And loud the tempest's roar.
　　　　　—BURNS : *Lord Gregory.*

'Twixt the gloaming and the *mirk*,
When the kye come hame.
　　　　　—JAMES HOGG.

Mirklins, the gloaming, inclining to be mirk or dark.

Mischant, a worthless person; from the French *mechant*, wicked.

Mischanter, a euphonistic name for the devil, synonymous with the English " old mischief,"

sometimes applied to the same personage. It is probable that *mischanter*, as applied to the devil, means the *mischief-maker*, or doer of mischief or wickedness.

Mishanter, misfortune, which is not of the same etymology as *mischanter*, is probably a corrupt abbreviation of misadventure.

Gin Rab Roy hae heard o' this lady's *mishanter*, he wadna be lang o' clearin' the house—Lord Lovat an' a', and letting her gang hame.—MACLEAY'S *Memoirs of the Clan MacGregor.*

Misleard, unmannerly, rude, mischievous, ill-conditioned.

Lord Lovat's sae *misleard* a chap that gin he ken't we were kind to her, he wad mak' whangs o' our hides to mend his Highland brogues wi'.—MACLEAY'S *Memoirs of the Clan MacGregor.*

Missie, a fondling term for a very young girl. The English word *miss*, of which, at first sight, *missie* would seem to be an affectionate diminutive, is of very uncertain derivation. It is commonly supposed to be the first syllable of *mistress*, the French *maitresse* (the feminine of *maitre*). *Miss* and *Missie* are peculiar to Scotch and English, and are unknown in any of the Teutonic and Romance languages. The Teutonic languages use the word *jungfrau*, and *fraülein ;* the French use *demoiselle*, or *mademoiselle ;* the Italians *signorina ;* and the Spanish *senorita.* Perhaps the graceful *miss* and *missie* in Scotch and English are from the Gaelic *maise*, beauty, grace, comeliness, or *maiseach*, pretty, beautiful, elegant. These are more appropriate as the designation of a young unmarried lady than *mistress* would be, implying, as that word does, a sense of command and mastery.

Mister, want, need, great poverty; *misterful*, necessitous.

> Unken'd and *misterful* in the deserts of Libye.
> —GAWIN DOUGLAS : *Translation of the Æneid.*

Misterfu' folk should nae be mensfu'.
(Needy people should not be too particular).—ALLAN RAMSAY's *Scots Proverbs.*

The original phrase of *misterfu'* beggars, or needy beggars, was afterwards corrupted into *masterful* beggars, *i.e.*, arrogant or sturdy beggars, as they are called in an edict of James VI., "the whole class of *maisterfull* and ydill beggaris, sornaris (sorners), fulis (fools), and bardis (wandering minstrels or balladsingers)." It is difficult to account for *mister* and *misterful*, unless they be derived from the Scottish Gaelic *misde*, the Irish Gaelic *miste*, the comparative of *olc*, bad or evil. *Mistear* and *mistire* signify a sly, cunning, and mean person, as well as a needy beggar. The corruption to *masterful* in the sense of arrogant is easily accounted for.

Mool, to have carnal intercourse; sometimes corrupted into *mow* or *mowe*.

> An' there'll be Alaster Sibbie
> That in wi' black Bessie did *mool*,
> Wi' snivellin' Lillie an' Tibbie
> The lass that sits aft on the stool.
>   (the cutty stool, q. v.)
> —*The Blythesome Bridal.*

Jamieson's Dictionary contains neither *mool* nor *mowe*, in the sense in which they are used in the too libidinous vernacular; but has *mool*, to crumble, and *mowe* or *mow*, dust or mould.

Moolins, refuse, grains of corn, husks, or chaff; sometimes crumbs of bread; from the Gaelic *muillean*, a husk or particle of chaff or grain; the waste of the meal at the miller's.

> The pawky wee sparrow will peck aff your floor,
> The bauld little Robin hops in at your door;
> But the heaven-soaring lark 'mang the cauld drift will dee,
> Afore he'll come cowerin' your *moolins* to pree.
>   —JAMES BALLANTINE : *Winter Promptings.*

Mools, from mould—earth, the grave.

> And Jeanie died. She had not lain i' the *mools*
> Three days ere Donald laid aside his tools,
> And closed his forge, and took his passage home.
>
> .   .   .   .   .   .
>
> But long ere forty days had run their round,
> Donald was back upon Canadian ground—
> Donald the tender heart, the rough, the brave,
> With earth and gowans for his true love's grave.—*All the Year Round.*

Moop and mell, to feed together; *mell*, to associate with; from the French *meler*, to mingle. Halliwell's Archaic Dictionary contains *mouch* — said to be a Lincolnshire word, signifying to eat greedily.

The auld West Bow sae steep and crookit,
Where bawbee pies wee callants *moopit.*
    —JAMES BALLANTINE.

But aye keep mind to *moop and mell*
Wi' sheep o' credit like thysel.
    —BURNS : *Poor Mailie.*

Guid ale hauds me bare and busy,
Gars me *moop* wi' the servant hizzie ;
Stand i' the stool when I hae done ;
Guid ale keeps my heart abune.
    —BURNS : *Good Ale Comes.*

Moop does not mean to keep company with (mell does, meddle with, have to do with), *moop* really means to eat, or rather to nibble, and, if I mistake not, is an old English word,—the present form of the word is *mump.*—R. DRENNAN.

Morn. The Scotch make a distinction between *the morn,* which means to-morrow, and *morn* (without the article), which means morning—thus, " the morn's morn " is to-morrow morning.

Mother-naked, stark-naked, utterly naked ; as naked as the new-born babe at the moment of birth. This word, though a compound of two English ones, has never been admitted into modern English dictionaries, and does not even appear in Nares, Halliwell, or Wright. If it were ever English, there remain no traces of it either in literature or in the common speech of the people. It is still current in the Scottish vernacular, and in poetical composition.

They'll shape me in your arms, Janet,
  A dove, but and a swan,
At last they'll shape me in your arms
  A *mother-naked* man.
Cast your green mantle over me,
  I'll be myself again.
    —*Ballad of the Young Tamlane.*

Readers of the " Arabian Nights' Entertainments " will remember the counterpart of the story of Young Tamlane, in that marvellous compilation of Eastern romance.

Mouter, fee paid to the miller for grinding corn ; old English, *multure ;* French, *moudre,* to grind.

It's good to be merry and wise,
Said the miller when he *moutered* twice.
    —ALLAN RAMSAY'S *Scots Proverbs.*

The quaker's wife sat down to bake
  Wi' a' her bairns about her,
Ilk ane gat a quarter cake
  And the miller gat his *mouter.*
    —CHAMBERS'S *Old Song.*

Mowes, jesting, mockery, grimaces ; to make *mowes,* to make faces.

Affront your friend in *mowes* and tine him in earnest.
    —ALLAN RAMSAY'S *Scots Proverbs.*

It has been supposed that *mowes,* which in this sense is only used in the plural, is derived from *mou',* a Scottish abbreviation of mouth. It would seem so at first blush ; but as the French have " faire la *moue,*" " grimace faite par mecontentement, en allongeant les levres," and as *moue* in that language does *not* signify a mouth, it is probable that the source of *mowes* is to be sought in the French and not in the Teutonic. Possibly both the Scottish *mowe* and the French *moue* have a common origin in the Celtic and Gaelic *muig*, a discontented look, an ill-natured frown. In English slang, *mug* signifies the face; and "ugly *mug*" is a common expression for an ugly face.

Muckle, mickle, meikle, great, large, big; *muckle-mou'd*, big-mouthed, wide-mouthed, clamorous, vociferous; *Muckle-mou'd Meg*, a name given to a cannon of large calibre. This word is akin to the English *much*, the Spanish *mucho*, the Greek *mega* and *megala*, and the Latin *magnus*—all implying the sense of greatness. The Gaelic has *meud*, [in which the final *d* is often pronounced *ch*], bulk, great size; and *meudaich*, to magnify.

Every little helps to mak a *muckle*.
—*Scots Proverb.*

Far hae I travelled,
And *muckle* hae I seen,
But buttons upon blankets
Saw I never nane.
—*Our Gudeman cam' Hame at E'en.*

Mull, a snuff or tobacco-box, as used in the Highlands. The Lowland Scotch sometimes call a snuff-box "a sneeshin *mill*," mill being a corruption of mull; from the Gaelic *mala*, a bag, the French *malle*, a trunk or box.

The luntin' pipe and *sneeshin mill*
Are handed round wi' right guidwill.
—BURNS: *The Twa Dogs.*

Jamieson says, with a non-comprehension of the origin of the word *mill* and its connection with *mull*, that the snuff-box was formerly used in the country as a *mill* for grinding the dried tobacco leaves! If so, the box must have contained some machinery for the purpose. But neither Jamieson, nor anybody else, ever saw a contrivance of that kind in a snuff-box.

Murgullie, to spoil, to mangle, to lacerate, to deform. Sometimes written *margulye*.

He wadna *murgullie* the howlet on the moudiewort either.—MACLEAY'S *Memoirs of the Clan MacGregor.*

Muslin-kail, an epithet applied by Burns to a purely vegetable soup, without animal ingredients of any kind, and compounded of barley, greens, onions, &c.

I'll sit down o'er my scanty meal,
Be 't water-brose or *muslin-kail*,
Wi' cheerfu' face,
As lang's the Muses dinna fail
To say the grace.
—*Epistle to James Smith.*

It has been supposed that the word *muslin* was applied to it on account of its thinness. The French call it *soupe maigre;* but as muslin was only introduced to Europe from Mosul in India in 1670, and vegetable broth was known for countless ages before that time in every part of the world, it is possible that *muslin* is an erroneous phonetic rendering of *meslin*, or *mashlum.* Both *meslin* and *mashlum* appear in Jamieson, who translates the former as "mixed corn," and the latter as "a mixture of edibles," but gives no etymology for either. *Mess* is a word that, with slight variations, appears in almost every language of Europe, and which, in its English form, is derived by nearly all philologists from *mensa*, a table. But that this is an error will appear on a little examination, for *mess* originally signified, in nearly every instance in which it was used, a dish of vegetables. The old translation of the Bible speaks of a *mess* of pottage, a purely vegetable compound. Milton speaks of

Herbs and other country *messes*,
Which the neat-handed Phillis dresses.

The Dutch and Flemish *moes* signifies a dish of herbs, or herbs reduced to what the French call a *purée ;* the Americans call oatmeal porridge, or any compound of mashed grain, a *mush*. The Gaelic *meas* signifies fruit or vegetables, and this, combined with the word *lan*, full, is doubtless the true root of *meslin* or *mashlum*, rendered *muslin* by Burns's printers. It may be observed that *mash*, to render into a pulp or *purée*, is exclusively used for vegetables, as *mashed* potatoes, *mashed* turnips, &c., and that *hash* or *mince* is the word employed by cooks

for the reduction of beef, mutton, and other flesh of animals into smaller portions or particles. *Muslin-kail* seems to be peculiar to Burns.

Mutch, a woman's cap or bonnet ; from the Flemish *muts*, the German *mützen*, which have the same meaning.

Their toys and *mutches* were sae clean,
They glancit in our ladies' e'en.
           —Allan Ramsay.

A' dressed out in aprons clean,
And braw white Sunday *mutches*.
—Sir Alexander Boswell : *Jenny Dang the Weaver*.

Mutchkin, a pint ; from the Flemish *mudde*, a *hectolitre*, a large quart ; or *muid*, a quart. An English traveller, who prided himself on his knowledge of the Scotch language, called at an inn in Glasgow for a *mutchkin* of whisky, under the idea that *mutchkin* signified a *gill*, or a small glass. "*Mutchkin ?*" inquired the waiter, "and a' to yoursel' ?" "Yes, a *mutchkin !*" said the Englishman. "I trow ye'll be gey an' fou," said the waiter, "an' ye drink it." "Never you mind," said the Englishman, "bring it." And it was brought. Great thereanent was the Englishman's surprise. He drank no more than a gill of it ; but he added meanwhile a new Scottish word to his vocabulary.

N

Nae-thing. The English language, or at least the rhymers who write English, have lost many rhymes by not being able to make *nothing* do duty for *no-thing*; whence they might have claimed it as a rhyme for *slow-thing*, *low-thing*, and many others too obvious to be specified. The Scottish language, in preserving *nae-thing*, has emphasised the etymology of the word. It is impossible to find a rhyme for the English *nothing*, but for the Scottish *nae-thing* Burns has found that there are many; among others, *ae-thing*, *claithing*, *graithing*, *gaything*, *plaything*, &c.

Napery, table-linen ; from the French *nappe*, a tablecloth, or the English *napkin*, a little cloth.

I thought a beetle or bittle had been the thing that the women have when they are washing towels and *napery*—things for dadding them with.—DEAN RAMSAY: *The Diamond Beetle Case.*

Nappy. This word was used by a few English writers in the eighteenth century, but was never so common in England as it was in Scotland. It always signified strong drink, particularly ale or beer, and not wine or spirits.

> Two bottles of as *nappy* liquor
> As ever reamed in horn or bicker.
> —ALLAN RAMSAY.

Care, mad to see a man sae happy,
E'en drowned himsel' among the *nappy*.
BURNS: *Tam o' Shanter.*

With *nappy* beer, I to the barn repaired.
—GAY's *Fables.*

The word is rendered in French by " capiteux, qui monte à la tete "—that is to say, heady. It seems derivable from the English slang *nob*, the head, as in the pugilistic phrase, " One for his *nob*," " One (blow) for his head ; " whence also the familiar *nopper*, the head. The original word was the German *knob*, a round lump, or ball, in allusion to the shape ; whence *knobby*, rounded or lumpy. *Nap-pie*, in the sense of strong drink that mounts to the head, be-comes, by extension of meaning, strong and vigorous ; " a *nappie* callant " is a strong, vigorous youth, with a good head on his shoulders.

Nappy.—Bailey's definition of this word in his English Dictionary is " Nappy-ale, such as will cause persons to take or knap pleasant and strong ale."—R. DRENNAN.

N e b, the nose. Flemish *sneb* (with the elision of the *s*), the nose, the beak ; a point, as the *neb* or *nib* of a pen.

> She holds up the *neb* to him,
> And arms her with the boldness of a wife.
> —SHAKSPEARE: *Winter's Tale.*

Turn your *neb* northwards, and settle for awhile at St. Andrews.
—SCOTT: *Fortunes of Nigel.*

Neep, a turnip; from the French *navet.*

A late Lord Justice-Clerk of the Court of Session, who was fond of sport, was shooting pheasants in a field of turnips, when the farmer, whose consent had not been asked, and who looked upon the sportsman as an illegal trespasser, rushed out of his house in a towering passion, and called out in a loud voice, "Come oot o' that you, sir! come oot o' that immediately." The Lord Justice-Clerk, unaccustomed to this style of address, confronted the angry man, and asked him if he knew to whom he was speaking? "I dinna ken, and I dinna care; ye'se come oot o' that, or I'll mak it the waur for ye." "I'm the Lord Justice-Clerk," said the legal dignitary, thinking to overawe the irate agriculturist. "I dinna care whose clerk ye are, but ye'se come oot o' my *neeps.*" How the altercation ended is not on record, though it is believed that his lordship left the field quietly, after enlightening the farmer as to his high status and position, and cooling his wrath by submission to an authority not to be successfully contested, without greater trouble than the contest was worth.—*Scottish Wit and Humour.*

Neuk, a corner; English a nook, a small corner. Both words are derived from the Gaelic *uig,* a corner, which, with the indefinite article *an* before it, was corrupted from an *ook,* or an *uig,* into a *neuk,* or a *nook.* The Flemish *uig* and *hoek,* and the German *eck,* a corner, are traceable to the same Celtic root.

The deil sits girnin' in the *neuk,*
Rivin' sticks to roast the Deuk.
—*Jacobite Ballad on the Victory of the Duke of Cumberland at Culloden.*

Nevermas, the time that never comes. This word, equivalent to the "Greek kalends," is formed after the model of Martinmas, Michaelmas, and Christmas. It does not occur in Jamieson. It is found in Armstrong's Gaelic Dictionary as the translation of *Là buain na lin,* the "day of the cutting of the flax," which has in the Highlands the meaning of "never," or "at no time," or "at a very uncertain time."

Nicher, to neigh, to snort; French, *nennir,* sometimes written *hennir;* Flemish, *nenniker,* or *ninniker.*

Little may an auld nag do that maunna
nicher.
—ALLAN RAMSAY'S *Scots Proverbs.*

Nick, Auld Nick, Nickie-Ben. All these names are used in Scotland to signify the devil; the third is peculiar to Scotland, and finds no place in English parlance.

But fare-you-weel, auld *Nickie-Ben!*
Oh, wad ye tak a thought an' men',
Ye aiblins might, I dinna ken,
    Still hae a stake!
I'm wae to think upon yon den,
    Even for your sake!
—BURNS: *Address to the Deil.*

Why *Nick* came to signify Satan in the British Isles has never been satisfactorily explained. Butler in *Hudibras* supposes that he was so called after Nicholas Macchiavelli.

Nick Macchiavel had no such trick,
Though he gave name to our *Old Nick.*

But the name was in use many ages before Macchiavelli was born; and the passage must, therefore, be considered as a joke, rather than as a philological assertion. It is remarkable, too, that *Nick* and *Old Nick*, whatever be the derivation, is a phrase unknown to any nation of Europe except our own. The derivation from Nicholas is clearly untenable; that from *Nikkr*, a water-sprite or goblin, in the Scandinavian mythology, is equally so; for the *Old Nick* of British superstition is reputed to have more to do with fire than water, and has no attributes in common with Satan, the prince of the powers of evil. To derive the word from *niger*, or *nigger*, black, because the devil is reputed to be black, is but perverted ingenuity. All the epithets showered upon the devil by Burns,

Oh thou, whatever title suit thee,
Auld Satan, Hornie, Nick, or Clootie,

are, with the exception of Satan, titles of irreverence, familiarity, and jocosity; *Hornie*, from the horns he is supposed to wear on his forehead, and *Clootie*, from his cloven hoofs, like those of a goat. It is probable that *Nick* and *Old Nick* are words of a similarly derisive character, and that *nick*, which appears in the glossaries to Allan Ramsay and to Burns, as *cheat* or *to cheat*, is the true origin, and that *Old Nick* simply signifies the *Old Cheat*. It may be mentioned, in connection with the idea of *cheat* or *nick*, that *old gentleman* is a name often

given to Satan by people who object to the word *devil*, and that the same name is descriptive, according to the Slang Dictionary, of a card almost imperceptibly longer than the other cards of the pack, used by card-sharpers for the purpose of cheating. To be out on the *nick* is, on the same authority, to be out thieving. The etymology of *nick* in this sense is doubtful. Dr. Adolphus Wagner, the learned editor of the German edition of Burns, derives it from the Greek Νεκω, and translates it "to bite or to cheat." In Wright's Dictionary of Obsolete and Provincial English, *nick* is "to deceive, to cheat, to deny; also, to win at dice unfairly."

Nidder, Nither, to lower, to depress; *niddered*, pinched with cold or hunger, with the vital energies depressed; also, stunted or lowered in growth. From the German *nieder*, low, or down; the Flemish *neder*, English *nether*, as in the Biblical phrase, "the upper and the *nether* millstone." *Netherlands*, the low countries; the French *Pays Bas.*

Nithered by the norlan' breeze,
The sweet wee flower aft dwines and dees.
—JAMES BALLANTINE.

Nieve, the fist, the closed hand; *nevel*, to strike with the fist, a blow with the fist. From the Teutonic *knuffen*, to beat with the fist, to cuff, to fisticuff.

Though here they scrape, and squeeze,
and growl,
Their worthless *nieve-fu'* o' a soul
May in some future carcass howl
    The forest's fright.

—BURNS: *Epistle to John Lapraik.*

Sir Alexander Ramsay of Fasque, showing a fine stot to a butcher, said, "I was
offered twenty guineas for that beast."
"Indeed, Fasque!" said the butcher, "ye
should hae steekit your *nieve* upon that."
—DEAN RAMSAY.

They partit manly with a *nevel;*
God wat gif hair was ruggit
    Betwixt thame.
        —*Christ's Kirk on the Green.*

He hasna as muckle sense as a cow could
had in her *nieve.*—ALLAN RAMSAY'S *Scots
Proverbs.*

Mark the rustic, haggis-fed,
The trembling earth resounds his tread,
Clap in his walie *nieve* a blade,
        He'll mak' it whissle;
And legs and arms and heads will sned
        Like taps o' thrissle.
        —BURNS: *To a Haggis.*

Niffer, to barter, to exchange.
Probably, according to Jamieson, from *nieve,* the fist or closed
hand—to exchange an article
that is in one hand for that
which is in the other. This etymology is doubtful, although no
better one has been suggested.

Ye'll no be *niffered* but for a waur, and
that's no possible.—ALLAN RAMSAY'S *Scots
Proverbs.*

Ye see your state wi' theirs compared,
    And shudder at the *niffer;*
But, cast a moment's fair regard,
    What maks the mighty differ?
        —BURNS: *To the Unco Guid.*

Nippit, miserly, mean, parsimonious, near; from *nip*, to pinch.
The English *pinch* is often applied in the same sense.

Noo or **the noo**, at the present
time, now.

On one occasion a neighbour waited on
a small laird in Lanarkshire, named Hamilton, and requested his signature to an
accommodation bill for twenty pounds at
three months' date, which led to the following characteristic colloquy:—

"Na! na!" said the laird, "I canna
do that."

"What for no, laird? Ye hae done the
same thing for others."

"Aye, aye, Tammas! but there's wheels
within wheels that ye ken naething about.
I canna do't."

"It's a sma' thing to refuse me, laird."

"Weel, ye see, Tammas, if I was to pit
my name till't, ye wad get the siller frae
the bank, and when the time cam round,
ye wadna be ready, an' I wad hae to pay't.
An' then me an' you wad quarrel. So we
may just as weel quarrel *the noo,* an' I'll
keep the siller in my pouch."—DEAN
RAMSAY.

Nowte, horned cattle; corrupted
in English into *neat.*

Mischief begins wi' needles and prins,
    And ends wi' horned *nowte.*
        —ALLAN RAMSAY.

Or by Madrid he takes the route,
To thrum guitars and fecht wi' *nowte.*
        —BURNS: *The Twa Dogs.*

Lord Seafield, who was accused by his brother of accept-
ing a bribe to vote for the union
betwixt England and Scotland,
endeavoured to retort upon him
by calling him a cattle-dealer.
"Ay, weel," replied his brother,
"better sell *nowte* than nations."

Noyt, **noit**, or **nowt**, to injure, to
hurt, to beat, to strike; from
the French *nuire*, to injure.

The miller was of manly mak,
    To meet him was na mowis,

They durst not ten come him to tak,
Sae *noytit* he their powis.
—*Christ's Kirk on the Green.*

Nugget, a word scarcely known to the English until the discovery of gold in California and Australia, when it was introduced by the miners to signify a large piece of the metal as distinguished from grains of gold dust. Many attempts have been made to trace its etymology, only one of which has found a qualified acceptance—that which affirms it to be a corruption of *ingot.* This is plausible, but not entirely satisfactory. In some parts of Scotland, the word for a *luncheon,* or a hasty repast taken at noon, is *noggit*—sometimes written *knockit*—which means a piece. In other parts of Scotland the word used is *piece,* as, " Gie the bairn its *piece,*" and the word *lunch* itself, from the Gaelic *lonach,* hungry, signifies the *piece* which is cut off a loaf or a cheese to satisfy the appetite during the interval that elapses before the regular meal.

When hungry thou stoodest, staring like an oaf,
I sliced the *luncheon* from the barley loaf.
—Gay.

All these examples tend to show that *nugget* simply means a lump or piece. In Kent, according to Wright's Archaic Dictionary, a lump of food is called a *nuncheon.*

Nyse, to beat, to pommel, a word in use among the boys of the High School of Edinburgh ; from the Gaelic *naitheas* (*t* silent), a mischief. " I'll *nyse* you," " I'll do you a mischief."

O

Ock, a diminutive particle appended to Scottish words, and implying littleness combined with the idea of tenderness and affection, as in lass, *lassock,* wife, *wifock.* This termination is sometimes combined with *ie,* thus making a double diminutive, as *lassockie,* often spelled *lassiekie,* and *wifockie, wifiekie.* *Ock* is probably derived from the Gaelic *og,* young.

Olyte, diligent, industrious, active. According to Mr. Halliwell, this word appears in the Harleian MS., and is still used in some parts of England. Jamieson spells it *olight* and *olite,* and derives it from the Swedish *offlaet,* "too light, fleet," but no such word is to be found in the Swedish dictionaries, nor in those of the other Teutonic languages. Possibly the true origin of the word is the Gaelic *oil,* to rear, educate, instruct, and *oilte,* instructed, *oilean,* instruction, good-breeding ; whence an *olyte* mother, in the proverb quoted

below, may signify a woman instructed in the due performance
of all her household duties, and
performing them so zealously as
to leave nothing for her daughter
to do. *Oileanta*, more commonly
written *ealanta*, signifies quick,
nimble, active.

An *olyte* mother makes a sweer daughter.
—ALLAN RAMSAY'S *Scots Proverbs.*

Oo aye ! An emphatic assertion
of assent.   The French *oui.*

Orra, all sorts of odds and ends,
occasional.

Where Donald Caird fand *orra* things.
—SCOTT.

She's a weel-educate woman, and if she
win to her English as I hae heard her do
at *orra* times, she may come to fickle us a'.
—SCOTT : *The Antiquary.*

Orra,—now and then, unusual, not frequently met with, almost always associated
with time.—R. DRENNAN.

Orra man.   A man employed to
do odd jobs on a farm, that are
not in the regular routine of
the work of the other farm
servants.

Oughtlins, pertaining to duty,
or to that which *ought* to be
done ; a word composed of
ought, a *debt* owing to duty,
honour and propriety, and *lins*
(see AIBLINS, WESTLINS, &c.), inclining towards.

If that daft buckie, Geordie Wales,
Was grown *oughtlins* douser.
—BURNS : *On Receiving a Newspaper.*

Ourie or **oorie**, cold, shivering.
This word, peculiar to Scotland,

is derived from the Gaelic *fuar*,
cold, which, with the aspirate,
becomes *fhuar*, and is pronounced *uar.*

I thought me on the *ourie* cattle.
—BURNS : *A Winter Night.*

The English *hoar-frost*, and
the *hoary* (white, snowy) hair
of old age, are traceable to the
same etymological root.   Jamieson, however, derives *oorie* from
the Icelandic *ur*, rain, and the
Swedish *ur*, stormy weather,
though the origin of both is to
be found in the Gaelic *uaire*,
bad weather or storm.

Outthrough, entirely or completely through.

They dived in through the one burn bank,
Sae did they *outthrough* the other.
—BUCHAN'S *Ancient Ballads.*

Out-cast, a quarrel, to " cast-out,"
to quarrel.

O dool to tell,
They've had a bitter black *cast-out*
Atween themsel.
—BURNS : *The Twa Herds.*

I didna ken they had *casten-out.*
—DEAN RAMSAY.

Outlers, cattle left out at night in
the fields, for want of byres or
folds to shelter them.

Amang the brackens on the brae,
Between her an' the moon,
The Deil or else an *outler quey*
Gat up and gae a croon.
Poor Lizzie's heart maist lap the hool—
Near lav'rock height she jumpit,
But miss'd a foot, and in the pool
Out owre the lugs she plumpit.
—BURNS : *Hallowe'en.*

Outside of the Loof, the back of the hand. "The outside of my loof to ye," is a phrase that signifies a wish on the part of the person who uses it to reject the friendship or drop the acquaintance of the person to whom it is addressed.

"If ye'll no join the Free Kirk," said a wealthy widow to her cousin, to whom she had often conveyed the hint that he might expect a handsome legacy at her death (a hint that never ripened into a fact), "ye'll hae the *outside* o' my loof, and never see the inside o't again."—C. M.

Outspeckle, a laughing-stock; and *kenspeckle,* to be easily recognised by some outer mark of singularity. These words have a common origin, and are derived either from *speck,* or *speckle,* a small mark or spot; or from *spectacle,* corrupted into *speckle;* but most probably from the former.

"Wha drives thir kye," gan Willie to say,
"To mak' an *outspeckle* o' me!"
—*Border Ballads: Jamie Telfer.*

Outwittens, unknowingly, without the knowledge of.

Outwittens of my daddie [*i.e.,* my father not knowing it].—JAMIESON.

Overlay or **owerlay,** the burden or chorus of a song; the *refrain.*

And aye the *owerlay* o' his sang
Was, wae's me for Prince Charlie.
—*Jacobite Ballad.*

The French *refrain,* recently adopted into English, is of Gaelic origin, from *ramh* or *raf,* an oar, and *rann,* a song; a sea song or boat-song, formerly chanted to the motion of the oars by Celtic boatmen in Brittany and the Scottish Highlands.

Ower Bogie, a proverbial phrase used in regard to a marriage which has been celebrated by a magistrate, and not by a clergyman. Synonymous in Aberdeenshire with the English Gretna Green marriages, performed under similar conditions. The origin is unknown, though it is supposed that some accommodating magistrate, at some time or other, resided on the opposite side of the river Bogie from that of the town or village inhabited by the lovers who desired to be joined in the bonds of matrimony without subjecting themselves to the sometimes inconvenient interrogations of the kirk. Jamieson erroneously quotes the phrase as *owre boggie.*

I will awa wi' my love,
I will awa' wi' her,
Though a' my kin' had sorrow and said,
I'll *ower Bogie* wi' her.
—ALLAN RAMSAY: *Tea Table Miscellany.*

Owergang, to surpass, to exceed.

You're straight and tall and handsome withal,
But your pride *owergangs* your wit.
—*Ballad of Proud Lady Margaret.*

Ower-word, a chorus or burden. A phrase often repeated in a song, the French *bourdon,* the English *burthen* of a song.

K

And aye the *ower-word* of his song
    Was, wae's me for Prince Charlie.
        —GLEN : *A Jacobite Song.*

The starling flew to the window stane,
    It whistled and it sang,
And aye the *ower-word* o' the tune
    Was " Johnnie tarries lang."
        —*Johnnie of Breadislee.*

Oxter, the armpit and the space between the shoulder and the bosom ; sometimes it is used incorrectly for the lap ; and to embrace, to encircle with the arms in fondness. From the Gaelic *uchd*, the breast or bosom ; whence also the Latin *uxor*, a wife, *i.e.*, the wife of one's bosom ; and *uxorious*, fondly attached to a wife ; *uchd mhac*, an adopted son, the son of one's bosom. Jamieson derives *oxter* from the Teutonic *oxtel*, but no such word is to be found in the German language. The Flemish and Dutch have *oksel*, a gusset, which Johnson defines as " an angular piece of cloth, inserted in a garment, particularly at the upper end of the sleeve of a shirt, or as a part of the neck." This word has a clear but remote connection with the Gaelic *uchd*.

He did like ony mavis sing,
    And as I in his *oxter* sat
He ca'd me aye his *bosome* thing.
        —ALLAN RAMSAY : *Tea Table Miscellany.*

Here the phrase " sitting in his *oxter* " is equivalent to sitting folded in his arms, or clasped to his bosom.

P

Pack, familiar, intimate, closely allied.

Nae doubt but they were fain o' ither,
And unco *pack* and thick thegither,
Wi' social nose whiles snuff d and howkit.
        —BURNS : *The Twa Dogs.*

    Pack is not only used as an adjective, but is common as a noun in colloquial English, as in the phrase, a *pack* of rascals, and a *pack* of thieves. In this sense it is derivable from the Gaelic *pac* or *pacca*, a troop, a mob.

Pad, to travel, to ride. Often in Scotland when a lady is seen on horseback in the rural districts, the children of the villages follow her, crying out, " Lady *pad !* lady *pad !* " Jamieson says that on *pad* is to travel on foot, that *pad*, the hoof, is a cant phrase, signifying to walk, and that the ground is *paddit* when it has been hardened by frequent passing and repassing. He derives the word from the Latin *pes*, *pedis*, the foot. It seems, however, to be more immediately derived from *path ; pad*, to go on the *path*, whether on foot or on horseback ; from the German *pfad*, the Flemish *pad*, and *voet - pad*, the foot - path. The English dictionaries erroneously explain *pad* in the word *foot-pad*, a highway thief. But *pad* by itself is never used in the sense of steal. Grose's Classical Dictionary of the Vulgar Tongue has *pad-borrowers*, horse-stealers, as if *pad* signified a horse. The phrase really means *path-borrowers*, *i.e.*, borrowers on the path or journey.

Padda, **Paddock**, a frog or toad; *paddock stool*, a toad-stool, a wild fungus or mushroom. Flemish *pad* and *padde*, a frog.

Says the mother, "What noise is that at the door, daughter?" "Hoot," says the lassie, "it's naething but a filthy *padda*." "Open the door," says the mother, "to the puir *padda*." Sae the lassie opened the door, and the *padda* cam loup, loup, loupin' in, and sat doun by the ingle side. —*Scottish Songs collected by* ROBERT CHAMBERS, 1829.

> Gowks and fools,
> Frae colleges and boarding schools,
> May sprout like summer *paddock-stools*,
>   In glen or shaw.
> —BURNS: *Verses written at Selkirk.*

Old Lady Perth, offended with a French gentleman for some disparaging remark which he had made on Scottish cookery, answered him curtly, "Weel! weel! some folk like parritch, and some like *paddocks*." —DEAN RAMSAY.

Paidle. This eminently Scottish word has no synonym in the English language, nor in any country where everybody, even the poorest, wears shoes or boots, and where, to go barefooted, would imply the lowest social degradation. But in Scotland, a land of streams, rivulets, and burns, that wimple down the hills and cross the paths and roads, to go barefooted is a

pleasure and luxury, and a convenience, especially to the children of both sexes, and even to young men and women verging upon manhood and womanhood. An Englishman may *paddle* his boat and his canoe, but a Scotsman *paidles* in the mountain stream. How the young children of England love to *paidle*, may occasionally be seen at the sea-side resorts of the southern counties in the summer season, but the Scottish child in the rural districts *paidles* all the year, and needs no holiday for the purpose.

> We twa hae *paidled* in the burn,
> Frae morning sun till dine,
> But seas between us braid hae roared,
> Sin' the days of auld lang syne.
>   —BURNS.

The remembrance of *paidlin'* when stirred by the singing of this immortal song by Scotsmen in America, in India, in Africa, or at the Antipodes, melts every Scottish heart to tenderness, or inspires it to patriotism, as every Scotsman, who has travelled much, very surely knows.

Paik, a beating, to beat, to thrash, to fight, to drub, to strike. Jamieson derives this word from the German *pauken*, to beat; but there is no such word in that language. *Pauke* in German, *pauk* in Flemish, signifies a kettle-drum; and *pauken*, to beat the kettle-drum, but not to beat in any other sense. The word is probably from the Gaelic *paigh*, to pay; and also, by an extension of meaning, to pay one's deserts by a beating, as in the proverb in Allan Ramsay—" He's sairest dung that is *paid* with his own wand," *i.e.*, he is sorest hit who is beaten with his own cudgel.

Paikie, a trull, a prostitute, a *fille de joie*, a euphemism from the Gaelic *peacadh* (*peaca*), a sinner. *Paik*, a sin ; the French *pecher ;* and the Italian *peccare.*

> In adulterie he was ta'en—
> Made to be punisht for his *paik.*
> —JAMIESON.

Pang, to fill full, to cram ; *pang-fu'*, as full as one can hold. Etymology unknown ; but possibly related to the French *panse*, belly ; *pansu*, large-bellied ; English *paunchy.*

> Leeze me on drink ; it gies us mair
> Than either school or college,
> It kindles wit, it waukens lair,
> It *pangs* us fu' o' knowledge.
> —BURNS : *The Holy Fair.*

Parle, a discourse ; from the French *parler*, to speak ; the Italian *parlare*. The Gaelic *beurla* signifies language, and more particularly the English language.

> A tocher's nae word in a true lover's *parle*,
> But gie me my love, and a fig for the warl.—BURNS : *Meg o' the Mill.*

Parritch or **porridge.** A formerly favourite, if not essential, food of the Scottish people of all classes, composed of oatmeal boiled in water to a thick consistency, and seasoned with salt. This healthful food is generally taken with milk, but is equally palatable with butter, sugar, beer, or wine. It is sometimes retained in middle and upper class families ; but among the very poor has unfortunately been displaced by the cheaper and less nutritious potato.

> The hailsome *parritch*, chief o' Scotia's food.
> —BURNS : *Cotter's Saturday Night.*

Partan, a crab, from the Gaelic ; *partanach*, abounding in crabs ; *partan-handit*, epithet applied to one who is hard-fisted and penurious, who grips his money like a crab grips with its claw.

> An' there'll be *partans* and *buckies*,
> An' singit sheeps' heads and a haggis.
> —*The Blithesome Bridal.*

Pash, the head, the brow, the forehead. Allan Ramsay, barber and wig-maker, sang of his trade :—

> I theek [thatch] the out, and line the inside,
> Of mony a douce and witty *pash*,
> And baithways gather in the cash.

A bare *pash* signifies a bald head, and mad-*pash* is equivalent to the English madcap. Latham's Todd's Johnson has *pash*, to push or butt like a ram or bull, with the head. *Pash* was current English in the time of Shakspeare, who uses it in the " Winter's Tale," in a passage which no commentator has been able to explain. Leontes, suspicious of the fidelity of his wife Hermione, asks his child Mamilius—

Art thou my calf?
To which Mamilius replies—

Yes! if you will, my Lord.

Leontes, still brooding on his imaginary wrong, rejoins moodily—

Thou wants a rough *pash* and the shoots that I have to be full like me.

It is amusing to note into what errors the English editors of Shakspeare have fallen, in their ignorance of this word. Nares thought that *pash* was something belonging to a bull —he did not know what—or a calf, and Steevens thought that it was the Spanish *paz*, a kiss. Mr. Howard Staunton, the editor of Shakspeare, had a glimpse of the meaning, and thought that *pash* meant a " *tufted* head." Jamieson acknowledged the word, but attempted no etymology. *Pash* is clearly derivable from the Gaelic *bathais* (pronounced *bash* or *pash*), and signifies the forehead. The allusion of the unhappy Leontes to the *shoots* on his rough *pash* (wrinkled brow) is to the horns that vulgar phraseology places on the foreheads of deceived and betrayed husbands. Read by this gloss, the much-mis-understood passage in the "Winter's Tale" becomes clear.

Paughty, proud, haughty, repulsive, but without having the qualities of mind or person to justify the assumption of superiority over others. Probably derived from the Flemish *pochen*,

to vaunt, to brag, and *pocher*, a braggadocio, a *fanfaron*.

An askin', an askin', my father dear,
An askin' I beg of thee;
Ask not that *paughty* Scottish lord,
For him ye ne'er shall see.
  —*Ballad of the Gay Goss-Hawk.*

Yon *paughty* dog
That bears the keys of Peter.
  —Burns: *A Dream.*

Paumie and **taws.** All Scottish school-boys, past and present, have painful knowledge of the meaning of these two words. *Paumie* is a stroke over the open hand, with a cane or the *taws.* The *taws* is a thong of leather cut into a fringe at the end, and hardened in the fire. It is, and was, the recognised mode of punishment for slight offences or breaches of discipline at school, when the master was unwilling to resort to the severer and more degrading punishment, inflicted *a posteriori*, after the fashion of Dr. Busby. *Paumie* is derived from the *palm* of the hand, the French *peaume*, and *taws* is the plural form of the Gaelic *taod*, a rope, a scourge.

Pawky, of a sly humour, wise, witty, cautious, discreet, and insinuating,—all in one. There is no synonym for this word in English. The etymology is unknown.

The *pawky* auld carle cam owre the lea,
Wi' mony good e'ens and good days to me.

Dear Smith, the slee'est, *pawkie* thief.
  —Burns: *To James Smith.*

Peat-Reek and **Mountain Dew**. *Peat-Reek* is the smoke of peat when dried and burned for fuel, the flavour of which used to be highly appreciated in Scottish whiskey, when made by illicit distillers in lonely glens among the mountains, out of the usual reach of the exciseman. From the solitary places of its manufacture, whiskey received the poetic name of *Mountain Dew*, or the "Dew off Ben Nevis," which it still retains.

Mountain Dew, *clear* as a Scot's understanding,
  Pure as his conscience wherever he goes,
Warm as his heart to the friends he has chosen,
  Strong as his arm when he fights with his foes !
In liquor like this should old Scotland be toasted,
  So fill up again, and the pledge we'll renew ;
Unsullied in honour, our blessings upon her—
  Scotland for ever ! and old *Mountain Dew !*—MACKAY.

Pech, to pant, to blow, for want of breath. Derived by Jamieson from the Danish *pikken*, to palpitate.

> My Pegasus I gat astride,
> And up Parnassus *pechin'*.
>   —BURNS: *To Willie Chalmers.*

There comes young Monks of high complexion,
Of mind devout, love and affection ;
And in his court their hot flesh dart (tame),
Fule father-like with *pech* and pant,
  They are sa humble of intercession,
Their errand all kind women grant,
  Sic tidings heard I at the session.

>   —ALLAN RAMSAY : *The Evergreen—
>   Frae the Session.*

Pechan, the stomach.

> Ev'n the ha' folk fill their *pechan*
> Wi' sauce, ragouts, and such like trashtrie,
> That's little short o' downright wastrie.
>   —BURNS : *The Twa Dogs.*

This word seems to be a corruption of the Gaelic *poc,* a bag, a poke ; and *pocan,* a little bag ; and to be ludicrously applied to the belly or stomach. The English slang *peckish,* hungry, is probably derived from the same root, and not from the beak, or peck of a bird.

Pedder-coffe, a pedlar. In Allan Ramsay's "Evergreen," a poem ascribed to Sir David Lyndsay is entitled a "Description of *Pedder-coffs,* their having no regard to honesty in their vocation." Both *pedder* and *coffe* are of Teutonic derivation ; *ped,* sometimes written *pad,* from the German *pfad ;* Flemish *pad,* a path ; and *coffe* or *koffe,* from *kaufen,* to buy ; whence a pedlar signified a walking merchant who carried his wares along with him. But it should be observed with regard to the Teutonic derivation, that in the Kymric, or ancient language of Wales, more ancient than the German, *padd* signifies one that keeps a course. Attempts have been made to trace *pedlar* to *ped,* a local word in some parts of England for a basket : but this derivation would not account for *pedder,* a mounted highwayman ; for foot-*pad,* a highway robber on foot, from the slang expression among thieves and beggars to go on the *pad, i.e.,* on the tramp.

Jamieson derives the Scottish *pedder* from the barbarous low Latin *pedarius,* i.e., *nudis ambulans pedibus.* Sir David Lyndsay in his poem was exceedingly indignant, both with the *Pedders* and the *Coffes,* who seem to have been in their mode of transacting business with the country people, whom they favoured with their visits on their peregrinations through districts afar from towns, the exact counterparts of the tallymen at the present day. He recommends, in the interest of the people, that wherever the " pedder knaves appear in a burgh or town where there is a magistrate, that their lugs should be cuttit off," as a warning to all cheats and regrators. A similar outcry is sometimes raised against the " tallymen," or travelling linen-drapers and haberdashers, who tempt the wives of working men, and poor people generally, to buy their goods at high prices, and accept small weekly payments on account, until their extortionate bills are liquidated.

Peel, a border tower, a small fortress, of which few specimens are now left standing. A very interesting one, however, still remains in the town of Melrose. Possibly a corruption of *bield,* a shelter.

And black Joan, frae Creighton-*peel,*
O' gipsy kith an' kin'.
—Burns : *The Five Carlins.*

An' when they came to the fair Dodhead
Right hastily they clam (climbed) the *peel,*
They loosened the kye out, ane and a',
An' ranshackled the house right weel.
—*Border Minstrelsy : Jamie Telfer.*

Peep, to utter a faint cry or sound, like an infant or a young bird. *Peepie-weepie,* a querulous and tearful child ; *peep-sma',* a feeble voice, a weak person who has to submit to the domination of one stronger; synonymous with the English " sing small." " He daurna play *peep,*" he must not utter a word in defence of himself. In Dutch and Flemish, *pipen* signifies to cry like an infant; and *piep-yong* is a word for a very young or new-born child. The etymology is that of *pipe,* or the sound emitted by a flute or pipe, when gently blown upon.

Peesweep, a lapwing, or plover ; *peesweep-like,* a contemptible epithet applied to a feeble, sharp-featured man or woman, with a shrill but not loud voice, like the cry of a plover.

Peerie, pearie or **perie,** a humming top; sometimes a peg-top; from the Gaelic *beur (b* pronounced as *p*), to hum, to buzz. Brand, in his well-known work on Popular Antiquities, quotes Jamieson as his authority. He defines it to mean a peg-top, and adds that the name was apparently derived from its close similarity to a pear, and that the Scotch originally called it a French pear or *pearie*, because it was first imported from France.

Peik-thank, is, according to Jamieson, an ungrateful person, one who returns little or no thanks for benefits conferred. *Peik* in this phrase seems to be a corruption and misspelling of the Gaelic *beag* (*b* pronounced as *p*), little. Jamieson derives it from the Italian *poco*.

The English *pick-thank* appears to have had a different origin and meaning, and signifies, according to the examples of its use in Nares, a sycophant, a favourite, a flatterer, who strove to pick up, acquire, or gather thanks from the great and powerful. Shakspeare has " smiling *pick-thanks*, and base newsmongers;" Fairfax, "a flatterer, a *pick-thank*, and a liar."

Possibly, however, the Scottish and English interpretations of the word may be more akin than might appear at first glance. Sycophants, flatterers, and parasites are proverbially ungrateful, unless it be, as La Rochefoucauld so wittily asserts, " for favours to come."

Pendles, ear-rings; from pendants.

She's got *pendles* in her lugs,
  Cockle-shells wad set her better ;
High-heel'd shoon and siller tags,
  And a' the lads are wooin' at her.

Be a lassie e'er sae black,
  Gin she ware the penny-siller,
Set her up on Tintock tap,
  The wind will blaw a man till her !
    —Herd's *Collection: Tibbie Fowler.*

Pennarts. Jamieson says this word means " revenge," and quotes the proverbial saying, " I'se hae *pennarts* o' him yet ; " suggesting that the derivation may be from *pennyworths*. It is more likely to be from the Gaelic *pein*, punishment ; *peanas*, revenge ; and *pein-ard*, high or great revenge.

Penny-fee, wages. *Penny* is commonly used in Scottish parlance for money generally, as in *penny-siller*, a great quantity of money ; *penny-maister*, the town-treasurer ; *penny - wedding*, a wedding at which every guest contributed towards the expense of the marriage festival ; *penny-friend*, a friend whose only friendship is for his friend's money. The French use *denier*, and the Italians *danari*, in the same sense.

Peny is ane hardy knyght,
Peny is mekyl of myght,
Peny of wrong he maketh ryght
  In every country where he go.
    —Ritson's *Ancient Songs and Ballads : A Song in Praise of Sir Peny.*

My riches a's my *penny-fee*,
And I maun guide it canny, O.
    —Burns : *My Nannie, O.*

Pensy, proud, conceited; above one's station. Probably a corruption of pensive or thoughtful.

Helen Walker was held among her equals to be *pensy*, but the facts brought to prove this accusation seem only to evince a strength of character superior to those around her.—SCOTT : *Heart of Midlothian.*

Perlins or **pearlins**, fine linen ornamented with lace work or knitted work.

Oh where, oh where, is her auld son,
    Spak out the Lammikin ;
He's gane to buy *pearlins*
    Gin our lady lye in.
These *pearlins* she shall never wear,
    Spak out the Lammikin.
        —HERD'S *Collection : Lammikin.*

Pernickitie (sometimes written *prig-nickitie*), precise about trifles ; finicking, over - dainty, trim, neat, nicely dressed, adorned with trifling articles of finery, or knick - knackets. Etymology doubtful.

The English are sae *pernickity* about what they eat, but no sae *pernickity* about what they drink.—*Noctes Ambrosianæ.*

Peuter or **peuther**, to canvass, to solicit votes, to thrust one's self forward in election times to ask for support ; from the Gaelic *put*, to thrust, and *putair*, one who thrusts ; and the Flemish *peuteren*, to poke one's fingers into other people's business,— rendered in the French and Flemish Dictionary (1868), " pousser les doigts, dans quelque chose."

He has *peuthered* Queensferry and Inverkeithing, and they say he will begin to *peuther* Stirling next week.—JAMIESON.

Philabeg or **fillabeg**, the kilt as worn by the Highlanders ; lite-

rally a little cloth ; from the Gaelic *fileadh*, a cloth, a woven garment, and *beag*, little.

Oh to see his tartan trews,
Bonnet blue, and laigh-heeled shoes,
Philabeg aboon his knee- –
That's the laddie I'll gang wi'.
        —GEDDES : *Lewie Gordon.*

I' faith, quo' John, I got sic flegs (frights)
Wi' their claymore and *philabegs*,
If I face them again, deil break my legs,
So I wish you a good mornin'.
        —*Jacobite Ballad : Hey Johnnie Cope.*

They put on him a *philabeg*,
An' up his dowp they rammed a peg,
How he did skip, and he did roar,
The deils ne'er saw sic fun before.

They took him niest to Satan's ha',
There to lilt wi' his grandpapa ;
Says Cumberland, I'll no gang ben
For fear I meet wi' Charlie's men.
        —*Jacobite Ballad : Bonnie Laddie
            Highland Laddie.*

Pickle, a small quantity ; from the Italian *piccolo*, small, akin to the Gaelic *beag* (or *peag*), little. *Pickle* in familiar English, as applied to a small, unruly, and troublesome boy, is of the same origin ; " a wee *pickle* saut," a very small quantity of salt ; " a *pickle* o' tow," a small quantity of flax or hemp for spinning into yarn. *Pickle* is sometimes used for *pilfer*, to steal small things. " To *pickle* in one's ain pock, or peuk," *i.e.*, to take grain out of one's own bag, is a proverbial expression signifying to depend on one's own resources or exertions. A hen is said to "*pickle* up" when she searches for and feeds on grain. The word, in these senses, is not from the same source as *pickle*, to preserve in salt or vinegar.

> She gies the herd a *pickle* nits
> And twa red-cheekit apples.
> —BURNS : *Hallowe'en.*

Pig, an earthen pitcher or other vessel, a flower-pot. *Piggerie,* a place for the manufacture of crockery and earthenware. *Pigman* and *pigwife,* hawkers of crockery, or keepers of shops where earthenware is sold ; from the Gaelic *pigeadh,* an earthen pot or jar ; *pigean,* a little pot ; *pigeadair,* a potter or manufacturer of crockery. The English *pig iron,* iron in a lump, before its final manufacturing by fire into a superior quality, seems to be derived from its coarse nature, as resembling the masses of clay from which crockery and earthenware are formed by the similar agency of fire.

> My Paisley *piggy*
> Contains my drink, but then, oh,
> No wines did e'er my brains engage
> To tempt my mind to sin, oh.
> —CHAMBERS'S *Scots Songs : The Country Lass.*

She that gangs to the well wi' ill-will
Either the *pig* breaks or the water will spill.
> —ALLAN RAMSAY'S *Scots Proverbs.*

Where the *pig's* broken, let the shards lie.
> —*Idem.*

An English lady, who had never before been in Scotland, arranged to spend the night at a respectable inn, in a small provincial town in the south. Desiring to make her as comfortable as possible, Grizzy, the chambermaid, on showing her to the bedroom, said—

"Would you like to hae a *pig* in your bed this cauld nicht, mem ?"

"A what ?" said the lady.

"A *pig*, mem ; I will put a *pig* in your bed to keep you warm !"

"Leave the room, young woman ; your mistress shall hear of your insolence."

"Nae offence, I hope, mem. It was my mistress bade me ask it, an' I'm sure she meant it oot o' kindness."

The lady was puzzled, but feeling satisfied that no insult was intended, she looked at the girl and then said pleasantly—

"Is it common in this country for ladies to have *pigs* in their beds ?"

"Gentlemen hae them tae, mem, when the weather's cauld. I'll steek the mouth o't an' tie it up in a clout."

A right understanding was come to at last, and the lady found the *pig* with hot water in her bed not so disagreeable as she imagined.—DOUGLAS'S *Scottish Wit and Humour.*

A rich Glasgow manufacturer, an illiterate man who had risen from the ranks, having ordered a steam yacht, sent for a London artist to decorate the panels in the principal cabin. The artist asked what kind of decoration he required ? The reply was, *Ony thing simple, just a pig wi' a flower.* Great was the surprise of the Glasgow body when the work was completed, to see that the decoration consisted of swine, each with a flower in its jaws, which had been painted on every panel. He made no complaint—paid the bill, and declared the effect to be satisfactory, though "it was no exactly what he had meant in ordering it." — *Traits of Scottish Life.*

Pike, to pick and steal ; *pikie,* one addicted to pilfering and petty thefts.

> By these *pickers* and stealers.
> —SHAKSPEARE : *Hamlet.*

Pinch and drouth, hunger and thirst.

> Nae mair wi' *pinch and drouth* we'll pine
> As we hae done—a dog's propine ;
> But quaff our draughts o' rosy wine,
> Carle ! an' the king come.
> —*Jacobite Song.*

Pinkie-small, the smallest candle that is made, the weakest kind of table beer, anything small. The word is also applied to the eye when contracted.

There's a wee *pinkie* hole in the stocking.—JAMIESON.

Possibly this word is from the Latin *punctus*, a point, or from the Dutch and Flemish *pink*, the little finger, and *pink-oogen*, to look with half-closed eyes. The Kymric *pinc* signifies a small branch or twig.

Pirrie-dog, a dog that follows at his master's heels; *pirrie*, to follow and fawn upon one, like a dependant, for what can be gained from or wheedled out of him. Jamieson derives this word from the Teutonic *paeren*, or *paaren*, to pair or couple; and refers to *parry*, an Aberdeenshire word, with a quotation, "When ane says *parry*, a' say *parry*," signifying that when anything is said by a person of consequence, it is echoed by every one else. The true origin both of *pirrie* and the Aberdonian *parry* seems to be the Gaelic *peire*, a polite word for the breech. A dog that follows at the *heels* is a euphemism for a less mentionable part of the person. Jamieson suggests that the Aberdeenshire *parry* is derived from the French *il parait ;* but the Gaelic *peire* better suits the humour of the aphorism.

Piss-a-bed, a vulgar name for the dandelion or taraxacum—a beautiful, though despised, wild flower of the fields. The word appears to have originated in Scotland, and thence to have extended to England. It is a corruption of the Gaelic *pios*, a cup, and *buidhe*, yellow—a yellow cup, not, however, to be confounded with buttercup, another wild flower—the companion in popular affection of the daisy.

The daisy has its poets,—all have striven
　　Its world-wide reputation to prolong ;
But here's its yellow neighbour !—who
　　has given
　　The dandelion a song?

Come, little sunflower, patient in neglect,
　　Will ne'er a one of them assert thy
　　claim,
But, passing by, contemptuously connect
　　Thee and thy Scottish name ?
—ROBERT LEIGHTON : *To a Dandelion.*

Several years before Robert Leighton strove to vindicate the fair fame of the dandelion, a couplet in its praise appeared in the *Illustrated London News*, in a poem entitled " Under the Hedge " : —

Dandelions with milky ring,
Coins of the mintage of the spring.

Pit-dark, dark as in the bottom of a pit.

'Tis yet *pit-dark*, the yard a' black about,
And the night fowl begin again to shout.
　　　　　　—Ross's *Helenore.*

It is very probable that *pit-dark* was the original form of the English *pitch-dark*, as dark as *pitch, i.e.,* as dark as *tar*, or coal tar. The etymology from pit, a hole, is preferable.

Pixie, a fairy. This Scottish word is used in some parts of England, particularly in the south and west. It has been supposed to be a corruption of *puck*, or *puckie*, little *puck*, sometimes called Robin Goodfellow. It is more probably from the Gaelic *beag* (peg), little, *sith* (shee), a fairy, anglicised into *pixie*, a little fairy, a fairy sprite. *Puck* is the name of one particular goblin and sprite in Shakspeare, and in popular tradition; but the *pixies* are multitudinous, and the words *puck* and *pixie* are from different sources. The English *puck* is the word that, in one variety or another, runs through many European languages. The Welsh or Kymric has *pwca* (pooca), a goblin, a sprite, the Gaelic *bocan*, and Lowland Scottish *bogie*, the Russian *bug*, the Dutch and Flemish *spook*, the German *spuk*, &c.

Pixie-rings are fairy-rings, supposed to be made in the grass by the footsteps, not of one *puck*, but of many little sprites that gamble by moonlight on the green *pixie-stool*, a popular name for the fungus, sometimes called toad-stool; *pixie-led*, bewildered and led astray by the *ignis fatuus*, Jack o' Lantern, or Will o' the Wisp.

Plack, an ancient Scottish coin of the value of one-twelfth of an English penny.

> There's your *plack* an' my *plack*,
> An' Jenny's bawbee.
> —*Old Song.*

> Nae howdie gets a social night,
> Or *plack* frae them.
> —BURNS : *Scotch Drink.*

> Stretch a joint to catch a *plack*,
> Abuse a brother to his back.
> —BURNS : *To Gavin Hamilton.*

The word is probably derived from the ancient Flemish coin, a *plaquette*, current before the introduction into the Netherlands of the French money, reckoned by francs and centimes.

Plea, a lawsuit; the substitution of the aggregate of law for the segregate. The English verb, *to plead*, has received in Scottish parlance a past tense which does not correctly belong to it, in the phrase, " he *pled* guilty," instead of " he *pleaded* guilty," as if *plead* were a word of Teutonic origin and subject to the Teutonic inflexion which governs most of the ancient English verbs, which are derived from the Dutch, German, or Danish, such as " bleed, bled ; " " blow, blew ; " " run, ran ; " " freeze, froze," &c. &c. Verbs derived from the Latin and French cannot be correctly conjugated in the past tense, except by the addition of *d* or *ed* to the infinitive, as in " coerce, coerced ; " " plead, pleaded."

Nae *plea* is best. (It is best not to go to law at all.)—*Old Proverb.*

> When neighbours anger at a *plea*,
> The barley bree
> Cements the quarrel.—BURNS.

Pliskie, a trick, a prank. From the Gaelic *plaosgach*, a sudden noise, a flash, a blaze.

> Her lost militia fired her blood,
> Deil na they never mae do guid,
> Played her that *pliskie*.
> —BURNS: *Author's Earnest Cry and Prayer.*

Ghaist! ma certie, I sall ghaist them! If they had their heads as muckle on their wark as on her daffins, they wadna play sic *pliskies!*—SCOTT: *St. Ronan's Well.*

Plooky, swollen, blotchy, pimpled. From the Gaelic *ploc*, a tumour, a bunch, a knob, a swelling. The English slang *bloke*, a swell, is probably from the same root.

> *Plooky, plooky* are your cheeks,
> And *plooky* is your chin,
> And *plooky* are your armis twa
> My bonnie queen's layne in.
> —SCOTT'S *Minstrels of the Scottish Border: Sir Hugh Le Blonde.*

Plotcock, the devil; the dweller in the pit of hell, the fiend, the arch enemy. This singular word, or combination of words, appears in Jamieson as "from the Icelandic *Blotgod*, a name of the Scandinavian Pluto; or *blotkok*—from *blot*, to sacrifice; and *koka*, to swallow—*i.e.*, the swallower of sacrifices." May not a derivation be found nearer home than in Iceland: in the Gaelic *blot* (pronounced *plot*), a pit, a cavern; and *cog*, to conspire, to tempt, to cheat?

Since you can *cog*, I'll play no more with you.
—SHAKSPEARE: *Love's Labour's Lost.*

> Lies, *coggeries*, and impostures.
> —NARES.

The Kymric has *coegiaw*, or *cogio*, to cheat, to trick. To *cog* dice was to load the dice for the the purpose of cheating; and *cogger*, in old English, signified a swindler, a cheat. This derivation would signify the cheat, the tempter who dwells in the *cavern* or bottomless pit of hell; and might have been included by Burns in his "Address to the Deil," among the other names which he bestows upon that personage.

Plout, plouter, to wade with difficulty through mire or water; akin to the English *plod*, as in the line in Gray's Elegy :—

> The ploughman homewards *plods* his weary way.

From the Gaelic *plodan*, a clod of mud or mire, a small pool of water; *plodanachd*, the act of paddling in the water or the mud.

> *Plouting* through thick and thin.
> —GROSE.

Many a weary *plouter* she cost him
Through gutters and glaur.
—JAMIESON: *Popular Ballads.*

Had it no been, Mr. North, for your *plowterin'* in a' the rivers and lochs o' Scotland, like a Newfoundland dog.
—*Noctes Ambrosianæ.*

Ploy, a plot, scheme, contrivance.

I wish he mayna hae been at the bottom o' the *ploy* himsel'.—SCOTT: *Rob Roy.*

Pluff, a slight emission or short puff of smoke, either from a tobacco-pipe or of gas from a burning coal; possibly of the same derivation as the English *puff*, a slight, short or sudden movement of the wind or the breath.

Pockpud, an abbreviation of the contemptuous epithet of *pockpudding* applied by the Scottish multitude to the English, in the bygone days when the English were as unpopular in Scotland as the Scotch still are among the more ignorant of the lower classes in England.

> They gloom, they glower, they look sae big,
> At ilka stroke they fell a Whig;
> They'll fright the fuds o' the *Pockpuds*,
> For mony a buttock 's bare coming.
> —*Jacobite Song*, 1745.

The English *pockpuddings* ken nae better.—SIR WALTER SCOTT: *Waverley.*

Pock-shakings, a humorous and vulgar term applied to the last born child of a large family, expressive of the belief that no more are to be expected.

Poind, to lay a distraint on a debtor's goods, to make a seizure for non-payment or arrears of rent. The word was once current in English, and survives in a corrupt form, as *impound*, and *pound*, an enclosure for stray cattle. The officer whose duty it was to *impound* was formerly called a *pindar*, a word that survives in tradition or legend in the "*Pindar* of Wakefield," celebrated in connection with the deeds, real or fabulous, of Robin Hood and his merry band of poachers and out-

laws. The etymology is from the French *poigne*, the closed fist, and *empoigner*, to seize. Multiple-*poinding* is a Scottish law-phrase, expressive of a series of *poindings*.

> An' was na I a weary wight,
> They *poin'd* my gear and slew my knight:
> My servants a' for life did flee,
> An' left me in extremitie.
> —*Lament of the Border Widow.*

" A puir *poind*" signifies a weak, silly person, metaphorically applied to one who is not substantial enough to take hold of, intellectually or morally ; one of no account or importance.

Point, an old Scottish word for state of body ; almost equivalent to the modern "form," which implies good condition generally of body, mind, and manners.

Murray said that he never saw the Queen in better health or in better *point*.— ROBERTSON : *History of Mary Queen of Scots.*

This is a French idiom, nearly allied to that which is now familiar to English ears, *en bon point.* "In better *point*" signifies more plump, or in fuller habit of body.— JAMIESON.

The word *point* has so many meanings, all derivable from and traceable to the Latin *punctus*, such as the *point* of a weapon ; *puncture,* the pinch of a sharp weapon ; *punctual,* true to the *point* of time, or the time appointed, &c., as to suggest that the etymology of *point*, in the sense of the French *en bon point,* and of the old Scotch, as used by Robertson in his reference to

Queen Mary, must be other than *punctus*. *En bon point* is euphemistic for stout, fat, fleshy, inclining to corpulency — all of which words imply the reverse of *pointed*. It is possible that the true root is the Gaelic *bun* (*b* pronounced as *p*), foundation, root; applied to one who is in solid and substantial health or condition of body; well formed and established, physically and morally. The word is indicative of stability rather than of sharpness or pointedness. The now current slang of " form," derived from the language of grooms, jockeys, and racing men, springs from the same idea of healthiness and good condition. The Gaelic *bunanta* signifies firm, well-set, and established. The colloquial and vulgar word *bum* is from the same root of *bun*, and produces *fundament;* the French *fondement,* the bottom, the foundation.

Post, to tramp, to tread. To *post* the linen was to tread upon it with the bare feet in the washing-tub, a common practice among the women of the working-classes in Scotland. Seen for the first time by English travellers in the far North, the fashion excited not only their surprise, but sometimes their admiration, by the display of the shapely limbs of the bonnie Highland and Lowland lassies engaged in the work, with their petticoats kilted up to the knee,

without the faintest suspicion of immodesty. *Post* is derived from the Gaelic, "to tread;" *postadh,* treading; *postanach,* a little child that is just beginning to walk or tread. The word is thus of a different origin and meaning from *post,* an office, a station, a place, which is derived from the Latin *positum.* The *post-office* and the postal service, words which are common to nearly all the European languages, are more probably traceable to the Gaelic and Celtic source, in the sense of tread and tramp, than to the Latin *positum.* The postman *treads* his accustomed rounds to the great convenience of the public in all civilised countries.

In scouring woollen clothes or coarse linen when the strength of arm and manual friction are found insufficient, the Highland women put them in a tub with a proper quantity of water, and then with petticoats tucked up commence the operation of *posting.* When three women are engaged, one commonly tramps in the middle, and the others tramp around her. This process is called *postadh.*—ARMSTRONG'S *Gaelic Dictionary,* 1820.

Pot, a deep pool, or eddy in a river.

> The neist step that she waded in,
>   She waded to the chin;
> The deepest *pot* in Clyde water
>   They gat sweet Willie in.
> —*Ballad of Willie and May Margaret.*

Pow or **powe,** the head; from the old English *poll.* The impost called the " Poll-tax," that created such great dissatisfaction in the days of Wat Tyler, was a personal tax on the *head* or *poll.*

There is little wit in his *pow*
That lights the candle at the low [or fire].
—ALLAN RAMSAY'S *Scots Proverbs.*

The miller was of manly make,
  To meet him was nae *mows* [joke];
There durst not ten cum him to take,
  Sae noytit [thumped] he their *pows.*
    —*Christ's Kirk on the Green.*

Fat pouches bode lean *pows.*—ALLAN RAMSAY'S *Scots Proverbs.*

Blessings on your frosty *pow,*
John Anderson, my jo.
        —BURNS.

Powsoudie. Sheep's head broth. This word occurs in the humorous ballad by Francis Semple, "Fy let us a' to the bridal," which contains an ample list of all the dainty eatables served up at a marriage-feast among the rural population of Scotland in the seventeenth century.

And there'll be fadges and bracken,
  And fouth o' gude gebbocks o' skate,
Powsoudie and drammock and crowdie,
  And caller nowte-feet on a plate.
    —WATSON'S *Collection,* 1706.

The word is compounded of *pow,* the head, and *soudie,* broth.

Powt, a young fowl or chicken; from the French, *poule* and *poulte;* in English, *poultry* and *poulterer.*

Ye peep (chirp or pipe) like a *powt,*
O Tammy, my man, are ye turned a saunt?
—HEW AINSLEE: *Tam o' the Balloch.*

Pree, to taste, to sip, "to *pree* the mou," to kiss the mouth. A story has long been current that

a young English nobleman, visiting at Gordon Castle, had boasted that during his six weeks' shooting in the north he had acquired so much Scotch that it was impossible to puzzle him. The beautiful and celebrated Duchess of Gordon took up his challenge, and defied him to interpret the sentence, "Come *pree* my bonnie mou, my canty callant." It was with intense disgust that he afterwards learned what a chance he had lost by his ignorance.

Ye tell me that my lips are sweet,
Sic tales I doubt are a' deceit,
At any rate it's hardly meet,
  To *pree* their sweets before folk.
    —CHAMBERS'S *Scotch Songs : Behave
      Yoursel before Folk.*

Preen, a pin; from the Gaelic *prine,* a pin; *prineachan,* a little pin; *prinich,* to secure with pins.

Prick-me-dainty, prick-ma-leerie. These two apparently ridiculous phrases have the same meaning, that of a finical, conceited, superfine person, in his manners or dress, one who affects airs of superiority—without the necessary qualifications for the part he assumes. Jamieson suggests that *prick-me-dainty* is from the English *prick-me-daintily !* Of *prick-ma-leerie,* he conjectures nothing. Both phrases seem to be traceable to the Gaelic *breagh,* fine, beautiful, braw ; and *deanta,* complete, finished, perfected ; and *leor* or *leoir,* enough, sufficient, entirely ; so that *prick-me-dainty* resolves itself into a corruption of *breagh-me-deanta*, I am beautifully perfect; and *prick - ma - leerie* into *breagh - ma-leor*, I am beautiful entirely. A comic and scornful depreciation underlies both phrases.

Prig, to cheapen, to beat down the price; whence the English word *prig*, a conceited person, who thinks he knows better than other people. The English, "to *prig*," in the sense of committing a petty theft, appears to have no connection with the Scottish word.

Men who grew wise *priggin'* ower hops and raisins.
   —BURNS: *The Brigs of Ayr.*

   Ane o' the street-musician crew
   Is busy *priggin'* wi' him now ;
   An' twa auld sangs he swears are new,
      He pawns on Jock ;
   For an auld hod o' coals half fou,
      A weel-matched troke.
   —JAMES BALLANTINE : *Coal Jock.*

Jamieson defines to *prig* as to haggle, and derives it from the Flemish *prachgen*, to beg ; French *briguer*, barter, from *brigue*, "rechercher avec ardeur."

Prig.—I don't know how this word in Scotch means to cheapen, and in English to steal ; perhaps there is some connection which a knowledge of the root from which it comes would help us to understand. *Prig*, as a conceited person, is purely a conventional use of the word. *Prig* in Scotch has also the meaning of earnestly to entreat. "I *prigged* wi' him for mair nor an' hour that he shouldna leave me." —R. DRENNAN.

Prink and **preen.** *Prink* signifies to adorn, to dress out in finery ;

preen or *prein*, a pin—or to pin ; and *preen-head*, a pin's head.

   She has *prinked* hersell and *preen'd* hersell
      By the ae light o' the mune,
   And she's awa to Castelhaugh
      To speak wi' young Tamlane.
      —*Minstrelsy of the Scottish Border :
         Ballad of the Young Tamlane.*

Prinkling, a slight pricking; a tingling sensation, either of pain or pleasure.

   Her wily glance I'll ne'er forget,
      The dear, the lovely blinkin' o't,
   Has pierced me through and through the heart,
      And plagues me in the *prinkling* o't.
   The parson kissed the tinker's wife,
      An' coudna preach for thinking o't.
      —CHAMBERS'S *Scottish Songs : Love's
         Like a Dizziness.*

Prog, to goad, to stab, to thrust, to prick, to probe; metaphorically, to taunt, to gibe, to provoke by a sarcastic remark; a sting, a lance, an arrow. From the Kymric *proc*, a thrust; and *prociaw*, to thrust or stab.

Propine, a gift, or the power of giving. Also drink-money — equivalent to the German word *trink-geld*, the French *pour boire*, and the English *tip.* To *propine* also means to pledge another in drinking, or to touch glasses in German fashion.

   If I were there and in thy *propine*,
   Oh, what wad ye do to me.
      —*Border Minstrelsy : Lady Anne.*

Puirtith, poverty.

   Oh *puirtith* cauld, and restless love,
      Ye wreck my peace atween ye ;
   Yet *puirtith* a' I could forgi'e,
      An' 'twerna for my Jeanie.
      —BURNS.

L

Punchy, thick, short, squat, and broad; applied to the human frame. From the Gaelic *bun*, foundation; and *bunaich*, to establish firmly on a broad foundation.

Purlicue, the unnecessary flourish which people sometimes affix at the end of their signatures; also, a whim, a caprice; and, in derision, the summing up of a judgment, and the peroration of a sermon or a speech. The French *par la queue*, by the tail or finish, has been suggested as the derivation.

Puslic (more properly *buslick*), a cow-sherd, gathered in the fields when dried by the weather, and stored for winter fuel by the poor. According to Jamieson, this is a Dumfriesshire and Galloway word, and used in such phrases as "dry as a *puslick*," and "as light as a *puslick*." It is compounded of the two Gaelic words *buac*, cow-dung; and *leag*, a dropping, or to drop or let fall: used in a similar sense to the English "horse-droppings," applied to the horse-dung gathered in the roads.

Pyle, a small quantity; small as a hair, or as a grain. From the Latin *pilus*, French *poil*.

> The cleanest corn that e'er was dight
> May hae some *pyles* o' caff in.
> —BURNS: *The Unco Guid.*

Pyot, a magpie; from the Gaelic *pighe*, a bird.

> I tent it a *pyot*
> Sat chatterin' on the house heid.
> —ANDREW SUTAR: *Symon and Janet.*

Q

Quarters, a place of residence or abode, a domicile, an apartment or lodging.

> An' it's oh for siccan *quarters*
> As I gat yesternight.
> —*King James V.: We'll Gang Nae Mair a-Rovin.*

Quarters, in this sense, is not derived from *quatuor*, or from the fourth part, as is generally asserted in the dictionaries, and exemplified by the common phrase, "From which *quarter* does the wind blow?" *i.e.*, from which of the *four* points of the compass? The true derivation of *quarter*, the French *quartier*, and of the military functionary, the Quarter-master General, is the Gaelic *cuairt*, a circle. "Paris," says Bescherelle in his French Dictionary, "was formerly divided into four quarters; it is now divided into forty-eight, which, if *quarters* were translated into *circle*, would not be an incongruous expression, as it is when *quarter* represents a fourth part only." The French use the word *arrondisse-ment* in the same sense, which supports the Gaelic etymology. The *quarter* or habitation of a bird is its nest, which is a *circle.* "The circle of one's acquaintance," and "the social circle," are common expressions; and the points of the compass are all points in a circle, which, as all navigators know, are considerably more than *four.*

Quean, wench, winklot. These are all familiar or disrespectful terms for a woman.

> I wat she was a cantie *quean,*
> And weel could dance the Highland
> walloch.
> *—Roy's Wife.*

> By that the dancin' was all done,
> Their leave took less or mair,
> When the *winklots* and the woers turn'd
> To see it was heart-sair.
> *—Peblis to the Play.*

Quean, like *queen,* seems to originate in the Greek γυν, a woman ; Danish *quinde,* a woman ; *quin-delig,* feminine ; Gaelic *gin,* to beget, to generate ; *gineal,* offspring. *Wench,* by the common change of *gu* into *w,* as in *war* for *guerre,* is from the same root. *Wink-lot,* or *wench-let,* as a little *wench* or *quean,* is of the same parentage.

Queer cuffin. English and Scottish gipsy slang—a justice of the peace. This phrase is of venerable antiquity, and is a relic of the Druidical times

when the arch-druid, or chief priest, was called *coibhi (coivi),* since corrupted into *cuffin.* The arch-druid was the chief administrator of justice, and sat in his *coir,* or court (whence *queer*), accessible to all suppliants ; like Joshua, Jephtha, Eli, and Samuel, judges of Israel. A Druidical proverb, referring to this august personage of the olden time, is still current among the Gaelic-speaking population of the Highlands, that "the stone is not nearer to the ground on which it rests, than is the ear of *Coibhi* to those who apply to him for justice."

Queet, an ankle ; sometimes written *cute* (which see).

> The firstan step that she stept in,
> She steppit to the *queet ;*
> "Ochone ! alas !" said that lady,
> "The water's wondrous deep."
> —BUCHAN's *Ancient Ballads : The
> Drowned Lovers.*

> I let him cool his *cutes* at the door.
> —JAMIESON : *Aberdeenshire Proverb.*

Quey, a young cow ; from the Danish *quay,* cattle, the German *vieh,* the Dutch and Flemish *vee.*

> Amang the brachans on the brae,
> Between her and the moon,
> The Deil, or else some outler *quey,*
> Gat up and gae a croon.
> —BURNS : *Hallowe'en.*

> The cow was eager to browse the pasturage on which she had been fed when she was a young and happy *quey.—Noctes Ambrosianæ.*

R

Rad, to fear, to be afraid, or to guess.

> I am right *rad* of treasonry.
> —*Song of the Outlaw Murray.*

> O ance ye danced upo' the knowes,
>   And ance ye lightly sang,
> But in herrying o' a bee byke
>   I'm *rad* ye gat a stang.
>   —BURNS : *Ye hae been a' wrang,
>   Lassie.*

Jamieson derives *rad* from the Danish *raed*, afraid, which meets the sense of the passage in which it is used by Burns. The sense, however, would be equally well rendered by a derivation from the Danish, Flemish, and Dutch *raad*, German *rathen*, to guess or conjecture.

Ram and **ran.** The Scottish language contains many expressive and humorous words commencing with the syllables *ram* and *ran*, which are synonymous, and imply force, roughness, disorder ; and which appear to be primarily derived from the Gaelic *ran*, to roar, to bluster. Among others are—*randy*, violent or quarrelsome ; *rampage*, a noisy frolic, or an outburst of ill-humour, a word which Charles Dickens revived and rendered popular in the English vernacular ; *ramgunshock*, rough, rugged, coarse ; *ramshackle*, old, worn out with rough usage.

> Our *ramgunshock* glum gudeman,
>   Is out and owre the water.
>   —BURNS : *Had I the Wyte.*

Rangunshock. This seems to be a corruption of the Gaelic *ran*, to roar ; *gun*, without ; and *seach* (pronounced *shach*), alternation, *i.e.*, to roar incessantly, without alternation of quiet.

Rant, to be noisily joyous ; *rants*, merry-makings, riotous but joyous gatherings ; *ranter*, a merrymaker. From the Gaelic.

> My name is Rob the *ranter*.
>   —*Maggie Lauder.*

> From out the life o' publick haunts,
> But thee, what were our fairs and *rants*,
> Ev'n godly meetings o' the saunts
>   By thee inspired.
> When gapin' they besiege, the tents
>   Are doubly fired.
>   —BURNS : *Scotch Drink.*

Rattan, rottan, a rat. In Flemish the word is written *rat* or *rot*. *Baudrons*, in the following quotation, is a familiar name for a cat.

> Then that curst carmagnole, old Satan,
> Watches like *baudrons* by a *rattan*,
> Our sinful souls to get a claut on.
>   —BURNS : *Colonel De Peysten.*

"Wonderful man, Dr. Candlish," said one clergyman to another. "What versatility of talent. He's fit for onything !" "Aye, aye ! that's true ; put him doon a hole, he'd make a capital *rottan !*"— *Anecdotes of Scottish Wit and Humour.*

Rax, to reach; *raught*, reached; a corruption, or perhaps the original of the modern English word.

Never *rax* aboon your reach.

The auld guidman *raught* down the pock.
　　　　—BURNS: *Hallowe'en.*

And ye may *rax* Corruption's neck,
And gi'e her for dissection.
　　　　—BURNS: *A Dream.*

"*Rax* me a spaul o' that bubbly Jock."
Reach me a wing of that turkey.—DEAN RAMSAY.

Ream, to froth like beer, or sparkle like wine, to effervesce, to cream; from the German *rahmen*, to froth; *rahm*, yeast; Flemish *room*.

Fast by an ingle, bleezing finely,
Wi' *reaming* swats that drank divinely.
　　·　　　·　　　·
The swats sae *reamed* in Tammy's noddle,
Fair play! he cared na deils a boddle.
　　　　—BURNS: *Tam o' Shanter.*

The nappy reeks wi' mantling *ream.*
　　　　—BURNS: *The Twa Dogs.*

That merry night we got the corn in,
Oh sweetly then thou *reams* the horn in.
　　　　—BURNS: *Scotch Drink.*

Reaming dish, a shallow dish for containing the milk until it is ready for being creamed.

Red-wud, stark, raging mad.

And now she's like to run *red-wud*
　　About her whisker.
　—BURNS: *Earnest Cry and Prayer.*

Red, used as an intensitive prefix to a word, is not uncommon in English and Scottish literature. *Red* vengeance is a vengeance that demands blood; and possibly *red-wud* may mean a madness that prompts blood.

In Gaelic the great deluge is called the *Dile Ruadh*, or red-flood.

Rede, advice, counsel.

Rede me noght, quod Reason,
No ruth to have
Till lords and ladies
Loves alle truth
And hates alle harlotrie.
　—*Vision of Piers Ploughman.*

Short *rede* is good *rede.*
—ALLAN RAMSAY'S *Scots Proverbs.*

I *rede* ye weel—tak care o' skaith—
　See there's a gullie!
　—BURNS: *Death and Dr. Hornbook.*

Ye gallants wight, I *rede* ye right,
　Beware o' bonnie Anne.
　　　　—BURNS.

This word was once good English, as appears from the extract from "Piers Ploughman," and was used by Chaucer, Gower, and Shakspeare. It is either from the Flemish and Dutch *raed*, counsel; the German *reden*, to speak; or the Gaelic *radh*, *raidh*, or *raite*, a saying, an aphorism.

Renchel, a tall, lean, lanky person; from the Gaelic *reang*, or *reing*, thin, lean; and *gillie*, a youth, a young man, a fellow.

He's naething but a lang *renchel*.
　　　　—JAMIESON.

Rhaim, Rhame. According to Jamieson, these words signify either a commonplace speech, a rhapsody; or "to run over anything in a rapid and unmeaning way," "to repeat by rote, to reiterate." He thinks it a corruption of *rhyme*, "because proverbs were anciently expressed in a sort of rhyme."

Is not the true derivation of the word the Teutonic *rahm*, the Flemish *room*, froth ; to *ream*, to cream, to froth, to effervesce like soda-water or champagne? "A *frothy* speaker" is a common expression of disparagement.

Rickle or **ruckle**, a loose heap ; *rickler*, a term of contempt applied to a bad architect or builder.

I'm grown so thin ; I'm naething but a *rickle* o' banes.—JAMIESON.

The proud Percy caused hang five of the Laird's henchmen at Alnwick for burning a *rickle* of houses.

SCOTT : *The Monastery.*

A wild goose out o' season is but a *ruckle* o' banes.—*Noctes Ambrosianæ.*

Rigging. In English this word is seldom used except in reference to ships, and the arrangements of their masts, spars, ropes, &c. In the Scottish language it is employed to signify the roof, cross-beams, &c., of a house.

This is no my ain house,
    I ken by the *rigging* o't ;
Since with my love I've changed vows,
    I dinna like the bigging [building] o't.
                —ALLAN RAMSAY.

There by the ingle-cheek
        I sat,
And heard the restless rattons squeak
        About the *riggin'*.
            —BURNS : *The Vision.*

The word is derived from the Teutonic *ruck*, the Flemish *rug*,

a ridge, top, or back ; whence the *ridge* at the top of the house, the roof. The *rigging* tree is the roof tree. The *rigging* of a vessel is in like manner the roof, or ridge of a ship, as distinguished from the hull. So the colloquial expression to "rig out," to dress, to accoutre, to adorn, to put the finishing touch to one's attire, comes from the same idea of completion, which is involved in the *rigging* of a ship or of a house.

Rigwoodie, old, lean, withered.

Withered beldams, auld and droll,
    Rigwoodie hags.
        —BURNS : *Tam o' Shanter.*

Rigwoodie.—" Old, lean, withered." Mr. Robert Chambers says it means "worthy of the gallows." Neither of these meanings is correct. *Rigwoodie* is the name of the chain or rope which passes across the saddle to support the shafts of a cart or other conveyance—what an Englishman would call the back band. This very likely was anciently made of twisted woodies or *saugh* or willow *wands*, now it is generally made of twisted chain and of iron. By a very evident metonomy Burns applied the twisted wrinkled appearance of a *rigwoodie* to these old wrinkled hags. —R. DRENNAN.

Rind or **rhynd**, hoar frost ; a corruption of the English *rime*, or possibly of the Kymric *rhym*, great cold ; *rhyme*, to shiver. Jamieson derives the Scottish *rhynd* and the English *rime* from the Anglo-Saxon *hrim*, and the Dutch and Flemish *rym ;* but in these languages *rym*—more correctly *rijm*—signifies rhyme, in versification, not *rime* or frost. *Rhind* is all but obsolete in Lowland Scotch, and has been superseded by *cranreuch*, sometimes written *crandruch*, a particularly cold and penetrating mist or fog. The etymology is uncertain, but the word is most probably a corruption and mispronunciation by the Lowland Scotch of the Gaelic *grainn*, horrible ; whence *cranreuch*, from *grainn* and *driugh*, penetrate, ooze, drip ; whence also the word *drook*, to saturate with moisture, and *drookit*, wet through. Jamieson derives *cranreuch* from the Gaelic *cranntarach*, but no such word is to be found in the Gaelic dictionaries of Armstrong, Macleod, and Dewar, MacAlpine, or the Highland Society of Edinburgh.

When hailstones drive wi' bitter skyte,
And infant frosts begin to bite
  In hoary *cranreuch* drest.
        —BURNS : *The Jolly Beggars.*

The French word for hoar-frost or *cranreuch* is *verglas*, which is also of Gaelic origin, from *fuar*, cold, and *glas*, grey.

Ringled-eyed, squinting.

He's out-shinned, in-kneed, and *ringled-
  eyed* too,
Auld Rob Morris is the man I'll ne'er
  lo'e.
        —ALLAN RAMSAY : *Auld Rob
                Morris.*

Rink, a space cleared out and set aside for sport or jousting, and in winter for curling or skating on the ice.

Trumpets and shalms with a shout
  Played ere the *rink* began,
And equal judges sat about
  To see wha tint or wan
    The field that day.
  —ALLAN RAMSAY : *The Evergreen.*

Then Stevan cam steppand in,
  Nae *rink* might him arrest.
        —*Christ's Kirk on the Green.*

Jamieson derives *rink* from the English *ring*, a circle ; but it is more probably from the Gaelic *rianaich*, to arrange, to set in order, to prepare.

Ripp, a handful of unthrashed ears of corn pulled out of the sheaf or stack to give to an animal ; from the Gaelic *reub*, to rend, to pull out.

A guid New Year I wish thee, Maggie ;
Hae ! there's a *ripp* to thy auld baggie.
        —BURNS : *Auld Farmer to his
                Auld Mare Maggie.*

An' tent their duty, e'en and morn,
Wi' teats o' hay and *ripps* o' corn.
        —BURNS : *Mailie, the Author's
                Pet Yowe.*

Rippet, a slight matrimonial quarrel. The word seems to be derived either from the Gaelic *riapaladh*, mismanagement, bungling, misunderstanding, or from *reubte*, a rent, from *reub*, to tear, to rend, to pull asunder ; the English *rip*, or *rip up*.

Mr. Mair, a Scotch minister, was rather short tempered, and had a wife named Rebecca, whom, for brevity sake, he called Beckie. He kept a diary, and among other entries this one was very frequent. " Beckie and I had a *rippet*, for which I desire to be humble." A gentleman who had been on a visit to the minister went to Edinburgh and told the story to a minister and his wife there, when the lady replied, "Weel, weel! he must have been an excellent man that Mr. Mair. My husband and I sometimes have *rippets*, but deil tak' me if *he's* ever humble."—DEAN RAMSAY'S *Reminiscences.*

Rippet means a noise or disturbance of any kind, not specifically and only a domestic quarrel between husband and wife. I have often been told by my mother, when a boy, to be "quate and no breed sic a *rippet.*"—R. DRENNAN.

Rispie, a bulrush; the badge of the clan Mackay, worn in the bonnet.

Among the greene *rispies* and the reeds. —ALLAN RAMSAY : *The Evergreen—The Golden Terge.*

Jamieson erroneously defines *rispie* to mean coarse grass, and derives the word from the English *rasp,* to scrape, with which, however, it has not the slightest connection. It seems to be derived from the Gaelic *rias,* or *riasg,* a moor, a fen, a marsh, where bulrushes grow; and thus to signify a marsh flower or bulrush.

Ritt, to thrust with a weapon, to stab. The etymology cannot be traced to the Gaelic, the German, the Flemish, or any other of the known sources of the Scottish language. Jamieson seems to think it signifies to scratch with a sharp instrument. It is possibly a corruption of *right;* "*ritted* it through " may mean, drove it *right* through.

Young Johnston had a rust-brown sword Hung low down by his gair [belt], And he *ritted* it through the young Colonel, That word he never spak mair. —MOTHERWELL'S *Collection: Ballad of Young Johnson.*

Roddins, the red berries of the hawthorn, the wild rose, the sweet briar, and the mountain ash, more commonly called *rowan,* or *rodden,* in Scotland; from the Gaelic *ruadh,* red. Jamieson confines the use of the word to the berries of the mountain ash, but in this he is mistaken, as appears from the following :—

I've mair need o' the *roddins,* Willie, That grow on yonder *thorn.*
. . . .
He's got a bush o' *roddins* till her That grew on yonder thorn, Likewise a drink o' Maywell water Out o' his grass-green horn. —BUCHAN'S *Ancient Ballads,* vol. ii. : *The Earl of Douglas and Dame Oliphant.*

Roop, roup, to call out, especially if the voice be harsh and rough ; *roopet* or *roupit,* rendered hoarse by cold or by violent vociferation. This word seems to be from the Flemish *roop,* to cry out ; the German *rufen,* to call.

Alas ! my *roupit* Muse is *hearse.* —BURNS : *Earnest Cry and Prayer.*

Here the poet is guilty of a pleonasm, unusual with one so terse in expression, of using in one line the two synonymous words of *roupit* and *hearse* (hoarse). But he was sorely in need of a rhyme for the coarse but familiar word in the third line of the poem. *Roup* also signifies a sale by auction, from the "crying out" of the person who offers the goods for sale.

Roose, rouse, to praise or extol ; and thence, it has been supposed, by extension of meaning, to drink a health to the person praised ; also, any drinking-bout or carousal. The etymology of *roose*, in the sense of to praise, as used in Scotland, is unknown. *Rouse*, in the sense of a drinking-bout, has been held by some to be a corruption of *carouse*, and by others, of the German exclamation, *heraus !* signifying " empty the cup or glass," drink it !

> *Roose* the ford as ye find it.
> *Roose* the fair day at e'en.
> —ALLAN RAMSAY'S *Scots Proverbs.*

> To *roose* ye up and ca' ye guid,
> An' sprang o' great an' noble bluid.
> —BURNS : *To Gavin Hamilton.*

> He *roos'd* my e'en sae bonnie blue,
> He *roos'd* my waist sae genty sma'.
> —BURNS : *Young Jockey.*

> Some o' them hae *roosed* their hawks,
> And other some their houndes,
> And other some their ladies fair.
> —MOTHERWELL'S *Ancient Minstrelsy.*

In all the above quotations the meaning of *roose* is clearly to praise or extol. But the English *rouse* has not that meaning.

> No jocund health that Denmark drinks to-day,
> But the great cannon to the clouds shall tell,
> And the kings *rouse*, the heavens shall bruit again,
> Bespeaking earthly thunder.
> —SHAKSPEARE : *Hamlet.*

> I have took since supper a *rouse* or two too much.
> —BEAUMONT AND FLETCHER.

It is thus clear that the Scottish *roose* and the English *rouse*

are of different origin. The German *rausch*, and the Dutch and Flemish *roes*, signify semi-intoxication ; *roesig*, in these languages, means nearly drunk, or, as the French phrase it, " entre deux vins," or, as the English slang expresses it, "half seas over." In Swedish, *rus* signifies drunkenness ; *taga rus*, to get drunk ; and *rusig*, inebriated. In Danish, *ruus* signifies drunkenness, and *ruse*, intoxicating liquor. Nares rightly suspected that the English *rouse* was of Danish origin. The passage in *Hamlet*, act i. scene 4—

> The king doth wake to-night and takes his *rouse*,

signifies the king takes his *drink*, and all the other instances quoted by Nares are susceptible of the same interpretation. Nares quotes from Harman's " Caveat for Common Cursitors," 1567 :—

> I thought it my bounden duty to acquaint your goodness with the abominable, wicked, and detestable behaviour of all these *rowsey*, ragged rabblement of rakehells.

He defines *rowsey* in this passage to mean *dirty*, but, in view of the Danish, Dutch, and Flemish derivations, it ought to be translated *drunken*.

Row, to enwrap, to entwine, to enfold, also to roll or flow onwards like the wavelets on the river ; from the Gaelic *ruith* (*rui*), to flow, to ripple.

Hap and *row,* hap and *row,*
Hap and *row* the feetie o't,
It is a wee bit eerie thing,
I downa bide the greetie o't.
                        —*Creech.*

Then round she *row'd* her silken plaid.
        —*Ballad of Fremmet Hall.*

Where Cart runs *rowan'* to the sea.
                        —BURNS.

Rowan, the mountain ash ; a tree
that grows in great perfection
in the Highlands of Scotland,
and named from its beautiful
red berries, *ruadh,* the Gaelic
for red.   This tree, or a twig of
it, is supposed, in the superstition of Scotland, to be a charm
against witchcraft.   Hence, it
has been supposed, but without sufficient authority, that
the phrase,"Aroint thee, witch,"
in Shakspeare, is a misprint for
"a *rowan-tree,* witch!"   The
word occurs in no author previous to Shakspeare.

The night was fair, the moon was up,
  The wind blew low among the gowans,
Or fitful rose o'er Athole woods,
  An' shook the berries frae the *rowans.*
        —*The Wraith of Garry Water.*

Rowan tree and red thread
Mak' the witches tyne [lose] their speed.
        —*Old Scottish Proverb.*

Rowt, to bellow or low like cattle ;
from the Gaelic *roiteach,* bellowing.   Nares erroneously renders
it " snore."   " The rabble *rowt,*"
i.e., the roaring rabble, the
clamorous multitude.

The kye stood *routin* in the loan.
        —BURNS : *The Twa Dogs.*

Nae mair thou'lt *rowte* out o'er the dale,
  Because thy pasture's scanty.
        —BURNS : *The Ordination.*

And the king, when he had righted
himself on the saddle, gathered his breath,
and cried to do me nae harm ; "for," said
he, "he is ane o' our Norland stots, I ken
by the *rowte* o' him ;" and they a' laughed
and *rowted* loud eneuch.—SCOTT : *Fortunes of Nigel.*

Rowth, plenty, abundance ; a
word formed from *roll* and *roll-
eth,* Scottish *row.*   It is expressive of the same idea as in the
English phrase, applied to a
rich man, "He *rolls* in wealth."
A peculiarly Scottish word
which never seems to have been
English.   It has been suggested
that it is derived from the Gaelic
ruathar, a sudden rush, onset,
or inpouring ; whence metaphorically, a sudden or violent
influx of wealth or abundance.

A *rowth* o' auld knick-knackets,
Rusty airn caps, and jingling jackets.
        —BURNS : *Captain Grose.*

The ingle-neuk, with *routh* o' bannocks
and bairns !—DEAN RAMSAY : *A Scottish
Toast or Sentiment.*

A *rowth* aumrie and a close nieve.—
JAMIESON.

It's ye have wooers mony a ane,
  An' lassie ye're but young, ye ken,
Then wait a wee, and cannie wale,
  A *routhie* butt, a *routhie* ben.
        —BURNS : *Country Lassie.*

God grant your lordship joy and health,
Long days and *routh* of real wealth.
        —ALLAN RAMSAY : *Epistle to
            Lord Dalhousie.*

A houndless hunter and a gunless
gunner see aye *rowth* o' game.—ALLAN
RAMSAY'S *Scots Proverbs.*

Fortune, if thou wilt give me still
Hale breeks, a scon, a whisky gill,
And *rowth* o' rhyme to rave at will,
  Take a' the rest.
        —BURNS : *Scotch Drink.*

Roxle, to grunt, to speak with a hoarse voice; Gaelic *roc*, a hoarse voice; French *rauque*, hoarse; English *rook*, a bird that has a hoarse voice in cawing; Gaelic, *rocair*, a man with a hoarse voice; *rocail*, croaking. Mr. Herbert Coleridge, in his dictionary of "The Oldest Words in the English Language," from the semi-Saxon period of A.D. 1250 to A.D. 1800, derives it from the Dutch *rotelen*, but the word does not appear in any Dutch or Flemish dictionary.

Royet, wild, dissipated, riotous, unruly. *Roit*, according to Jamieson, is a term of contempt for a woman, often conjoined with an adjective, denoting bad temper; as, "an *ill-natured roit*." The resemblance to the English *riot* suggests its derivation from that word, but both *royet* and *riot* are traceable to the Gaelic *raoit*, noisy, obstreperous, or indecent mirth and revelry; and *ruidhtear*, a loud reveller; *riatach*, indecent, immodest. Jamieson, however, derives it from the French *roide*, stiff, which he wrongly translates fierce, ungovernable.

> *Royet* lads may make sober men.
> —ALLAN RAMSAY'S *Scots Proverbs.*

Ruddy, to roar like thunder, or to rumble like wind in the stomach. Derivation uncertain, but possibly akin to *rowte* or *rowtin*, the bellowing of cattle.

> I in its wame heard Vulcan *ruddy*.
> —BEATTIE: *John o' Arnha'.*

Rude, the complexion; the ruddy face of a healthy person. From the Flemish *rood*, red, which has the same meaning; Gaelic *ruath*, red, corrupted by the Lowland Scotch into *Roy*, as in Rob *Roy*, Gilde*roy*, and applied to the hair as well as to the complexion.

> Of all their maidens myld as meid
> Was nane sae gymp as Gillie,
> As ony rose her *rude* was reid,
> Her lyre was like the lillie.
> —*Christ's Kirk on the Green.*

> She has put it to her *roudes* lip,
> And to her *roudes* chin,
> She has put it to her fause, fause mouth,
> But never a drap gaed in.
> —*Border Minstrelsy: Prince Robert.*

Sir Walter Scott, in a note to this ballad, glosses *roudes* by "haggard." Surely this is wrong?

Rug, to pull. Derivation uncertain.

> Trying to *rug* them off, tae an' heel.—
> *Noctes Ambrosianæ.*

Rugg, a great bargain, a thing ridiculously cheap; to spoil, to plunder, to seize. From the Gaelic *rug*, the past tense of *beir*, to take hold of.

> When borrowers brak, the pawns were *rugg*,
> Rings, beads of pearl, or siller jug,
> I sold them off—ne'er fashed my lug
> Wi' girns or curses;
> The mair they whinged, it gart me hug
> My swelling purses.
> —ALLAN RAMSAY: *Last Speech of a Wretched Miser.*

Rule the roast. This originally Scottish phrase has obtained currency in England, and excited much controversy as to its origin. It has been derived from the function of a chief cook, to be master or mistress in the kitchen, and as such, to "rule the *roasting.*" It has also been derived from the mastery of the cock among the hens, as ruling the place where the fowls *roost* or sleep. In the Scottish language *roost* signifies the inner roof of a cottage, composed of spars or beams reaching from one wall to the other ; the highest interior part of the building. Hence, to rule the *roast,* or *roost,* or to rule the house, to be the master.

Rummel, to make a confused sound ; from *rumble.*

> Your crackjaw words of half an ell,
> That *rummel* like a witch's spell.
> —GEORGE BEATTIE : *John o' Arnha'.*

Rump, to break ; *rumpit,* broken ; or in English slang " to be cleaned out," or exhausted of money by losses at gambling. " Perhaps," says Jamieson, " in allusion to an animal whose tail has been cut off near the *rump !* " The etymology did not need the " perhaps " of the non-erudite author, and is to be found in the French *rompre,* to break, and *rompu,* broken.

Rumple-bane, the lowest bone of the spine.

> At length he got a carline grey,
>   And she's come hirplin ' hame, man,
> And she fell o'er the buffet stool,
>   And brak her *rumple-bane,* man.
> —JOHNSON's *Musical Museum.*

Rung, a cudgel, a staff, a bludgeon, the step of a ladder ; any thick strong piece of wood that may be wielded in the hand as a weapon. From the Gaelic *rong,* which has the same meaning. The modern Irish call a bludgeon a *shillelah ;* also a Gaelic word for *seileach,* a willow, and *slaith* (*sla*), a wand.

> Auld Scotland has a raucle tongue,
> She's just a deevil wi' a *rung.*
> —BURNS.

Runk, to whisper secret slanders, also a term of opprobrium applied to an old woman, a gossip, or a scandal-monger. From the Gaelic *runach,* dark, mysterious, also a confidant ; *run,* a secret, a mystery ; and by extension of the original meaning, a scandal repeated under the pretence of a secret and confidential disclosure.

Runt, a deprecatory or contemptuous name for an old woman ; from the German *rind,* and the Flemish *rund,* an ox, or a cow that calves no longer ; also, the hard stalk of kail or cabbage left in the ground, that has ceased to sprout.

Ruther. This word, according to Jamieson, means to storm, to bluster, to roar, also an uproar or commotion. It is probably from the Gaelic *rutharach,* quarrelsome, contentious, and *rutharachd,* quarrelsomeness.

Ryg-bane, or **rig-bane,** the spine or backbone ; from the Flemish *rug*, the German *rucken*, the back, and *bein*, a bone. The original meaning of *rug* and *rucken* is that of extension in length; from the Gaelic *ruig*, to extend, to reach, and *ruigh*, or *righe*, an arm; *ruighe* (the English *ridge*) is the extension of a mountain, or of a series of hills forming, as it were, the spine or backbone of the land.

S

Saikless, innocent, guiltless; from the Teutonic *sach*, the cause; whence *sachless*, or *saikless*, without cause.

. "Oh, is this water deep," he said,
    "As it is wondrous dim;
Or is it sic as a *saikless* maid,
    And a leal true knicht may swim?"
            —*Ballad of Sir Roland.*

Leave off your douking on the day,
    And douk upon the night,
And where that *saikless* knight lies slain,
    The candles will burn bright.
    —*Border Minstrelsy: Earl Richard.*

Sain, to bless, to preserve in happiness; from the German *segnen*, to bless, and *segen*, a benediction; Flemish *zegenen*— all probably from the Latin *sanus*.

Sain yoursel frae the deil and the laird's bairns.
    —ALLAN RAMSAY'S *Scots Proverbs.*

Sairing, enough, that which satisfies one; used both in a favourable and unfavourable sense. "He got his *sairin*," applied to a drubbing or beating; in the ironical sense, he got enough of it, or, as Jamieson phrases it in English, "he got his bellyfull of it." A corruption of *serve*, or serve the purpose—therefore, a sufficiency.

You couldna look your *sairin* at her face,
So meek it was, so sweet, so fu' o' grace.
            —Ross's *Helenore.*

Sairy or **sair**, very, or very great; from the German *sehr*, as in *sehr schön*, *sehr gut*, very fair, very good; sometimes used in English in the form of *sore;* as, "sore distressed," very much distressed.

And when they meet wi' *sair* disasters,
Like loss o' health or want o' masters.
            —BURNS: *The Twa Dogs.*

It's a *sair* dung bairn that mauna greet.
    —ALLAN RAMSAY'S *Scots Proverbs.*

    It's a *sair* field where a' are slain.
            —*Idem.*

The state of man does change and vary:
Now sound, now sick, now blythe, now sary,
Now dansand merry, now like to dee.
    —ALLAN RAMSAY: *The Evergreen.*

Sak, saik, sake, blame, guilt; whence *sachless, sackless, saikless*, guiltless, innocent; and also, by extension of meaning, foolish, worthless, as in the corresponding English word, "an innocent," to signify an imbecile.

The root of all these words appears to be either the German *jach* (see SAIKLESS, *ante*), or the Gaelic *sag*, weight; whence also *sag*, to weigh or press down, and *sack*, a bag to carry heavy articles. The idea of weight, as applied to guilt and blameworthiness, is obvious, as in the line quoted by Jamieson, " Mary was *sackless* o' breaking her vow," *i.e.*, she was not *burthened* with the guilt of breaking her vow. A *saikless* person, or an imbecile, in like manner, is one who is not weighted with intellect. *Sag*, in English, is said of a rope not drawn tightly enough, and weighed down in the middle. It also signifies to bend or give way under pressure of weight.

The heart I bear
Shall never *sag* with doubt or shake with fear.—SHAKSPEARE.

" It is observable," says Dr. Johnson, "that *sack* (in the sense of a bag for carrying weight) is to be found in all languages, and is therefore conceived to be antediluvian." The phrase " sair *saught*," quoted by Jamieson, and defined as signifying " much exhausted, and especially descriptive of bodily debility," is traceable to the same root, and might be rendered, sorely weighed down by weakness or infirmity. There is, however, in spite of these examples, much to be said in favour of the derivation from the German *sach*.

Sandie, Sanders, Sawney, Sannock, abbreviations of the favourite Scottish Christian name of Alexander ; from the last two syllables. The English commonly abbreviate the first two syllables into *Aleck*. In the days immediately after the accession of James VI. to the English throne, under the title of James I., to the time of George III. and the Bute Administration, when Scotsmen were exceedingly unpopular, and when Dr. Samuel Johnson — the great Scoto-phobist, the son of a Scotch bookseller at Lichfield— thought it prudent to disguise his origin, and overdid his prudence by maligning his father's countrymen, it was customary to designate a Scotsman as a *Sawney.* The vulgar epithet, however, is fast dying out, and is nearly obsolete.

An', Lord ! remember singing *Sannock*,
Wi' hale breeks, saxpence, and a bannock.
BURNS : *To James Tait.*

Sanshagh or **sanshach.** Jamieson defines this word as meaning wily, crafty, sarcastically clever, saucy, disdainful, and cites— " ' He's a *sanshach* callant, or chiel,' is a phrase used in Aberdeenshire and the Mearns." He thinks it is derivable from the Gaelic *saobh-nosach*, angry, peevish, irascible ; but it is more probable that it comes from *sean*, old, and *seach* (*shach*), dry or caustic, an old man of a cynical temper.

Sant or **saunter**. Jamieson defines this word as meaning " to disappear, to vanish suddenly out of sight," and quotes it as in use in Ettrick Forest. " It's *santed*, but it will, may be, cast up again." In Wright's " Dictionary of Obsolete and Provincial English," *saunt*, a northern word, is said to signify to vanish; and *saum*, to wander lazily about. The word is nearly, if not quite obsolete, and does not appear either in Burns or Allan Ramsay. *Sant* was formerly current in the same sense as *saunter*, to roam idly or listlessly about ; to *saum*, to disappear from, or neglect one's work or duty. Johnson derived *saunter* from an expression said to have been used in the time of the crusades, in application to the idle vagabonds and impostors who roamed through the country and begged for money to help them on their way to the Holy Land, or *La Sainte Terre*. *Saunter*, as now used in English, is almost synonymous with the Scottish *dauner*, q.v. But no authoritative derivation has yet been discovered, either for *sant* or *saunter*, unless that given by Mr. Wedgwood, from the German *schlendern*, can be deemed satisfactory. In Sheffield, Duke of Buckingham's Essay on "Satire," *saunter* is used in a curiously unusual sense, an investigation of which may possibly throw light on the original meaning of the word.

While *sauntering* Charles betwixt so mean
 a brace [of mistresses],
Meets with dissembling still in either place,
Affected humour or a painted face ;
In loyal libels we have often told him
How one has jilted him, the other sold him.
. . . . . .
Was ever Prince by two at once misled,
Foolish and false, ill-natured and ill-bred ?

 Sir Walter Scott cites from the same author, in reference to the *sauntering* of Charles II. :—

In his later hours, there was as much laziness as love in all those hours he passed with his mistresses, who, after all, only served to fill up his seraglio, while a bewitching kind of pleasure called *sauntering* and talking without restraint, was the true sultana he delighted in.

 In Gaelic *sannt*, and *sanntaich*, signifies to covet, to desire, to lust after ; and if this be the true derivation of the word, the passage from the Duke of Buckingham would be exceedingly appropriate. To *saunter* was applied to idle men who followed women about the streets, with libidinous intent of admiration or conversation ; *sanntaire*, a lustful man. The French have a little comedy entitled " Un monsieur qui suit les femmes," which expresses the idea of *saunterer*, as applied to Charles II.

Sap, a fool, a simpleton, a ninny. The English has *milk-sop*, an effeminate fool. *Sap* and *sop* are both derived from the Gaelic *saobh*, silly, foolish, as well as the English slang, *soft*, apt to be imposed upon.

Sark, the linen, woollen, silken, or cotton garment worn next to the skin by men and women; a shirt or shift; the French *chemise,* the German *hemde.* Weel-*sarkit,* well provided with shirts.

> The last Hallowe'en I was wauken,
> My droukit *sark*-sleeve as ye ken.
> —BURNS : *Tam Glen.*

> They reel'd, they sat, they crossed, they cleekit,
> Till ilka carlin swat and reekit,
> And coost her duddies to the wark,
> And linkit at it in her *sark!*
> .   .   .   .   .   .
> Tam tint his reason a' thegither,
> And roar'd out, "Weel done! *Cutty sark!*"
> And in an instant a' was dark.
> —BURNS : *Tam o' Shanter.*

Being asked what was the difference between Presbyterian ministers, who wear no surplices, and Episcopalians, who do, an old lady replied, "Well, ye see, the Presbyterian minister wears his *sark* under his coat, the Episcopalian wears *his sark* aboon his coat."—DEAN RAMSAY.

The phrase, "*sark-alane,*" is used to signify nude, with the exception of the shirt; and "a *sarkfu*' o' sair banes," to express the condition of a person suffering from great fatigue, or from a sound beating. The etymology of the word, which is peculiar to Scotland and the North of England, is uncertain. Attempts have been made to trace it from the Swedish, the Icelandic, the Anglo-Saxon, and the Greek, but without success.

In the "Dictionaire de la Langue Romane, ou du Vieux Langage Française" (Paris, 1768), the Scottish word *sark* is rendered *serecote,* and *serecot,* "une camisole, une chemisette."

Saugh, a willow; the French *saule,* Gaelic *seileag.*

> The glancin' waves o' Clyde
> Through *saughs* and hanging hazels glide.
> —PINKERTON : *Bothwell Bank.*

Saulie, a hired mourner, a mute, or undertaker's man. The word seems to have been employed to express the mock or feigned sorrow assumed in the lugubrious faces of these men, and to be derived from the Gaelic *sall,* mockery, satire, derision ; *samhladh,* an apparition, a ghost, has also been suggested as the origin of the word. The derivation of Jamieson from *salve reginam* is scarcely worthy of consideration.

Saur, to flavour ; *saurless,* insipid, tasteless ; supposed to be a corruption of savour. The French for a red herring is *saure ;* and *saurir,* or *saurer,* is to flavour with salt.

Scaff-raff, rubbish, refuse.

If you and I were at the Witherspoon's Latch, wi' ilka ane a gude oak hipple in his hand, we wadna turn back—no, not for half-a-dozen o' your *scaff-raff.*—SCOTT : *Guy Mannering.*

Jamieson, unaware of the indigenous roots of these words, derives them from the Swedish *scaef,* a rag, anything shaved off ; and *rafa,* to snatch away. The true etymology, however, is from the Gaelic. *sgamh* (pronounced *scav*), dross, dirt, rubbish; and *rabh* (*raff*), coarse, idle, useless.

Scag, to shrivel in the heat, or by exposure to the weather, to split, to crack in the heat; a term applied in the fishing villages of Scotland to fish, dried or fresh, that have been kept too long. " A *scaggit* haddie " is a haddock spoiled by long exposure. Jamieson hesitates between the Icelandic *skacka*, *inquare ;* and the Gaelic *sgag*, as the derivation of this word. *Sgag*, in Gaelic, signifies to shrivel up, to crack, to split, or to spoil and become putrid by long keeping ; *sgagta*, lean, emaciated.

Scance, skance. To reflect upon a person's character or conduct by charge or insinuation ; to censure, to taunt indirectly ; to glance at a subject cursorily in conversation; also, a transient look at anything. These words are not used in English, though *askance*, a recognised English word, appears to be from the same root. The ordinary derivation of *askance* is either from the Italian *schianco*, athwart, or from the Flemish and Dutch *schuin*, oblique, to squint. The latter etymology, though it meets the English sense of the word, does not correspond with the variety of meanings in which it is employed in Scotland. Neither does it explain the English *scan*, to examine, to scrutinise,—still less the *scan-*

ning, or *scansion* of the syllables or feet in a verse.

Perhaps the Gaelic *sgath*, a shadow, a reflection in the water or in a glass, *sgathan* (*sga-an*), a mirror, and *sgathanaich*, to look in a glass, may supply the root of the Scottish, if not the English words. Tried by these tests, *scance* might signify to cast a shadow or a reflection upon one, to take a rapid glance as of one's self in a glass ; and to *scan*, to examine, to scrutinise, " to hold the mirror up to nature," as Shakspeare has it. In these senses, the word might more easily be derivable from the Gaelic, which does not imply obliquity, than from the Flemish and Dutch, of which obliquity is the leading, if not the sole idea, as in the English *squint*.

Then gently *scan* your brother man,
  Still gentler sister woman ;
Though they may gang a kennin' wrang,
  To step aside is human.
      —BURNS : *Address to the Unco Guid.*

To *scan* a verse, to examine or scrutinise whether it contains the proper number of feet or syllables, or is otherwise correct, may possibly be an offshoot of the same idea ; though all the etymologists insist that it comes from the Italian *scandio*, to climb.

Scarnoch. A *scarnoch o' words* signifies a multitude of words, such as are unnecessarily used by wordy lawyers and by over garrulous Members of Parliament, who use them, as Solomon

M

said in old times, "to darken counsel," and as a wise and cynical man of more modern days—the late Prince Talleyrand—said with equal appropriateness, "pour deguiser la pensée" (to disguise their thoughts). *Scarnoch* also signifies a tumultuous din, the murmur or shouting of a crowd, and *scarochin*, a great noise. Jamieson derives these words from the Swedish *skara*, a crowd, a cohort, but the true root is the Gaelic *sgairn*, to howl as dogs, wolves, or other animals, and *sgarneach*, howling, shrieking, roaring, &c.

Scart, a scratch; *scart-free*, without a scratch or injury. *Scart* is also a name given, in most parts of Scotland, to the rapacious sea-bird, the cormorant. *Scart*, to scratch, is a softer rendering of the harsher English word; and *scart*, a cormorant, is a corruption of the Gaelic *sgarbh*, which has the same meaning.

They that bourd wi' cats may count upon *scarts*.—ALLAN RAMSAY.

"To *scart* the buttons," or draw one's hand down the breast of another, so as to touch the buttons with one's nail, is a mode of challenging to battle among Scottish boys.—JAMIESON.

Like *scarts* upon the wing by the hope of plunder led.
—*Legends of the Isles.*

D'ye think ye'll help them wi' skirlin' that gate, like an auld *skart* before a flaw o' weather?—SCOTT: *The Antiquary.*

Scaur, a steep rock, a cliff on the shore; *skerrie*, a rock in the sea. Scarborough, a watering-place

in England, signifies the town on the cliff or rock; *Skerrievore*, or the great rock or *skerrie*, from *sgeir* and *mhor*, is the name of the famous lighthouse on the West Coast of Scotland. The *skerries* are rocks in the sea among the Scilly islands. Both *scaur* and *skerrie* are traceable to the Gaelic *sgeir*, a rock in the sea, and *sgor*, a steep mountain side; whence also the English *scar* in Scarborough.

Ye that sail the stormy seas
Of the distant Hebrides.
.   .   .   .   .   .
By lordly Mull and Ulva's shore
Beware the witch of *Skerrievore.*
—*Legends of the Isles.*

Where'er ye come by creek or *scaur*,
Ye bring bright beauty.
—JAMES BALLANTINE.

Schacklock. Jamieson imagines this word to mean a pickpocket or burglar, or one who *shakes* or loosens *locks*. It is, however, a term of contempt for a lazy ne'er-do-weel, like the similar English word, *shackaback*, and is derivable from the Gaelic *seac* (*shack*), useless, withered, dried up, and *leug*, dull, sluggish, or incorrigibly lazy.

Schore, a man of high rank; *schore-chieftain*, a supreme chief. Jamieson derives *schore* from the German *schor* or *schoren*, "altus eminens"—a word which is not to be found in any German dictionary, nor in Dutch or Flemish, or any other Teutonic speech. The etymology is unknown or difficult to discover, unless it be presumed that the word was used metaphorically for *high*, in the sense of an eminence; from the Gaelic *sgor*, a steep rock, a cliff.

Schrew (sometimes written *schrow*), to curse; allied to the English *shrew*, a scolding and ill-tempered woman, and usually derived from the German *besch-reien*, to curse. A *screw*, in English slang, signifies a mean, niggardly person, who, in American parlance, would be called "a mean cuss," or curse. A miserable old horse is called a *screw*, not as the Slang Dictionary says, "from the *screw-like* manner in which his ribs generally show through the skin," but from the original sense of *shrew*, to curse—*i.e.*, a horse only fit to swear at —or possibly from the Gaelic *sgruit*, old, wrinkled, thin, meagre. *Schrewit* signifies accursed, also poisonous, which is doubtless the origin of the slang English *screwed*, intoxicated. The kindred English word *scrub*, a mean person, and *scrubbed*, vile, worthless, shabby, as used by Shakspeare in the phrase, "a little *scrubbed* boy," is evidently derived from the Gaelic *sgrub*, to act in a mean manner, and *sgrubair*, a churl, a niggard, or a despicable person. The true derivation of the Scottish *schrew* remains obscure.

In its form of *shrew* or *schrow* the word was formerly used in reference to the male sex, in the sense of a disagreeable and quarrelsome person; as in *shrewd*, an epithet applied to a man of penetration and sharp common sense. These words, whether *schrew* or *schrow* be the correct form, have given rise to many discussions among etymologists, which are not yet ended. *Shrew* or *schrow* has been derived not only from the Teutonic *schreien*, to shriek, to call out lustily, but from the little harmless animal called the *shrew* mouse, which was fabled to run over the backs of cattle and do them injury by the supposed venom of its bite. Some of these apparently incongruous or contradictory derivations are resolvable by the Gaelic *sgruth* (*sru*), to run, to flow. A *shrew* is a scold, a woman whose tongue *runs* too rapidly, or a man, if he have the same disagreeable characteristic; *shrewd* is an epithet applied to one whose ideas *run* clearly and precisely. The *shrew* mouse is the *running* mouse.

Sclaurie, to bespatter with mud; also metaphorically, to abuse, revile, to asperse, make accusation against, on the principle of the English saying, "Throw mud enough; some of it will stick." The lowland Scotch *claur*, or *glaur*, signifies mud, q.v. This word is derived from the Gaelic *clabar* (aspirated *clab-har* or *claur*), filth, mire, mud; "A gowpen o' *glaur*," or *claur*, the two hands conjoined, filled with mud. When the initial *s* was either omitted from or joined to the root-word, is not discoverable.

Scogie or **scogie-lass**, a kitchen drudge, a maid-of-all-work, a "slavey;" one unskilled in all but the commonest and coarsest work. From the Gaelic *sgog*, a fool, a dolt, one who knows nothing.

Scoil, shriek; akin to the English *squeel*.

> An' smellin' John he gaed a *scoil*,
> Then plunged and gart the water boil.
> —*John o' Arnha'*.

> Till echo for ten miles around
> Did to the horrid *scoil* resound.
> —*Ibid.*

Scold or **skald**. Fingal and the other warriors whose deeds are commemorated by Ossian, drank out of shells (scallop shells), doubtless the first natural objects that in the earliest ages were employed for the purpose. *Scold* is an obsolete word, signifying to drink a health, evidently derived from *shell*, or scallop; the Teutonic *schale*, a shell or a cup; the Danish *skiall*, the French *escaille* or *ecaille*, the Flemish and Dutch *schelp* and *schaal*, the Norse *skul*, the Greek *chalys*, the Latin *calix*, a shell or cup. Possibly the tradition that the Scandinavian warriors drank their wine or mead out of the *skulls* of their enemies whom they had slain in battle, arose from a modern mis-

conception of the meaning of *skul* — originally synonymous with the skull or cranium, or shell of the brain. *Skul* is used by the old Scottish poet, Douglas, for a goblet or large bowl.

To *scold* or *scoll*, to drink healths, to drink as a toast; *scolder*, a drinker of healths; *skul*, a salutation of one who is present, or of the respect paid to an absent person, by expressing a wish for his health when one is about to drink it.
—JAMIESON.

Skeolach (sgeolach), the name of one of Fingal's drinking cups.—MACLEOD AND DEWAR: *Gaelic Dictionary.*

The custom of drinking out of shells is of great antiquity, and was very common among the ancient Gael. Hence the expression so often met with in the Fingalian poets, "the hall of *shells*," "the chief of *shells*," "the *shell* and the song." The *scallop* shell is still used in drinking strong liquors at the tables of those gentlemen who are desirous to preserve the usages of their ancestors.—ARMSTRONG'S *Gaelic Dictionary*, 1828.

Scon or **scone**, a barley cake; from the Gaelic *sgonn*, a lump or mass.

> Leeze me on thee, John Barleycorn,
>   Thou King o' grain,
> On thee auld Scotland chaws her cood,
> In souple *scones*, the wale o' food.
> —BURNS: *Scotch Drink.*

Sconfice, discomfit, beaten, led astray, subdued; from the Gaelic *sgon*, bad, and *fios*, knowledge.

I'm unco wae for the puir lady; I'm feart she'll grow wud gin she be lang in yon hole, for it would *sconfice* a horse, forbye a body.—MACLEAY'S *Memoirs of the Clan MacGregor.*

Scoot, a tramp, a gad-about, a vagrant, a term of opprobrium given to a low woman; from

the Gaelic *sguit*, to wander.
The English *scout*, a person employed by an army to recon-
noitre, by travelling or wandering to and fro, so as to observe
the motions of the enemy, is
obviously from the same root.

Scottis bed. "This phrase," says
Jamieson, "occurs in an Aberdeen Register, but it is not easy
to affix any determinate meaning to it." May it not mean a
ship's bed, or a hammock; from
scothach, a small skiff?

Scouk, to sneak, to loiter idly or
furtively; either a corruption
of the English *skulk*, or a derivation with an allied meaning;
from the Gaelic *sguga*, a coarse,
ill-mannered, ungainly person.

They grin, they glower, they *scouk*,
they gape.
—*Jacobite Relics.*

Scouth or **skouth**, elbow-room,
space, scope, room for the arm
in wielding a weapon so as to
cut off an enemy or an obstruction at a blow; from the Gaelic
sgud, to lop, to cut off; *sgudadh*,
act of cutting down by a sudden
blow.

An' he get *scouth* to wield his tree,
I fear you'll both be paid.
—*Ballad of Robin Hood.*

By break of day he seeks the dowie
glen,
That he may *scouth* to a' his morning
len' (lend).
—ALLAN RAMSAY: *Pastoral on the
Death of Matthew Prior.*

They tak religion in their mouth,
They talk o' mercy, grace, and truth—

For what? to gie their malice *scouth*
On some poor wight,
An' hunt him down, o'er right and ruth,
To ruin straight.
—BURNS: *To the Rev. John M'Math.*

"*Scouth* and *routh*" is a proverbial phrase for elbow-room
and abundance.

That's a good gang for your horse, he'll
have *scouth* and *routh.*—JAMIESON.

Scowf, a blustering, low scoundrel. Dutch and Flemish *schoft.*
Explained in Dutch and French
dictionaries as "*maroufle, coquin,
maraud,*" *i.e.*, a low scoundrel, a
rogue, an impudent blackguard.

He's naething but a *scouf;* Danish
scuffer, to gull, to cheat, to shuffle; a cheat,
a false pretender.—JAMIESON.

Scran or **skran**, odds and ends
or scraps of eatables, broken
victuals; also applied derisively
to food or daily bread.

Scranning is a phrase used by school-
boys when they spend their pocket-money
at the pastry-cook's.—JAMIESON.

Scran-pock, a beggar's wallet to
hold scraps of food. The word
scran is derived from the Gaelic
sgrath (pronounced *sgra*), to peel,
to pare, to take off the rind or
skin, and *sgrathan* (*sgra-an*), a
little peeling or paring. In the
sense of food, the word occurs
in the Irish objurgation, "Bad
scran to ye!"

Screed, a lengthy discourse or
written article. This word is
defined in a note to a passage
in the "Noctes Ambrosianæ"
as a "liberal allowance of anything."

A man, condemned to death for rape and murder at Inverness, requested that the editor of the *Courier* might be permitted to see him the night before his execution. After some talk, the criminal said, "Oh, Mr. Carruthers, what a *screed* you'll be printin' in your next paper about me!"—M.

Screik (or **scraigh**) **o' day**, the early dawn, the first flush of the morning light. Jamieson says the radical word is *creek;* from the Teutonic *krieche,* "aurora rutilans." It has been suggested that *screich,* or shriek, of day, means the shrill cry of the cock at early morn, but it is more probable that the phrase is from the Flemish *krieken van den dag,* which the French translate *l'aube du jour, l'aurore,* the dawn of day.

Scrieve, to roll or move or glide easily; from the Gaelic *sgriob,* to scrape, to draw a line or a furrow, to go on an excursion or journey.

The wheels o' life gae down-hill *scrievin'.*
—BURNS: *Scotch Drink.*

Scrimp, bare, scarce; *scrimply,* barely, scarcely.

Down flowed her robe, a tartan sheen,
Till half a leg was *scrimply* seen.
And such a leg! my bonnie Jean
   Alone could peer it.
      —BURNS: *The Vision.*

Scrog, a stunted bush, furze; *scroggy,* abounding in underwood, covered with stunted bushes or furze like the Scottish mountains; from the Gaelic *sgrogag,* stunted timber or underwood.

The way toward the cite was stony, thorny, and *scroggy.*—*Gesta Romanorum.*

As I came down by Merriemass,
   And down among the *scroggs,*
The bonniest chield that e'er I saw
   Lay sleeping 'mang his dogs.
      —*Johnnie of Bredislee.*

Sir Walter Scott, when in his last illness in Italy, was taken to a wild scene on the mountains that border the Lago di Garda. He had long been apathetic, and almost insensible, to surrounding objects; but his fading eyes flashed with unwonted fire at the sight of the furze bushes and scrogs that reminded him of home and Scotland, and he suddenly exclaimed, in the words of the Jacobite ballad—

Up the *scroggy* mountain,
   And down the *scroggy* glen,
We dare na gang a hunting,
   For Charlie and his men.

Scroggam and ruffam. These two words occur as a kind of chorus in a song attributed, but on doubtful authority, to Robert Burns. It is wholly unworthy of his genius, and appears—if he had anything at all to do with it—to have been slightly mended, to make it more presentable in decent company. Burns was almost wholly unacquainted with Gaelic, though he occasionally borrowed a phrase or a word from that language without quite comprehending its meaning.

There was a wife wonn'd in Cockpen,
      Scroggam!
She brewed guid ale for gentlemen,
Sing, Auld Coul lay ye down by me,
      Scroggam, my dearie, *ruffam.*

Scroggam is the Gaelic for *sgroggam*, let me put on my bonnet; and *ruffam* is *rubham*, or (*ruffam*) let me rub or scratch. An obscene meaning is concealed in the words.

Scrub, a term of contempt for a mean, niggardly person; a Scottish word that has made good its place in the English vernacular. *Scroppit*, sordid, parsimonious; from the Gaelic *scrub*, to hesitate, to delay, especially in giving or paying; *sgrubail*, niggardly; *scrubair*, a churl, a miser.

Scrunt, a worn-out broom; *scrunty*, a Northern word, signifying, according to Halliwell, short, stunted. Jamieson gives a second interpretation—"a person of slender make, a walking skeleton." Possibly the word is a corruption of the English *shrink, shrank*. There is no trace of it either in the Teutonic or the Gaelic.

Scuddy, stark naked; from the Gaelic *sguad*, to strip or lay bare.

Strip a country lass o' laigh degree perfectly *scuddy*, and set her beside a town belle o' a noble blood, equally naked, and wha can tell the ewe-milker frae the duchess?—*Noctes Ambrosianæ.*

Scug or **skug**, to hide, to take shelter, to run to sanctuary, to overshadow.

That's the penance he maun dree
To *scug* his deadly sin.
—*Border Minstrelsy: Young Benjie.*

In this quotation, *skug* seems to mean expiate, rather than hide or take refuge from the consequence of the deadly sin. Jamieson derives this word from the Gothic-Swedish *skugga*, a shade. It does not, however, appear in modern Swedish dictionaries. *Skug* and *scuggery* are noted both by Halliwell and Wright as northern English words for secret, hidden, and secrecy. In a note to the ballad of "Young Benjie," in the "Minstrelsy of the Scottish Border," Sir Walter Scott states that *scug* means to shelter or expiate. Possibly, if the interpretation of "shelter" can be accepted as connected, the etymology of the word is the Gaelic *sgathach*, pronounced *sgach*, or *skug*, a screen.

Scunner or **sconner**, a very expressive word, significant of a loathing or aversion to a thing or person, for which it is sometimes difficult or impossible to account.

And yill and whisky gie to cairds
Until they *scunner.*
—BURNS: *To James Smith.*

From the Gaelic *sgonn*, bad, also rude, boorish, ill-mannered. It enters also into the composite of the English word *scoundrel*, and the Italian *scondruels*, evidently of Celtic and Tuscan origin. Or it may perhaps be derived with equal propriety from *sgeun*, a fright, and *sgeunaich*, to frighten.

Scutch, to bruise or beat, to beat or dress flax. The error of Shakspeare's printers in spelling *scutch* as *scotch*, has led to the all but incorrigible mispronunciation of the word—"We have *scotched* the snake, not killed it"—and to the idea that the word has something to do with Scotland, and with the habits of the Scottish people. *Squids*, pronounced *scuitch* or *scutch*, is the Gaelic for to bruise, to beat; *sguidseadh*, the act of dressing flax. The word *scutch* is still used in the northern counties of England.

Sea-maw, the sea-gull, or sea-mew; the beautiful white bird of the ocean.

Keep your ain fish-guts to feed your ain sea-maws.—ALLAN RAMSAY's *Scots Proverbs*

The white sea-mew, and not the white dove, was considered by the Druids the bird that Noah let fly from the ark on the subsiding of the Deluge. The name of *pigeon*, sometimes given to the dove, signifies in Gaelic the bird of security; from *pighe*, bird, and *dion* (*di* pronounced *ji*), security, protection. The coincidence is curious.

Seile, happiness; from the German *selig*, happy.

Seile o' your face! is a phrase in Aberdeenshire, expressive of a blessing on the person to whom it is addressed.—DEAN RAMSAY

Sok and seil is best—the happiness that is earned is best—*i.e.*, earned by the plough; from *sock*, the ploughshare, and here used metaphorically for labour of any kind.—FERGUSON's *Scots Proverbs*.

Selkouth or **selcouth,** seldom seen or known; rendered "wondrous" by Sir Walter Scott, in the notes to "Thomas the Rhymer." The word is of the same origin as the English uncouth, strange, or unknown; from *kythe*, to show, or appear.

By Leader's side
A *selkouth* sight they see,
A hart and hind pace side by side
As white as snow.
—*Thomas the Rhymer.*

Sell or **selle,** a seat, a chair, a stool. Latin *sedile*, French *selle*, a saddle, the seat of a rider. This was once an English as well as a Scottish word, though obsolescent in the Elizabethan era. Shakspeare uses it in *Macbeth*—

Vaulting ambition that o'erleaps *itself,*
And falls on the other—

which, to render the image perfect, as Shakspeare meant—and no doubt wrote—ought to be read—

Vaulting ambition that o'erleaps its *sell,*
And falls on the other *side.*

The London compositors of Shakspeare's time, ignorant of the word *sell*, insisted upon making *self* of *it*, and in omitting "side." Ambition, in the guise of a horseman, vaulting to the horse's back, could not fall on the other side of itself; though it might well fall on the other side of the *sell* or saddle, and light upon the ground, which is the true Shakspearian metaphor.

Shacklebane, the wrist; a word apparently first applied to a prisoner who was handcuffed, or manacled.

Shadow-half, the northern exposure of land. Sir Walter Scott built Abbotsford on the wrong side of the Tweed—in the shadow-half. Land with a southern exposure is called the *sunny-half*, or the *sunnyside*.

S h a g h l e, sometimes written *shaucle*, to walk clumsily, to shuffle along, to drag or shackle the feet as if they were painfully constrained by the shoes; to distort from the original shape, to wear out.

Had ye sic a shoe on ilka foot, it wad gar ye *shaghle*.
—ALLAN RAMSAY'S *Scots Proverbs*.

And how her new shoon fit her auld *shachl't* feet.
—BURNS: *Last May a Braw Wooer*.

Schachled is metaphorically applied to a young woman who has been deserted by her lover. She is, on this account, compared to a pair of shoes that have been thrown aside, as being so put out of shape as to be unfit to be worn any longer.
—JAMIESON.

Jamieson derives this word from the Icelandic *skaga*, deflectere; *skaggrer*, obliquus. If he had looked at the Gaelic, he would have found *seac* (*shak*), dried up, worn out, without substance, decayed.

Shairnie-faced, a contemptuous epithet applied to a person with a very dirty face; from *sharn*, or *shairn*, dung, more especially cow-dung, sometimes called in English cow-*sherd*, a word, in all probability, from the same source.

Flae luggit, *shairnie-faced.*
—*The Blithesome Bridal.*

Shalk, a servant, a workman, a farm-servant; from the Gaelic *sgalag*, corrupted in America into *scalawag*, and used as a term of opprobrium. The word enters into the components of the French *marechal*, and the English *marshal;* from the Gaelic *maor*, a bailiff, overseer, steward, or superintendent; and *sgalag*, a servant or workman, whence *marechal*, one in charge of workmen or servants.

Shang, a vulgar term for a hasty luncheon or "snack," and for what Scottish children call a "piece;" *shangie*, thin, meagre, lean.

A *shang* o' bread and cheese, a bite between meals. In Icelandic *skan*, a crust, a rind.—JAMIESON.

The root is probably the Gaelic *seang* (*sheang*), lean, hungry; thence, by extension of meaning, a piece taken to satisfy hunger.

Shangie-mou'd, hare-lipped, or with a cleft mouth; from *shangan*, a cleft stick, or anything cleft or divided.

Shangie-mou'd, haluket Meg.
—*The Blithesome Bridal.*

The word *haluket* in this derisory line appears to be a form of *halse*, a giddy, thoughtless girl.

Shank, the leg. This noun is sometimes used as a verb in Scotland, and signifies to depart, to send away, to dismiss. To *shank* a person is to send him away; equivalent in English, to give him the sack; to *shank* one's self away is to leave without ceremony. The English phrase, to go on *shank's* or *shanks's mare*, *i.e.*, to walk, is rendered in Scottish—to go on *shank's naigie*, or little nag. Jamieson absurdly suggests that the English, to travel by the *marrow-bone* stage, *i.e.*, to walk, or go on *shank's* mare, may be derived from the parish of Marylebone, in London. The etymology of *shank* is the Gaelic *seang* (*shank*), lean, slender, like the tibia, or bone of the leg.

Shannach, or **shannagh**, a word explained by Jamieson in the phrase, "'It's ill *shannagh* in you to do this or that,' *i.e.*, it is ill on your part, or it is ungracious in you to do so." In Gaelic *seanacach* signifies wily, cunning, sagacious, which is clearly the root of *shannagh*, so that the phrase cited by Jamieson signifies it is not wise, or it is ill wisdom on your part to do so.

Shard (more properly *sharg*), a contemptuous epithet applied to a little, weazened, undergrown, and, at the same time, petulant and mischievous child. From the Gaelic *searg* (*s* pronounced as *sh*), a withered, insignificant person or animal, one shrivelled or dried up with age, sickness, or infirmity; *seargta*, withered, dried up, blasted.

Shargar, **sharg**, a lean, scraggy, cadaverous person. *Shargie*, thin, shrivelled, dried up; from the Gaelic *searg*, a puny man or beast, one shrivelled with sickness or old age; also, to wither, to fade away, to dwindle or dry up, from want of vitality.

Sharrow, sharp, sour or bitter to the taste. Flemish *scherp*, French *acerbe*, Gaelic *searbh*, bitter; *searbhad*, bitterness; *searbhag*, a bitter draught.

Shathmont, a measure, of which the exact length is uncertain, but which is evidently small.

As I was walking all alane
  Atween the water and the wa',
There I spied a wee, wee man,
  The wee'est man that e'er I saw,
His leg was scarce a *shathmont* lang.
    —*Ballad of the Wee, Wee Man.*

This obsolete English, as well as Scottish word, is sometimes written *shaftmond*, and *shaftman*. It appears in "Morte Arthur," and other early English poems. The etymology has never been satisfactorily traced. *Shacht*, which is also written *schaft*, is Flemish for the handle of a pike, or hilt of a sword; and *mand* is a basket or other piece of wickerwork; whence *schacht-mand*, a basket-hilt, or the length of a basket hilt of a sword, which may possibly be the origin of the word. The length of a *shathmont* is stated to be the distance between the outstretched thumb and little finger — a distance which corresponds with the position of the hand, when grasping the sword-hilt. *Maund*, for basket, is not yet entirely obsolete.

Shaver, a droll fellow, a wag, a funster, or one who indulges in attempts at fun ; *shavie*, a trick.

> Than him at Agincourt wha shone,
> Few better were or braver,
> And yet wi' funny, queer Sir John,
> He was an unco *shaver*.
>   —Burns : *A Dream.*

> But Cupid shot a shaft
> That played the dame a *shavie*.
>   —Burns : *The Jolly Beggars.*

It has been suggested that *shaver*, in the sense of a wag or funster, is derived from Figaro the barber, as the type of a class who were professionally funny in amusing their customers, when under their hands for hair-cutting or hair-dressing. The words are possibly corruptions of the old English *shaver*, described by Nares as a low, cunning fellow, and used by the writers of the early decades of the seventeenth century. *Shaver*, in the United States, signifies a bill discounter who takes ex-

orbitant interest, and a *shave* means a swindle or an imposition. Some have derived the word from *shave*, to cut the beard, itself a word of very uncertain etymology, and not necessarily connected with any idea of dishonesty. The more likely derivation is from the Gaelic *saobh* (or *shaov*), dissemble, prevaricate, take unfair advantage of, also, foolish.

Shaw, a small wood, a thicket, a plantation of trees ; from the Teutonic. This word was once common in English literature. It still exists in the patronymics of many families, as *Shawe*, *Aldershaw*, *Hinshaw*, *Hackshaw*, *Hawkshaw* (or *Oakshaw*), and others, and is used by the peasantry in most parts of England and every part of Scotland.

> Whither ridest thou under this green
>   *shawe ?*
> Said this yeman.
>   —Chaucer : *The Frere's Tale.*

> Gaillard he was as goldfinch in the *shaw*,
> Brown as a berry, a proper short fellow.
>   —Idem. : *The Coke's Tale.*

> Close hid beneath the greenwood *shaw*.
>   —Fairfax.

> In summer when the *shaws* be shene,
>   And leaves be fair and long, .
> It is full merry in fair forest,
>   To hear the fowles' song.
>   —*Ballad of Robin Hood.*

> To all our haunts I will repair,
>   By greenwood, *shaw*, and fountain.
>   —Allan Ramsay.

> The braes ascend like lofty wa's,
> The foaming stream deep roaring fa's,
> O'erhung wi' fragrant spreading *shaws*,
>   The birks of Aberfeldy.
>   —Burns.

Gloomy winter's now awa,
Saft the westlin breezes blaw ;
'Mang the birks o' Stanley *shaw,*
    The mavis sings fu' cheery, oh.
                        —TANNAHILL.

There's nae a bonnie flower that springs
    By fountain, *shaw,* or green,
There's nae a bonnie bird that sings,
    But minds me o' my Jean.
            —BURNS : *Of a' the Airts.*

Shear. The primary meaning of *shear* is to cut or clip. In this sense it is used by English agriculturists, for the operation of cutting or clipping the fleece of sheep. In Scotland it is used in the sense of reaping or cutting the corn in harvest. On the occasion of the first visit of Queen Victoria and the Prince Consort to the Highlands of Scotland, it was duly stated in the *Court Circular* that Her Majesty visited the *shearers,* and took much interest in their labours. In the following week, a newly-started pictorial journal, in opposition to the *Illustrated London News,* published a wood engraving, in which Her Majesty, the Prince, and several members of the Court in attendance, were represented as looking on at the *sheep - shearing.* The Cockney artist, ignorant alike of the seasons of agricultural operations and of the difference between the Scottish and English idioms, and who had no doubt, wished the public to believe that he was present on the occasion on which he employed his pencil, must have been painfully convinced, when his fraud

was discovered, of the truth of the poetic adage, that " a little knowledge is a dangerous thing ; " and that *shearing* and *reaping* had different meanings in England and Scotland.

> In hairst, at the *shearing,*
> Nae youths now are jeering,
> At fairs or at preaching,
> Nae wooing and fleeching.
>   —*The Flowers o' the Forest.*

Sheuch, a drain, a furrow or trench.

> I saw the battle sair and teuch,
> And reekin' red ran mony a *sheuch.*
>   —BURNS : *The Battle of Sheriffmuir.*

Shiel or **shielin,** a hut, a shed, or small cottage on the moor or mountain for the shelter of cattle or sportsmen ; derived by Jamieson from the Icelandic *skala,* a cottage ; probably a corruption of *shield,* or *shielding,* a place where one may be *shielded* or *sheltered* from the weather. *Wintershielins,* winter quarters.

> No ; I shall ne'er repent, Duncan,
>   And shanna e'er be sorry ;
> To be wi' thee in Hieland *shiel*
>   Is worth the lands o' Castlecary.
>   —*Ballad of Lizzie Baillie.*

> The craik among the clover hay,
>   The paitrick whirrin' o'er the lea,
> The swallow jinkin' round my *shiel,*
>   Amuse me at my spinnin' wheel.
> —BURNS : *Bess and her Spinnin' Wheel.*

Shill. Appears to be a contraction for the sake of euphony of the harsher English word *shrill.* The etymology of *shrill* is doubtful, though some derive it from the

Scottish *skirl*, which they call an *onomatopeia*, or imitation of the sound. This also is doubtful, more especially if the Teutonic *schreien*, and the Dutch and Flemish *schreuwen*, to cry out discordantly, are taken into consideration.

The westlin' wind blaws loud and *shill*,
The night's baith mirk and rainy, O.
　　　　—BURNS: *My Nannie, O.*

Shilpit, insipid, tasteless, dull, stale, flat; applied to liquor and sometimes to persons, metaphorically to signify that they are spiritless, timid, cowardly, and of no account.

A *shilpett* (*shilpit*) wretch, a heart stripped of manliness.—JAMIESON.

The Laird of Balmawhapple pronounced the claret *shilpit*, and demanded brandy with great vociferation.—SCOTT : *Waverley.*

According to Jamieson, *shilpit* is used to designate ears of corn that are not well filled. He derives it from the German *schelp*, signifying a reed, a bulrush, which is possibly the word that he referred to. But neither *schelp*, which Jamieson renders by the Latin *putamen*, a paring, a husk, a shell, or *schilp*, a bulrush, can be considered the root of *shilpit*, as applied to the insipidity or flatness of a liquor. The origin of *shilpit* remains unknown, though it may possibly have some remote connection with the Gaelic *sile* (*shile*), saliva, or drivel.

Shool, a shovel.

If honest nature made you fools,
　What sairs your grammars ?
Ye'd better ta'en up spades and *shools*
　An' knappin' hammers.
　　　　—BURNS : *To Lapraik.*

Shoon, the old plural of shoe, still used in Scotland, though almost obsolete in England.

If ever thou gave hosen or *shoon*,
　Every night an awle,
Sit thee down and pass them on,
　And Christ receive thy saule.
　—Funeral Dirge, in use in England
　　　before the Reformation, quoted
　　　in AUBREY'S Miscellanies.

Short, to divert, to amuse, to shorten the time by agreeable conversation ; *shortsome*, diverting, as opposed to *langsome*, or *longsome*, tedious, wearisome. In English, *short* is often applied to a hasty or quick temper. In Scottish parlance, *shortly* or *shortlie*, signifies tartly, peevishly, ill-naturedly.

Shot, shote, a puny or imperfect young animal, especially a pig or lamb. The Americans, who have acquired many words from the Scottish and Irish immigrants, have *shote*, a weakly little pig, and apply the word metaphorically to man or woman as an epithet of contempt or derision. It is derived from the Gaelic *seot* (pronounced *sheot*, or *shote*), a stunted animal, a short tail, a tail that has been docked ; and, generally, an incumbrance, impediment, or imperfection ; *scotair* signifies an idle, lazy,

useless person, a drone; a
vaurien, a good-for-nothing.

Seth Slope was what we call down East
a poor *shote*, his principal business being
to pick up chips and feed the pigs.—
Bartlett's *Dictionary of Americanisms*.

Shouther, the shoulder; "Highlanders! *shouther* to *shouther!*"
the motto of some of the Highland regiments in the British
service.

When the cloud lays its cheek to the flood,
And the sea lays its *shouther* to the shore.
—Chambers's *Scottish Songs: Hew
Ainslie*.

Shue, to play at see-saw; *shuggie-
shue*, a swing.

Sib, related, of kin by blood or
marriage. Hence the English
gossip, from *god-sib*, related by
baptismal union. From the
German *sippe*, which has the
same meaning; and *sippschaft*,
relationship.

He was *sibbe* to Arthur of Bretagne.
—Chaucer.
He was no fairy born or *sib* to elves.
—Spenser.

A boaster and a liar are right *sib*.

A' Stewarts are no *sib* to the king.

It's good to be *sib* to siller.
—Allan Ramsay's *Scots Proverbs*.

We're no more *sib* than sieve and riddle,
Though both grew in the woods together.
—*Cheshire Proverb*.

Siccan, such; *sic like*, such like,
or *such a*, as an adjective; *sic
like* a time, such a time; *sic like*
a fashion, in such a way or
fashion; generally used in the
sense of inopportune, improper,
unseemly.

What the deil brings the laird here
At *sic like* a time?
—*The Laird o' Cockpen*.

Wi' *siccan* beauties spread around,
We feel we tread on holy ground.
—James Ballantine: *Darnick Tower*.

Sicker, siccar, firm, safe, secure;
sickerly, safely; *sickerness*, safety,
security; to *sicker*, to make certain; *lock sickar*, lock securely,
or safely—the motto of the
ancient Scottish family, the
Earls of Morton. *Mak sickar* is
another motto of historic origin
in Scotland.

Toddlin' down on Willie's mill,
Setting my staff wi' a' my skill
To keep me *sicker*.
—Burns: *Death and Dr. Hornbook*.

Sick-saired, nauseated by reple-
tion, served with food to excess,
and to consequent sickness and
loathing.

Simmer (or **summer**) **couts**, the
gnats or midges which live for
one summer day, born ere noon
and dying ere sunset, and which
seem to pass their brief life in
whirling and dancing in the sun-
shine. The word, a *summercout*,
is often applied affectionately
to a very troublesome and merry
young child. Jamieson suggests
that *couts* may be a corruption
of *colts*, in which supposition he
is possibly correct, though the
comparison of the tiny midge
with so large an animal as a
young horse is not easy to explain. According to Wright's
Dictionary of Provincial English,
cote signifies a swarm of bees,

which seems to approach nearer to the idea of the midges. In Gaelic, *cutha* signifies frenzy, delirium ; and *cuthaich*, frantic dancing of the midges or other ephemeral flies, allied in idea to the phrase of Shakspeare—"a midsummer madness." This may be the real origin of the phrase.

Sindle, seldom ; from the Teutonic *selten.*

> Kame *sindle*, kame sair.
> —ALLAN RAMSAY'S *Scots Proverbs.*

Skalrag, of a shabby appearance ; from the Gaelic *sgail*, to cover, and *rag*, which is both Gaelic and English. *Skalrag* is synonymous, as Jamieson states, with *tatterdemalion*, one covered with rags, though he is incorrect in the etymology from *skail*, to scatter, and the explanation that it signifies one who "gives his rags to the wind."

Skedaddle, to disperse suddenly. A long obsolete Scottish word, revived unexpectedly in the army of the Potomac during the great American Civil War at the battle of Bull's Run, in 1862, when the Federal troops were seized with unreasonable panic, or alarm, and fled, when there was no pursuit. The word is said to be still occasionally used in Dumfriesshire, and to be applied to the wasteful overflow of the milk in the pails, when the milkmaids do not balance them properly, when carrying them from the byre to the farm. It has been generally considered to be an American coinage, on account of the incident of the retreat at Bull's Run, which brought it into notoriety, but was in reality employed either by the Gaelic-speaking Irish or Scottish soldiers under General MacClellan's command, and derived from the two Gaelic words *sguit*, to wander, to disperse, and *allta*, wild, irregular, ungovernable ; or else from *sgath* (*ska*), to lop or cut off, and *adhl*, a hook ; though some hold that it is derivable from the Greek σκεδαζω, to disperse. It is still doubtful which of these derivations, or either of them, is correct.

Skeigh, proud, scornful, disdainful, mettlesome, insolent in the pride of youth.

> When thou and I were young and *skeigh.*
> —BURNS : *Auld Farmer to his Auld Mare, Maggie.*

> Maggie coost her head fu' heigh,
> Looked asklent and unco *skeigh.*
> —BURNS : *Duncan Gray.*

From the Gaelic *sgeig*, to taunt, deride, scorn ; *sgeigeach*, disdainful. Jamieson has *skeg*, which he says is not clear, though he quotes "a *skeg*, a scorner, and a scolder"—words which might have helped him to the meaning.

Skeely, for skilful, but implying much more than the English word ; sagacious, far-seeing.

Out and spak Lord John's mother,
And a *skeely* woman was she,
" Where met ye, my son, wi' that bonnie
    boy
That looks sae sad on thee?"
       —*Ballad of Burd Helen.*

  Where will I get a *skeely* skipper
  To sail this ship o' mine?
    —*Ballad of Sir Patrick Spens.*

Skeerie, easily scared or frightened, timid, shy; from *scare*.

Skellum and blellum. These words are directed against Tam o' Shanter by his wife, in Burns' immortal poem:

She tauld thee weel thou wast a *skellum*,
A bletherin', blusterin', drunken *blellum*.

They are explained in the glossaries as signifying the first, " a worthless fellow;" the second, " an idle, talkative fellow." *Skellum* was used by English writers in the seventeenth century, among others by Taylor, the water-poet, and by Pepys in his diary. It is traceable to the German, Dutch, and Flemish *schelm*, a rogue, a rascal, a bad fellow; and also to the Gaelic *sgiolam*, a coarse blackguard; and *sgiolomach*, addicted to slander and mischief - making. *Blellum* is also from the Gaelic, in which *blialum* signifies incoherent, confused in speech; especially applied to the utterances of a drunken man.

Skelp, to smack, to administer a blow with the palm of the hand; to *skelp* the doup (breech), as used to be the common fashion of Scottish mothers.

I'm sure sma' pleasure it can gie,
    E'en to a deil,
To *skelp* and scaud puir dogs like me,
    And hear us squeal!
    —BURNS: *Address to the Deil.*

This word, of which the English synonym is *spank*, to strike with the palm of the hand in a quick succession of blows, appears to be derived primarily from the Gaelic *sgealbh*, to dash into small pieces, fragments, or splinters; and to have been applied afterwards, by extension of meaning, to the blows that might be sufficient to break any brittle substance. The English *spank* is to strike with the open hand, and the Scottish *spunk*, a match, signifies a splinter of wood, in which the same extension of meaning, from the blow to the possible results of the blow, is apparent. *Skelp* also means to walk or run at a smart pace, and the slang English phrase, "A pair of *spanking* tits" (a pair of fast-trotting or galloping horses), shows the same connection between the idea of blows and that of rapid motion.

    And, barefit, *skelp*
  Awa' wi' Willie Chalmers.
       —BURNS.

Three hizzies, early at the road,
  Cam *skelpin'* up the way.
    —BURNS: *The Holy Fair.*

Tam *skelpit* on thro' dub and mire,
Despising wind and rain and fire.
    —BURNS: *Tam o' Shanter.*

Skelpie-limmer, a violent woman, ready both with her hands and tongue.

Ye little *skelpie-limmer's* face,
I daur ye try sic sportin'.
—BURNS : *Hallowe'en.*

Skene-occle, a dagger, dirk ; from the Gaelic *sgian*, a knife, concealed in the *achlais*, under the arm, or in the sleeve ; *achlasan*, anything carried under the arm ; from whence the verb *achlaisich*, to cherish, to fold to the bosom, or encircle with the arm.

" Her ain sell," said Callum, "could wait for her a wee bit frae the toun, and 'kittle her quarters wi' his *skene-occle*."—
" *Skene-occle!* what's that ?" Callum unbuttoned his coat, raised his left arm, and, with an emphatic nod, pointed to the hilt of a small dirk, snugly deposited under the wing of his jacket.
—SCOTT : *Waverley.*

Skin, a vituperative term applied to a person whom it is wished to disparage or revile. " Ye're naething but a nasty *skin.*" Jamieson suggests that this word is a figurative use of the English *skin*, as denoting a *husk.* It is more likely to be a corruption of the Gaelic *sgonn*, a blockhead, a dolt, a rude clown, an uncultivated and boorish person, a dunce ; from whence *sgonn bhalaoch*, a stupid fellow ; *sgon* signifies vile, worthless, bad ; whence the English *scoundrel*— from *sgon*, and *droll*, or *droil*, an idle vagabond.

Skincheon o' drink, a drop of drink, a dram ; a pouring out of liquor. *Skincheon* is a misprint for *skinkin'.*

Skink, to pour out ; *skinker*, a waiter at a tavern who pours out the liquor for the guests, a bar tender. From the Flemish and German *schenken*, to pour out. This word is old English as well as Scotch, and was used by Shakspeare, Ben Jonson, and their contemporaries. *Skink* is sometimes contemptuously applied to soup or broth when not of the accustomed flavour or consistency, imparted by vegetable ingredients, such as barley, peas, &c.

Sweet Ned, I give thee this pennyworth
of sugar, clapt even now into my hand by
an under-*skinker*.
—SHAKSPEARE : *Henry IV.*

Such wine as Gannymede doth *skink* to
Jove.—SHIRLEY.

Ye powers wha mak mankind your care,
And dish them out their bill o' fare ;
Auld Scotland wants nae *skinking* ware
That jaups i' luggies,
But if ye wish her grateful prayer,
Gie her a haggis.
—BURNS : *To a Haggis.*

The wine ! there was hardly half a
mutchkin,—and poor fushionless *skink* it
was.—SIR WALTER SCOTT.

In many of the editions of Burns which have been printed in England, the compositors, or printers' readers, ignorant of the word *skink*, have perverted it in the " Lines to a Haggis," into *stink.*

Auld Scotland wants nae *stinking* wares.
—*Complete Works of* ROBERT BURNS,
edited by Alexander Smith. London : Macmillan &° Co., 1868.

" These editions," says Mr James M'Kie of Kilmarnock in his Bibliography of Robert Burns, " are known to collectors as the *stinking* editions."

Skipper, the captain of a ship, but properly any sailor; *skip*-man, a ship man. This word is fast becoming English, and promises to supersede captain as the designation of officers in the mercantile marine. *Skipper* is from the Danish *skiffer*, the German, Dutch, and Flemish *schiffer*.

> The king sat in Dunfermline tower,
>   Drinking the blood-red wine;
> Oh whaur 'll I get a skeely *skipper*,
>   To sail this ship o' mine.
>   —Sir Patrick Spens.

It is related of the late eminent sculptor, Patric Park, that, on an excursion through the beautiful lakes that form the chain of the Caledonian Canal, he was annoyed by the rudeness of the captain of the steamer, and expressed his sense of it in language more forcible than polite. The captain, annoyed in his turn, inquired sharply — "Do you know, sir, that I'm the captain of the boat?" "Captain be hanged!" said the irate man of genius, "you're only the *skipper*, that is to say, you're nothing but the driver of an aquatic omnibus!" The *skipper* retired to hide his wrath, muttering as he went that the sculptor was only a *stone mason!*

Skirl, to shriek, to cry out, or to make a loud noise on a wind instrument.

> Ye have given the sound thump, and he the loud *skirl* (*i.e.*, you have punished the man, and he shows it by his roaring).
>   —Allan Ramsay's *Scots Proverbs.*

> When *skirlin'* weanies see the light,
> Thou mak's the gossips clatter bright.
>   —Burns: *Scotch Drink.*

A family belonging to the Scottish Border, after spending some time at Florence, had returned home, and, proud of the progress they had made in music, the young ladies were anxious to show off their accomplishments before an old confidential servant of the family, and accordingly sang to her some of the finest songs which they had learned abroad. Instead, however, of paying them a compliment on their performance, she showed what she thought of it, by asking with much *naïveté*—"Eh, mem! Do they ca' *skirling* like yon, singing in foreign parts?"—Dean Ramsay's *Reminiscences.*

Skirl-naked, stark naked; naked as a child that *skirls* or squalls at the moment of its birth. *Skirl* is allied to screech, shriek, and shrill, and comes immediately from the Gaelic *sgreuch*, a shrill cry, and *sgreuchail*, shrieking.

Sklent, oblique, slanting; to deviate, to slant off the right line of truth, to cast obliquely; to push away, to look away, to squint.

> Now, if yer ane o' warld's folk,
> Who rate the wearer by the cloak,
> And *sklent* on poverty their joke,
>   Wi' bitter sneer.
>   —Burns: *To Mr. John Kennedy.*
> One dreary, windy, winter night,
> The stars shot doun wi' *sklentin'* light.
>   —Burns: *Address to the Deil.*
>   The city gent
> Behind a kist to lie and *sklent*,
> Or purse-proud, big with cent. per cent.
>   An' muckle wame.
>   —Burns: *Epistle to Lapraik.*
> Ye did present your smootie phiz
>   'Mang better folk,
> And *sklented* on the man of Uz
>   Your spiteful joke.
>   —Burns: *Address to the Deil.*

Skrae, or **scrae**, a thin, skinny, meagre person, a skeleton; *skrae-shankit*, having skinny legs; English *scrag*, and *scraggy;* Gaelic *sgraidh - teach* (*dh* silent), shrivelled, dried up; *sgraidht*, a lean, shrivelled, ugly old woman.

> But gin she say, lie still ye *skrae*,
>   That's Water Kelpie!
>   —Jamieson's *Border Minstrelsy:*
>   *Water Kelpie.*

In the glossary appended by Sir Walter Scott to Jamieson's ballad written in imitation of the antique, *skrae* is glossed as a skeleton.

Skreigh, or **screigh**, a shrill cry, a shriek, a screech.

The *skreigh* o' duty, which no man should hear and be inobedient.—Scott : *Rob Roy.*

It's time enough to *skreigh* when ye're strucken.—Allan Ramsay's *Scots Proverbs.*

When thou and I were young and skeigh,
An' stable meals at fairs were dreigh,
' How thou would prance and snort, and *skreigh,*
    An' tak the road.
        —Burns: *Auld Farmer to his Auld Mare, Maggie.*

Skulduddery. This grotesque word has been held to signify indulgence in lust, or illicit passion; but it also signifies obscene language or conversation, or, as it is sometimes called in English, *smut.* Jamieson suggests the Teutonic *shuld*, fault or crime, as the origin of the first syllable, and the Gaelic

sgaldruth, a fornicator, as the origin of the whole word. *Scaldruth*, however, has long been obsolete, and seems to have been a compound of *sgald*, to burn or scald ; and *druis*, lust ; whence the modern Gaelic *druisear*, a fornicator. If the Gaelic etymology be accepted, the word would resolve itself into a corruption of *sgald-druis*, burning lust, or burned by lust. From the Gaelic *druis* came the old English *druery*, for courtship, intercourse of the sexes, gallantry ; and *drossel*, an unchaste woman. The French, who have inherited many Celtic words from their ancestors, the Gauls, formerly used the word *dru* for a lover (*un ami*), and *drue* for a sweetheart (*une amie*). *Drú*, as an adjective, signified, according to the "Dictionaire de la Langue Romane" (Paris 1768), "un amant vigoureux et propre au plaisir." *Druerie*, in the sense of courtship and gallantry, occurs in the "Roman de la Rose." Another French word, *sgaldrine*, still more akin to the Scottish *skulduddery*, is cited in the "Dictionaire Comique de Le-Roux," as a "terme d'injure pour une femme de mauvaise vie ; femme publique affligée d'une maladie brulante."

And there will be Logan Macdonald—
    Skulduddery and he will be there !
        —Burns: *The Election.*

That can find out naething but a wee bit *skulduddery* for the benefit of the Kirk Treasury.—Scott : *Rob Roy.*

Skybald, apparently the same as the English *skewbald* and *piebald*, terms to designate a horse of two colours, marked as cows and oxen more usually are. Both *skybald* and *piebald*, as well as the English *skewbald*, have their origin in the Gaelic. *Sky* and *skew* are corruptions of *sgiath*, a shade, a dark shade; *pie* comes from *pighe*, a *pie*, or mag*pie*, a bird whose black plumage is marked with a white streak; *bald* is derived from the Gaelic *ball*, a mark or spot; whence *skybald* is shade-marked, and *piebald* is marked like a bird. Jamieson says that, in Scotland, *skybald* signifies a base, mean fellow, a worthless person, and that it is also applied to a man in rags and tatters. Possibly this metaphorical use of the word arises from the fact that the rags of such a person are often of various colours. Locke, the celebrated English metaphysician, uses *piebald* in a similar sense, "a *piebald* livery of coarse patches." In Yorkshire, according to Wright's Provincial Dictionary, *skeyl'd* signifies parti-coloured, which is apparently from the same Gaelic root as *sky* and *skew*.

Skyre. Jamieson renders this word, pure, mere, utter. The Flemish and German *schier* signifies nearly, almost; while the Danish *skier* means clear, pure, limpid. Thus the Danish, and not the German or Flemish, seems to be the root of this Scottish word.

Skyte or **skite**, to eject liquid forcibly, a flux, or diarrhœa. This vulgar word is often, both in a physical and moral sense, applied in contempt to any mean person. A *skyte* of rain is a sudden and violent shower; *skyter* is a squirt, a syringe, so called from the violent ejection of the liquid. *Bletherum skyte*—more properly, *blether and skyte* (see BLETHER, *ante*)—is a colloquial phrase very often employed by people who are unaware of the grossness of its original meaning, and who are impressed by its aptness as descriptive of the windy trash of conversation and assertion which it but too powerfully designates. The word is derivable either from the English *scud*, fast motion, or the Gaelic *sgud*, to cut, a cutting wind.

> When hailstanes drive wi' bitter *skyte*.
> —BURNS : *The Jolly Beggars.*

Slack, **slug**, a pass, opening, or gap between two hills; from the Gaelic *sloc*, and *slochd*, a hollow, a cavity, a ravine. *Slochd muigh*, or the gap of the wild swine, is a wild pass in the Grampians between Perth and Inverness.

> But ere he won the Gate-hope *slack*,
> I think the steed was wae and weary.
> —*Minstrelsy of the Border:*
> *Annan Water.*

Slanky, slimy.

> Twa *slanky* stanes seemed his spule banes.
> —*Border Minstrelsy: The Water*
> *Kelpie.*

Slap, a breach, or casual opening in a hedge or fence.

At *slaps* the billies [fellows] halt a blink [a
   little while],
Till lassies strip their shoon.
      —BURNS : *The Holy Fair.*

Slawpie, slaipie, indolent, slovenly ; derived by Jamieson from the Icelandic *slapr,* homuncio sordidus. It is rather from the Gaelic *slapach,* slovenly, *slapair* and *slaopair,* a slovenly man, a drawler, an idler ; and *slapag,* a slut, a lazy, dirty, slovenly woman or girl ; and *slapaireachd,* slovenliness.

Sleuth-hound, a blood-hound, a hound trained to follow by the scent the track of man or beast. From the Gaelic *slaod,* a trace, a trail ; and *slot, sliogach,* subtle, keen scented.

Wi' his *sleuth*-dog in his watch right
   sure ;
Should his dog gie a bark,
He'll be out in his sark,
And die or win.
      —*Ballad of The Fray of Suport.*

Slid, smooth ; *sliddery,* slippery.

Ye had sae saft a voice, and a *slid*
   tongue.
      —ALLAN RAMSAY : *The Gentle
         Shepherd.*

Sliddery, slippery ; from *slide. Slidder,* unstable, changeable in thought or purpose, not to be depended upon.

There's a *sliddery* stane afore the ha'
   door.
[It is sometimes dangerous to visit
   great houses.]
      —ALLAN RAMSAY'S *Scots
         Proverbs.*

Though I to foreign lands must hie,
Pursuin' fortune's *sliddery* ba'.
      —BURNS : *Farewell to his Native
         Country.*

Slink, a tall, idle person ; a term of depreciation. The word is usually associated with *lang,* as, a *lang slink.* It is sometimes written and pronounced *slunk.* It is derived apparently from the Teutonic *schlang,* the Dutch and Flemish *slang,* a snake. *Slinken* means to grow long, thin, and attenuated ; and Jamieson has the adjective *slunk,* lank and slender ; and the substantive *slink,* a starveling.

Slint or **slinter,** a slovenly, untidy, awkward man, corresponding with the English *slut* as applied to a woman ; from the Gaelic *slaod,* to draggle or trail lazily along the ground ; *slaodag,* a slut ; *slaodair,* a sluggard. Jamieson derives it from the Teutonic *slodde,* a dirty female ; but the word is not to be found in German dictionaries, though it possibly exists in the vulgar patois.

Sliver, a slice, a small piece. The word was employed in this sense by Chaucer, and is akin to the English *slice,* and to the Gaelic *slios,* a side. Stormonth derives it from the Anglo-Saxon *slifan,* to cleave or split. Shakspeare uses the word three times.

Slivered in the moon's eclipse.
      —*Macbeth,* act iv. scene 1.
An envious *sliver* broke.
      —*Hamlet,* act iv. scene 7.
Sliver and disbranch.
      —*Lear,* act iv. scene 2.

Slocken, to slake, to allay thirst, to extinguish.

> Foul water may *slocken* fire.
> —ALLAN RAMSAY'S *Scots Proverbs.*

It *slockened* not my drouth, but aggravated a thousandfold the torrent o' my greed.—*Noctes Ambrosianæ.*

The Rev. John Heugh of Stirling was one day admonishing one of his people on the sin of intemperance : " Man ! John ! you should never drink except when you're dry." " Weel, sir," said John, " that's what I'm aye doin', but I'm never *slocken'd.*"—DEAN RAMSAY.

Slogan, the war-cry of a Highland clan.

> Our *slogan* is their lyke-wake dirge.
> —SIR WALTER SCOTT.

When the streets of high Dunedin,
Saw lances gleam and falchions redden,
And heard the *slogan's* deadly yell.
SCOTT : *Lay of the Last Minstrel.*

Jamieson has this word as *slughorn*, and derives it from the Irish Gaelic *sluagh*, an army, and *arm*, a horn. Jamieson might have found the true etymology in the Scottish Gaelic *sluagh*, the people, the multitude, the clan ; and *gairm*, a cry, a shout, a loud call. The *slogan* was not made on a horn ; and *arm* does not signify a horn in Gaelic. *Slogan*, the war-cry, has been used by English writers as synonymous with *pibroch*, especially in a play that enjoyed considerable popularity a quarter of a century ago, on the siege and relief of Lucknow during the Indian Mutiny. When General Havelock approaches with his gallant Highlanders,

Jeanie, the heroine of the piece, who hears the music of the pibroch from afar, exclaims, " Oh ! hear ye not the *slogan ?* " But the " pock puddings," as one of Sir Walter Scott's characters called the English, knew no better, and always applauded the *slogan.*

Slogger, to swallow broth, porridge, or spoon meat awkwardly and voraciously; from the Gaelic *sluig*, to swallow ; *slugair*, or *slogair*, a glutton. Synonymous with the local English *slorp.*

Sloom, a deep sleep, whence the English word *slumber*, a light sleep ; from the Flemish *sluimeren*, to sleep; *sluimerig*, sleepy.

Sloomy, lethargic.

Slorp, slotter, to eat or drink greedily, and with a guttural and vulgar noise ; from the Flemish and Dutch *slorpen*, which has the same meaning.

There's gentle John, and Jock the *slorp*,
And curly Jock, and burly Jock,
And lying Jock himsel'.
—HOGG'S *Jacobite Relics.*

Slort, a sloven ; *sloeter*, to work in an idle, slovenly, and bungling manner ; akin to the English *slut*, applied in the same manner to a woman. From the Gaelic *slaodair*, a sluggard ; a lazy, careless person.

Slounge, to go idling about, to go sorning (q.v.), or seeking for a dinner, lounging about and coming into the house of a friend or acquaintance at or near dinner time, as if accidentally. Apparently a corruption of the Gaelic *slugair*, a glutton ; *sluganach*, a voracious person, and *slugan*, the gullet.

Slunk, sometimes written **slung**, an Aberdonian word, which according to Jamieson signifies a tall, cadaverous-looking person of inferior intellect, " a lang, toom, haiverilly kind o' chiel." He derives it from the Icelandic *slani*, an imbecile. The word, however, seems akin to the English *slink*, as its past participle *slunk*, and to be derivable from the German *schlang*, a snake that *slinks* away, and is hence, by association of ideas, applied metaphorically, in the same way as the English *sneak*, which has a similar origin.

Sma' drink, a weak liquor ; the English say *small beer*, for weak beer or ale, and the French *petit vin*, for inferior wine. To " think nae sma' drink o' himsel'," is a phrase applied to any one who thinks too much of his own dignity or importance.

Smaik, a mean, low fellow, a poltroon, a puny fellow, a person of small moral or physical account.

"Oh, I have heard of that *smaik*," said the Scotch merchant ; "it's he whom your principal, like an obstinate auld fule, wad mak a merchant o'—wad he, or wad he no !"—SCOTT : *Rob Roy*.

This false, traitorous *smaik*. I doubt he is a hawk of the same nest.—SCOTT : *Fortunes of Nigel*.

From the Teutonic *schmach*, insult, ignominy ; *schmächtig*, slender, lank.

Smeddum, spirit, pith, energy. Also dust, powder ; from the Gaelic *smodan*, small dust.

Now and then ye may overhaul an article that's ower lang and ower stupid, and put some *smeddum* into it.—*Noctes Ambrosianæ*.

> Oh, for some rank mercurial rozet,
> Or pale red *smeddum*,
> I'd gie ye sic a hearty dose o't
> Wad dress your droddum.*
> —BURNS : *To a Louse*.

Smeerless, pithless, marrowless ; from the Gaelic *smior*, marrow.

> I mark him for a *smeerless* dolt,
> Who'd jink to eschew a thunderbolt.
> —GEORGE BEATTIE : *John o' Arnha'*.

Smergh, marrow, vigour, pith ; strength either of body or of mind ; *smerghlers*, weak, marrowless, pithless, vapid, insipid ; from the Gaelic *smior*, marrow, and *smiorach*, marrowy, or full of marrow and pith. The Teutonic *mark*, marrow, seems to be of this origin, with the omission of the initial *s*, though Jamieson traces it to the Teutonic *mergh*, which does not mean marrow, but marl.

Smervy, fat and marrowy.

They scum'd the cauldron, fed the fuel,
They steer'd and preed, the *smervy* gruel.
—GEORGE BEATTIE : *John o' Arnha'*.

* *Droddum*, a ludicrous word for the posterior of a child.

Smiddle, to work by stealth; derivation uncertain, but possibly related to *smith*, *smithy*, and *smiddy*.

Smird, to gibe, to jeer. Jamieson derives this word from the Icelandic *sma'* (the Scottish *sma'* and the English *small*), and *ord*, a word, and supposes it to mean small and contemptuous language. It is more probably from the Gaelic *smioradh* or *smiuradh*, smearing, or besmearing; used metaphorically for *larding* with abuse or ill-natured jests.

Smirl, a roguish or mischievous trick. Jamieson derives this word from the German *schmieren*, illudere; but in the German dictionaries it is defined as "to smear." It is more probably from the Gaelic *smiorail*, strong, active, lively; and "I'll play him a *smirl* for that yet," as quoted by Jamieson, simply means, "I'll play him a *lively* trick for that yet."

> And in some distant place,
> Plays the same *smirle*.
> —T. SCOTT.

Smirtle, a slight, or half-suppressed laugh or smile.

> And Norie takes a *glack* of bread and cheese,
> And wi' a *smirtle* unto Lindie goes.
> —Ross's *Helenore*.

This word is akin to the English *smirk*, but without any depreciatory meaning.

Smit, the noise, clash, or clank of smitten metal; from the English *smite*.

> As she was walking maid alane
> Down by yon shady wood,
> She heard a *smit* o' bridle reins
> She wished might be for good.
> —*Border Minstrelsy: Lord William.*

Smitch or **smytch**, a term of contempt or anger applied to an impudent boy; from *smut*, dirt, a stain, an impurity. German *schmützig*, dirty; Flemish and Dutch *smotsen*, to soil, to dirty, to defile; the English *smudge*.

Smolt, an epithet applied to the weather when fair and calm, with a blue sky.

> Merry maidens, think na lang,
> The weather is fair and *smolt*.
> —*Christ's Kirk on the Green.*

This word is used, according to Messrs. Halliwell and Wright, in Sussex and other parts of England. It is probable that the root is the Teutonic *schmalte*, deep blue, applied to the unclouded sky.

> O'er Branxholme Tower, ere the morning hour,
> Where the lift is like lead so blue,
> The smoke shall roll white on the weary night,
> And the flame shine dimly through.
> —*Border Minstrelsy: Lord Inglis.*

Smook, to prowl stealthily about a place, with a view to pilfer small articles; from the Flemish *smuig*, furtive, secret.

Smookie, addicted to petty larceny.

> The *smookie* gipsy i' the loan.
> —Ross's *Helenore*.

Smoor, abbreviation and corruption of smother.

> What's the matter, quo' Willie,
> Though we be scant o' claes,
> We'll creep the closer thegither,
> An' we'll *smoor* a' the fleas.
> —*Woo'd an' Married an' A'*.

Smyte, a small particle; possibly derived from the spark of an anvil when smitten; *smytrie*, a large collection of little things, or little children.

> A *smytrie* o' wee duddie weans.
> —BURNS.

Snack, a slight repast, a cut from the loaf, refreshment taken hastily between meals; to go *snacks*, to share with another. From the Gaelic *snaigh*, to cut. *Snack*, and to go *snacks*, are still used in colloquial English, and are derived by Worcester and others from *snatch*, *i.e.*, as much of a thing as can be snatched hastily. An etymology which may apply to *snack*, a lunch, but scarcely applies so well as the Gaelic *snaigh*, to the phrase of go *snacks*, or shares in any thing.

Snag, to chide, to taunt, to reprove, to snarl; *snaggy*, sarcastical, apt to take offence. This word, with the elision of the initial *s*, remains in English as *nag*, the form of scolding or grumbling, which is peculiarly attributed to quarrelsome women. It is one of the numerous family of words commencing with *sn*, which, in the Scottish and English languages, generally imply a movement of the lips and nose, expressive of anger, reproof, scorn, and in inferior animals, of an inclination to bite; such as snarl, snub, sneer, snort, snap, snack, or snatch (as an animal with its jaws), and many others, all of which, inclusive of snore, sniff, snuff, sneeze, snigger, snivel, snout, have a reference to the nose. They appear to be derivable primarily from the Gaelic *sron*, pronounced *strone*, the nose. The Teutonic languages have many words commencing with *schn*, which also relate to the action of the nose, and are possibly of the same Celtic origin.

Snaggerel, a contemptuous term for a puny, deformed child; from *snag*, a broken bough.

Snash, impertinence, rebuff, rebuke.

> Poor bodies . . .
> . . . thole (endure) a factor's *snash*.
> —BURNS: *The Twa Dogs*.

Sneck or **snick**, the latch, bolt, or fastening of a door. The etymology is uncertain, and cannot be traced to any branches of the Teutonic, either High Dutch, Low Dutch, or Danish and Swedish. The English has *snacket* and *snecket*, a fastening, a hasp; as well as *sneck* and *snick*, with the same meaning as the Scotch, but the words are local, not general.

And you, ye auld *sneck*-drawing dog,
Ye came to Paradise incog.
　　—BURNS: *Address to the Deil.*

Sneeshin', snuff; from *sneeze*; *sneeshin'-mull*, a snuff-box.

Snaped haddocks, wilks, dulse an' tangles,
An' a mull o' gude *sneeshin'* to prie;
When weary wi' eatin' and drinkin'
We'll up an' we'll dance till we die.
　　—*The Blithesome Bridal.*

Snell, keen, bitter, sharp, quick; from the Flemish *snell*, and the German *schnell*, swift.

And bleak December's winds ensuing
Baith *snell* and keen.
　　—BURNS: *To a Mouse.*

Sir Madoc was a handy man, and *snell*
In tournament, and eke in fight.
　　—*Morte Arthur.*

Shivering from cold, the season was so *snell*.
　　—DOUGLAS: *Eneid.*

The winds blew *snell*.
　　—ALLAN RAMSAY.

Snelly the hail smote the skeleton trees.
　　—JAMES BALLANTINE.

Snirtle, to laugh slily, or in a half suppressed manner.

He feigned to *snirtle* in his sleeve,
When thus the laird addressed her.
　　—BURNS: *The Jolly Beggars.*

Snood or **snude**, a ribbon, a band worn by young unmarried women in or around the hair.

To tyne one's *snude* is a phrase applied in Scotland to a young woman who has lost her virginity. It is singular that the ancient Romans had the same figure.—JAMIESON.

The word and the fashion appears to be peculiar to the Celtic nations. In Gaelic, *snuadh* signifies beauty and adornment, and thence an ornament, such as the *snood* of the Scottish maidens. The word appears in Snowdon, the ancient name of Stirling, which signifies the fair or beautiful hill. The Kymric and Welsh has *ysnoden*, a fillet, a lace, a band, evidently from the same root. The much despised English patronymic *Snooks*, sometimes alleged to be a corruption of *screnoaks*, is probably of Celtic origin, from *snuadhach* (*snu-ach*), beautiful.

Snool, to flatter abjectly, to cringe, to crawl. This word also means to snub, to chide ill-naturedly and unduly.

They *snool* me sair and haud me down,
And gar me look like bluntie, Tam;
But three short years will soon wheel roun',
And then comes ane and twenty, Tam.
　　—BURNS.

Is there a whim-inspired fool,
Ow're blate (shy) to seek, ow're proud to *snool*.
　　—BURNS: *A Bard's Epitaph.*

Your *snools* in love and cowards in war,
Frae maidens' love are banished far.
　　—*John o' Arnha'.*

The etymology of this word is uncertain. It seems to have some relation to the nose and mouth, and expression of the features in an unfavourable sense; like many words in the English language commencing with *sn*. (See SNAG, *ante*.) The most probable derivation is that given by Jamieson from the

Danish *snofle*, to reprimand un-necessarily, continually, and un-justly—the French *rabrouer*.

Snoove, to glide away easily, like a worm or snake ; to sneak. Probably from the Gaelic *sniomh* (pronounced *sni-ov*), to twist, to twine, to wriggle,

But just thy step a wee thing hastit,
    Then *snoov't* away.
        —BURNS : *Auld Farmer to his
            Auld Mare, Maggie.*

Snowk, to snuff, to smell, to scent.

Wi' social nose they snuffed and *snowket*.
        —BURNS : *The Twa Dogs.*

Snuit, to go about in a careless, half-stupefied manner ; *snuitit*, having the appearance of sleepy inebriety.

He was gaun *snuitin* down the street ;
he came *snuitin* in.—JAMIESON.

Jamieson traces the word to the Dutch and Flemish *snuit*, the snout. The Gaelic has *snot*, to smell, to snuff up the wind, to turn up the nose suspiciously ; and *snotach*, suspecting, inclined to suspicion.

Snurl, to ruffle the surface of the waters with a wind ; meta-phorically applied to the temper of man or woman.

Northern blasts the ocean *snurl*.
        —ALLAN RAMSAY.

Sockdologer, a heavy, knock-down blow. This word is usually considered to be an Americanism. But it clearly

comes from the " old country," from the Gaelic *sogh*, easy ; and *dolach*, destructive ; *dolaidh*, harm, detriment, injury, de-struction ; thus a *sockdologer* means a blow that destroys easily.

Sodger or **sojer**, a soldier ; *swad-die* or *swad*, a familiar and vulgar name for a soldier.

My humble knapsack a' my wealth,
    A poor but honest *sodger*.
        —BURNS.

The Scottish word *sodger* is possibly not a mere corruption or mispronunciation of the Eng-lish *soldier*, or the French *soldat*, as it is generally considered to be. The old Teutonic for soldier was *kriegsman*, warman, or man of war ; a word which was not adopted by the early English of German, Danish, and Flemish descent. The English soldiers were called bowmen, spearmen, archers, &c. The commonly accepted derivation of soldier is from *solde*, pay,—*i.e.*, one who is paid. But in early times, before the establishment of standing armies, people who took up arms in defence of their country were not mercenaries, but patriots and volunteers, or retainers of great territorial chieftains. *Sodger*, as distin-guished from *soldier*, dates from a period anterior to the inven-tion of gunpowder and the use of fire-arms, when bows and arrows were the principal wea-pons of warfare over all Eu-rope ; may be derived from the

Gaelic *saighead*, an arrow; and *saighdear*, an arrower, an archer, a bowman; the same as the Latin *saggitarius*. Thus the Scottish *sodjer* appears to be a word of legitimate origin and of respectable antiquity. Soldier, from the French *soldat*, is comparatively modern, and does not appear in the "Dictionary of the First or Oldest Words in the English Language, from the Semi-Saxon Period from A.D. 1250 to 1300," by Herbert Coleridge, published in 1862. It is worthy of mention that Jamieson's Scottish Dictionary does not contain *sodger* or *sojer*, but has *sodgerize*, to act as a soldier, or go a soldiering; and the strange term *sodgertheed*, which he explains to be a low word meaning one that has little or no money, or having "the *thigh* of a soldier!" Had Jamieson, before hazarding this suggestion, looked to another page of his own dictionary, he would have found the word *thig*, to beg, and might have explained the phrase in the sense of a disbanded soldier, begging from door to door, without any particular reference to his *thigh*.

Sokand seil. An old Scottish proverb says, "*Sokand seil* is best." Dean Ramsay, who quotes it, defines it to mean, "The plough and happiness is the best lot." The translation is too loose to be accepted. *Soc* is, indisputably, a ploughshare, in Gaelic, in French, in Flemish (in Latin *soccus*), and other languages. No trace, however, has hitherto been discovered of its employment as a verb, signifying to plough. It would seem, nevertheless, from the terminal syllable in *sockand*, that it was in old time so used in Scotland. *Seil* is from the Gaelic *sealbh*, signifying good fortune, good luck, happiness, — whence the Teutonic *selig*, happy. Ploughing, in the proverb, may be taken to mean labouring generally; and then the proverb might be rendered, "Labouring happiness, or the happiness that results from labour, is the best."

Sonk, a stuffed seat, or a couch of straw; *sonkie*, a gross, coarse, unwieldy man, of no more shapely appearance than a sack of straw. The root of these two words seems to be the Gaelic *sonnach*, anything thick, bulky, or strong; *sonn* is a stout man, also a hero; and *sonnach*, a fat, ill-shaped person.

> The Earl of Argyle is bound to ride,
> And all his habergeons him beside,
> Each man upon a *sonk* of strae.
> —*Introduction to Border Minstrelsy.*

Sonse, happiness, good luck; *sonsie*, strong, happy, pleasant; from the Gaelic *sona*, happy, and *sonas*, happiness. *Sonas agus donas*, happiness and unhappiness.

> His honest, *sonsie*, baws'nt face
> Aye gat him friends in ilka place.
> —Burns: *The Twa Dogs.*

Sook, a suck, a drop, a sup or sip, a taste of liquor. *Sooch* or *sook* is defined by Jamieson as "a copious draught."

> There sat a bottle in a hole,
> Ayont the ingle low ;
> And aye she took the ither *sook*,
> To drook the stoury tow.
> —*The Weary Pund o' Tow.*

Sool (sometimes written *soul*), a sufficiency of food, also, a relish taken with insipid food to render it more palatable. " *Sool* to a potatoe," often applied to a finnan haddie, or a red herring; sometimes ludicrously used by the Irish as, "potatoes and point," a potato pointed at a red herring hanging from the roof, to whet the imagination with the unattainable flavour of the *sool.*

> I have, sweet wench, a piece of cheese as good as tooth may chaw,
> And bread and wildings *souling* well.
> —WARNER : *Albion's England.*

Sool, anything eaten with bread, such as butter, cheese, &c.—WRIGHT'S *Dictionary of Obsolete English.*

Soul, French *saouler*, to satisfy with food. *Soul*, silver, the wages of a retainer, originally paid in food.—*Idem.*

The French have *soul*, full; and *se souler*, to get drunk, *i.e.*, full either of meat or of liquor. The Gaelic *sult* seems to be of kindred derivation, and signifies fat, full, replenished with good things.

Sooth. Old English for *truth*, still preserved in such phrases as, " in *sooth*," " *for-sooth*," &c. In Scottish, *sooth* is used as an adjective, and signifies "true."

A *sooth* boord is nae boord (*i.e.*, a jest with too much truth in it it may be no jest at all).—ALLAN RAMSAY'S *Scots Proverbs.*

Sorn, to go to a person's house, without invitation, and fasten yourself upon him to feast or lodge. The English synonym is " to sponge upon ; " a very inferior form of expression, partaking of the character of slang, and not to be compared for force and compactness to the Scottish word. Mr. John Thompson, private secretary to the Marquis of Hastings in India, in his "Etymons of English Words," defines *sorn* to be a corruption of *sojourn.* The true etymon appears to be the Gaelic *saor*, free, and *saoranach*, one who makes free or establishes himself in free quarters. It is related of a noble Scottish lady of the olden time, who lived in a remote part of the Highlands, and was noted for her profuse and cordial hospitality, that she was sometimes overburdened with habitual *sorners.* When any one of them out-stayed his welcome, she would take occasion to say to him at the morning meal, with an arch look at the rest of the company—" Mak' a guid breakfast, Mr. Blank, while ye're about it ; I dinna ken whar' ye'll get your dinner." The hint was usually taken, and the *sorner* departed.

Soss, an incongruous, miscellaneous mixture of eatables.

Soss-poke, a ludicrous term for the stomach; usually derived from *sal* and *salsum*, because the ingredients are salted; but the word is more likely to have originated in *soss*, the old French *sause*, the Flemish *sass*, the modern *sauce*, compounded of several ingredients, all blending to produce a particularly piquant flavour. *Soss* is used in colloquial and vulgar English in the Scottish sense of a mixed mess; and *sorzle*, evidently a corruption of *soss*, is, according to Mr. Wright's Archaic Dictionary, a word used in the East of England to signify " any strange mixture."

Soudie, broth; from the old English *seethe*, to boil. (See POWSOUDIE, *ante*.)

Sourocks, wild sorrel; any sour vegetable.

Souter, a shoemaker, a cobbler. This word occurs in early English literature, though it is now obsolete.

> Ploughmen and pastourers.
> And other common labourers,
> *Souters* and shepherds.
> 　　　—*Piers Ploughman.*

> The devil maks a reeve to preach,
> Or a *souter*, a shipman, or a bear.
> 　　—CHAUCER: *Canterbury Tales.*

" Mair whistle than woo,"
As the *souter* said when he sheared the soo.
　—ALLAN RAMSAY'S *Scots Proverbs.*

> *Souters'* wives are aye ill shod.
> 　　　　—*Idem.*

Sowens, flummery; a mixture of oatmeal and sour milk.

Sowie, diminutive of *sow*. An implement of war for demolishing walls, which the English call a *ram*, and the French *un belier*, or a *battering ram;* the Scotch call it a *sow*, from its weight and rotundity.

> They laid their *sowies* to the wall
> 　Wi' mony a heavy peal ;
> But he threw ower to them again
> 　Baith pitch and tar-barrel.
> 　　　—SCOTT'S *Border Minstrelsy:*
> 　　　　　　*Auld Maitland.*

Sowth, to try over a tune with a low whistle, to hum a tune to one's self involuntarily.

> On braes when we please, then,
> 　We'll sit and *sowth* a tune,
> Syne rhyme till't ; we'll time till't,
> 　And sing't when we hae done.
> —BURNS: *To Davie, a Brother Poet.*

Sowther, or **soother**, to solder, to make amends for, to cement, to heal.

A towmond o' trouble, should that be my fa',
Ae night o' good fellowship *sowthers* it a'.
　　—BURNS: *Contented wi' Little.*

Spae, to tell fortunes, to predict. Etymology uncertain; derived by Jamieson from the Icelandic, but probably connected with *spell*, a magic charm or enchantment, or with *spes*, hope; *spae-wife*, a fortune-teller; *spae-book*, magic book, a fortune-teller's book.

The black *spae-book* from his breast he took,
　Impressed with mony a warlock spell;

And the book it was wrote by Michael
    Scott,
He held in awe the fiends o' hell.
    —LORD SOULIS : *Border Minstrelsy.*

Spae, which in Scottish means
to prophesy, has no connection
with the English *spae,* written
by Johnson *spay,* to castrate a
female animal for the purpose
of producing barrenness.

Be dumb, you beggars of the rhyming
    trade,
Geld your loose wits, and let the muse be
    spay'd.

A singular misconception of
the true meaning of a *spay'd,* or
one who is *spay'd,* has led to a
current English proverb, that
will doubtless drop out of use as
soon as its true origin is understood. In Taylor's works (1630),
quoted by Halliwell, occurs the
couplet :—

I think it good plaine English without
    fraude
To call a *spade* a *spade,* a bawd a bawd.

The juxtaposition of *bawd* and
spade in this passage suggests
that the true reading should be
spay'd. In Dr. Donne's satires,
anterior to the works of Taylor,
there appears the line :—

I call a *bawd* a *bawd,* a *spae'd* a *spae'd.*

Nares in his Glossary asks
very naturally, " why the *spade*
(rather than the poker, or hoe,
or plough, or pitchfork, or any
other implement) was especially
chosen to enter into this figurative expression is not clear."
If he had known the true meaning of the word *spay'd* or *spae'd,*

the obscurity would have been
cleared up.

Spairge, to sprinkle, to scatter
about as liquids. From the
French *asperger,* to sprinkle
with water.

When in yon cavern grim and sootie,
    Closed under hatches,
Spairges about the brimstane cootie.[*]
    —BURNS : *Address to the Deil.*

Spank, to move rapidly ; *spanker,*
one who walks with a quick
and lively step ; *spanky,* frisky,
lively, sprightly. The phrase
" a *spanking* tit " is still employed by the sporting brother-
hood of the lower classes to
signify a fast horse. The English *spank,* to beat, to slap,
seems to be derivable from the
same idea of rapidity of motion
which pertains to the Scottish
word, and to be suggestive of
the quick and oft-repeated motion of the hands in *spanking* or
slapping the posterior. *Spanker-
ing,* nimble, active, alert. The
word is derived by Jamieson
from the Teutonic *spannen,* to
extend. The German word,
however, does not exactly mean
extend, but to put the horses to
a carriage, as the French *átteler.*

Spargeon, plaister ; *spargeoner,*
a plaisterer ; from the French
asperger, to sprinkle.

Spartle, from the Flemish *sparteln,*
to move the limbs quickly or

---

[*] Cootie signifies a large dish, and also
the broth or other liquor contained in it.

convulsively, to kick about help-
lessly or involuntarily. *Sprattle*,
to struggle or sprawl.

Listening the doors and windows rattle,
I thought me on the ourie cattle,
Or silly sheep, wha bide this brattle
　　O' winter war,
And through the drift deep-lairing *sprattle*,
　　Beneath a scaur.
　　　　　—BURNS : *A Winter Night.*

　No more was made for that lady,
　For she was lying dead ;
　But a' was for her bonnie bairn,
　Lay *spartling* at her side.
　　.—BUCHAN'S *Ancient Ballads.*

Spatch-cock, a fowl split open,
to be broiled in haste, on a
sudden demand for dinner from
an unexpected guest ; a corruption of *dispatch*-cock, a cock
quickly cooked. The word is
common in the United States.

Spate, a flood or freshet, from the
overflow of a river or lake ; also
metaphorically an overflow of
idle talk.

The water was great and mickle o' *spate.*
　　　　　—*Kinmont Willie.*

Even like a mighty river that runs down in
　spate to the sea.
—W. E. AYTOUN : *Blackwood's Magazine.*

He trail'd the foul sheets down the gait,
　Thought to have washed them on a
　　stane,
The burn was risen out of *spate.*
　　—RITSON'S *Caledonian Muse : The
　　　　Wife of Auchtermuchty.*

While crashing ice, borne on the roaring
　spate,
Sweeps dams an' mills an' brigs a' to the
　gate.
　　　　　—BURNS : *The Brigs of Ayr.*

And doun the water wi' speed she ran,
　While tears in *spates* fa' fast frae her e'e.
—*Border M.nstrelsy : Jock o' the Side.*

The Laird of Balnamoon was a truly
eccentric character. He joined with his
drinking propensities a great zeal for the
Episcopal Church. One Sunday, having
visitors, he read the services and prayers
with great solemnity and earnestness.
After dinner, he, with the true Scottish
hospitality of the time, set to, to make
his guests as drunk as possible. Next
day, when they took their departure, one
of the visitors asked another what he
thought of the laird. "Why, really," he
replied, "sic a *spate* o' praying, and sic a
spate o' drinking, I never knew in all the
course of my life."—DEAN RAMSAY'S *Reminiscences.*

　Spate, or *spaite*, is from the
Gaelic *speid*, a mountain torrent
suddenly swollen by rain. In
the North of England, according to Messrs. Halliwell and
Wright, a *spait* signifies a more
than usually heavy downpour of
rain ; and in the county of Dur-
ham it signifies a pool formed
by the rain.

Spaul, sometimes written *spald*, a
shoulder ; from the French *es-
paule*, or *épaule*, often used to
signify a leg or limb. "To
spaul," according to Jamieson,
"is to push out the limbs like
a dying animal."

The late Duchess of Gordon sat at
dinner next to an Englishman, who was
carving, and who made it a boast that he
was thoroughly master of the Scottish
language. Her Grace turned to him and
said, "Rax me a *spaul* o' that bubbly-
jock !" The unfortunate man was completely nonplussed.—DEAN RAMSAY.

　The gander being longer in the *spauld.*
　　　　　—*Noctes Ambrosianæ.*

　Wi' spur on heel, or splent (armour) on
　spauld.
　—*Border Minstrelsy : Kinmont Willie.*

The Scotch employ the French word *gigot* for a leg of mutton; but they do not say a *spaul* of mutton for a shoulder.

Spean (sometimes spelled *spane* or *spayn*), to wean. The English *wean* is derived from the German *wohnen*, or *entwohnen;* and the Scottish *spean* from the Flemish and Low Dutch *speen*, which has the same meaning. *Speaning-brash*, an eruption in children, which often occurs at weaning-time.

> Withered beldams auld and droll,
> Rigwoodie hags wad *spean* a foal,
> Louping and flinging on a crummock,
> I wonder did na turn thy stomach.
> —Burns: *Tam o' Shanter.*

The meaning of *spean*, as used by Burns, implies that the hags were so very hideous, that, had they been brood mares, a foal would in disgust have refused to imbibe nourishment from them.

Speer-windit or **spier-windit**, out of breath or wind from asking too many questions, tired of asking; a word most applicable to impudent barristers cross-examining a witness; from *speer*, or *spier*, to inquire.

Spell, an interval. The Scotch and the Americans say: "a *spell* of work," "a *spell* of idleness," "a *spell* of bad weather," "a *spell* of good weather," "a *spell* of amusement," &c. The derivation of the word is supposed to be from the Dutch and

Flemish *spel*, the German *spiele*, to play. Possibly, though not certainly, the root is the Gaelic *speal*, to mow, cut down; and thence a *stroke, i.e.*, a stroke of good or bad weather, &c. The word has recently become current in English.

Spence, a store-room next to a kitchen, where the provisions are kept; an inner apartment in a small house. The word is supposed to be derived from *dispense*, to distribute; whence *dispensary*, the place where medicines are distributed.

> Wi' tottering step he reached the *spence*,
> Where soon the ingle blazed fu' hie;
> The auld man thought himself at hame,
> And the tear stood twinkling in his e'e.
> —Pickering: *Dornocht Sea, or the Auld Minstrel.*

> Our Bardie lanely keeps the *spence*
> Sin' Mailie's dead.
> —Burns: *Poor Mailie's Elegy.*

"Edward," said the sub-Prior, "you will supply the English knight here, in this *spence*, with suitable food and accommodation for the night."—Scott: *The Monastery.*

The word is still used in the north of England for a buttery, also for a cupboard, a pantry, and a private room in a farm house.

> Yet I had leven she and I
> Were both togydir secretly
> In some corner in the *spence*.
> —Halliwell.

Spier, to inquire, to ask after; of unknown etymology. The derivation from the Gaelic *speur*, clear, whence by extension of

O

meaning, an inquiry, to make clear, is scarcely satisfactory.

Mony a ane *spiers* the gate he knows full well.—ALLAN RAMSAY'S *Scots Proverbs.*

> I am Spes, quoth he,
> And *spier* after a knight,
> That took me a mandement
> Upon the mount of Sinai.
> —*Piers Ploughman.*

I *spiered* for my cousin fu' couthie and sweet.
—BURNS : *Last May a Braw Wooer.*

When lost, folks never ask the way they want,
> They *spier* the gait.
—ROBERT LEIGHTON : *Scotch Words.*

A very expressive derivation of *spier* is *back-spier,* meaning to cross-examine.— R. DRENNAN.

Her niece was asking a great many questions, and coming over and over the same ground, demanding an explanation how this and that had happened, till at last the old lady lost patience, and burst forth—" I winna be *back-spiered,* noo, Polly Fullerton."--DEAN RAMSAY.

Sperthe, a spear, a javelin, or, more properly, a battle-axe; a word that might well be rescued from oblivion for the use of rhymers, often hardly pushed for a rhyme to earth, birth, girth, and mirth—all well, or too well worn.

> His helmet was laced,
> At his saddle girth was a good steel *sperthe,*
> Full ten pound weight and more.
> —*Border Minstrelsy: The Eve of St. John.*

Spin-drift, sometimes corruptly written and pronounced *speen-drift* and *spune-drift,* snow driven by the wind in whirls or spinnings in the air, and finally accumulates on the ground when the force of the wind is exhausted.

Spirlie, a person with slender legs; *spindle-shanked,* slim, thin, often combined with *lang ;* as, " A lang spirlie," a tall slender person. From the Gaelic *speir,* a shank, a claw; *speireach,* having slender limbs.

Spleuchan, a Highland purse; from the Gaelic *spliuchan,* an outside pouch or receptacle of small matters, and *spliuch,* anything that hangs down.

> Deil mak' his king's-hood [scrotum] in a *spleuchan.*
> —BURNS : *Death and Dr. Hornbook.*

Splore, a riotously merry meeting; to make a *splore,* to create a sensation. The Americans have *splurge,* a word with the same meaning. The derivation is unknown.

> In Poosie Nancy's held the *splore.*
> .   .   .   .   .   .
> Wi' quaffing and laughing,
> They ranted and they sang.
> —BURNS : *The Jolly Beggars.*

The squads o' chiels that lo'ed a *splore,*
> On winter evenings never ca' ;
Their blythesome moments now are o'er,
> Since Rabbie gaed an' left them a'.
> —RICHARD GALL : *On the Death of Burns.*

Splute, to exaggerate in narrative, to indulge in fiction. Jamieson derives this word from the French *exploit,* but it is more probably a corruption of the Gaelic *spleadh,* a romance, a boast, a gasconade, a vain-glorious assertion; *spleadhaich,* hyperbolical.

Spoacher, a poacher, one who steals game. The Scottish word seems to have been the origi-nal form, and to have become poacher by the elision of the initial *s*, a not uncommon result in words from the Celtic, as the Welsh *hen*, old, is the same as the Gaelic *sean;* the English *nag* is the same as *snag,* to snarl or say provoking things, as is the custom with spiteful women if they wish to quarrel with their husbands. The English *poacher* is usually derived from *poke*, the French *poche*, a pocket, pouch, or bag, because the poacher, like the sportsman, *bags* his game. But if the Scot-tish *spoacher* be the elder word, it will be necessary to account for the lost *s*. This is supplied in the Gaelic *spog,* to seize vio-lently, as birds of prey do with their claws and talons, and *spogadh,* seizure. Jamieson was of opinion that the *s* was *added* in the Scottish word; but this would be a singular instance, contradicted by all previous ex-perience of similar cases.

Spoutie, a word of contempt for a too fluent orator, or a garru-lous boaster; one who, accord-ing to a wealthy Scottish phil-anthropist, is too plentifully endowed with "the pernicious gift of the gab—the curse of all free countries, especially of

Great Britain and the United States." To *spout* is a common English vulgarism that signifies to talk at an inordinate length to a public meeting. The Ame-ricans derisively call it to *orate.*

Sprack, lively, alert, animated; common in Scotland and pro-vinces in the south of England.

Spraikle, sprackle, sprauchle, to clamber up a hill with great exertion and difficulty. From the Gaelic *spracail,* strong, ac-tive. The English words *sprawl* and *sprag* seem to be of the same parentage.

> I, rhymer Robin, *alias* Burns,
>   October twenty-third;
> A ne'er-to-be-forgotten day,
> Sae far I *sprachled* up the brae,
>   I dinnered wi' a lord.
> —Burns: *The Dinner with Lord Daer.*

Wad ye hae naebody *spraickle* up the brae but yoursel, Geordie.—Scott: *For-tunes of Nigel.*

Spring, a lively tune.

> Sae rantingly, sae wantonly,
> He played of *spring*
> Beneath the gallows tree.
> —*Old Song: Macpherson's Farewell.*

Let him play a *spring* on his ain fiddle (*i.e.,* let him have his own way; let him ride his own hobby.)—Dean Ramsay.

Ye are as lang in tuning your pipes as anither man wad be in playing a *spring.*— *Scottish Proverb.*

Sproage. This eccentric-looking word signifies, according to Jamieson, to go out courting at night, to wander by the light of the moon or stars. Alexander Ross, in "Helenore, or the

Fortunate Shepherdess," has the lines :—

> We maun marry now ere lang ;
> Folk will speak o's, and fash us wi' the kirk,
> Gin we be seen thegither in the mirk.

Neither Burns, Allan Ramsay, nor Scott employs this word, and its origin is wholly unknown, unless the Gaelic *sporach*, to incite, excite, or instigate, may supply a clue.

Spulzie, to despoil, to ravage, to devastate, to lay waste; from *depouiller*, to spoil, or despoil.

> *Spulzie* him, *spulzie* him ! said Craigievar,
>   *Spulzie* him presentlie,
> For I wad lay my lugs in pawn,
>   He'd nae gude will at me.
>   —Buchan's *Ancient Ballads: The
>   Death of John Seton.*

Spune-hale, in such restored health as to be able to take one's ordinary food, one's kail or parritch, with a good appetite. *Parritch-hale* and *meat-hale* are synonymous.

Spung, a purse that fastens with a clasp; *sporan*, the large purse worn by the Highlanders on full-dress occasions.

> But wastefu' was the want of a',
> Without a yeuk they gar ane claw,
> When wickedly they bid us draw
>   Our siller *spungs*,
> For this and that to mak them braw
>   And lay their tongues.
>   —Allan Ramsay : *Last Speech of
>   a Wretched Miser.*

Spunk, a match, a spark; *spunkie*, fiery, high spirited; also an "ignis fatuus" or will o' the wisp. The word is derived by Jamieson from the Gaelic *spong*, rotten wood, or tinder, easily inflammable; but it is questionable whether the root is not the Teutonic *funk*, a sparkle of light; *funkeln*, to sparkle; and *ausfunkeln*, to sparkle out, to shine forth. *Ausfunk* is easily corrupted into *sfunk* and *spunk*.

> Erskine, a *spunkie* Norland billie,
>   And mony ithers ;
> Whom auld Demosthenes and Tully,
>   Might own as brithers.
>   —Burns : *Earnest Cry and Prayer.*

> If mair they deave us wi' their din
>   O' patronage intrusion ;
> We'll light a *spunk*, and every skin
>   We'll rin them aff in fusion,
>   Like oil some day.
>   —Burns : *The Ordination.*

> And oft from moss-traversing *spunkies*,
> Decoy the wight that late and drunk is.
>   —Burns : *Address to the Deil.*

Spurtle or **parritch spurtle**, a rounded stick or bar of hard wood, used in preference to a spoon or ladle for stirring oatmeal porridge in the process of cooking. Jamieson—who seldom dives deeper than the Teutonic—derives the word from *spryten*, the Latin *assula*. The Gaelic has *sparr* or *sparran*, a little wooden bar or bolt; and the Flemish has *sport*, with the same meaning; and also that of the rung of a ladder (a bar of wood which a Scottish housewife, in default of any better *spurtle*, might conveniently use for the purpose). Good bairns in the olden times when oatmeal porridge was the customary food

of the peasantry, were often re-
warded by having the *spurtle* to
lick in addition to their share of
the breakfast.

> Our gudeman cam' hame at e'en,
>   And hame cam' he ;
> And there he saw a braw broad sword,
>   Where nae sword should be.
>
> How's this ? gude wife,
>   How's this, quo he,
> How came this sword here
>   Without the leave o' me ?
>
> A sword ! quo she,
>   Aye, a sword, quo he ;
> Ye auld blind doited bodie,
>   And blinder may ye be,
> 'Tis but a parritch *spurtle*,
>   My minnie gied to me.
>
> Far hae I travelled,
>   And muckle hae I seen,
> But scabbards upon *spurtles*,
>   Saw I never nane !
>   —*Our Gudeman.*

Staffa, the name of the well-
known island of the West that
contains the " cave of Fingal."
Colonel Robertson, in " The
Gaelic Topography of Scotland," has omitted to give the
etymology of the word. Many
people suppose it to be English, and akin to *Stafford*. It
is, however, pure Gaelic, and
accurately descriptive of the
natural formation of the cave,
being compounded of *stuadh* (*dh*
silent), a pillar or pillars, column
or columns; and *uamh* (*uav* or
uaf), a cave, whence *stua-uaf*
or *staffa*, the cave of pillars or
columns.

Staig, a young, unbroken stallion.
In the North of England, this
word *stag*, or *staig*, is applied to

any young male quadruped, and,
in contempt, to a strong, vulgar,
romping girl, whose manners are
masculine. The word is also
applied to the Turkey cock and
the gander. From the German
steigen, to mount, to raise, to
stick up, to stand erect. In the
old Norse, *steggr* signifies male.

> It's neither your *stot* nor your *staig* I
>   shall crave,
> But gie me your wife, man, for her I
>   must have.
>   —BURNS : *The Carle o' Kellyburn
>   Braes.*

Stance, situation, standing-place,
or foundation. This word has
not yet been admitted into the
English dictionaries.

> No ! sooner may the Saxon lance,
> Unfix Benledi from his *stance*.
>   —SCOTT : *Lady of the Lake.*

We would recommend any Yankee be-
liever in England's decay to take his
stance in Fleet Street or any of our great
thoroughfares, and ask himself whether it
would be wise to meddle with any member
of that busy and strenuous crowd.—*Blackwood's Magazine,* June 1869.

Stank, a pool, a ditch, an en-
trenchment filled with water
for the defence of a fortress.
This word, with the elision of
the initial letter, becomes the
English *tank*, a receptacle for
water. *Stankit*, entrenched.
From the French *etaing*, or
estaing; the Gaelic *staing*, a
ditch, a pool ; *staingichte*, entrenched.

> I never drank the Muses *stank*,
>   Castilia's burn and a' that ;
> But there it streams, and richtly reams,
>   My Helicon, I ca' that.
>   —BURNS : *The Jolly Beggars.*

Clavers and his Highland men
　　Cam down among the raw, man;
Ower bush, ower bank, ower ditch, ower
　　stank,
She flang amang them a', man.
　　　　　—*Battle of Killiecrankie.*

Stanners, gravel, small stones on
the banks of a stream, shingle
on the sea shore.

Yestreen the water was in spate,
　　The *stanners* a' were curled.
—*Border Minstrelsy: Water Kelpie.*

Stark, strong; from the German.
The word, however, is English,
with a different meaning, as in
the phrase, *stark naked*, utterly
naked.

Fill fu' and hand fu' maks a *stark* man.
—*Old Proverb.*

S t a u m r e l, a stupid person;
saumer, to stutter, to be incoherent in speech, to stammer;
from the German *stumme*, dumb;
and *stumpf*, stupid, the Flemish
and Dutch *stumper*, a fool, a silly
and idle person.

Nae langer, thrifty citizens, an' douce,
Meet owre a pint or in the council house,
But *staumrel*, corky-headed gentry,
The herriment and ruin of the country.
　　　　—BURNS: *The Brigs of Ayr.*
The lad was aye a perfect *stump*.
　　　　　　—JAMIESON.

Staves. "To go to *staves*" is a
proverbial expression used in
Scotland to signify to go to
ruin, to fall to pieces like a
barrel, when the hoops that
bind the staves together are
removed.

Staw, to surfeit, to disgust. Etymology uncertain; not Flemish,
as Jamieson supposes, but probably from the Gaelic *stad* or
stadh (pronounced *stà*), to desist,
or cause to desist.

Is there that o'er his French ragout,
Or olio that wad *staw* a sow.
　　　　—BURNS: *To a Haggis.*

Curryin's a grand thing, when the edge
o' the appetite's a wee turned, and ye're
rather beginnin' to be *stawed.—Noctes
Ambrosianæ.*

Steek, to close, to shut, to fasten
with a pin.

Sages their solemn e'en may *steek*.
　　　　—BURNS: *Cry and Prayer.*

　　Steek the awmrie.
—SIR WALTER SCOTT: *Donald Caird.*

Ye're owre bonnie! ye're owre bonnie!
Sae *steek* that witchin' e'e,
It's light flees gleamin' through my brain.
　　　　　—JAMES BALLANTINE.

Your purse was *steekit* when that was
paid for.

When the steed's stown *steik* the stable-
door.
　　—ALLAN RAMSAY'S *Scots Proverbs.*

Steeks, the interstices of any woven or knitted fabric, stitches;
steek, probably from *stitch*, as *kirk*
from *church*.

He draws a bonnie silken purse,
As lang's my tail, where, through the *steeks*,
The yellow-lettered Geordie [guinea] keeks.
　　　　—BURNS: *The Twa Dogs.*

Steenies, guineas, foreign or other
gold coins; derivation unknown,
unless the term be a mock depreciation of the precious metal,
from *stone*, or *stein*, applied upon
the same principle that money
is called dross or filthy lucre.

What though we canna boast of our
     guineas, O,
We've plenty of Jockies and Jeanies, O,
     An' these, I'm certain, are
     More daintier by far
Than a pock full of yellow *steenies*, O.
          —Rev. JOHN SKINNER: *The Old
               Man's Song.*

Steeve, or **steive**, firm, erect,
stout; from the English *stiff*,
and the Flemish *stijf*.

> Sit ye *steeve* in your saddle seat,
> For he rides sicker who never fa's.
>   —JAMES BALLANTINE.

Sten, to spring to one side, a sudden motion in the wrong direction; to turn away, to twist, to
bend; *stennis*, a sprain. From
the Gaelic *staon*, awry, askew;
and *staonaich*, to bend, to twist,
to turn. Jamieson erroneously
derives *sten* from *extend*.

> Yestreen at the valentines' dealing,
>   My heart to my mou' gied a *sten*,
> For thrice I drew ane without failing,
>   And thrice it was written Tam Glen.
>   —BURNS: *Tam Glen.*

Stevin or **steven**. Before the introduction from the Latin *vox*,
and the French *voix*, of the
word *voice* into the English and
Scottish languages, the word
stevin was employed. It was
used by Chaucer in England,
and by Gawin Douglas in Scotland. From its resemblance
to the Teutonic *stimme*, a voice,
and *stimmen*, voices, the Flemish
stem, it is probable that it was a
corruption or variation of that
word.

> With dreary heart and sorrowful *steven*.
>   —*Morte Arthur.*

Betwixt the twelfth hour and eleven,
I dreamed an angel cam frae heaven,
With pleasant *stevin* sayand on hie,
Tailyiors and soutars, blest be ye!
          —DUNBAR: ALLAN RAMSAY'S
                         Evergreen.

Lang may thy *steven* fill with glee
The glens and mountains of Lochlee.
     —BEATTIE: *To Mr. Alexander Ross.*

Quoth Jane, " My *steven*, sir, is blunted
     sair,
And singing frae me frighted off wi' care;
But gin ye'll tak' it as I now can gie't,
Ye're welcome til't—and my sweet blessing
     wi't."
                    —Ross's *Helenore.*

The rhymes to "heaven" in
Scottish and English poetry are
few, and *stevin* would be an
agreeable addition to the number if it were possible to revive it.

Steward, a director, a manager,
an administrator. As a patronymic, the word is sometimes
spelled *stewart* and *stuart*, and
has been derived from the Teutonic *stede-ward*, one who occupies the place delegated to him
by another; or from the Icelandic *stia*, work, and *weard*, a
guard or guardian. It seems,
however, to have an indigenous
origin in the Gaelic *stiuir*, to
lead, direct, guide, steer, super-
intend, manage, &c.; and *ard*,
high or chief. The "*Steward*
of Scotland*" was in early times
the chief officer of the crown,
and next in power and dignity
to the king. There was a similar functionary in England:—

> The Duke of Norfolk is the first,
> And claims to be high *Steward*.

The attributes of the "*Steward* of Scotland" are set forth by Erskine as quoted in Jamieson ; and the last holder of the office —who became king of Scotland —gave the name of his function to his royal descendants. In its humbler sense, of the *steward* of a great household, or of a ship, the name is still true to its Gaelic derivation, and signifies the chief director of his particular department.

It has been suggested in the "Gaelic Etymology of the Languages of Western Europe," that the true etymon of *stew* or *stu* (the first syllable of *steward* and *stuart*) is the Gaelic *stuth*, pronounced *stu*, which signifies any strong liquor, as well as food, sustenance, or nourishment for the body ; and that consequently *steward* means chief butler, or provider of the royal household. There is much to be said in favour of this hypothesis, but the derivation from *tiar* seems preferable.

The Irish Gaelic spells *steward* in the English sense *stiobhard*. The Scottish Gaelic has it *stiubhard* ; but the words thus written have no native etymology, and are merely phonetic renderings of an obsolete Gaelic term, re-borrowed from the modern English. The suggested Teutonic etymology of *steward* from *stede-ward*, has no foundation in the Teutonic languages. *Steward* in Germany is *Verwalter*, administrator or director ; and *Haushofmeister*, master of the household. In Flemish, *bestieren* signifies to administer, to direct ; and *bestierder*, an administrator, a director, a steward.

Stey, steep, perpendicular. In Cumberland and Westmoreland, a mountain of peculiar steepness is called a *sty ;* and in Berkshire, *sty* signifies a ladder. *Stey* and *sty* are both from the German *stiegen*, and the Flemish *stijgen*, to mount, to climb.

> Set a stout heart to a *stey* brae.—ALLAN RAMSAY'S *Scots Proverbs.*

> The *steyest* brae thou wouldst hae face't at.
>   —BURNS : *The Auld Farmer to His Auld Mare, Maggie.*

Stickit minister, a term of obloquy in Scotland for a candidate for holy orders who has failed to pass the necessary examination, or to give satisfaction to the congregation before whom he preached the probationary sermon. The phrase is akin to the vulgar English—"old *stick* in the mud."

> Puir lad ! the first time he tried to preach, he *stickit* his sermon.—JAMIESON.

> A speech is *stickit* when the speaker hesitates and is unable to proceed.—*Idem.*

Still. This word is sometimes employed in the Scottish vernacular in a sense which it possesses no longer in English, that of taciturn, or reticent of speech. "A *still* dour man," signifies a taciturn, reserved, and hard man.

Stirk, a bullock ; *stirkie*, a bull calf.

There's aye water where the *stirkie* drowns (*i.e.*, there's a reason or cause for everything ; or there's never a smoke without fire).

Stob, to push the foot accidentally against a stone or other impediment in the ground. " I have *stobbed* my toe," said the late President Lincoln, in explanation of his temporary lameness ; from the Gaelic *stob*, a stake, a thrust, or anything thrust in the ground ; a stick, a stump, any stalk broken or cut and still projecting from the ground ; whence the English word *stubble*.

Stoit, to stagger.

> And aye as on the road he *stoitit*,
> His knees on ane anither *knockit*
> [knocked together].
> —GEORGE BEATTIE : *John o' Arnha'.*

Stound, a moment, a very short space of time ; also, a quick sudden momentary pain. From the German *stund*, an hour.

> Gang in and seat you on the sunks a' round,
> And ye'se be sair'd wi' plenty in a *stound*.
> —·Ross's *Helenore.*

> And aye the *stound*, the deadly wound,
> Came frae her e'en sae bonnie blue.
> —BURNS : *I Gaed a Waefu Gate.*

Stoup or **stoop**, a flagon, a pitcher, a jug. *Pint-stoup*, a bottle or jug containing a pint. This word was used by Shakspeare, Ben Jonson, and other dramatists of the Elizabethan era ; it has long been obsolete in England, but survives with undiminished vitality in Scotland.

> Come, ;Lieutenant ! I have a *stoop* of wine, and here without are a brace of Cyprian gallants, that would fain have a measure to the health of black Othello.—*Othello.*

Set me the *stoup* of wine upon that table.
> —*Hamlet.*

> And surely ye'll be your *pint-stoup*,
> As sure as I'll be mine.
> —BURNS : *Auld Lang Syne.*

> Water-*stoups ?* quo' he ;
> Aye, water-*stoups*, quo' she—
> Far hae I ridden,
> And muckle I hae seen ;
> But silver spurs on water-*stoups*
> Saw I never nane !
> —HERD'S *Collection : Our Guidman.*

The etymology of *stoup* or *stoop* has long been contested. Johnson derives it from the Dutch and Flemish *stop*, a cork or stopper of a bottle ; the German *stöpsel ;* but this can scarcely be the origin of the Scottish word, for a milk-*stoup*, a water-*stoup*, a can, a pitcher, a bucket, a pail, are not corked or stopped. In some Scottish glossaries a *stoup* is said to be a tin pot, and in others it is defined as a jug with a handle ; while in Northumberland, according to Wright's Provincial Dictionary, a *stoop* signifies a barrel. In Gaelic, *stop* means a wooden vessel for carrying water, a measure for liquids, or a flagon ; and *stopan* signifies a small flagon. Between the Flemish and Gaelic derivations it is difficult to decide ; but the Gaelic, which applies the word to wide and open utensils, seems to be preferable, at least in comprehensiveness.

Stour, dust in motion, and metaphorically trouble, vexation, or
disturbance; *stourie*, dusty. The
word is akin to the English *stir*,
and in its metaphorical sense is
synonymous with the Scottish
steer, as in the song "What's a'
the *steer*, kimmer?" what's the
disturbance, or in the broad
vernacular, what's the row?
"To kick up a dust" is a slang
expression that has a similar
origin.

> Yestreen I met you on the moor,
> Ye spak na, but gaed by like *stour;*
> Ye geck at me because I'm poor.
> 　　　—Burns: *Tibbie, I hae Seen*
> 　　　　　*the Day.*

After service, the betheral of the strange
clergyman said to his friend the other
betheral, "I think our minister did weel.
He aye gars the *stour* flee out o' the
cushion." To which the other replied,
with a calm feeling of superiority, "*Stour*
out o' the cushion! Hoot! our minister,
sin' he cam' wi' us, has dung [knocked or
beaten] the guts out o' twa Bibles."—Dean
Ramsay.

> How blithely wad I bide the *stoure*,
> 　A weary slave frae sun to sun,
> Could I the rich reward secure
> 　Of lovely Mary Morrison.
> 　　　　　—Burns.

Burns uses the word in the
sense of mould, earth, or soil, as
in his "Address to the Daisy:"—

> Wee, modest, crimson-tippet flower,
> Thou'st met me in an evil hour,
> For I man crush amang the *stour*,
> 　Thy slender stem.

Stour, in the sense of strife,
was a common English word in
the time of Chaucer and his
predecessors.

Stowlins, stownlins, by stealth,
stealthily, or stolen moments
unobserved, or expecting to be
unobserved.

> Rob *stowlins* pried her bonnie mou,
> Fu' cosie in the neuk for't
> Unseen that night.
> 　　　—Burns: *Hallowe'en.*

Stoyte, stoiter, to stagger,
stumble, or walk unsteadily;
from the Flemish *stooten*, to
push against, to stumble or
cause to stumble.

> When staggirand and swaggirand,
> They *stoyter* hame to sleep.
> 　—Allan Ramsay: *The Vision.*

> Blind chance let her snapper and *stoyte*
> on the way.
> 　　　—Burns: *Contented wi' Little.*

> At length wi' drink and courtin' dizzy,
> He *stoitered* up and made a face.
> 　　　—Burns: *The Jolly Beggars.*

To *stoitle* over, in consequence of infirmity, without being much hurt. To
tyne or lose the *stoyte*, is a metaphor for
being off the proper line of conduct.—
Jamieson.

Strae death, straw death, death
in bed, natural death. This
strong but appropriate expression comes from the Middle
Ages, when lawlessness and
violence were chronic.

Strappan or **strappin'**, strong, tall,
burly, well-grown; the English
strapping, a strapping youth.

> The miller was *strappin'*, the miller was
> ruddy.
> 　　　—Burns: *Meg o' the Mill.*

> Wi' kindly welcome Jenny brings him
> ben,
> A *strappin'* youth—he taks the mother's
> eye.
> 　　　—Burns: *Cotter's Saturday Night.*

This word comes from the Gaelic *streap*, to climb up, *i.e.*, in stature, to grow tall.

Streik, to stretch; from the Dutch and Flemish *strekken*, German *strechen*, to extend. This word is used in a variety of ways, unknown to or unfrequent in English; as, "Tak' your ain *streik*," take your own course; *streikin*, tall and active; *streik*, to go quickly, *i.e.*, to stretch out in walking; tight or tightly drawn, *i.e.*, excessively drawn, stretched out, or extended.

Strone or **stroan**, a ludicrous word for the habitual urination of dogs when out on their rambles. It is introduced by Burns in his description of the rich man's dog, Cæsar, the fine Newfoundland, who was the friend and companion of Luath, the poor man's dog:—

Though he was of high degree,
The fient o' pride, nae pride had he.

. . . . .

Nae tauted tyke, though e'er sae duddie,
But he wad stan't as glad to see him,
And *stroan't* on stanes and hillocks wi' him.

The word seems to have been originally applied to the action of the dog in first smelling the place where another dog has been before for a similar purpose, and to be derived from the Gaelic *srone* (pronounced *strone*), a nose; and *sronagaich*, to trace by the scent as dogs do.

Stroop, a spout. *Stroopie*, the spout of a kettle; also a gutter or watercourse.

Struishle, to struggle pertinaciously, and in vain, against continually recurring difficulties; from the Femish *struikelen*, to stumble, to fall down.

A tradesman employed to execute a very difficult piece of carved work, being asked how he was getting on, answered—" I'm *struishling* awa' like a writer [lawyer] tryin' to be honest !"—*Laird of Logan.*

Strunt, alcoholic liquor of any kind ; a fit of ill-humour ; also, an affront, or a sturdy, arrogant walk.

Strunt and sturt are birds of ae feather,
And aft are seen on the wing thegither.
—*Scots Proverb.*

Burns makes the disagreeable insect that he saw on a lady's bonnet at church " *strunt* rarely over her gauze and lace." The word, in this sense, seems to be a corruption of the English *strut*. *Stront* is a low Teutonic word for *stercus humanum;* but this can scarcely be the root of *strunt* in any of the senses in which it is used in the Scottish language ; though *strunty*, an epithet applied to any one in a fit of such ill-humour as to be excessively disagreeable to all around him, may not be without some remote connection with the Teutonic idea.

Study or **brown study.** This expression seems to have first appeared in literature in the

" Case Altered " of Ben Jonson, who was of Scottish parentage, though born in London :—

Faiks ! this *brown study* suits not with your black ; your habit and your thought are of two colours.

(See BROWN STUDY, *ante*, p. 19.)

Stug. This Scottish word is used in a variety of senses—all allied to the idea of stiffness, erectness, rigidity, hardness, prickliness, &c., as the English *stiff*, *stick*, *stock*, *stuck up*, and the corresponding verb derived from the noun ; as *stug*, to stab or stick with a sharp weapon ; *stug*, the trunk or fragment of a decayed tree projecting above the ground; *stug*, a hard, masculine woman ; *stug*, obstinate ; *stugger*, an obstinate person ; *stug*, a thorn ; *stugs*, stubble. From the Dutch and Flemish *stug*, inflexible, stiff, obstinate ; the German *stich*, to stab, to pierce ; *sticheln*, to prick, to sting.

Sturt, strife, contention, disturbance ; also, to strive, to contend ; a word apparently akin to *stour* in its poetical sense of confusion. It is akin to, and possibly derived from, the German *stürzen*, to disturb, to overthrow.

And aye the less they hae to *sturt* them, In like proportion less will hurt them.
　　　—BURNS : *The Twa Dogs.*

I've lived a life of *sturt* and strife, I die by treachery.

　　　—*Macpherson's Farewell.*

Styme, a particle, an iota, an atom; the least possible quantity; a blink, a gleam, a glimpse.

He held, she drew, fu' steeve that day, Might no man see a *styme*.
　　　—*Christ's Kirk on the Green.*

I've seen me daz't upon a time, I scarce could wink or see a *styme*.
　　　—BURNS : *Naething like Nappy.*

The faintest form of an object ; a glimpse or transitory glance, as, " There's no a *styme* o' licht here."—JAMIESON.

From *styme* is formed *stymie*, one who sees indistinctly ; and *stymel*, which, according to Jamieson, is a name of reproach given to one who does not perceive quickly what another wishes him to see. Jamieson hints, rather than asserts, that *styme* is from the Welsh *ystum*, form, or figure ; but as *styme* is the absence of form and figure, something faint, indistinct, and small, rather than a substantial entity, the etymology is unsatisfactory. The word seems to have some relationship to the Gaelic *stim*, or *stiom*, a slight puff, or wreath of smoke ; and thence to mean anything slight, transitory, and indistinct.

Sugh. or **sough**, a sigh, a breath. Greek *psyche*, the breath of life, the soul. To keep a calm *sugh*, is to be discreetly silent about anything, not to give it breath ; *sugh-siller*, erroneously printed *sow-siller* by Jamieson, means hush-money.

Sunkets, scraps of food, scrans (q. v.).

In Scotland there lived a humble beggar,
He had neither house nor hauld nor hame,
But he was weel likit by ilka body,
And they gied him *sunkets* to rax his wame ;
A nievefu' o' meal, a handfu' o' groats,
A daud o' a bannock, or pudding bree,
Cauld parritch, or the licking o' plates,
Wad mak him as blithe as a body could be.
  —*Tea Table Miscellany.*

Sunket-time is meal-time. The etymology of *sunket* is uncertain. Herd derived it from *something.*—Jamieson.

Whenever an uncertain etymology in English or Lowland Scotch is avowed, it would be well if the dubious philologists would look into the Gaelic, which they seldom do. In the case of *sunket* they would have found something better in that language than the English *something. Sanntach* signifies a dainty, or something that is desired, coveted, or longed after ; and *sanntaichte,* that which is desired. This word would be easily convertible by the Lowland Scotch into *sunket.* Halliwell, in his Archaic Dictionary, has *sun-cote,* a dainty, which he says is a Suffolk word.

Sumph, a stupid or soft-headed person. Jamieson derives the word from the German *sumpf,* and Flemish *somp,* a bog, a marsh, a morass ; a possible but not a convincing etymology. Halliwell has *sump,* a heavy weight, whence he adds, a heavy stupid fellow is so called.

The soul of life, the heaven below,
  Is rapture-giving woman ;
Ye surly *sumphs* who hate the name,
  Be mindfu' o' your mither.
    —Burns.

Sumph, an admirable word.—*Noctes Ambrosianæ.*

Swack, to deal a heavy blow ; akin to the vulgar English *whack,* to beat severely ; a swashing blow, a heavy blow; etymology uncertain. The Teutonic *schwach,* weak, has an opposite meaning, though there may be some connection of idea between a heavy blow and a blow that *weakens* him on whom it falls.

When Percy wi' the Douglas met,
  I wat he was fu' fain,
They *swakkit* their swords till sair they swat,
  And the blood ran doun like rain.
    —*Battle of Otterbourne.*

In another stanza of this vigorous old ballad, occur the lines :—

Then Percy and Montgomery met,
  That either of other were fain ;
They *swappit* swords, and they twa swat,
  And the blood run doun between.

Here *swappit* seems employed in the same sense as *swakkit,* and is possibly a variation of *swoop,* to come down with a heavy blow.

Swacken, to grow weak ; from the German *schwach,* weak.

Wi' that her joints began to *swacken,*
And she scour'd like ony *maukin* (hare).
    —George Beattie : *John o' Arnha'.*

Swagers, men married to sisters. Jamieson goes to the Swedish and Icelandic for the derivation of this word, but it is to be found nearer home in the Flemish *zwager*, and the German *schwager*, a brother-in-law.

Swank, active, agile, supple; *swankie*, an active, clever young fellow, fit for his work, and not above it; from the Flemish and German. Halliwell says that *swanky* is a northern English word for a strong, strapping fellow; and *swanking* for big, large.

Thou ance was in the foremost rank,
A filly, buirdly, steeve, and *swank*.
　　—BURNS: *The Auld Farmer to his Auld Mare, Maggie.*

At e'en at the gloaming,
Nae *swankies* are roaming,
Bout stackin' the lassies at bogle to play.
　　—*The Flowers of the Forest.*

The etymological root of *swankie* is apparently the Teutonic *schwank*, droll; used in a sense equivalent to the French *drôle*, which means a funny fellow, a droll fellow, or a fellow in a contemptuous and depreciatory sense. Mr. Thomas Wright, in his Archaic Dictionary of Local and Provincial English, says that *swankie* is a northern word for a strapping fellow; and that *swamp* signifies lean, unthriving, which suggests that possibly *swampie* is a corruption of *swankie*, with a slight shade of difference in the phrase; the meaning for "a strapping fellow," though suggestive of strength, may be also suggestive of tallness and leanness. The Danish has *svang*, withered, lean; but it also has *svanger*, which means large-bellied, and is applied to a pregnant woman; the Flemish and Dutch have *swanger* with the same meaning.

Swankies young in braw braid claith,
Are springin' owre the gutters.
　　—BURNS: *The Holy Fair.*

Swarf, to faint, to swoon, to stupefy, or be stupefied; also, a fainting fit, a swoon.

And monie a huntit poor red coat,
　For fear amaist did *swarf*, man!
—BURNS: *The Battle of Sherriff-Muir.*

He held up an arrow as he passed me; and I *swarf'd* awa wi' fright.—SCOTT: *The Monastery.*

Ye hae gar'd the puir wretch speak till she *swarfs*, and now ye stand as if ye never saw a woman in a *dwam* before.—SCOTT: *St. Ronan's Well.*

The etymology of *swarf* is uncertain; the author of "Piers Ploughman" has *swowe*, to swoon, akin apparently to the Gaelic *suain*, to fall asleep. By some *swarf* has been derived from the Teutonic *auswerfen*, to throw out, or throw off; and as to fall in a fainting fit is to throw off temporarily the semblance of life, it is probable that the derivation is correct. *Dwam*, in the same sense as used by Sir Walter Scott, was formerly written *dualm*, and *dwalm*. These latter words are evidently allied to the old English *dwale*, one of the popular names of the plant bella donna, or deadly night-shade; a word employed by the early poets Gower and Chaucer, and still in use in the Lowlands of Scotland, and the Northern counties of England.

Swatch, a specimen, a sample. Etymology uncertain.

On this side sits a chosen *swatch*,
Wi' screwed-up, grace-proud faces.
—BURNS: *The Holy Fair.*

That's just a *swatch* o' Hornbook's way;
Thus goes he on from day to day,
Thus does he poison, kill, and slay,
  An's weel paid for't.
—BURNS: *Death and Dr. Hornbook.*

Swats, new ale or beer.

Tam had got planted unco right
Fast by an ingle bleezing finely,
Wi' reaming *swats* that drank divinely.
—BURNS: *Tam o' Shanter.*

I gie them a skelp as they're creeping along,
Wi' a cog o' guid *swats* and an auld Scottish sang.
—BURNS: *Contented wi' Little.*

This word seems to be a ludicrous derivation from the Gaelic *suath*, to mix liquids, to rub or press barley; and *suathadh*, a mode of threshing barley; and thence, by extension of meaning, the juice of the barley. According to Jamieson, *swats*, or *swaits*, signifies new ale only. He derives it from the Anglo-Saxon *swate*, ale or beer; but the anterior root seems to be the Gaelic *suath.*

Sweer, difficult, heavy, slow, wearied; from the German *schwer*, heavy, hard, difficult.

Sweer to bed, and *sweer* up in the morning.—ALLAN RAMSAY'S *Scots Proverbs.*

Sweere-arse and **sweer-tree** are, according to Jamieson, the names of a sport among Scottish children, in which two of them are seated on the ground, and, holding a stick between them, endeavour each of them to draw the other up from the sitting posture. The heaviest in the posterior wins the game.

Sweine, a swoon, a trance; from the Gaelic *suain*, sleep.

Sometimes she rade, sometimes she gaed
As she had done before, O,
And aye between she fell in a *sweine*
Lang ere she cam to Yarrow.
—*The Dowie Dens o' Yarrow.*

Swick or **swyke**, to deceive; also, a trick, a fraud, a deception; *swicky* and *swickful*, deceitful. Apparently from the Danish *svige*, to deceive, to cheat, to defraud; and *svig*, fraud, imposture.

"He played them a *swick;* I had nae *swick o't,*" I had no blameableness in it.— JAMIESON.

Swiff, the English *whiff,* a puff of smoke, a breath, a short interval, as a *swiff* of sleep amid pain, a passing odour; *swiff,* the sound of an object passing rapidly by, as of an arrow or bullet in its flight. Whether the English *whiff,* or the Scottish *swiff,* were the original form, it is hopeless to inquire. The Scottish word seems to be a variety of the old English *swippe,* which Halliwell's Archaic Dictionary defines, to move rapidly; and *swipper,* nimble, quick.

Swine. "The *swine's* gone through it," is a proverbial expression which signifies that a marriage has been postponed or unduly delayed. Why the swine should have anything to do with a marriage is so incomprehensible as to suggest that the word does duty for some other, of which it is a corruption. Such a word exists in the Gaelic *suain*, a sleep, a deep sleep, a lethargy, whence the English *swoon*. *Suain* also signifies to entwine, to wrap round, to envelop, to tie up, to twist a cord or rope round anything; and hence may, in the proverbial saying above cited, signify an impediment. Either of the two meanings of *suain* would meet the sense of the phrase better than *swine*.

Swipes, a contemptuous term for small and weak beer; probably first given to it on account of its thinness, and the difficulty, or impossibility, of getting drunk upon it. From the Flemish *zuipen*, to drink to excess; the German *saufen*, to drink as animals do, who, however, wiser in this respect than men, never drink to excess. *Sowf*, to drink, to quaff, and *souffe*, a drunkard, are Scottish words from the same root.

Die Juden sind narren die fressen kein schwein,
Die Turken sind narren die *saufen* kein wein.
[The Jews are fools, they eat no swine ;
The Turks are fools, they *swite* no wine.]
        —*Old German Song ; attributed to*
                MARTIN LUTHER.

Swirl, to turn rapidly, to eddy, to curl.

                        His tail
Hung o'er his hurdies wi' a *swirl*.
        —BURNS : *The Twa Dogs.*

The mill wheel spun and *swirl'd*,
And the mill stream danced in the morning light,
    And all its eddies curl'd.
        —*The Lump of Gold.*

Swither, fear, doubt, perplexity, hesitation, dread. The etymology is doubtful, but is possibly from the German *zwischen*, between, *i.e.*, between two conflicting opinions.

I there wi' something did foregather,
That put me in an eerie *swither*.
    —BURNS : *Death and Dr. Hornbook.*

Syde, long or low, largely applied to a gown or dress.

Jeanie she gaed up the gate,
Wi' a green gown as *syde* as her smock,
Now, sirs, Jeanie has gotten her Jock.
        —CHAMBERS'S *Scottish Songs.*

Syke, a ditch, a northern English word, according to Halliwell, for a gutter; probably a corruption of *soak* or *suck*. A *sike*, according to Jamieson, is a rill, or a marshy bottom with a small stream in it.

Through thick and thin they scoured about,
Plashing through dubs and *sykes*.
    —ALLAN RAMSAY : *Continuation of
            Christ's Kirk on the Green.*

Syne, since, time past, a time ago. (See AULD LANG SYNE, p. 3.)

Here's a health to them that were here short *syne*,
    And canna be here the day.
        JOHNSON'S *Musical Museum.*

T

Tabean birben, a comb ; probably a side-comb for the adornment of a woman's hair. It occurs in the ancient version of the song entitled " Lord Gregory." Jamieson is of opinion that the phrase, a *" tabean birben* kame " means a comb made at Tabia, in Italy. " Shall we suppose," he adds, "that *birben* is a corruption of *ivour,* or *ivory-bane* (or bone) ? " Shall we not rather suppose, as Tabia was not known as a place of manufacture for combs, that the word is of native Scotch origin, and that, uncouth as it looks, it is resolvable into the Gaelic *taobh,* a side ; *taobhan,* sides ; *bior,* a pin, a point, a prickle, the tooth of a comb ; and *bean,* a woman, whence *taobhan bior bean* (corrupted into *tabean birben*), the side-comb of a woman ?

Tack, a lease, a holding ; *tacksman,* a leaseholder ; from *tack,* to hold, to fasten.

> Nae man has a *tack* o' his life.
> —ALLAN RAMSAY'S *Scots Proverbs.*

Taigle, to tease, to perplex, to banter ; from the Gaelic *teagamh,* doubt, perplexity.

Two irreverent young fellows determined to *taigle* the minister. Coming up to him in the High Street of Dumfries, they accosted him with much solemnity, " Maister Dunlop, hae ye heard the news ? " " What

news ? " " Oh, the deil's dead ! " " Is he ? " replied Mr. Dunlop. " Then I maun pray for twa faitherless bairns."—DEAN RAMSAY'S *Reminiscences.*

Taigle, " to tease, perplex, banter." I never heard these meanings ;—*teigle* is to delay, to hinder—dinna *taigle* me—I was sair *taigled* the day. In the quotation from Dean Ramsay, I suspect that *taigle* is improperly put for *tackle,* or, as pronounced in Scotland, *tackle,* meaning to seize upon, lay hold on. In a description of a meeting of the U.P. Presbytery of Edinburgh, that had what is called the Dalkeith heresy case before it, it was stated that Dr. Peddie proceeded to *tackle* Mr. Ferguson upon his heretical views.—R. DRENNAN.

Tairge, or **targe,** to cross-question severely and rigidly ; of uncertain etymology, though possibly connected with the Gaelic *tagair,* to plead, to argue, to dispute.

> And aye on Sundays daily, nightly,
> I on the questions *tairge* them tightly ;
> Till, fack, wee Davock's grown so gleg,
> Though scarcely larger than my leg,
> He'll screed you aff Effectual Calling
> As fast as ony in the dwalling.
> —BURNS : *The Inventory.*

I'll gie him a *tairgin'.*—JAMIESON.

Tait, joyous, gay ; a word used by the old Scottish poet, Douglas, in his translation of the " Eneid." Jamieson derives it " from the Icelandic *teitr,* hilares, exultans ; " but its more obvious source is the Gaelic *taite,* which has the same mean-

P

ing. The English exclamation of *hoity-toity*, or *hoite cum toite*, the name of a favourite dance in the reign of Charles II., is from the same Gaelic root—*aite chum taite*—in which *aite* and *taite* are almost synonymous, and signify joy, merriment, pleasure. *Hoyt*, in the sense of revelry, was used by the Elizabethan writers, Donne, Beaumont and Fletcher, and others.

Hoity-toity, whisking, frisking.
—BICKERSTAFFE : *Love in a Village.*

He sings and *hoyts* and revels among his drunken companions. — BEAUMONT AND FLETCHER.

The modern English slang *tight*, applied to a person who is joyously intoxicated, or semi-intoxicated, seems to be of the same Gaelic derivation.

Taity, taitey, matted like hair, entangled. *Tait* (sometimes written *tate* and *tett*), a lock of matted hair.

At ilka *tait* o' his horse's mane
There hung a siller bell,
The wind was loud, the steed was proud,
And they gied a sindry knell.
—*Ballad of Young Waters.*

Her skirt was o' the grass-green silk,
Her mantle o' the ermine fine,
At ilka *tett* o' the horse's mane
Hung fifty siller bells and nine.
—*Ballad of True Thomas.*

The etymology of this word is uncertain, unless it is to be found in the Gaelic *taod*, a rope, a string ; from the ropy, stringy appearance of hair in this condition. There is an old

Scottish song entitled "Taits o' Woo'."

Tak' tellin', take telling ; a phrase that implies that a person either requires or is amenable to advice or admonition, or the reverse.

He wad na *tak tellin*, he would not be advised. . . . She's a clever servant in a house, but she *taks tellin*, *i.e.*, she needs to be reminded of what ought to be done. —JAMIESON.

Tandle (sometimes written *tawnle*), a bonfire ; from the Gaelic *tein*, fire, and *deal*, friendly. From the root of *teine* comes *teind*, or *tynd*, to kindle ; and *tin-egin* (sometimes rendered by the Teutonic *neid-fire*), a fire of emergency, produced by friction of two pieces of dried wood. *Neid-fire* also means a beacon ; possibly a misprint for "need-fire." Jamieson translates *tin-egin*, a force fire, but gives no etymology. *Egin* is from the Gaelic *eigin* or *eiginn*, force, violence, compulsion. See BELTANE, *ante.*

Tangle, long, tall, and feeble, not well jointed ; from the Gaelic *tean*, long, thin, drawn out, extended ; and *gille*, a lad ; also the popular name of the long seaweed, *tangle*, often used in conjunction with dulse, for seaweed generally. Dean Ramsay quotes the saying of an old Scottish lady, who was lifted from the ground after a fall, happily not severe, by a very tall, young lieutenant, who addressed him when she afterwards met him—"Eh, but ye're a *lang lad !*"

The English *tangle* and *entangle* are words of a different meaning, and probably a corruption of the Gaelic *seangal*, to tie up, to fasten, to enchain, to fetter. The American phrase applied to whisky or other spirit, when indulged in too freely, of *tangle-foot* and *tangle-footed*, unable to walk steadily from intoxication, is both humorous and appropriate.

Tangleness, contradiction, confusion, dishonesty, entanglement of truth and falsehood.

Donald's the callant, that brooks nae
 tangleness,
Whiggin' and priggin' and a' new fangle-
 ness,
They maun be gane, he winna be baukit,
 man,
He maun hae justice, or faith he will tak
 it, man.
—James Hogg, *the Ettrick Shepherd.*

Tanterlick, a severe beating. Probably this word is derivable from the Gaelic *deann* (*teann*, see Tantrum), or *dian*, fierce, hot. This, combined with *lick*, the English slang to beat (a good *licking*, a good beating), and the Gaelic *leach*, a stone, would signify, in the first instance, a stoning, one of the earliest methods adopted in the quarrels of boys for the conquest or punishment of an opponent.

Tantin', hard pressing, squeezing ; *rantin'-tantin'*, ranting and raving ; or *ranting* and pressing

hard upon or against, from the Gaelic *teantann*, a pressing, a squeezing. A minister in his Sabbath service, asked by his congregation to pray for fine weather during a long continuance of rain that threatened to be injurious to the harvest, put up the following prayer :—

"O Lord, we pray thee to send us wind, no a *rantin'-tantin'*, tearin' wind, but a soughin' (sighing), winnin' wind." More expressive words than these could not be found in any language.—Dean Ramsay.

Tantrum. This word, borrowed by the English from the Scotch, is generally used in the plural ; and the phrase, "to be in the *tantrums*," most commonly applied to a woman, signifies that she is in a violent fit of ill-temper. Jamieson explains it as "high airs," and derives it from the French *tantrans*, nicknacks. This etymology cannot be accepted — firstly, because there is no such word in the French language ; and secondly, because if there were, the meanings are not in the slightest degree related. The "English Slang Dictionary" derives it from a dance called, in Italy, the *tarantula*, because persons in the *tantrums* dance and caper about ! The word is composed of the Gaelic *deann*, haste, violence, hurry ; and *trom*, heavy, whence violent and heavy, applied to a fit of sudden passion.

Tapetless, heedless, foolish ; probably from the Gaelic *tapadh*, activity, cleverness; and *ta-paidh*, quick, active, manly, bold, with the addition of the English *less*, want of cleverness or activity.

The *tapetless*, ramfeezled hizzie,
She's saft at best, and something lazy.
      —BURNS : *To John Lapraik.*

Tap-oure-tail, top-over-tail, or topsy-turvy (erroneously printed in Jamieson tap-*our*-tail), has the same meaning as *tapsalteerie*, and the English *head-over-heels*.

Tappiloorie, top-heavy; or *tappie-tourie*, round at the top. From the Flemish, Dutch, and English *top;* and the Flemish and Dutch *loer*, French *lourd*, heavy; *tourie*, from the Flemish, *toere*, round about; the French *tour* and *autour*.

Tappit-hen, a crested hen, or a hen with a top tuft of feathers; a phrase applied to a large bottle or jar of wine or spirits.

Blythe, blythe, and merry was she,
   Blythe was she but and ben,
Weel she loo'ed a Hawick gill,
   And leuch to see a *tappit-hen.*
—*Tea Table Miscellany : Andrew
      and his Cuttie Gun.*

Come, bumpers high, express your joy,
   The bowl we maun renew it,
The *tappit-hen* gae bring her ben,
   To welcome Willie Stewart.
                  —BURNS.

Their hostess appeared with a huge pewter measuring pot, containing at least three English quarts, familiarly termed a *tappit-hen.*—SCOTT : *Waverley.*

Blithe, blithe, and merry are we,
   Pick and wale o' merry men,
What care we though the cock may crow,
   We're masters o' the *tappit hen.*
   —CHARLES GRAY : *Whistle Binkie.*

" This term," says Jamieson, " denoted in Aberdeen a large bottle of claret, holding three magnums or Scots pints; " but as regards the quantity opinion differs. All agree, however, that a *tappit-hen* held considerably more than an ordinary bottle.

Tapsalteerie, in confusion, upside down, topsy-turvy. Possibly from the Gaelic *toabh*, the side; and *saltair*, to tread, to trample. *Topsy-turvy* is apparently from the same source, and not from "top-side the t'other way," as some etymologists have suggested.

Gie me a cannie hour at e'en,
   My arms about my dearie, O,
And warldly cares and warldly men
   May a' gang *tapsalteerie*, O !
               —BURNS.

In an excellent translation into German of Burns's " Green grow the rashes, O ! " appended as a note in Chambers's " Scottish Songs," the two lines in which *tapsalteerie* occurs are well rendered :—

Mag Erdenvolk and Erdenplag,
Kopfuber dann, *Kopfunter* gehen.

Tapthrawn, perverse, obstinate, unreasonably argumentative; from *tap*, the head or brain, metaphorically the intellect; and *thrawn*, twisted wrongly.

Tartar. To catch a *Tartar*, to be
overpowered in argument or in
fight, by one whose prowess had
been denied or unsuspected;
to get the worst of it. *Tartar*,
says the Slang Dictionary, is
" a savage fellow, an ugly cus-
tomer." To "catch a *Tartar*,"
is to discover, somewhat un-
pleasantly, that a person is by
no means so mild or good tempered as was supposed.

This saying originated from the story
of an Irish soldier in the imperial service,
who, in a battle against the Turks, called
out to his comrade that he had caught a
Tartar. "Bring him along then," said
he. "He won't come," said Paddy.
"Then come along yourself," replied his
comrade. "Bedad!" said he, "but he
won't let me!" A *Tartar* is also an adept
at any feast or game. "He is quite a
tartar at cricket or billiards."—GROSE'S
*Classical Dictionary of the Vulgar
Tongue.*

Grose's story was evidently invented. Philology had no need
to travel into Tartary to explain
the source of a peculiarly British
phrase, which has no equivalent
in any language but English and
Scotch: inasmuch as it is of
native origin, from the Gaelic
tartar, a great noise, clamour,
bustle, confusion; *tartarach*,
bustling, noisy, uproaring, unmanageable.

Tartarian is a word used by the
dramatists of the Elizabethan
era to signify a strong thief, or
a noisy blustering villain.

Tass, a small heap of earth or
cluster of flowers; from the
French *tas*, a parcel or pack.

There lived a lass in Inverness,
　She was the pride of a' the toun,
Blythe as the lark on gowan *tass*
　When frae the nest it's newly flown.
　　　　—ALLAN CUNNINGHAM.

Tatshie, according to Jamieson,
signifies dressed in a slovenly
manner; and *tattrel*, a rag.

Tatterdemalion, a ragged, miserable object. A colloquial word
introduced into England by the
Scotch; and supposed by English philologists to be from the
Icelandic *tetur*, a torn garment.
The roots, however, are derivable from the Gaelic; that of
tatter is from *dud*, a rag; from
whence the provincial English
dud, meaning a scarecrow.
Malion comes from *meall* and
meallan, a lump, a heap of confused objects; from whence the
primary meaning of *tatterdemalion* would seem to be a
"heap of rags," applied contemptuously to the wearer of
them. Mr. James M'Kie, of
Kilmarnock, quotes in his Bibliography of Burns, "The Jolly
Beggars, or *Tatterdemalions*, a
cantata by Robert Burns. Edinburgh, Oliver & Boyd, 1808."

**Tavern sign of the Dog and
Duck.** This is usually explained in the English sense of
a "Dog" and a "Duck," with
a representation on the sign-
board of a sportsman shooting
wild ducks, followed by a dog
ready to spring into the water.
It is probable, however, that the
sign is of greater antiquity than

the conquest of England by the Danes and Saxons; and that it dates from the Celtic period, and was originally *Deoch an Diugh*, or "Drink to-day," an invitation to all travellers and passers by to step in and drink; and that it was not by any means confined to the shooters of ducks, or to the watery districts in which such sports were possible. The perversions of the word *deoch* (drink), by the English and Lowland Scotch, are very numerous. One of them in particular deserves to be cited, *dog's nose*, which is, or used to be, a favourite drink of the populace in London, composed of beer and gin. Charles Dickens, in Pickwick, describes *dog's nose* as a warm drink; but the compiler of Hotten's Slang Dictionary affirms it to be a cold drink—so called, because it was "as cold as a dog's nose." The true derivation is most probably from the Gaelic *deoch* and *nos*, custom; and *nosag*, customary, or usual; and thus signifies the "usual drink." Another common and equally ludicrous perversion of the Gaelic is "Old Tom," which is used by the publicans of London, illustrated by a large tom-cat sitting on a barrel of gin. The origin of the phrase is *ol*, drink, and *taom*, to pour out; whence, to pour out the favourite liquor.

Tavey's locker, Davy's locker, Davy Jones's locker. These singular phrases, used princi-

pally among sailors, all signify death simply, or death by drowning in the sea. Their origin has never been very satisfactorily explained or accounted for; and no one has yet told the world whether *Tavey* or *Davy* was a real or a fabulous person, or who *Jones* was, and what was signified by his *locker*. The Teutonic roots of the English and Scotch languages fail to give the slightest hint or clue to the etymology of the expression, and thus compel inquirers to look to the Celtic for a possible solution of the mystery. In Gaelic is found *taimh* (*taiv* or *taif*), death; and *tamh* (*tav*), the ocean; *ionadh*, a place; and *lochd*, sleep, or a closing of the eyes. *Taimh* or *tamh* may account for the corruption into *Tavey* or *Davy*, *ionadh* for *Jones*, and *lochd* for *locker*. This explanation supplies an intelligible and appropriate meaning to *Davy Jones's locker*, the grotesque combination of words in Scotch and English which has become proverbial among seafaring people.

According to Wright's "Provincial English Dictionary," *David Jones* is a name given by sailors to a "sea-devil." But whether the "sea-devil" had or had not a *locker* we are not informed. Nares, in his Glossary, says that one "Davy" was a proficient in sword and buckler exercise, celebrated at the close of the sixteenth century. It does not appear, however, that any of these allusions can shed any light on the origin of *Davy's locker.*

Tawdy, a term of contempt for a child; *tawdy-fee,* a fine for illegitimacy; also, a depreciatory epithet for the *podex.* The etymology is unknown, but may be connected with the Gaelic *todhar,* excrement, and, by extension of meaning, to the senses in which it is applied to the *podex,* or to a child. *Todhar* also signifies a field manured by folding cattle upon it. *Taudis,* in French, signifies a miserable and dirty hole or hovel. In Irish Gaelic, *tod* or *todan* signifies a lump, a clod, a round mass, which may also have some remote connection with the idea of the *podex.*

Tawie, tame, peaceable, friendly, easily led. Gaelic *taobhach (taovach),* friendly, partial, inclined to kindness; erroneously derived from *tow,* a rope, or to be led by a rope.

> Hamely, *tawie,* quiet, cannie,
>   An' unco sonsie.
> —Burns: *Auld Farmer's Address.*

Tawpie, a foolish person, especially a foolish girl.

> Gawkies, *tawpies,* gowks and fools.
> —Burns: *Verses Written at Selkirk.*

This word is usually derived from the French *taupe,* a mole —erroneously supposed to be blind; but the Gaelic origin is more probable, from *taip,* a lump, a lumpish or clumsy person.

> Dans le royaume des *taupes,* les *borgnes* sont rois.—*French Proverb.*

Teen, tene, teyne, provocation, anger, wrath, From the Gaelic *teine,* fire; *teintidh,* fiery, angry.

> Last day I grat wi' spite and *teen,*
>   As poet Burns cam' by:
> That to a bard I should be seen,
>   Wi' half my channel dry.
> —Burns: *Humble Petition of Bruar Water.*

Teethie, crabbed, ill-natured, snarling; applied metaphorically from the action of a dog which shows its teeth when threatening to bite. The English word *toothsome,* which has no relation in meaning to *teethie,* is often used instead of *dainty,* from the erroneous idea that *dainty* is derived from *dens,* a tooth. The real derivation of *dainty* is from the Gaelic *deanta,* complete, perfect, well formed, and finished. When Shakspeare speaks of his "*dainty* Ariel," or a man praises the *dainty* hand or lips of his beloved, he does not mean that the teeth should be employed upon them, but that they are well-formed, complete, or beautifully perfect.

Teind, a tax, a tribute, a tithe, a tenth; *teind-free,* exempt from tithes or taxation.

> But we that live in Fairy Land
>   No sickness know, nor pain,
> I quit my body when I will,
>   And take to it again;
> And I would never tire, Janet,
>   In Elfin land to dwell:

But aye at every seven years' end,
They pay the *teind* to hell ;
And I'm sae fat and fair of flesh,
I fear 'twill be mysel.
　　—*Border Minstrelsy : The Young
　　　　Tamlane.*

Tendal knife. Jamieson cites from an inventory, " two belts, a *tendal knife*, a horse comb, and a burning iron ; " and at a loss to account for the word, asks : " Shall we suppose that knives celebrated for their temper had been formerly made somewhere in the dale, or valley of Tyne, in England ? It might, however, be the name of the maker ? " These are, no doubt, ingenious suppositions, but both appear to be wrong if tested by the Gaelic, in which *tean* signifies long and thin ; and *tail*, or *taile*, strong ; whence *tendal knife*, a knife with a long, thin, strong blade.

Tent, to take heed, to act cautiously and warily, to be attentive. From the French *tenter*, to try, to attempt. *Tentie*, cautious, wary ; *to tak tent*, to take care, to beware ; *tentless*, careless.

When the tod preaches tak *tent* o' the lambs.
　　—ALLAN RAMSAY : *Scots Proverbs.*

But warily *tent* when ye come to court me,
And come na unless the back yett be ajee.
Syne up the back stair and let naebody see,
And come as ye were na comin' to me.
　　—BURNS : *Oh Whistle and I'll come to
　　　　you, my Lad.*

I rede you, honest man, tak *tent*,
Ye'll show your folly.
　　—BURNS : *Epistle to James Smith.*

The time flew by wi' *tentless* heed,
Till 'twixt the late and early,
Wi' sma' persuasion she agreed
To see me through the barley.
　　—BURNS : *Corn Rigs and Barley Rigs.*

See ye take *tent* to this !
　　—BEN JONSON : *Sad Shepherdess.*

Teribus ye teri odin, the war cry of the men of Hawick at the battle of Flodden, and still preserved in the traditions of the town. The full chorus is often sung at festive gatherings, not only in the gallant old border town itself, but in the remotest districts of Canada, the United States, and Australia, wherever Hawick men and natives of the Scottish Border congregate to keep up the remembrance of their native land, and the haunts of their boyhood.

Teribus ye teri odin,
Sons of heroes slain at Flodden,
Imitating Border bowmen,
Aye defend your rights and common.

Attempts have been frequently made to connect this Border ballad with the names of the Scandinavian and Norse demigods, Thor and Odin ; but these heroes were wholly unknown to the original possessors of the Scottish soil, and but very partially known to the Danish and Saxon invaders, who came after them. The ballad, of which these mysterious words form the burden, is one of patriotic " defence and defiance " against the invaders of the soil. *Teribus ye teri odin* is an attempt at a phonetic rendering of the Gaelic

Tir a buaidh's, tir a dion, which, translated, means " Land of victory, and Land of defence."

Teth, spirit, mettle, humour, temper, disposition; usually employed in the sense of high-spirited. The word was English in the Elizabethan era, and was pronounced and written *tith*, from the Gaelic *teth*, hot.

She's good mettle, of a good stirring strain, and goes *tith*.—BEAUMONT AND FLETCHER.

Take a widow—a good staunch wench that's *tith*.—*Idem.*

Ill-teth'd, ill-humoured.—JAMIESON.

Teuch, a drink, a draught of liquor. This word has been derived by Jamieson and others from the Teutonic *tog*, and *teughe*, to draw or pull. As no such words are to be found in the Teutonic languages, it is possible that Jamieson meant the German *zug*, the English *tug*, to pull or draw; whence, in vulgar language, a long *pull* at the bottle or tankard, a deep draught. It seems more probable, however, that the Lowland Scotch word is a corruption of the Gaelic *deoch*, a drink, as in the phrase, " *deoch* an' doruis," a drink at the door, a stirrup cup. (See DEUK, *ante*, p. 42.)

Tevoo. This nearly obsolete word was formerly used by women in contemptuous depreciation of a male flirt, fond of their society, but who was never serious in his attentions to them.

It has been supposed to be somehow or other derived from the French, but no word similar to it appears in that language. It is probably from the Gaelic *ti*, a person, a creature; and *fu*, an abbreviation of *fuachaidh*, a flirt, a jilt, a deceiver.

Tew is a word of many meanings in Scotland, but most commonly signifies to work hard. It also signifies to struggle, to strive, to fatigue, to overpower, to make tough. " Sair *tews* " signifies old or sore difficulties or troubles; *tewing on*, toiling on; sair *tewd*, greatly fatigued, are common expressions. Jamieson derives the word from the French *tuer*, to kill; Nares cites instances in which it is used in the sense of *tow*, to pull along by a rope. Possibly, however, it is but a misspelling of the Scottish *teuch* (with the omission of the guttral *j*, the English *tough*, in which the omitted guttral is replaced by the sound of *f*, as *tuff*). The Gaelic *tiugh*, thick, stiff, strong, is doubtless an allied word.

Thack and raip, from the thatch of a house; and *rope*, the binding or fastening which keeps the thatch in its place. Hence, metaphorically, the phrase applied to the conduct of an unreasonable and disorderly person, that he acts " out of a' *thack and raip*," as if the roof of his house were uncovered, and let in the wind and weather;

or, in vulgar slang, as if he had "a slate or a tile loose."

Thairms, the strings of a violin, harp, or other instrument for which wire is not used, called in England cat-gut. The word is derived from the German, Dutch, and Flemish *darm*, gut, intestines ; the German plural *därme*.

Oh, had M'Lachlan, *thairm*-inspiring sage,
Been there to hear this heavenly band en-
gage.
   —Burns : *The Brigs of Ayr.*
Come, screw the pegs wi' tunefu' cheep,
And ower the *thairms* be trying.
     —Burns : *The Ordination.*

The word, though immediately derived from the Teutonic, may, in the sense of gut or entrails, have some connection with the practice of divination by the ancient Augurs, who studied the intestines of sacrificed birds to foretell future events. But this is a mere conjecture founded upon the fact, that the Gaelic *tairm*, or *thairm*, signifies divination.

From *thairm*, string made from gut, may probably come the Scottish words *thrum*, to play on a stringed instrument, and, in a contemptuous sense, *thrummer*, an inferior fiddler. Possibly the English *strum* is a corruption and euphemism of *thrum*.

Thane, a very ancient title of nobility in Scotland, equivalent in rank to an English earl. Macbeth, according to Shakspeare,

was Thane of Cawdor. Jamieson suggests its derivation from the Anglo-Saxon *thegn*, a servant ; but as the title was peculiar to the Gael, wholly unknown to the Saxon, and implied rather mastery and dominion than servitude, a Celtic etymology is most probable ; that etymology is found in *tanaistear*, a governor, a lord, a prince ; one second in rank to the king or sovereign ; and *tanaisteach*, governing, acting as a thane, or master.

The noo, or **the now**, a common Scotticism for just now, immediately, presently, by and by.

Theak, theek, to thatch a house. Greek θηκη (*thēkē*), a small house, a repository ; German *dach*, a roof ; old English *theccan*, to cover ; Gaelic *tigh* and *teach*, a house.

Bessie Bell and Mary Gray,
  They were twa bonnie lasses,
They biggit a bower on yon burn brae,
  And *theekit* it o'er wi' rashes.
—*Ballad : Bessie Bell and Mary Gray.*

Ye'll sit on his white hause bane,
  And I'll pike out his bonnie blue een ;
Wi' ae lock o' his gowden hair
We'll *theek* our nest when it grows bare.
  —*Minstrelsy of the Scottish Border :*
    The Twa Corbies.

The cozy roof *theekit* wi' moss-covered
strae.
    —James Ballantine.

Them, they, those. These plural pronouns are often used in Scotland instead of the singular *it*, especially when applied to oatmeal porridge, brose, hotchpotch, and broth, or soup. The idea of plurality seems to be attached to porridge, from the multiplicity of the grains of meal, of which the dish is compounded, and to hotch-potch, barley broth, and other soups, for the same reason of their numerous ingredients.

Why dinna ye sup ye're parritch, Johnnie?
Johnnie—I dinna like *them*.
—GALT.

Once at the annual dinner to his tenants, given by the Duke of Buccleuch, the Duchess pressed a burly old farmer, to whom she wished to show attention, to partake of some pea-soup. "Muckle obleeged to your Grace," said the farmer, "but I downa tak' *them. They're* owre wundy!"—*The Ettrick Shepherd.*

Each true-hearted Scotsman, by nature jocose,
Can cheerfully dine on a dishfu' o' brose,
And the grace be a wish to get plenty of *those;*
And it's O for the kail brose o' Scotland,
And O for the Scottish kail brose.
—ALEXANDER WATSON : *Old Song.*

Then-a-days, in former time, as opposed to the English and Scottish phrase, *now-a-days*, in the present time.

Thepes, gooseberries, or more properly *gorse* or thorn berries ; in Dutch and Flemish *doorn*, or thorn-berries. Mr. Halliwell, in his Archaic Dictionary, cites *thepes* as an Eastern Counties word, used in Sir Thomas Brown's works. It is also current in the Lowlands of Scotland. The derivation is unknown.

Thetes, traces or harness of a horse drawing a vehicle. To

be " out of the traces," is to be out of rule, governance, or control.

To be quite out of the *thetes, i.e.*, to be disorderly in one's conduct. . . . To be out of *thete* is a phrase applied to one who is rusted as to any art or science from want of practice.—JAMIESON.

The word is derived by Jamieson from the Icelandic *thatt'r*, a cord, a small rope ; but is more probably from the Gaelic *taod ;* aspirated *thoad*, a rope.

Thief - like, ugly, disagreeable. This Scottish phrase does not signify dishonest-looking, but simply repulsive, or disagreeable ; possibly because the Lowland Scotch who made use of it suffered but too often from the incursions of the Highland cattle-stealers into the pastures and sheep-folds, associated in their minds with all that was most offensive, morally and physically.

That's a *thief-like* mutch ye have on, *i.e.*, that's an ugly cap you have on.—JAMIESON.

Thief-like occurs in two common proverbial phrases—the *thiefer-like* the better soldier ; the aulder the *thiefer-like.* Ye're like the horse's bains, the aulder ye grow the *thiefer-like.*—JAMIESON.

Thig, to beg or borrow ; sometimes written *thigger.*

The father buys, the son biggs (builds),
The oye (grandson) sells, and *his* son *thigs.*
—ALLAN RAMSAY'S *Scots Proverbs.*

And if the wives and dirty brats,
E'en *thigger* at your doors an' yetts.
—BURNS : *Address of Beelzebub.*

Think-lang, to grow weary, to be impatient of another's absence ; to think the time long.

But *think* na' *lang*, lassie, tho' I gang awa',
The summer is comin', cauld winter's
  awa',
And I'll come back and see thee in spite
  o' them a'.
    —*Song : Logie o' Buchan.*

Thistlecock or **thrustlecock**, the thrush, more poetically called the *mavis*, both in Old English and Scottish poetry.

The primrose is the fairest flower
  That springs on muir or dale ;
An' the *thistlecock* is the bonniest bird
  That sings on the evening gale.
    —*Ballad of Proud Lady
      Margaret.*

Thivel, a cudgel, a large shillelagh. Etymology unknown.

    An' for a *thivel* they did use
    A sturdy stump o' knotty spruce.
      —*John o' Arnha'.*

Tholeable, tholesome, tolerable, that may be endured ; *tholance*, sufferance, endurance. *Thole* is doubtless from the same root as the Latin *tolerare*, and the Gaelic *dolas*, sufferance, dolour, pain.

Thowless. Perhaps a corruption of *thewless*, weak ; without *thews* and sinews. Gaelic *tiugh*, thick, strong ; whence *thowless*, without strength or thickness.

For fortune aye favours the active and
  bauld,
But ruins the wooer that's *thowless* and
  cauld.
    —ALLAN RAMSAY.

Her dowff excuses pat me mad,
Conscience—says I, ye *thowless* jad,
I'll write, and that a hearty blaud
    This very night.
    —BURNS : *Epistle to Lapraik.*

Thraine. According to Jamieson, this word signifies to be constantly harping on one subject, and is derived from the Teutonic or Swedish *traegen*, assiduous. He is of opinion also that *rane*, to cry the same thing over and over again, is synonymous, and of the same origin. But more probably, in the sense of harping continually on one subject, of complaint, *thraine* is from the Greek *threnos*, a lamentation. *Rane* is probably from the Gaelic *ran*, to roar.

Thram, to thrive, to prosper. Etymology uncertain. Jamieson supposes it to be from the Icelandic.

Well wat your honour, *thram* for that,
  quo' she.
    —Ross's *Helenore.*

Can you expect to *thram*,
That hae been guilty o' so great a wrang ?
    —*Ibid.*

Thrang, busy, crowded with work or occupation ; from the English *throng*, to crowd, and the German *drang*, pressure, *drängen*, to press, and the Flemish *dringen*, to press, to squeeze.

Upon a bonnie day in June,
When wearin' through the afternoon,
Twa dogs that were nae *thrang* at hame,
Foregathered ance upon a time.
    —BURNS : *The Twa Dogs.*

The deil sat grim amang the reek,
Thrang bundling brimstone matches!
—*Jacobite Song: Awa', ye Whigs,
Awa'.*

Thrapple, the throat; akin to the English *throttle*.

As murder at his *thrapple* shored;
And hell mixed in the brulzie [broil].
—BURNS: *Epistle to Robert Graham.*

When we had a Scots Parliament,—deil
rax their *thrapples* that reft us o't.
SCOTT: *Rob Roy.*

Thraw, a twist, a fit of ill-humour; *thrawn*, twisted, contorted. *Thrawn-gabbit*, with a twisted or contorted *gab*, or mouth; and, metaphorically, a cantankerous, morose person who is always grumbling. *Gabbit* is from the Gaelic *gab*, a mouth; whence the English slang, "the gift of the *gab*," the gift of eloquence, or power of much speaking. *Thrawart*, perverse, obstinate; *thraw*, to contradict; *thraws*, *throes*, twists or contortions of pain; also, a little while, or a turn of time, a twist.

She turns the key wi' cannie *thraw.*
—BURNS: *Hallowe'en.*

When I a little *thraw* had made my moan,
Bewailing mine misfortune and mischance.
—*The King's Quair.*

There are twa hens into the crib,
Have fed this month and mair;
Make haste and *thraw* their necks about,
That Colin weel may fare.
—MICKLE: *There's nae Luck About the House.*

He's easy wi' a' body that's easy wi' him; but if ye *thraw* him, ye had better *thraw* the deevil.—SCOTT: *Rob Roy.*

Thraw seems akin to the English *throe*, a throb, a twist of pain, and is probably from the Teutonic.

Threpe, or **threap**, to argue, to contend pertinaciously in argument, to assert obstinately in spite of reason; from the Gaelic *drip*, or *trip*, to contend, to fight.

It's not for a man with a woman to *threep*,
Unless he first give owre the plea:
As we began we'll now leave off—
I'll tak my auld cloak about me.
—*Old Ballad, quoted by* SHAKSPEARE.

Some herds, weel learned upon the beuk,
Wad *threap* auld folk the thing mistook.
—BURNS: *Epistle to Simpson.*

Threapin's no' provin'.
—ALLAN RAMSAY.

This is na *threapin'* ware [*i.e.,* this is genuine ware, not to be argued about].—
ALLAN RAMSAY.

Thrimle, thrimmel, to press, to squeeze; *thrimp, thrump*, to press as in a crowd, to push. Etymology uncertain, but possibly from the Flemish *drempel*, an entrance—whence to force an entrance, to press through, to push through.

Through. This word, the Gaelic *troimh*, the Kymric *trw*, and the Teutonic *durch*, enters more largely into its structure of Scottish compound terms and phrases, than was ever the case in England. Thus the Scotch have *through-gang*, perseverance; *through-gaun*, and *through-ganging*, persevering, also wasteful, prodigal, going through

one's means ; *through-pit*, activity, energy, that *puts* a thing
through; through-fare, or *through-
gang*, a thoroughfare; *through-
ither*, confused ; *through-stone*,
a stone as thick as the wall;
through-pittin', or *through-bearin'*,
a bare subsistence, enough to
get through the world with;
and the verb *to through*, or *thruch*,
to penetrate, to go through.
Sir Walter Scott uses *through-
gaun* in Rob Roy, in the sense
of a severe exposure of one's
life and conduct, during a rigid
cross-examination.

Throwther, higgledy - piggledy,
helter - skelter, in confusion ;
possibly a corruption of *through-
ither*, or *through-each-other*.

> Till—skelp—a shot ! they're aff a'
>   *throwther*,
>   To save their skin.
> —BURNS : *Earnest Cry and Prayer.*

Thrum, a musical sound, also
a thread. *Gray thrums*, the
popular phrase in Scotland for
the purring of a cat, the sound
of a spinning-wheel, the thread
remaining at the end of a web;
apparently derived from the
Gaelic *troimh*, through.

> Come out wi' your moolins, come out wi'
>   your crumbs,
> And keep in slee baudrons [the cat] to
>   sing ye *gray thrums.*
> —JAMES BALLANTINE : *A Voice from the
>   Woods.*

Thud, a dull, heavy blow : etymology unknown. Lord Neaves
considered it a *comic* word,
though it is difficult to see

why, especially when such
serious use of it was made
by Gawin Douglas and Allan
Ramsay :—

> The fearful *thuds* of the tempestuous tide.
> —GAWIN DOUGLAS : *Translation of
>   the Enid.*

> The air grew rough with boisterous *thuds*.
>   ALLAN RAMSAY : *The Vision.*

> Swith on a hardened clay he fell,
> Right far was heard the *thud*.
>   —*Hardyknute.*

Tid, tid - bit, tydy. All these
words, like the English *tide*, are
derivable from the idea of time,
the German *zeit*, the Dutch
and Flemish *tijd*. *Tid*, in the
Scottish language, signifies season ; the English *tid-bit* is a
seasonable bit. *Bit* is from
the Gaelic *biadh*, food, and not
from the English *bite*, or that
which is bitten. The French
morceau, the English *morsel*, is
unquestionably derived from
mordre, to bite. *Tydy*, seasonable; " a *tydy* bride " is a phrase
applied to an unmarried girl who
is about to become a mother,
and in that state is married and
taken home to her bridegroom's
house, in order that the coming
child may be born after wed-
lock, and thus become legiti-
mised.

Tift, English *tiff*, a slight quarrel, a fit of ill-humour ; *tip*, a
slang word for money given to
a servant as a small gratuity
to procure drink or otherwise ;
called by the French a *pour
boire*, and by the Germans *trink-*

geld. No English or Scottish etymologist has succeeded in tracing these words to their sources. Jamieson derives *tift* from the Icelandic *tyfta*, to chastise; Johnson declares *tiff*, a quarrel, to be "a low word, without etymology;" Richardson has *tiff*, a drink, which he thinks a corruption of *tipple*, an allied word; Ash defines *tiff* to be a corruption of the Teutonic *tepel*, a dug or teat, while the ancient author of "Gazophylacium Anglicanum" surpasses all his predecessors and successors in ingenuity by deriving *tipsy* and *tipple* from the Latin *tipula*, a water-spider, because that insect is always drinking! Mr. Halliwell, without entering on the etymological question, says that in English provincial dialects *tiff* has three meanings— small beer, a draught of any liquor, and to fall headlong from the effects of drink.

There are several derivatives in the Scottish language from *tift*, a quarrel, viz., *tifty*, quarrelsome, apt to take offence; *tifting*, an angry scolding; and "to be in a *tifter*," *i.e.*, in a difficult and disagreeable position where one is likely to be severely reprimanded. Possibly the Scottish *tift* (a quarrel), the English *tiff* (a fit of ill-humour), are as closely allied in meaning as they are in sound.

Tig, a twitch, a touch, a sharp stroke; also a slight fit of ill-temper; possibly, in both senses,

derived from the Gaelic *taoig*, anger, and *taoigeach*, angry, and as such disposed to strike a blow.

A game among children. He who in this game gives the stroke, says to the person to whom he has given it, "Ye bear my *tig.*"—JAMIESON.

Tillie-soul. According to Jamieson, this word signifies "a place to which a gentleman sends the horses and servants of his guests, when he does not choose to entertain them at his own expense." He derives it from the French *tillet*, a ticket; and *solde*, pay. There is, however, no such word as *tillet*, a ticket, in the French language. There is *tiller*, which means, "detacher avec la main les filaments du chanvre," *i.e.*, to remove with the hand the filaments of hemp. But this operation has certainly nothing to do with the explanation given to *tillie-soul.* The true derivation appears to be from the Gaelic *till*, to turn away; and *sult*, feeding, fatness, good bodily entertainment; whence *tillie-soul* or *till sult*, to turn away for entertainment elsewhere.

Timmer, timber; from the Flemish *timmer*. This word is used not alone as signifying wood, but in the sense of building or constructing out of wood; and, by extension of meaning, into constructing or fashioning generally; and, by still wider extension, into doing or performing. "To give one a *timmerin'*" signifies to beat one with a stick (or piece of timber). *Timmer*-breeks and *timmer*-sark were ludicrous terms for a coffin. *Timmerman*, in the Flemish, and *zimmerman*, in the German, signified a carpenter, an artificer in wood, and also a woodmonger, or woodman.

Timmer up the flail, *i.e.*, to wield the flail; *timmer* up the floor with a dishclout, *i.e.*, to clean it. . . . To *timmer* up the lesson, *i.e.*, to be busily employed in learnit. . . . Oh, as he *timmers* up the Latin! *i.e.*, what a deal of Latin he employs.—JAMIESON.

> And who in singing could excel
> Famed Douglas, Bishop of Dunkel';
> He *timmer'd* up, though it be lang,
> In gude braid Scots a Virgil's sang.
> —INGRAM'S *Poems.*

Tine, to lose; *tint*, lost. This ancient English word has long been confined to Scottish literature and parlance.

> What was *tint* through tree,
> Tree shall it win.
> —*Piers Ploughman.*

He never *tint* a cow that grat for a needle.

Where there is nothing the king *tines* his right.

All's not *tint* that's in danger.

Better spoil your joke than *tine* your friend.

Tine heart—all's gone.
—ALLAN RAMSAY'S *Scots Proverbs.*

> Next my heart I'll wear her,
> For fear my jewel *tine.*—BURNS.

Tinkle - sweetie. According to Jamieson, *tinkle-sweetie* was a name formerly given in Edinburgh to a bell that was rung at eight o'clock in the evening. A previous bell, which was rung at two in the afternoon, was called the "kail bell," *i.e.*, the dinner bell. *Tinkle-sweetie* was superseded as a phrase by the "aucht hour bell." Jamieson, at a loss for the etymology, says "it was thus denominated because the sound of it was *sweet* to the ears of apprentices and shopmen, because they were then at liberty to shut up for the night." The conjecture is no doubt ingenious; but it may be asked whether the kail or dinner bell might not have been as justly entitled to be called sweet as the bell that announced the cessation of labour? The word is apparently a relic of the very old time when the kings and nobles of Scotland and the merchants of Edinburgh all spoke or understood Gaelic. In that language *diun* (*d* pronounced as *t*) signified to shut up, to close; *glaodh* (pronounced *glao*) signified a cry, a call; and *suaiteachd*, labour, work, toil; whence *duinglao* (*tuinglao*, quasi *tinkle*) and *suaiteachd* corrupted into *sweetie*. Thus the phrase would mean a call or summons, to cease from labour, or, in modern parlance, "to shut up shop."

Tinsel, loss; from *tine*, to lose.

> My profit is not your *tinsel.*
> —ALLAN RAMSAY'S *Scots Proverbs.*

Tippenny, from twopence; whence *tippenny,* at the price of two pence; twopenny ale.

> Wi' *tippenny* we'll fear nae evil,
> Wi' usquebae we'll face the devil.
> —BURNS: *Tam o' Shanter.*

Mr. Loève Weimaurs, a once noted French author, who translated or paraphrased Burns into French, rendered the first of these lines by "Avec deux sous, nous ne craindrons rien," with twopence we'll fear nothing, thus leaving the ale out of the question.

Tirl, to turn the knob, the pin, or other fastening of a door. The word is of constant occurrence in the ballad poetry of Scotland.

> Oh he's gone round and round about
> And *tirled* at the pin.
> —*Willie and May Margaret.*

Tirl, to spin round as in a whirlwind, to unroof with a high wind.

> Whyles, on the strong-winged tempest flying,
> *Tirling* the kirks.
> —BURNS: *Address to the Deil.*

This word has been supposed to be a corruption of the English *twirl,* to turn round; and, by extension of meaning, "*tirling* the roof of the kirk," *i.e.,* sending the materials whirling or twirling in the storm. To *tirl* the pin or knob of a door, is doubtless from twirl, in the English sense; but to *tirl* the roof of a kirk, as in the line of Burns, is more probably from the Gaelic *tuirl,* and *tuirlin,* to rush rapidly with a great noise.

Tirlie-wirlie, intricate or trifling ornaments.

> Queer, *tirlie-wirlie* holes that gang out to the open air, and keep the air as caller as a kail-blade.—SCOTT: *The Antiquary.*

> It was in and through the window broads
> And a' the *tirlie-wirlies* o't,
> The sweetest kiss that e'er I got
> Was frae my Dainty Davie.
> —HERD'S *Collection: Dainty Davie.*

From the English *twirl* and *whirl,* though Jamieson goes to the Swedish in search of the etymology.

Tirr, a fractious child; *tirran,* one of a perverse and complaining humour; *tirrie,* querulous, peevish. These words seem all to be derived from the Gaelic *tuir,* to moan, to lament, to weep; and *tuireadh,* moaning, complaining, lamentation. Jamieson, however, derives *tirr* from the Greek *tyrannos,* a tyrant, or the Teutonic *terghen,* to irritate; though the latter word is not to be found in German or in any of its dialects. *Tire lire* is often used in French poetry for the song or lament of the nightingale.

Tittie, a sister.

> He had a wee *tittie* that loved na me
> Because I was true and trim as she.
> —LADY GRIZZEL BAILLIE.

Tittie-billie, according to Jamieson, who denounces it as vulgar.

Q

This phrase signifies an equal, a match, as in the proverbial saying which he quotes, "Tam's a great thief, but Willie's *tittie-billie* wi' him ; " and derives it from *tittie*, a sister ; and *billie*, a brother. The true meaning of *billie* is a fellow ; from the Gaelic *balaoch*, a mate, or close companion ; and *tittie*, in all probability, is a corruption of *taite*, joyousness, jolliness. *Tittie-billie* would thus be synonymous with the English phrase, "a jolly good fellow." (See BILLIES, *ante*, page 8.)

Tocher, a dowry, but principally used as applicable to the fortunes of persons in the middle and lower ranks of life, who are too poor to give their daughters *dowries*. A *tocher* may be either a large or a small one. There is no other *Scotch* word for a daughter's portion. *Tocherless*, fortuneless.

> A cow and a calf,
> An ox and a half,
> Forty good shillings and three ;
> Is not that enough *tocher*
> For a shoemaker's daughter ?
> —J. O. HALLIWELL : *Nursery Rhymes of England.*

The bonnie lass *tocherless* has mair wooers than chances of a husband.

The greatest *tochers* make not ever the greatest testaments.

Marry a beggar and get a louse for your *tocher.*

Maidens' *tochers* and ministers' stipends are aye less than they are ca'd.

—ALLAN RAMSAY'S *Scots Proverbs.*

Oh meikle thinks my love o' my beauty,
And meikle thinks my love o' my kin,

But little thinks my love I ken brawly,
My *tocher's* the jewel has charms for him.
　　　　　　　　　　　—BURNS.

Philologists are at variance as to the origin of *tocher*, which is purely Scottish, and has no relation to any similar word in the Teutonic or in the Romance languages of Europe. The French has *dot*, the German *braut-schätz* (bridal treasure), and the Dutch and Flemish *bruid schat.* Dr. Adolphus Wagner, editor of a German edition of Burns (Leipzig, 1825), suggests "the Icelandic *tochar*," which he thinks is either corrupted from the Latin *douarium*, or from *daughter*, the German *tochter*, or the Greek θυγατηρ. The real root of the word is the Gaelic *tacar* or *tocar*, provision or store, a marriage portion ; *tocharachd*, well or plentifully dowered ; *toic*, wealth, fortune ; *toic ard*, high fortune ; and *toic-each*, rich.

Tod, usually considered to signify a bush ; *ivy tod*, a bush or bunch of ivy. The derivation seems to be from the Dutch and Flemish *tod*, a rag, a fringe ; and the Gaelic *dud*, a rag ; or *taod*, a string ; from the string-like and ragged appearance of ivy when it has grown as high as possible on the supporting tree or wall, and has then fallen downwards. *Tod* also signifies a fox ; *tod-laurie* is a jocose word for the same animal.

Ye're like the *tod ;* ye grow grey before you grow guid.

The *tod* ne'er sped better than when he gaed on his ain errand.
—ALLAN RAMSAY'S *Scots Proverbs.*

The King rose up, wiped his eyes, and calling, "*Todlaurie*, come out o' your den [Fox, come out of your hole]," he produced from behind the arras the length of Richie Moniplies, still laughing in unrestrained mirth. — SCOTT : *Fortunes of Nigel.*

Toddy, a mixture of whisky with hot water and sugar. It has been generally supposed that the name was introduced into Scotland by some retired East Indian, from *toddy*, a juice extracted from various species of palm trees, especially from the *cocos nocifera*, which, when fermented and distilled, was known as *arrack*. But this is doubtful. In Allan Ramsay's poem of "The Morning Interview," published in 1721, occurs a description of a sumptuous entertainment or tea-party, in which it is said "that all the rich requisites are brought from far ; the table from Japan, the tea from China, the sugar from Amazonia, or the West Indies ; but that

Scotia does no such costly tribute bring,
Only some kettles full of *Todian* spring."

To this passage Allan Ramsay himself appended the note— "The Todian spring, *i.e.*, *Tod's well*, which supplies Edinburgh with water." Tod's well and St. Anthony's well, on the side of Arthur's seat, were two of the wells which very scantily supplied the wants of Edinburgh ;

and when it is borne in mind that whiskey (see that word) derives its name from water, it is highly probable that *Toddy* in like manner was a facetious term for the pure element. The late Robert Chambers, when this etymology was first propounded to him by the present writer, rejected the idea, but afterwards adopted it on the strength of Allan Ramsay's poem.

Tol-lol, a slang expression, common to Scotland and England, as a reply to an inquiry after one's health. "How are you?" "Oh, *tol-lol!*" *i.e.*, pretty well. The word is usually supposed to be a corruption of *tolerable*, or *tolerably well.* Perhaps it comes more probably from the Gaelic *toileil*, substantial, solid, sound, in good condition.

Toman or **tommack**, a small hill, a hillock, a mound of earth ; from the Gaelic *tom*, a hill. This primitive monosyllable is widely spread over all the languages of Western Europe, and enters into the composition of numberless words that imply the sense of swelling above the surface ; as in the Latin *tumulus*, a mound of earth that marks a grave ; the English *tomb*, the French *tombeau*, the Keltic and Kymric *tom*, a mound, a heap ; the Latin *tumor*, *tume*faction, a pimple, a swelling of the flesh ; *tumescere*, to swell up ; the English and French *dome*, the Italian *duomo*.

the German, Dutch, and Flemish *dom*, the Latin and Greek *doma*, the rounded roof or cupola, swelling over a church or cathedral, and also the cathedral itself; as "il *duomo*" at Milan, and the "*Dom* kirke" at Cologne. *Tom*, in the secondary sense, signifies large, from the primary idea of that which is swollen; a *tom* cat is a large cat; *tom* noddy is a great noddy or simpleton; *tom* fool is a great fool; and *tom-boy*, when applied as a reproach to a romping or noisy girl, signifies that she acts more like a great boy than like a girl.

Singing a song to the Queen o' the Fairies, among the *tomans* o' the ancient woods.—*Noctes Ambrosianæ.*

Tongue - ferdy, glib of tongue, loquacious, over ready of speech. From the German *zung*, Flemish and Dutch *tong*, the tongue; and *fertig*, ready.

Tongue-tackit, tongue-tied, either from natural impediment, or from nervous timidity and inability to speak when there is occasion to declare one's self; also, undue reticence, when there is a necessity for speaking out.

Toom or **tume**, empty, poured out; from the Gaelic *taom*, to pour out, the English *teem*, to produce, to pour out progeny. *Toom - handit*, empty - handed; *toom*-headit, brainless, empty-headed; a *toom* pock, an empty purse. The word is used in Lancashire, according to Tim Bobbin's Glossary.

Better a *toom* house than an ill tenant.
　　—ALLAN RAMSAY'S *Scots Proverbs.*

Scotland greetin' owre her thrissle,
Her mutchkin stoup as *toom*'s a whistle.
　　—BURNS: *Earnest Cry and Prayer.*

Mr. Clark of Dalreoch, whose head was vastly disproportioned to his body, met Mr. Dunlop one day. "Weel, Mr. Clark, that's a great head o' yours." "Indeed, it is, Mr. Dunlop; I could contain yours inside o' my own." "Just so," echoed Mr. Dunlop, "I was e'en thinking it was gey an *toom*."—DEAN RAMSAY.

On being called upon to give his vote in the choice of a chaplain to the prison of Dunfermline, David Dewar signified his assent to the election of the candidate recommended by the Board, by saying, "Weel, I've no objection to the man, for I understand that he has preached a kirk *toom* already; and if he be as successful in the jail, he'll maybe preach it vacant as weel."—DEAN RAMSAY.

A *toom* pouch maks a sair heart. But why should it? Surely a heart's worth mair than a pouch, whether it's *toom* or brimming ower?—DONALD CARGILL.

"Set on them, lads!" quo' Willie, then,
　"Fie, lads! set on them cruellie,
For ere they win to the Ritterford
　Mony a *toom* saddle there sall be."
　　—JAMES TELFER: *Border Minstrelsy.*

Toot, or **tout**, to noise a thing abroad, to spread a rumour or a scandal; also, to blow a horn.

It was *tootit* through a' the country.
. . . The kintra claiks were *tootit* far and wide.—JAMIESON.

But now the Lord's ain trumpet *touts*,
　Till a' the hills are rairin'.
　　—BURNS: *The Holy Fair.*

An auld *tout* in a new horn.

Every man can *tout* best on his ain horn.

It's ill making a *touting* horn of a tod's tail.
　　—ALLAN RAMSAY'S *Scots Proverbs.*

In English slang, a *tout* is one stationed outside of a shop or place of amusement, to entice people to enter ; metaphorical for blowing the trumpet, *i.e.*, praising the goods, or entertainment, to be had within. From the Gaelic *dud*, a trumpet ; *dudair*, a trumpeter. The Germans call the bagpipe a *dudelsack*, *i.e.*, a trumpet sack.

Toothills—or hills where in early times a horn was blown to give warning of danger — are frequently mentioned in old records, and the name still subsists. *Tothill* or *Toothill* Fields in London was so called from an eminence of the kind in the borough of Southwark.

Tory, a word of contemptuous anger for a child, equivalent to *brat*. Jamieson cites it as an Ayrshire expression—" Get out of my sight, ye vile little *tory*." It is obvious that the word has no political origin, and is possibly from the Gaelic *torrach*, pregnant, and *toradh* (*dh* silent), the fruit or produce of pregnancy, *i.e.*, a child.

Tosh, neat, trim, cozy, comfortable ; *toshach*, a neat, tidy-looking girl ; *tossie*, warm and snug, —almost synonymous with *cozie*. Of uncertain etymology. Jamieson derives it from the Flemish *dossen*, to dress, to adorn ; but the Gaelic offers *dos*, a bush, a thicket, a bield, a shelter, which has become slang among Eng-

lish tramps and vagrants, to signify a lodging. It is possible that the idea of comfortable shelter, in the sense of the proverb, " Better a wee bush than nae bield," lies at the root of *tosh* and *tozie*.

She works her ain stockings, and spins her
ain cleedin',
And keeps herself *tosh* frae the tap to the
tae.
—JAMES BALLANTINE : *Auld Janet.*

Tot, a fondling name for a child that is learning to walk ; from whence *tottle*, and *toddle*, to walk with slow, feeble, and uncertain step. From the Gaelic *tuit*, to fall. (See TOTUM.)

Tottie, warm, snug, comfortable. From the Gaelic *teth*, warmth ; *teodh*, to warm ; and *teodhaichte*, warmed ; whence also *tottle*, to boil, or the bubbling noise made by boiling liquids.

Totum, a term of affection for a child just beginning to walk, and sometimes falling in the process ; from the Gaelic *tuit*, to fall. From the same root comes the name of the spinning and falling toy, the *teetotum ;* and English *tot*, a child.

Twa-three toddlin' weans they hae,
The pride o' a' Strabogie ;
Whene'er the *totums* cry for meat,
She curses aye his cogie.
—*Song : There's Cauld Kail in Aberdeen.*

The Scotch have carried the word *totum* with them to the United States. It occurs in a ridiculous rhyme concerning the negroes—

> De Lord He lub de nigger well,
> He know de nigger by um smell ;
> And when de nigger *totums* cry,
> De Lord He gib 'em possum pie.

The English word *teetotum*, is a child's toy, or kind of top to be twisted round by the fingers and spun on a table. Stormonth's Dictionary defines it, in addition to its ordinary use as a toy, to mean " any small thing in contempt," and suggests that the word is probably imitative of its unsteady movements when nearly spent. *Teetotum* is an amplification of the Gaelic, from its tendency to fall ; *tuiteam*, let me fall.

Toun's Bairn, a name affectionately applied to the native of a town or city, after he has risen to distinction and established a claim to the respect of the inhabitants.

Toustie, quarrelsome, irascible, contentious, twisty. From the Gaelic *tuas*, and *tuasaid*, a quarrel ; *tuasaideach*, quarrelsome.

Mr. Treddles was a wee *toustie*, when you rubbed him against the hair, but a kind, weel-meaning man.—Scott : *Chronicles of the Canongate.*

Touttie, totey, irritable, irascible, of capricious and uncertain temper. Derived by Jamieson from the Flemish *togtig*, windy, a word which is not to be found in the Dutch or Flemish dictionaries.

Tove, to associate kindly as friends or lovers ; to " *tove* and crack," to hold amorous or friendly discourse. *Tovie*, comfortable ; a *tovie* fire, a snug, cozy, or comfortable fire. From the Gaelic *taobh* (pronounced *taov*), a side, a liking, partiality, friendship ; *taobhach*, kindly, friendly. *Tovie* is an epithet sometimes used to signify that a man is garrulously drunk.

Tow, a rope, also the hemp of which ropes are made ; to pull by a rope. *Towing-path* by a canal, the path by which men or horses *tow* or pull the vessels through the water. To wallop in a *tow*, to dangle from the gallows.

> And ere I wed another jade,
> I'll wallop in a *tow.*
> —Burns : *The Weary Pund*
> *o' Tow.*

I hae another *tow* on my rock [I have other business to attend to].—*Scots Proverb.*

Jamieson derives *tow* from the Swedish *tog*, the substance of which ropes are made. It is more likely from the Gaelic *taod*, a rope, a string, a halter.

Towdy, a jocular term for the breech, fundament, podex, or doup, especially when abnormally large. From this word comes the English *dowdy*, applied to an ill-dressed and unshapely woman, large in the hips. The derivation is possibly from the Gaelic *doideach*, fleshy, muscular.

Towhead, a head with flaxen or very light - coloured hair. A term used in America, according to Bartlett's Dictionary of Americanisms, for "a flaxenheaded urchin."

Towmond, a twelvemonth.

How 'twas a *towmond* auld, sin' lint was i' the bell.
　　　—BURNS : *Cotter's Saturday Night.*

Surrounded wi' peat an' wi' heather,
Where muircocks and plovers were rife.
For mony a long *towmond* together
There lived an auld man an' his wife.
　　　—ANDREW SCOTT : *Symon and Janet.*

Towzie, rough, hairy, shaggy ; whence *towzer*, the name sometimes applied in England to a terrier.

His *touzie* back
Weel clad wi' coat o' glossy black.
　　　—BURNS : *The Twa Dogs*

A *touzie* tyke, black, grim, and large,
To gie them music was his charge.
　　　—BURNS : *Tam o' Shanter.*

Toy, a woman's cap. This word is probably from the Gaelic *toil*, pleasure, applied to the finery with which it is the *pleasure*, and often the *toil*, of women to adorn or attire themselves, and was originally given to the ordinary *mutch* or indoor head-dress when bedizened with ribbons.

Toyte, to dawdle, to take things easily ; from the Gaelic *taite*, ease, pleasure.

We've won to crazy years thegither,
We'll *toyte* about wi' ane anither,
Wi' tentie care I'll flit thy tether

To some hain'd rig,
Where ye may doucely rax your leather
Wi' sma' fatigue.
　　　—BURNS : *Auld Farmer to his Auld Mare, Maggie.*

Traik, to lounge, to gad about, to follow idly after women ; from the Flemish *trekken*, to walk, to draw or pull along.

There is not a huzzy on this side of thirty that ye can bring within your doors, but there will be chiels, writer lads, 'prentice lads, and what not, come *traiking* after them for their destruction.—SCOTT : *Heart of Midlothian.*

Trattle. The resemblance of this word to *prattle*, from *prate*, has led Jamieson and others to suppose that its meaning is identical. But it is by no means clear that the supposition is well founded, or that *trattle*, *prattle*, and *rattle* are related in meaning, notwithstanding the similarity of sound. The word seems to be akin to, or to be derived from, the German *trotzen*, the Flemish *trots*, to dare, to defy, to be arrogant or presumptuous ; *trotzig*, violent.

Oh better I'll keep my green cleiding
Frae gude Earl Richard's bluid,
Than thou canst keep thy clattering tongue
That *trattles* in thy head.
　　　—EARL RICHARD : *Border Minstrelsy.*

Against the proud Scots clattering
That never will leave their *trattling*.
　　　—SKELTON : *Against the Scottis,* quoted *by* SIR WALTER SCOTT *in Border Minstrelsy.*

The German and Flemish *trotzen* would more fully meet the meaning and spirit of the epithet than any derivation from *prattle* could pretend to.

Treacherous as Garrick, false as Garrick, deep as Garrick. These phrases are current in England as well as in Scotland, and can have no possible connection with the name of Garrick, or to the renowned actor who bore it in the last century. The true origin is unknown. It is possible, however, that *treacherous as Garrick* may mean treacherous as a *caoireagh* (or *caoireach*), Gaelic for a blazing fire. This suggestion is offered *faute de mieux*. A Highlander, however, is of opinion that *Garrick* is a corruption of *coruisg*, a deep, gloomy, and treacherous loch in the island of Skye. " Who shall decide when doctors disagree ? "

Trig, neat, clean, attractive ; usually derived from the English *trick* or *tricky*, which has not the same meaning. Also, a fop, or a person giving too much attention to his personal appearance.

> It is my humour : you are a pimp and a *trig*,
> An Amadis de Gaul, or a Don Quixote.
> —BEN JONSON : *The Alchemist.*

> And you among them a', John,
> Sae *trig* from top to toe.
> —BURNS : *John Anderson.*

The word seems to be derived from the Dutch and Flemish *trek*, to attract. Though Jamieson derives it from the English *trick*, or *trick* out, to dress

gaudily or finely, it is possibly either from the Welsh or Kymric *trig*, firm-set, or the Gaelic *triathach* (*th* silent, *triac*), splendid.

Trimmer, trimmie, disrespectful terms applied to a scolding or irascible woman. From the Gaelic *dream*, or *tream*, to snarl, to grin angrily ; *dreamach*, morose, peevish, ill-natured ; *dreamag*, or *dréimeag*, a vixen, a shrew.

Troggin, wares exchanged with servant girls for the odds and ends of a household by travelling pedlars ; *trog*, old clothes ; *trogger*, or *trocker*, a pedlar, one who deals in old clothes. It is doubtful whether these words are from the French *troquer*, to barter, the English *truck*, or from the Dutch and Flemish *troggelen*, to beg under pretence of selling trifles that nobody requires. The word appears as *troke* in Halliwell's Archaic Dictionary.

> Buy braw *troggin*,
> Frae the banks o' Dee ;
> Wha' wants *troggin*,
> Let him come to me.
> —BURNS : *An Election Song.*

Trolollay, a term which, according to Jamieson, occurs in a rhyme sung by young people in Scotland at Hogmanay, the last day of the old year, and the morning of the new. " It has," he says, " been viewed as a corruption of the French *trois rois* *allais*, three kings are come!" In this sentence the word *allais* is ungrammatical and incorrect, for *trois rois sont venus*. But independently of the bad French, the etymology is entirely wrong. The word, or words, are part of a very ancient Druidical chorus, sung two thousand years ago at the dawning of the day, in honour of the sunrise : *trà là là!* From the Gaelic *tràth* (*tra*), early ; and *là*, day, signifying not " the three kings are come," but " Day ! early day !" equivalent to the " Hail, early morn !" of a well-known modern song.

Tron. There is a *Tron* Church in Edinburgh and another in Glasgow ; but the Scottish Glossaries and Jamieson's " Scottish Dictionary " make no mention of the word. It would appear from a passage in Hone's " Every-day Book " that *Tron* signified a public weighing-machine, or scale in a market-place, where purchasers of commodities might, without fee, satisfy themselves that the weight of their purchase was correct. Hence a " *Tron* Church " was a church in the market-place near which the public weighing - machine was established. The word is derived from the Gaelic *trom*, heavy, or a weight.

Tronie, a tedious story that has been often repeated, and that causes a sense of weariness in the person condemned to listen to it. From the Gaelic *trom* or *tron*, heavy, tedious. The same epithet is applied to a boy who is unable to learn his lessons.

Trow or **drow**, the evil one. From the Gaelic *droch*, evil, bad, wicked. *Sea trowes*, evil spirits of the sea ; to *trow*, or *drow*, to wish evil, to imprecate.

Trullion, a low, base, dirty fellow. The English has *trull*, the feminine of this word, applied to an immoral woman of the lowest class. The origin is the Gaelic *truaill*, to pollute, to debase ; and *truilleach*, a base, dirty person.

Tryste, an appointed place of meeting, a rendezvous ; of the same origin as *trust*, or confidence, from the idea that he who appoints a *tryste* with another *trusts* that the other will keep or be faithful to it. The word occurs in Chaucer, and in several old English MSS. of his period ; but is not used by Spenser, Shakspeare, or later writers. " To bide *tryste*," to be true to time and place of meeting.

"You walk late, sir," said I. " I bide *tryste*," was the reply, "and so I think do you, Mr. Osbaldistone?"—SIR WALTER SCOTT : *Rob Roy*.

The tenderest-hearted maid
That ever bided *tryste* at village stile.
—TENNYSON.

By the wine-god he swore it, and named
  the *trysting*-day.
          —Lord Macaulay.

No maidens with blue eyes
Dream of the *trysting* hour
Or bridal's happier time.
          —*Under Green Leaves.*

When I came to Ardgour I wrote to
Lochiel to *tryste* me where to meet him.—
Hogg's *Jacobite Relics: Letter from Rob
Roy to General Gordon.*

Tuath de Danaan. This name
has been given to a colony of
northmen who early settled in
Ireland, and afterwards passed
into Argyllshire. From *tuath*,
north; *tuathach*, northern; and
dan, bold, warlike; and *danfher*,
(*dan-er*), a warrior, a bold man;
and also a *Dane*. *Tuath de Danaan* is a corruption, in which
the second word *de* ought to
have no place of *tuathaich* and
dan or *dana*. The Very Rev.
Canon Bourke, in his work on
the Aryan origin of the Gaelic
language, says "The *Tuath de
Danaans* were a large, fair-
complexioned, and very remarkable race, warlike, energetic,
progressive, musical, poetical,
skilled in Druidism," &c. Mr.
Pym Yeatman, in "The Origin
of the Nations of Europe," who
quotes these and other passages,
is of opinion that the *Tuath de
Danaans* were Scandinavians, a
supposition which their Gaelic
designation fully corroborates.
Of course they brought with
them their own language, many
of the words of which were in
course of time incorporated
with the speech of the people
with whom they amalgamated.

This accounts for the many
Danish words both in modern
Gaelic and in Lowland Scotch.

Tuilyie or **toolzie**, a broil, a
struggle, a quarrel; *tuiliesome*,
quarrelsome; *tuilzeour*, a quarrelsome person, a wrangler.
Though Jamieson derives *tuilzie*
from the French *touiller*—a word
which is not to be found in the
French dictionaries—to stir or
agitate water, it is probably derived from the same source as
the quasi-synonymous English
tussle, and akin to the Gaelic
tuisleach, a tumult, a quarrel
among several persons; and
tuileas, riot; whence, also, *towzle*,
to pull about roughly, to dis-
hevel or disorder.

A *toolying* (*toolzieing*) tyke comes limping hame.—Allan Ramsay's *Scots Proverbs.*

The *toolzie's* teugh 'tween Pitt and Fox,
And our gude wife's wee birdie cocks.
      Burns: *Elegy on the Year* 1783.

But though dull prose folk Latin splatter
    In logic *tulzie*,
I hope we bardies ken some better
    Than mind sic *brulzie*.
      —Burns: *To William Simpson.*

What verse can sing, what prose recite,
The butcher deeds of bloody fate
Amid this mighty *tulzie*.
    —Burns: *Epistle to Robert Graham.*

Tulcan. Mr. Gladstone, during
his electioneering raid into Midlothian, in November 1879, explained at Dalkeith the meaning
of *tulcan*.

My noble friend, Lord Rosebery, speaking to me of the law of hypothec, said that
the bill of Mr. Vans Agnew on hypothec
is a *Tulcan Bill*. A *tulcan*, I believe, is

a figure of a calf stuffed with straw, and it is, you know, an old Scottish custom among farmers to place the *tulcan calf* under a cow to induce her to give milk.

Jamieson writes the word *tulchane*, and cites the phrase a *tulchane bishop*, as the designation of one who received the episcopate on condition of assigning the temporalities to a secular person. In some parts of Scotland the people say a *tourkin calf*, instead of a *tulcan calf*, and it is difficult to say which of the two words is the more correct, or in what direction we must look for the etymology. *Tulcan*, in the Gaelic, signifies a hollow or empty head, that of the mocked calf stuffed with straw, from *toll*, hollow, and *cean*, a head; while *tourkin* would seem to be derived from *tur*, to invent, and *cean*, a head; therefore signifying a head invented for the occasion, to deceive the mother.

A *tourkin calf*, or lamb, is one that wears a skin not its own. A *tourkin lamb* is one taken from its dam, and given to another ewe that has lost her own. In this case, the shepherd takes the skin of the dead lamb, and puts it on the back of the living one, and thus so deceives the ewe that she allows the stranger to suck.— JAMIESON.

Tumbler, a drinking-glass of a larger size than is ordinarily used for wine. The derivation may be from *tumble*, to fall over ; as in the deep drinking days, happily passed away, glasses were round at the base, without stems, and a drinker who held one full in his hand had to drink off the contents, before he could set it down, without spilling the liquor. "Tak' a tumbler," *i.e.*, take a glass of toddy, is a common invitation to convivial intercourse. "Three *tumblers* and an eke" were once considered a fair allowance for a man after dinner, or before retiring to rest. A Highland writer once suggested that the derivation was from *taom*, pour out or empty, and *leor*, enough. This was apt, and may perhaps be the true etymology. Jamieson has *tumbler*, the French *tombril*, a cart ; but this can have no relation to the convivial glass.

Tum-deif. Jamieson suggests that perhaps this word means *swooning*, and refers it to the Icelandic *tumba*, the English *tumble*, to fall to the ground. It seems, however, to be no other than a mis-spelling of *dumb-deaf*, or *deaf and dumb*.

Tumph, a blockhead. From the German *dumm*, stupid, the Dutch and Flemish *dom*. *Tumfie*, or *tumphie*, is diminutive of *tumph*.

Lang Jamie was employed in trifling jobs on market days, especially in holding horses for the farmers. He was asked his charge by a stranger to the town. "Hoot ! I hae nae charge ; sometimes a *tumph* offers me twa bawbees, but a gentleman like you always gies me a saxpence !"— *Laird of Logan.*

Tunag, a kind of jacket worn by women in the Highlands

of Scotland and in Ireland, and covering the shoulders, back, and hips ; a *tunic.* " If not derived from the Latin *tunica,*" says Jamieson, " *it may be from the same root.*" It *is* from the same root in a language much older than the Latin —the Celtic and Gaelic *ton,* the posterior, the hips. The Greeks called that part of the body πυγη, whence, in the learned slang of the English universities, the coat-tails were called " pygastoles," and by some irreverent undergraduates, " bum curtains." The word in Scottish Gaelic is *tonag,* and in Irish Gaelic *tonach.*

Turnimspike, a name given by the Highlanders to a high road or turnpike road when first made to the north of Inverness. Great consternation is said to have been excited in Ross-shire when a sheriff's officer and a tollcollector first appeared in Tain. " Lord preserve us ! " said one townsman to his neighbour, " what'll come next ? The law has reached Tain ! "

Another law came after this,
  She never saw the like, man,
They mak a lang road on the crund
              (the ground)
  An' ca' him *turnimspike*, man.

But she'll awa to Highland hills
  Where deil a ane can turn her,
And no come near to *turnimspike*,
  Unless it be to burn her.
        —*Jacobite Songs and Ballads.*

Tutti, tatie, according to Jamieson, is an interjection equiva-

lent to the English *pshaw !* But *Hey ! tuttie tatie* is the name of an old Scottish martial air, to which Burns adapted his noble song of " Scots wha hae wi' Wallace bled." To this spirited melody, according to tradition, the troops of King Robert Bruce marched to the great victory of Bannockburn. The words are derived from the Gaelic, familiar to the soldiers of Bruce, *aite dudach taite!* from *dudach*, to sound the trumpet, and *taite*, joy, and may be freely translated, " Let the joyous trumpets sound ! " The battle of Bannockburn was fought in an age when the bagpipe had not become common in Scotland, and when the harp was pre-eminently the national instrument in peace as the trumpet was in war. Jamieson, not quite sure of *Pshaw* as an interpretation, adds that " the words may have been meant as imitative of the sound of the trumpet in giving the charge."

It may be remarked that possibly there may be a remote connection between Jamieson's idea of *Pshaw* and that of the blast of trumpets. *Fanfare* in French signifies a blast on a trumpet, and a *fanfaron* is a braggadocio, a vain boaster, a braggart, or one who blows the trumpet of his own praises. For such a one in the full flow of his self-laudation, the impatient interjection, *Pshaw !* would be equally appropriate and well-merited.

When you hear the trumpet sound
   Tutti tatti to the drum,
Up your sword, and down your gun,
And to the loons again !
   —*Jacobite Relics :* WHEATLEY'S
      Reduplicated Words in the
      English Language.

Tut-mute and **tuilzie mulzie**, described in Wheatley's Dictionary of Reduplicated Words " as a muttering or grumbling between parties that has not yet assumed the form of a broil." This odd phrase, signifying a fierce quarrel that had but slight beginning, is presented in the proverb—

   It began in a laigh *tute-mute*,
   An' it rose to a wild *tuilzie mulzie.*
      —JAMIESON.

Tut is the Gaelic *dud*, the sound or *toot* upon a wind instrument, a horn, a flute, a whistle or a trumpet—and *mute* is a corruption of *maoth*, soft, gentle. *Tuilzie* is a brawl, a scuffle, a fight, from the Gaelic *tuaileas*, riot, disorder, conflict, tumult ; *tuaileasag*, a quarrelsome, foulmouthed woman ; a scold, and *mileadh*, battle. The proverb expresses a meaning similar to that in Allan Ramsay—" It began wi' needles and pins, and ended wi' horned nowte."

Twasome, threesome, foursome. The numerals two, three, and four, with the addition of the syllable *some*, are used in a sense of which they are not susceptible in English. A *twasome* walk, or a *twasome* interview, is often rendered in English by the French phrase *tête-à-tête.*

Threesome and *foursome* reels, dances in which three or four persons participate.

There's *threesome* reels and *foursome* reels,
   There's hornpipes and strathpeys, man,
But the best dance in a' the toun
, Is the Deil's awa' wi' the Exciseman.
      —BURNS.

Tway, a pair, a couple, the English *twain ;* two, sometimes written *twa.*

Every knight had a lady bright,
   And every squire a May ;
Her own self chose Lord Livingstone—
   They were a lovely *tway.*
      —BUCHAN'S *Ancient Ballads : Lord*
         Livingstone.

Twime and **thrime**, a couplet and a triplet. These are words that have not yet been admitted into the dictionaries.

Twine, to rob, to deprive ; to part with, to relinquish. Etymology uncertain ; supposed to be from the English *twain*, two, thence to separate into two.

The fish shall swim the flood nae mair,
   Nor the corn grow through the day,
Ere the fiercest fire that ever was kindled
   Twine me and Rothiemay.
      —*Ballad of the Fire of Frendraught.*

   My duddie is a cankert carle
      Will no *twine* wi' his gear.
         —JAMES CARNEGIE.

         Brandy . . .
Twines many a poor, doylt, drucken hash
   Of half his days.
      —BURNS : *Scotch Drink.*

Tyke, a mongrel, a rough dog ; originally a house dog ; from the Gaelic *tigh*, or *taigh*, a house. The word is common in Yorkshire, and in all the Northern Counties of England.

Tyke-tyrit or **tired.** Tired or wearied, as a dog or *tyke* after a long chase.

> Base *tyke*, call'st thou me host?
> —SHAKSPEARE: *Henry V.*

Nae tawted (uncombed) *tyke.*
> —BURNS: *The Twa Dogs.*

He was a gash and faithful *tyke.*
> —*Idem.*

I'm as tired of it as a *tyke* of lang kail.

You have lost your own stomach and found a *tyke's.*
> —ALLAN RAMSAY'S *Scots Proverbs.*

U

Ug. ugg, to feel extreme loathing or disgust. *Ugsome,* frightful; *ugsomeness,* frightfulness, horror.

> They would *ug* a body at them.
> — JAMIESON.

> *Ugsome* to hear was her wild eldrich shriek.
> .　　.　　.　　.　　.　　.
> The *ugsomeness* and silence of the night.
> —DOUGLAS: *Translation of the Enid.*

> Who dang us and flang us into this *ugsome* mire.
> —ALLAN RAMSAY: *The Vision.*

This word seems to be akin to the English *ugly,* which all the philologists who ignore the Gaelic as one of the sources of the English language, derive either from the Danish *huggern,* to shiver, or from other equally improbable Teutonic roots. In Gaelic *aog* (quasi *ug*), signifies death, a ghost, a skeleton, and *aogail,* ghastly, deathlike, *ugly.*

Ultimus eekibus, the very last glass of whisky toddy, or *eke,* one drop more at a convivial gathering before parting for the night; the last of the *ekes.*

Umbersorrow, hardy, rough, rude, uncultivated. This corrupt word, of which Jamieson cites a still corrupter, " a *number sorrow*," is clearly derived from the Flemish and Teutonic *unbesorgt,* uncared for, wild, neglected, growing in the strength of nature without human assistance. Jamieson cites its use in the Lothians in the sense of " rugged, of a surly disposition," applied to one whose education has been neglected, and who is without good manners.

Umquhile or **umwhile,** at one time, formerly; used also in the sense of departed or late, in such phrases as, " my late husband," " my departed wife," my *umquhile* husband, my *umquhile* wife; from the Flemish *om,* past, and *wijl,* a short time, the same as the English *while,* a short time past, a short while ago.

Unco, strange, unknown, a wonder, a strange thing; an abbre-

viation of *uncouth. Unco guid,*
extremely good, very good.

The *unco* guid, and the rigidly righteous.
　　　　　　　　—BURNS.

　　An *unco* cockernony.—GALT.

Nae safe wading in *unco* waters.

Like a cow in an *unco* loan.
　—ALLAN RAMSAY'S *Scots Proverbs.*

Each tells the *uncos* that he sees or hears.
　—BURNS : *Cotter's Saturday Night.*

Unfurthersome, unpropitious; applied to the weather, if too cold,
or too rainy, and preventing the
due ripening of the crops.

Ungainly, awkward, uncouth, insufficient, clumsy ; *gainly,* pleasant, fit, proper, pleased ; *gane,*
to serve, to suffice, to fit, to be
appropriate ; *unganed,* inappro-
priate. *Gainly* and *ungainly*
are not exactly synonymous in
Scottish parlance with the English word. *Gainly* is nearly
obsolete in England ; and *ungainly* merely signifies awkward,
clumsy. The root of the words
in the Scottish sense is the Gaelic *gean,* good-humour, fitness,
comeliness ; *geanail,* comely, fit,
proper, pleasant, serviceable.
In the following quotation *gane*
means to serve or suffice :—

　But there is neither bread nor kale
　　To *gane* my men and me.
　—*Battle of Otterbourne, Old Version.*

Unkensome, not to be known or
recognised, not to be traced.

　A smith ! a smith ! Dickie, he cries,
　A smith, a smith right speedilie !
　To turn back the caukers o' our horses'
　　shoon
　For its *unkensome* we wad be.
　—*Border Minstrelsy : Archie o' Ca'field.*

Unmackly, mis-shapen, deformed.

　Up then sterts the stranger knight,
　　Said Ladye be not thou afraid,
　I fight for thee with this grim Soldan
　　Though he's sair *unmackly* made.
　　　—*Ballad of Sir Cauline.*

Untholeable, intolerable, unen-
durable, insufferable ; from *thole.*
to endure.

　He got *untholeably* divertin', and folk
complained o' pains in their sides wi
laughin'.—*Noctes Ambrosianæ.*

Updorrock, worn out, bankrupt.
According to Jamieson, a Shetland word, which he derives
from " Icelandic *app* and *throka,*
also *thruka,* urgere, primere."
It seems to be rather from the
Flemish *op drogen,* dried up.
exhausted.

Uppil, to clear up ; applied to the
weather.

　When the weather at any time has been
wet, and ceases to be so, we say it is *uppled.*
—JAMIESON.

　From the Teutonic *aufhellen*—
auf, up ; *hellen,* to become clear.
to clear up.

Upon luck's head, by chance.
" I got it on *luck's head,*" I got
it by chance.

Urisk, according to Jamieson,
was a name given in the Highlands of Scotland to a satyr. It
was in reality the name given
to a *Brownie* or Puck, the Robin
Goodfellow of Englith fairy mythology ; from the Gaelic *uirisg,*
a goblin. (See WIRRY-COW.

V

Vanquish, a disease among sheep and lambs, caused by their eating a certain unwholesome grass. Jamieson says the disease is so called because it *vanquishes* the sheep! He might as well account for the name of Kilmarnock, by stating that one Marnock was killed there. *Vanquish* is a corruption of the Gaelic *uain*, pale green, and *cuiseach* or *cuiseag*, a species of rank grass with a long stalk that grows on wet soil and is deleterious to cattle, and especially to sheep. *Cuiseach* is possibly the same as *couch* grass, described in Halliwell's Archaic and Provincial Dictionary as a kind of coarse grass that grows very quickly, and is sometimes called *twitch* grass.

Vaudy or **vaudie**, gay, showy; a corruption of the English *gaudy*.

Our land shall be glad, but the Whigs shall be sorry
When the King gets his ain, and heaven gets the glory;

The rogues shall be sad, but the honest man
　　　vaudie
When the throne is possessed by our ain
　　bonnie laddie.
　　　　　—Jacobite Relics of Scotland.

Vauntie, proud, vain, also a braggart ; from the French *vanter*, to boast.

　　　　Her cutty sark
　In longitude though sorely scanty,
　It was her best, and she was *vauntie*.
　　　　—BURNS: *Tam o' Shanter.*

Vir, force, vigour. Sometimes written *bir*, a vein; from the Latin *vis, vires.* Possibly the English *burly*, strong, is of kindred origin.

Swith with *vir* he whirled her round.
—GEORGE BEATTIE: *John o' Arnha'.*
Wi'vengeful *vir*,and Norland twang.—*Ibid.*

Vlonk, or **Wlonk**, splendidly dressed, richly attired ; from the "Anglo Saxon" or old English *vlonke*, which has the same meaning. Possibly this may be the origin of the modern word *flunkey*, in contemptuous allusion to the grayish colours of the liveries of male servants in great ostentatious families. (See FLUNKEY, *ante*, p. 60).

W

Wa', abbreviation of wall. "His back is at the *wa'*," *i.e.*, he is driven into a corner ; his back is at the wall, fighting against opposing enemies or creditors.

Wabster, a weaver ; from weave and web.

Willie Wastle dwalt on Tweed,
　The spot they ca'd it Linkum-doddie,
Willie was a *wabster* gude.
　　　　　　BURNS.

An honest *wabster* to his trade,
Whose wife's twa nieves were scarce weel bred.
　　　　　—BURNS : *Death and Dr.*
　　　　　　　Hornbook.

Wad, to wager, to bet; from the Flemish *wedden*, which has the same meaning. *Wads* also signify forfeits; a game at *wads*, a game at forfeits; *wad-set*, a mortgage; *wad*, a pledge.

The gray was a mare and a right good mare,
But when she saw the Annan water,
She could not hae ridden a furlong mair,
    Had a thousand merks been *wadded* at her.
    —*Minstrelsy of the Scottish Border:
        Annan Water.*

Wads are nae arguments.
    —ALLAN RAMSAY'S *Scots Proverbs.*

My Sunday's coat she has laid it in *wad*,
And the best blue bonnet e'er was on my head;
At kirk or at market I'm covered but barely,
Oh that my wife would drink hooly and fairly.
    —HERD'S *Collection: The Drucken
        Wife o' Galloway.*

Waddie, vigorous, willing, alert, ready to do.

What fee will you give me for now and for aye—
Was e'er a young laddie sae *waddie* as I.
    —BUCHAN'S *Ancient Ballads: The
        Rigwoodie Carlin'.*

Wae's! woe is; unlucky, unhappy, in ill plight.

Wae's the wife that wants the tongue,
but wee's the man that gets her.
    —ALLAN RAMSAY'S *Scots Proverbs.*

And aye the o'erword o' his sang
Was—*wae's* me for Prince Charlie.
    —*Jacobite Song.*

Waesuck! wae's-heart! wae's-me! Interjections or expressions of surprise or sorrow, like *alas!*

Waesuck! for him that gets nae lass,
Or lasses that hae naething.
    —BURNS: *The Holy Fair.*

The derivation of *wae's-heart* and *wae's-me*, from *wae*, sorrow, is obvious; that of *waesuck* is not so clear. It is probably from the Flemish *wee*, sorrow or love, and *sugt* or *zucht*, a sigh. Jamieson derives it from the Danish *usig*, woe to us; *vae nobis*, woe to us. The word, however, is not to be found in Danish dictionaries.

Waff, wauf, waft. A freak, a whiff, a wave of sound or of wind, a sudden and slight impression upon the senses, a transient glance, a glimpse, a passing odour. "A *waff* o' cauld" is a slight attack of cold. "I had a *waff* o' him i' the street;" I had a glimpse of him. "There was a *waff* o' roses;" there was a sudden odour of roses. The primitive idea at the root of the word is sudden and of short duration, rising and subsiding like a wave.

Waff, worthless, or shabby in appearance and conduct; idle, dissipated; *waffie*, a loafer, an idler, a vagrant, a vagabond; *waff-like*, resembling a vagabond in manners and appearance; *waffinger*, a confirmed vagrant and idler. These words are of uncertain etymology, though it is probable that they are all from the same root as the English *waif*, a stray, a vagrant, one who, like the

R

Italian *traviato* and *traviata*, has gone astray from the right and respectable path, and formed on the same principle from *way off*, or off the way. Another possible root is the Flemish *zwerfen* (with the elision of the initial *z*), to go astray, to vagabondise.

Wa'gang or **awa'-gang**, departure; *ganging awa'*, going away; an escape.

> Winter's *wa'gang*.
> —James Ballantine.

A *wa'gang* crop is the last crop gathered before a tenant quits his farm; also the name given to the canal, through which the water escapes from the mill wheel.—Jamieson.

> Its dowie in the end o' hairst,
>   At the *wa'gang* o' the swallow,
> When the wind grows cauld and the burn
>   grows bauld,
>   And the weeds are hanging yellow;
> But oh, it's dowier far to see
>   The *wa'gang* o' her that the heart gangs
>   wi'.
>   —Hew Ainslie.

Waghorn. In the North of Scotland it is a proverbial phrase to say of a great liar that "he lies like *Waghorn*," or is "waur than *Waghorn*," that "he is as false as *Waghorn*, and *Waghorn* was nineteen times falser than the devil." Jamieson records that "*Waghorn* is a fabulous personage, who being a greater liar than the devil, was crowned King of Liars." Why the name of *Waghorn*, any more than that of *Wagstaffe*, both respectable patronymics, should be selected to adorn or to disfigure the

proverb is not easy to explain, except on the supposition that the traditionary "*waghorn*" is a corruption of a word that has a more rational as well as a more definite meaning. And such it is found to be. In Gaelic *uaigh* (quasi *wag*) signifies the grave, the pit, and *iutharn* (*iuarn*, quasi *horn*) signifies hell, whence he lies like *Waghorn*, would signify he "lies like hell" or like the "pit of hell," consequently worse than the devil, who is supposed to be but one, while the other devils in the pit are supposed to be multitudinous.

Waif, a derelict, a wanderling; one found by accident after having been lost or gone astray. The word in this sense has lately been adopted into English literature as a noun; but in Scotland it is employed both as a noun and an adjective.

> Wi' her I will get gowd and gear,
>   Wi' thee, I sall get nane;
> Ye cam to me as a *waif* woman,
>   I'll leave thee as the same.
>   —Herd's *Collection: Fair Annie.*

This word, sometimes written and pronounced *waff*, *waffie*, and *waffinger*, signifies a wanderer, a strolling vagabond, lost to civilised life and society; *wafflike*, of vagabond and disreputable appearance.

Waith, to wander, a wandering and straying. The English *waif*, waifs and strays, things or persons that have wandered or gone astray. The etymology is doubtful; perhaps from *waft*, to be blown about by the wind, or carried by the waters.

Wale, to choose, to select, a choice ; *waly*, choice. From the German *wahlen*, to choose.

> Scones, the *wale* o' food.
> —BURNS : *Scotch Drink.*

> There's auld Rob Morris that wons in yon glen,
> He's the king o' guid fellows and *wale* o' auld men.
> —BURNS.

The Laird of Balnamon, after dinner at a friend's house, had cherry brandy put before him in mistake for port. He liked the liquor, and drank freely of it. His servant Harry or "Hairy" was to drive him home in a gig. On crossing the moor, whether from greater exposure to the blast, or from the Laird's unsteadiness of head, his hat and wig fell to the ground. Harry got off to pick them up and restore them to his master. The Laird was satisfied with the hat, but demurred to the wig. "It's no my wig, Harry lad ; it's no my wig." "Ye'd better tak it, sir," said Harry ; "for there's nae *wale* o' wigs on the moor."—DEAN RAMSAY's *Reminiscences.*

> He *wales* a portion wi' judicious care,
> And let us worship God, he says, wi' solemn air.
> —BURNS: *Cotter's Saturday Night.*

Wallageous. This obsolete word is used by the ancient Scottish poet, Barbour, in the sense of sportive, wanton, lustful. It is evidently a corruption of the Gaelic *uallach*, which has the same meaning; *uallachās*, cheerfulness, gaiety, frolicksomeness, conceitedness, wantonness; *uallachag*, a coquette.

Wallie, a toy ; a *bonnie wallie*, a pretty toy ; from *wale*, choice ; from the Teutonic *wahlen.*

Walloch, a name applied in the Lowlands to the Highland fling, or other dance, and not to the reel, which is less active and boisterous. The word also means a *frisk* or *kick*. The word seems to be derived from the Gaelic *uallach*, joyous, frisky.

> I wat she was a cantie quean,
> And weel could dance the Highland *walloch.*
> —*Roy's Wife of Aldivalloch.*

> Auld Roy look'd as he gaed by,
> And oh ! he gaed an unco *walloch;*
> And after them he soon did hie,
> And followed through the braes of Balloch.
> —BUCHAN's *Collection of Old Scottish Ballads.*

The word is sometimes written *wallop*, as in the favourite song of " Maggie Lauder " : —

> Meg up and *wallop'd* o'er the green,
> For brawly she could frisk it.

Walloch-goul, an abusive epithet applied to a wanton or arrogant blusterer ; from the Gaelic *uallach*, and *guil*, to cry out. (See YOWL.)

Wallop, to dangle, to hang, to sway about with quick motion, to swing.

> Now let us lay our heads thegither,
> In love fraternal ;
> May Envy *wallop* in a tether,
> Black fiend, infernal !
> —BURNS : *To Lapraik.*

Wallow, to fade away ; *wallowed*, faded, withered by cold, blight, or natural decay ; the etymon doubtless of the word *wilt*, in common use in America, and in some parts of England, of which a ludicrous example is given by the humorist, Artemus Ward : " I said to her, *wilt* thou ? and she *wilted*." The derivation is uncertain, though probably from the Teutonic *welken*.

> The last time that I saw her face
> She ruddy was and red,
> But now, alas ! and woe is me,
> She's *wallowed* like a weed.
> —SCOTT's *Border Minstrelsy : Ballad of the Gay Goss-Hawk.*

Waly ! waly ! an interjection of sorrow ; *alas !* or, *woe is me !* Derived from *wail*, to lament, or *wail* ye ! lament ye ; the Teutonic *weh*, woe, and *wehlich*, woful.

> Oh *waly ! waly !* but love is bonnie,
> A little time while it is new ;
> But when it's auld it waxes cauld,
> And fades awa' like morning dew.
> —*Ballad of the Marchioness of Douglas.*

> Oh *waly ! waly !* up the bank,
> And *waly ! waly !* down the brae,
> And *waly ! waly !* yon burn side,
> Where I and my love wont to gae.
> —*Lady Anne Bothwell's Lament.*

Wame, the belly ; also the English word *womb*, which is from the same etymological root. The Scottish derivatives of *wame* are numerous ; among others, *wamie*, having much *wame*, *i.e.*, corpulent ; *wamieness*, corpulency ; *wamyt*, pregnant ; *wame-tow*, a belly-band or girth, from *wame*,

the belly, and *tow* (the Gaelic *taod*), a rope, a band ; *wamefu'*, a bellyfull.

I never liked water in my shoon ; and my *wame's* made o' better leather.

Wae to the *wame* that has a wilfu master.
—ALLAN RAMSAY'S *Scots Proverbs.*

Food fills the *wame*, and keeps us livin',
Though life's a gift no worth receivin',
When heavy dragged wi' pine and grievin'.
—BURNS : *Scotch Drink.*

A *wamefu'* is a *wamefu'*, whether it be of barley-meal or bran.—SCOTT : *St. Ronan's Well.*

Wame has disappeared from English literature, but still survives in the current speech of the northern counties. *Womb*, in English, was formerly applied to the male sex, in the sense of the Scottish *wame*, or belly, as appears from Piers Ploughman :—

> Paul, after his preaching,
> Paniers he made,
> And wan with his handes
> What his *wombe* needed.

(Gained with his hands what his belly needed.) In recent times the word is restricted in its meaning to the female sex, though used metaphorically and poetically in such phrases as the "*womb* of Time."

The earth was formed, but in the *womb* as yet
Of waters, embryon immature.
—*Paradise Lost.*

Caves and *womby* vaultages of France
Shall chide your trespass.
—SHAKSPEARE : *Henry V.*

Among the three interpretations of the word, as given by

Johnson, the last is "a cavity." The only traces of anything like *wame*, or *womb*, that appears in any of the Teutonic languages, or in high or low Dutch, is the Swedish *wam*, signifying tripe. Though Johnson derives *womb* from the Anglo-Saxon and from Icelandic, it may be suggested that the more ancient Celtic and Gaelic provides the true root of both *wame* and *womb* in *uaimh* and *uamh*, a cavity, a cave, a hollow place. The Shakspearean adjective *womby* finds its synonym in the Gaelic *uamhach*, abounding in cavities or hollows.

Wan, pale green, as applied to the colour of a river in certain states of the water and the atmosphere. Many philologists have been of opinion that *wan*, both in English and Scotch, always signifies pale. Jamieson, however, thought differently, and translated *wan* as "black, gloomy, dark-coloured, or rather filthy," not reflecting, however, that these epithets, especially the last, were hardly consistent with the spirit or dignity of the tender or tragical ballads in which *wan* occurred. The etymology of the English *wan* has been traced to *wane*, to decrease in health and strength, as well as in size, whence *wan*, the pallor of countenance that attends failing health. That of the Scottish *wan*, as applied to the colour of the streams, was for the first time suggested in "The Gaelic

Etymology of the Languages of Western Europe." It is from the Gaelic *uaine*, a pale blue, inclining to green. This is the usual colour of the beautiful streams of the Highlands, when not rendered "drumlie" or muddy by the storms that wash down sand and earth from the banks.

On they rade, and on they rade,
  And a' by the light o' the moon,
Until they came to the *wan* water,
  And then they lighted down.
            —The Douglas Tragedy.

Deep into the *wan* water
  There stands a muckle stane.
            —Earl Richard.

The ane has ta'en him by the head,
  The ither by the feet,
And thrown him in the *wan* water
  That ran baith wide and deep.
            —Lord William.

There's no a bird in a' this forest
  Will do as muckle for me
As dip its wing in the *wan* water,
  And straik it ower my e'e bree.
            —Johnnie o' Bradislee.

In English, *wan* is never used as an epithet except when applied to the countenance, as in such phrases—"His face was pale and *wan*," and occasionally by poetic license, to the face of the moon, as in the beautiful sonnet of Sir Philip Sidney.

With how sad steps, oh moon! thou
    climb'st the sky,
How silently, and with how *wan* a
    face.

Wanchancie, unlucky, mischanceful.

Wae worth the man wha first did shape
That vile *wanchancie* thing—a rape.
            —BURNS : Poor Mailie's Elegy.

Wandought, weak, deficient in power; from *dow*, to be able; *doughty*, brave; and *wan*, or *un*, the privative particle. *Wandocht*, a weak, silly creature.

By this time Lindy is right well shot out
'Twixt nine and ten, I think, or thereabout,
Nae bursen-bailch, nae *wandought* or mis-
    grown,
But plump and swack, and like an apple
    roun'.
            —Ross's *Helenore.*

Wanhope, despair. Jamieson incorrectly renders it "delusive hope." This is an old English word which is nearly obsolete, but still survives in Scotland.

I sterve in *wanhope* and distress,—
Farewell, my life, my lust and my
    gladnesse.
    —CHAUCER: *The Knight's Tale.*

Good Hope that helpe shulde
To *wanhope* turneth.
            —*Piers Ploughman.*

Some philologists, misled by the prefix *wan*, have imagined that the word was synonymous with *wane*, and have interpreted *wanhope* as the "waning of hope." But *wan* is the Dutch and Flemish negative prefix, equivalent to the English and German *un*. Among other beautiful Scottish words which follow the Flemish in the use of the negative prefix, are *wanearthlie*, preternatural or unearthly; *wanfortune*, ill-luck; *wangrace*, wickedness, ungraciousness; *wanrest*, inquietude; *wanworth*, useless, valueless; *wanthrift*, prodigality, extravagance; *wanuse*, abuse; *wanwit* or *wanwith*, ignorance.

An' may they never learn the gaets (ways)
Of ither vile *wanrestful* pets.
            —BURNS: *Poor Mailie.*

Wanwierd, misfortune, ill-luck, calamity.

Nor wit, nor power, put off the hour
For his *wanwierd* decreed.
    —*Border Minstrelsy: The Water
        Kelpie.*

Wap, in England written *wad*, a bundle of straw, a wisp, used in the Scottish sense in the North of England; from the Flemish *hoop*, a bundle, a pile of hay or straw. To be in the *wap* or *wad*, to lie in the straw.

Moll i' the *wap* and I fell out,
I'll tell ye what 'twas a' about,—
She had siller and I had nane,
That was the gait the steer began.
            —*Gipsy Song.*

The English version among the gipsies is—

Moll i' the *wad* and I fell out,
She had money and I had none,
That was the way the row began.

Ware, to spend, to guide, to control or guide one's expense discreetly.

My heart's blood for her I would freely
    ware,
Sae be I could relieve her of her care.
            —Ross's *Helenore.*

But aiblins, honest Master Heron
Had at the time some dainty fair one,
To *ware* his theologic care on.
            —BURNS: *To Dr. Blacklock.*

This word is most probably a corruption of the Teutonic *führen*, the Flemish *voeren*, to lead or guide.

Ill-won gear is aye ill *wared.*
—ALLAN RAMSAY'S *Scots Proverbs.*
[Ill-acquired money is always ill guided or spent.]

The best o' chiels are whyles in want,
While cuifs on countless thousands rant,
And ken na how to *ware't.*
BURNS : *Epistle to Davie.*

Warklike, Warkrife, industrious, fond of work.

Warklume, a tool, a working tool. The second syllable of this word remains in the English *loom*, part of the working apparatus of the weaver. In Scotland *lume* signifies any kind of tool or implement with which work can be done. Burns uses it in a very ludicrous sense in the "Address to the Deil."

Thence mystic knots mak great abuse
On young gudemen fond, keen, and crouse,
When the best *warklume* i' the house
By cantrip wit,
Is instant made na worth a louse
Just at the bit.

This peculiar superstition prevails among all the Celtic peoples of Europe, and is thought to be the favourite and most malignant diversion of the devil and his instruments, the wizards and witches, to prevent the consummation of marriage on the bridal night. A full account of the alleged practices of several sorcerers who were burnt at the stake in France in the Middle Ages, for their supposed complicity in this crime, appears in the "History of Magic in France," by Jules Garinet, Paris,

1818. The name given in France to the "cantrip" mentioned by Burns was *nouer l'aiguillette*, or, tie the little knot. One unhappy Vidal de la Porte, accused of being a *noueur d'aiguillette* by repute and wont, was in the year 1597 sentenced to be hung and burned to ashes for having bewitched in this fashion several young bridegrooms. The sentence was duly executed, amid the applause of the whole community.

Warld's gear, worldly wealth ; a word used for any valuable article of whatever kind, as in the phrases " I have nae *warld's gear*," I have no property whatever ; "there's nae *warld's gear* in the glass but cauld water," nothing more costly than cold water.

But *warld's gear* ne'er fashes me,—
My thocht is a' my Nannie, O.
—BURNS.

Warlock, a wizard. The Scottish word, though admitted into the English dictionaries, is not common either in English conversation or literature.

She prophesied that late or soon
Thou would be found deep drowned in Doon,
Or catch'd by *warlocks* in the mirk,
By Alloway's auld haunted kirk.
—BURNS : *Tam o' Shanter.*

In the ancient time of Druidism, a wizard, an augur, a prophet, or fortune-teller, was called a Druid, a name that is still retained in modern Gaelic. The Lowland Scotch *warlock* is derived, according to Jamieson, from the Icelandic *vardlokr*, a magic song or incantation for calling up evil spirits. Mr. Stormonth, in his Etymological Dictionary, refers the word to the Anglo-Saxon *waer*, wary, and *loga*, a liar. It is more probable, however, that the word had not this uncomplimentary meaning; and that as *wizard* is derived from the German *weise* or *wise*, *warlock* has its root in a similar idea, and may come from the Gaelic *geur*, sharp, acute, cunning; and *luchd*, folk. It was not customary in the days when witches and fairies were commonly believed in, to speak disrespectfully of them. The fairies were "the good folk," the wizard was "the wise man," and the witch, in Irish parlance, was the Banshee (*Bean-sith*), or woman of peace; and *warlock*, in like manner. was an epithet implying the sagacity rather than the wickedness of the folk so designated. The change of the syllable *geur* into *war* is easily accounted for. The French *guerre* becomes *war* in English by the change—not uncommon —of *g* into *w*, as in *wasp*, from the French *guespe* or *guêpe*. Another possible derivation is suggested in the "Gaelic Etymology of the Languages of Western Europe," from *barr*, head, top, chief; and *loguid*, a rascal; but the first is preferable.

Warple, to entangle, to intertwine wrongly. From the English *warp*, to twist or turn aside, as in the phrase, "His judgment is *warped*." The root of both the Scottish and English is the Flemish *werwele*, to turn, or turn aside.

That yarn's sae *warplit* that I canna get it redd.
—JAMIESON.

Warsle, to wrestle, to contend. also to tumble violently after a struggle to keep the feet.

Upon her cloot (hoof) she coost (cast) a hitch
And ower she *warsled* in the ditch.
—BURNS: *Poor Mailie.*

Wast, west; often used in the north-east of Scotland for beyond, further off.

Sir Robert Liston, British Ambassador at Constantinople, found two of his countrymen who had been especially recommended to him in a barber's shop, waiting to be shaved in turn. One of them came in rather late, and seeing he had scarcely room at the end of the seat, addressed the other—"Neebour, wad ye sit a wee bit *wast?*" What associations must have been called up in his mind by hearing, in a distant land, such an expression in Scottish tones!"—DEAN RAMSAY.

Wat, to know, to wit. Obsolete English *wot*; Dutch and Flemish *weten*. *Watna*, wits not. knows not.

Little *wats* the ill-willy wife what a dinner may haud in't.

Dame! deem warily; ye *watna* wha wytes yoursel.

Mickle water runs by that the miller *wats* na of.
—ALLAN RAMSAY'S *Scots Proverbs.*

Wath, a ford; a shallow part of the river that may be waded across. Either from the Flemish *waad*, or the Gaelic *ath*, a ford. Scotis-*wath* is the name given to the upper part of the Solway Firth, where, in certain states of the tide, people from the English side can wade across to Scotland.

Watter, water. The word is used in Scotland in the sense of a stream, a brook, a river; as in the phrase, "the *water* of Leith," and the Glasgow phrase, "Down the *water*," signifying down the Clyde. It is recorded of the noted Edinburgh advocate, John Clerk, afterwards Lord Eldin, that, in arguing a case of water privilege in Scotland before Lord Chancellor Eldon, he annoyed his lordship by constantly repeating the word *watter* with a strong Scottish accent. " Mr. Clerk," inquired his lordship, " is it the custom in your country to spell water with two *t's* ? " " No, my lord," replied Clerk ; " but it's the fashion in *my* country to spell *manners* wi' twa *n's*."

Wattie - wagtail. From *Walter Wagtail*, a name given to the beautiful little bird, the *hochequeue* of the French; the *motacilla yarrellie* of the naturalists. The English have corrupted the word, not knowing its Scottish origin, into "*water-wagtail*." *Walter*, or *Wattie*, is a fond alliteration formed on the same principle as that of *Robin Redbreast. Water-wagtail* is an appellation given by the English to the pretty little creature, founded on the erroneous notion that it is an aquatic bird, or that it frequents the water more than it does the land. It comes with the flies and departs with the flies, which are its only food, and, unlike many other attractive birds, does no harm to fruit, blossoms, seeds, or any kind of vegetation. In some parts of Scotland it is called " *Wullie*," or " *Willie-wagtail*."

Wauchle, to weary; also, to puzzle, to sway from side to side ; English, to *waggle ;* Flemish *waggelen*, to vacillate, to stagger.

The road *wauchlit* him sair (made him stagger with fatigue).

That question *wauchlit* him (staggered him.
—JAMIESON.

Waught, a large deep draught of liquor. The etymology is uncertain. In most of the glossaries to Burns' Poems the word is erroneously joined with " willy," and converted into " willy-*waught*," and described as meaning " a hearty draught." The line in " Auld Lang Syne," usually printed—

We'll drink a right gude willy-*waught*,

should be

We'll drink a right gude-willie *waught :*

i.e., we'll drink with right good will a deep or hearty *waught* or draught.

Dean Ramsay, whose undoubted knowledge and appre

ciation of the Scottish language should have taught him better, has fallen into the mistake of quoting *willie - waught* as one word in the following lines :—

Gude e'en to you a', and tak your nappy,
A " *willywaught*," a gude night cappy.

The word is introduced with fine effect in a translation from the Gaelic, by the Ettrick Shepherd, of the Jacobite Ballad, " The Frasers in the Correi : "—

Spier na at me !
Gae spier at the maiden that sits by the
    sea,
The red coats were here, and it was na for
    good,
And the ravens are hoarse in " the *waught-
ing*" o' blood.

And meantime gies a *waught* o' caller
    whey,
The day's been hot, and we are wondrous
    dry.
            —Ross's *Helenore.*

I'm sure 'twill do us meikle guid, a *waucht*
    o' caller air.
A caller douk, a caller breeze, and caller
    fish and fare.
  —*Whistle Binkie : Doun the Water.*

Wauk, to render the palm of the hand hard, callous, or horny, by severe toil.

I held on high my *waukit* loof,
To swear by a' yon starry roof,
That henceforth I wad be rhyme proof,
    Til my last breath.
      --BURNS : *The Vision.*

Waukrife, watchful, wakeful, unable to sleep; the suffix *rife*, as in cauld*rife*, very cold, is used as an intensitive, so that *wauk-rife* signifies not only unable

to sleep, but unable in an intense degree.

What time the moon, wi' silent glower,
    Sets up her horn,
Wail through the dreary midnight hour,
    Till *waukrife* morn.
    —BURNS : *Elegy on Captain Matthew
        Henderson.*

'Tis hopeless love an' dark despair,
    Cast by the glamour o' thine e'e,
That clouds my *waukrife* dreams wi' care,
An' maks the daylight dark to me.
        —JAMES BALLANTINE.

Waullies or **waulies**. Jamieson defines *wallies* as meaning the intestines. The word is not to be confounded with *waly* or *walie*, choice, large, ample, as Burns uses it.

But mark the rustic haggis-fed,
The trembling earth resounds his tread ;
Clap in his *walie* nieve a blade,
    He'll mak it whistle.
        —*To a Haggis.*

In "Jacob and Rachel," a song attributed to Burns, published in an anonymous London edition of his songs, dated 1825, the word occurs in the following stanza :—

Then Rachel, calm as ony lamb,
    She claps him on the *waulies*,
Quo' she, " ne'er fash a woman's clash."

In this song, omitted on account of its grossness from nearly all editions of his works, the word is not susceptible of the meaning attributed to it by Jamieson, nor of that in the poem in praise of "The Haggis." Jamieson has the obsolete word *wally*, a billow, a wave, which affords a clue to its derivation.

The name of *waulie* was given to the hips or posteriors on account of their round and wavy form, as appears from the synonymous words in Gaelic— *tonn*, a wave, and *ton*, the breech. The idea is involved in the words, now seldom used, which are cited by Jamieson, *wallie-drag*, and *wallie-dragglie*, signifying a woman who is corpulent and heavy behind, and makes but slow progress in walking. The connection with *wallies*, intestines, as rendered by Jamieson, is exceedingly doubtful.

Waur, worse. To *waur*, or *warr*, to conquer, to give an enemy the worst of the conflict ; from *worst*, to put a person in the wrong, or in a worse position.

> Up and *waur* them a', Willie.
> —*Jacobite Ballad.*

An advocate was complaining to his friend, an eminent legal functionary of the last century, that his claims to a judgeship had been overlooked, adding acrimoniously, "And I can tell you, they might have got a *waur*," to which the only answer was a grave "*whaur?*"—DEAN RAMSAY.

> Sax thousand years are near hand fled,
> Sin I was to the butcherin' bred,
> And mony a scheme in vain's been laid
> To stop or scaur me,
> Till ane Hornbook's ta'en up the trade,
> An faith he'll *waur* me.
> —BURNS : *Death and Dr. Hornbook.*

Want o' wit is *waur* than want o' wealth.

In his case, the water will never *waur* the widdie.
> —ALLAN RAMSAY'S *Scots Proverbs.*

(*i.e.*, in his case the water will never get the better of the gallows ; equivalent to the English saying, "He that's born to be hanged will never be drowned").

Wax, to grow, or increase ; the reverse of *wane*, to decrease. *Wax* is almost obsolete ; but *wane* survives, both in Scotland and England, as in the phrases : "the *waning* moon," "the *waning* year," "his *waning* fortunes." *Wax* remains as a Biblical word, in the noble translations of the Old Testament by Wickliffe and the learned divines of the reign of James I., which has preserved to this age so many emphatic words of ancient English, which might otherwise have perished. It is derived from the German *wachsen;* the Flemish *wassen*, to grow.

> The man *wox* well nigh wud for ire.
> —CHAUCER.

> And changing empires wane and *wax*,
> Are founded, flourish and decay.
> —SIR WALTER SCOTT : *Translation of Dies Irae.*

Wazie, jolly, brisk ; probably a variation for *gaucie* (q.v.), with the common change of *g* into *w*, as in *war* for *guerre*, &c.

> Right *wazie* wax'd an' fou' o' fun,
> They whistled down the setting sun.
> —BEATTIE : *John o' Arnha'.*

Wean, a little child ; a *weanie*, a very little child—from "wee ane," little one. This word has not yet been admitted to the dictionaries, though becoming common in English parlance.

A smytrie o' wee duddie *weans*
    (a lot of little ragged children).
            —BURNS : *The Twa Dogs.*

When skirlin' *weanies* see the light.
            —BURNS : *Scotch Drink.*

Wearin' awa', decaying gradually.

I'm *wearin' awa'*, Jean,
Like snaw when it's thaw, Jean,
I'm *wearin' awa'*
    To the Land o' the Leal.
                —LADY NAIRNE.

Hope's star will rise when
    Life's welkin grows grey,
We feel that within us which ne'er can
        decay,
And Death brings us Life as the
Night brings the Daw' [dawn],
    Though we're *wearin' awa'*, an'
        we're *wearin' awa'*.
                —JAMES BALLANTINE.

Weatherie, stormy or showery
weather ; a word formed on the
same principle as the Teutonic
ungewitter, very bad weather.
Weather gleam, a streak of light
on the horizon in cloudy weather.

Wee, little, diminutive, very little ;
generally supposed to be derived
from the first syllable of the
German *wenig*. This word
occurs in Shakspeare, and is
common in colloquial and familiar English, though not in literary composition. It is often
used as an intensification of littleness, as " a little *wee* child,"
" a little *wee* bit."

            A *wee* house well filled,
            A *wee* farm well tilled,
            A *wee* wife well willed,
                Mak' a happy man.

A *wee* mouse can creep under a great
haystack.
            —ALLAN RAMSAY'S *Scots Proverbs.*

Weed or **weeds**, dress, attire,
clothing. The only remnant of
this word remaining in modern
English is the phrase, a
" widow's *weeds*," the funeral
attire of a recently bereaved
widow.

They saw their bodies bare,
Anon they pass'd with all their speed,
Of beaver to mak themselves a *weed*,
    To cleith (clothe) them was their care.
—*On the Creation and Paradyce Lost,*
        by SIR RICHARD MAITLAND, *in*
        ALLAN RAMSAY'S *Evergreen.*

Weed is in many Etymological
Dictionaries said to be derived
from *weave*, the Teutonic *weben*.
Possibly it comes from the
Gaelic or *eudadh*, a dress or
garment, also the armour of a
knight. The author of the
Scottish poem of " Paradyce
Lost," which appears in the
" Evergreen," was born in 1496,
and died in 1586, at the advanced age of 90, and was
consequently long anterior to
Milton, who afterwards adopted
the same title, and rendered it
as enduring as the English language.

Weeder-clips, shears for clipping
weeds.

The rough burr thistle spreading wide
    Among the bearded bear,
I turned the *weeder-clips* aside
    And spared the symbol dear.
                —BURNS.

The patriotic poet turned the
clips aside in order that he might

not cut down a thistle, the floral badge of his country.

Weeks or **weiks** of the eye or mouth signify, according to Jamieson, the corners of the mouth or eyes. To hang by the *weeks* of his mouth, is to keep hold of a thing or purpose to the utmost, to the last gasp; an exaggerated phrase similar to that in Holy Writ to " escape by the skin of the teeth." *Week* or *weik* is a corruption of the Gaelic *uig*, a corner. The word occurs in Tim Bobbin's Yorkshire Glossary.

Weigh-bauk, the cross beam of a balance.

> Come like a *weigh-bauk*, Donald
> MacGillivray,
> Come like a *weigh-bauk*, Donald
> MacGillivray,
> Balance them fairly, balance them
> cleverly,
> Off wi' the counterfeit, Donald Mac-
> Gillivray.
> —JAMES HOGG, *the Ettrick Shepherd.*

Weil or **wele,** an eddy in the water; a whirlpool.

Weil-head, the centre of an eddy. These words appear to be a corruption of *wheel* or *whirl*, having a circular motion, and to have no connection with *well*, a spring of water.

> They doukit in at a *weil-head.*
> —*Border Minstrelsy: Earl Richard.*

Weill, good fortune, the English *weal*, as in the phrase, " Come weal, come woe."

> He is na worth the *weill* that canna thole the wae.—*Old Proverb.*

Weir, war; *wierman*, a soldier, a man of war, a combatant; *wierlike*, warlike; *weirigills*, quarrels; *wedded weirigills*, disputes between husband and wife; from the French *guerre*, the Italian *guerra*, with the change of the *gu* into *w*. The primary root seems to be the Flemish *weeren*, to defend; the English *be ware!* *i.e.*, be ready to defend yourself;—a noble origin for resistance to oppressive and defensive war, that does not apply to offensive war—the "bella, horrida bella," of the Latin, and the *krieg* of the Teutonic, which signify war generally, whether offensive or defensive;—the first a crime, the second a virtue.

Weir or **wear,** to guard, to watch over, to protect, to gather in with caution, as a shepherd conducts his flock to the fold.

> Erlinton had a fair daughter;
> I wat he *wiered* her in a great sin,
> And he has built a high bower,
> And a' to put that lady in.
> —*Ballad of Erlinton.*

Motherwell translates "*wiered* her in a great sin," placed her in danger of committing a great sin, which is clearly not the meaning. But the whole ballad is hopelessly corrupt in his version.

Weird or **wierd.** Most English dictionaries misdefine this word, which has two different significations: one as a noun, the other as an adjective. In English literature, from Shakspeare's time downwards, it exists as an adjective only, and is held to mean unearthly, ghastly, or witch-like. Before Shakspeare's time, and in Scottish poetry and parlance to the present day, the word is a noun, and signifies "fate" or "destiny"—derived from the Teutonic *werden*, to become, or that which *shall* be. Chaucer, in "Troilus and Cressida," has the line —

O Fortune! executrice of *wierdes* !

and Gower, in a manuscript in the possession of the Society of Antiquaries, says—

It were a wondrous *wierde*
To see a king become a herde.

In this sense the word continues to be used in Scotland :

A man may woo where he will, but he maun wed where his *wierd* is.

She is a wise wife that kens her ain *wierd.*—ALLAN RAMSAY's *Scots Proverbs.*

Betide me weel, betide me woe,
That *wierd* shall never danton me.
     —*Ballad of True Thomas.*

The *wierd* her dearest bairn befel
By the bonnie mill-dams o' Binnorie.
—SCOTT's *Minstrelsy of the Border.*

Shakspeare seems to have been the first to employ the word as an adjective, and to have given it the meaning of unearthly, though pertaining to the idea of the Fates :—

The *wierd* sisters, hand in hand,
Posters of the sea and land.
          —*Macbeth.*

Thane of Cawdor! by which title these *wierd* sisters saluted me.—*Idem.*

When we sat by her flickering fire at night she was most *wierd.*—CHARLES DICKENS : *Great Expectations.*

No spot more fit than *wierd*, lawless Winchelsea, for a plot such as he had conceived.—*All the Year Round*, April 2, 1870.

It opened its great aisles to him, full of whispering stillness, full of *wierd* effects of light.—*Blackwood's Magazine*, April 1870.

Jasper surveyed his companion as though he were getting imbued with a romantic interest in his *wierd* life.—CHARLES DICKENS : *The Mystery of Edwin Drood.*

She turned to make her way from the *wierd* spot as fast as her feeble limbs would let [permit] her.—T. A. TROLLOPE : *The Dream Numbers.*

Wierd is sometimes (but rarely) used as a verb, signifying to doom.

I *wierd* ye to a fiery beast,
And relieved sall ye never be.
     Border Minstrelsy : Kempion.

Weise, to direct, to guide, to draw or lead on in the way desired. This word is akin to the English *wise*, a way or manner, as in the phrase, "Do in that *wise*," and in the word *likewise*, in a like manner, and is derived from the French *viser* and the Dutch and Flemish *wijzen* or *wyzen*, to indicate, to show or point the way.

Every miller wad *weise* the water to his ain mill.—ALLAN RAMSAY's *Scots Proverbs.*

Weise also signifies to use policy for attaining any object, to turn to art rather than by strength, to draw or let out anything cautiously so as to prevent it from breaking, as in making a rope of tow or straw one is said to *weise* out the tow or straw.—JAMIESON.

The wean saw something like a white leddy that *weised* by the gate.—SCOTT : *The Monastery.*

Wem, a scar; *wemmit*, scarred, *wemless*, unscarred; and, metaphorically, blameless or immaculate. Probably from the Flemish and English *wen*, a tumour or swelling on the skin.

Wersh, insipid, tasteless; from the Gaelic *uiris*, poor, worthless, trashy.

A kiss and a drink o' water are but a *wersh* disjune.—ALLAN RAMSAY.

Why do ye no sup your parritch? I dinna like them; they're unco *wersh*. Gie me a wee pickle saut!—JAMIESON.

That auld Duke James lost his heart before he lost his head, and the Worcester man was but *wersh* parritch, neither gude to fry, boil, nor keep cauld.—SCOTT: *Old Mortality.*

The word was English in the seventeenth century, but is now obsolete, except in some of the Northern Counties, where it survives, according to Brocket's Glossary, in the corrupted form of *welsh*.

Her pleasures *wersh*, and her amours tasteless. — *Translation of Montaigne*, 1613.

Helicon's *wersh* well.—ALLAN RAMSAY.

Wet one's whistle. *Whistle* is a ludicrous name for the throat, whence to "*wet one's whistle*" signifies to moisten the throat or take a drink.

But till we meet and *weet our whistle*, Tak' this excuse for nae epistle.
        —BURNS: *To Hugh Parker.*

Whalp, to bring forth young dogs or *whelps*. Burns says of Cæsar, the Newfoundland dog

in his well-known poem of the " Twa Dogs " that he was—

Whalpit some place far abroad, Where sailors gang to fish for cod.

The Jacobite ballad-singers and popular poets of the '45, when Prince Charles Edward made his forlorn but gallant attempt to regain the throne of his ancestors, made frequent derogatory and contemptuous allusions to the family name of the House of Hanover, which they persisted in calling *Whelp* instead of *Guelph*.

Now our good king abroad is gone, A German *whelp* now fills the throne, *Whelps* that are desired by none, They're brutes compared wi' Charlie.

Oh, Charlie, come an' lead the way, No German *whelp* shall bear the sway; Though ilka dog maun hae his day, The right belongs to Charlie.
        —PETER BUCHAN'S *Prince Charlie and Flora Macdonald.*

Whalpit is the past tense of the verb to *whelp*, or bring forth *whelps* or young dogs. In Dutch and Flemish, *welp* signifies the cub of the lion or the bear, but in Scotch and English the word, though formerly applied to the progeny of the wolf and the fox, is now almost exclusively confined to that of the dog. Dr. Wagner, in his Glossary to the German edition of Burns, conjectures that the word is derivable from the Latin *vulpes.*

Whang, a large slice, also a thong of leather, and by extension of meaning, to beat with a strap or thong, or to beat generally.

Wi' sweet-milk cheese i' mony a *whang*,
And farlies baked wi' butter.
—BURNS : *Holy Fair.*

Ye cut large *whangs* out of other folk's leather. — ALLAN RAMSAY'S *Scots Proverbs.*

Whang, in the sense of to beat with a strap, is local in England, but in the sense of a large slice, or anything large, it is peculiar to Scotland ; and in one odd phrase, that of *slang-whanger*, to the United States of America. According to to Bartlett's " Dictionary of Americanisms " it signifies political vituperation largely intermingled with *slang* words. It appears, however, in Hood's " Ode to Rae Wilson : "—

No part I take in party fray
With tropes from Billingsgate's *slang-whanging* Tartars.

To which Mr. Bartlett appends the note, " If the word, as is supposed, be of American origin, it has been adopted in the mother country."

This day the Kirk kicks up a stour,
Nae mair the knaves shall wrang her ;
For Heresy is in her power,
And gloriously she'll *whang* her,
Wi' pith this day.
—BURNS : *The Ordination.*

The Glossaries translate *whang*, by beat, belabour ; but it is probably derived from the Teutonic *wanke*, the Flemish *wankelen*, to shake, to totter, to stagger, or cause to shake and stagger.

What ails ye at ? This question signifies, what is the matter with a thing named ? What dislike have you to it ? as to a child that does not eat its breakfast, "*What ails ye at your parritch ?*"

Lord Rutherford having, when on a ramble on the Pentlands, complained to a shepherd of the mist, which prevented him from enjoying the scenery, the shepherd, a tall grim figure, turned sharply round upon him. "*What ails ye at* the mist, sir ? It weets the sod, slockens the yowes, and " —adding with more solemnity—" it is God's wull."—DEAN RAMSAY.

An old servant who took charge of everything in the family, having observed that his master thought that he had drank wine with every lady at the table, but had overlooked one, jogged his memory with the question, "*What ails ye at* her wi' the green gown?"—DEAN RAMSAY.

Whaup, a curlew.

The wild land-fowls are plovers, pigeons, curlews, commonly called *whaups.—Statistical Account of Scotland,* article ORKNEY.

Whaup-nebbit, having a nose like the neb or bill of a curlew.

Wheen, a lot, a small quantity.

What better could be expected o' a *wheen* pock-pudding English folk?— SCOTT : *Rob Roy.*

A young girl (say at St. Andrews) sat upon the cutty stool for breach of the seventh commandment, which applies to adultery as well as to the minor, but still heinous, offence of illicit love, was asked who was the father of her child ? " How can I tell," she replied artlessly, " among a *wheen* o' divinity students ?"—DEAN RAMSAY.

But in my bower there is a wake,
And at the wake there is a *wane ;*
But I'll come to the green wood ere morn.
—*Border Minstrelsy : Erlinton.*

Wane means a number of people, a *wheen folk.*—SIR WALTER SCOTT.

The derivation, which has been much disputed, seems fairly traceable to the Teutonic *weniy*, little or few.

Wheep, a sharp, shrill cry or whistle. *Penny-wheep*, a contemptuous designation for sour, weak, small beer, sold at a penny per quart or pint, and dear at the money ; so called, it is supposed, from its acidity, causing the person who swallows it, thinking it better than it is, to make a kind of whistling sound, expressive of his surprise and disgust. Formed on the same principle as the modern word " penny dreadful," applied to a certain description of cheap and offensive literature. *Wheep* seems to be akin to *whoop*, a shrill cry, and *whaup*, the cry of the curlew or plover.

Be't whisky gill or penny-*wheep*,
  Or ony stronger potion,
It never fails, on drinking deep,
  To kittle up our notion.
          —BURNS : *The Holy Fair.*

Wheeple, the cheep or low cry of a bird ; also, metaphorically, the ineffectual attempt of a man to whistle loudly.

A Scottish gentleman, who visited England for the first time, and ardently desired to return home to his native hills and moors, was asked by his English host to come out into the garden at night to hear the song of the nightingale, a bird unknown in Scotland. His mind was full of home, and he exclaimed, " Na, na ! I wadna gie the *wheeple* o' a whaup (curlew) for a' the nightingales that ever sang."—*Statistical Account of Scotland.*

Wheericken or **queerikens**, a ludicrous term applied to children who are threatened with punishment, signifying the two sides of the breech or podex, the soft place appropriate for " skelping." Apparently derived from the Gaelic *ciùrr*, to hurt, to cause pain.

Whid or **whud**, an untruth, a falsehood, a lie ; usually applied to a departure from veracity which is the result of sudden invention or caprice, rather than of malicious premeditation.

Even ministers they hae been kenn'd,
  In holy rapture,
A rousin' *whid* at times to vend,
  An' nail't wi' Scripture.
    —BURNS : *Death and Dr. Hornbook.*

In the first edition of Burns the word *whid* did not appear, but instead of it—

Even ministers they hae been kenn'd,
  In holy rapture,
Great lies and nonsense baith to vend,
  And nail't wi' Scripture.

This was ungrammatical, as Burns himself recognised it to be, and amended the line by the more emphatic form in which it now appears.

The word *whid* seems, in its primary meaning, to be applied to any sudden and rapid movement, or to a deviation from the straight line. It is akin to the English *scud*. According to Jamieson, to *yed* is to fib, to magnify in narration. This word is probably a variety or hetero-

S

graphy of *whid,* and has the same meaning.

An arrow *whidderan!*
—*The Song of the Outlaw Murray.*

Paitricks scraichin' loud at e'en,
An' mornin' poussie *whiddin* seen.
[Partridges screeching, and the early hare scudding along.]
—BURNS : *To Lapraik.*

Connected with the idea of rapidity of motion are the words *whidder,* a gust of wind ; *whiddie,* a hare ; *whiddy,* unsteady, shifting, unstable ; to *whiddie,* to move rapidly and lightly ; to *twidder* the thumbs, in English twiddle the thumbs. The derivation is uncertain, but is probably from the Teutonic *weit,* the English *wide,* in which sense *whid,* a falsehood, would signify something wide of the truth, and would also apply in the sense of rapid motion through the wideness of space.

Whid, a lie. Bailey has "*whids,* many words"—a cant word, he says. Does not Burns speak of amorous *whids,* meaning, or rather I should say referring to, the quick rapid jumpings about of rabbits? *Whid* certainly has in Scotch the meaning of frisking about; and applied to statements, it is obvious how *whid* could come to mean a lie.—R. DRENNAN.

Whigmaleeries, whims, caprices, crotchets, idle fancies ; also fanciful articles of jewellery and personal adornment, toys and trifles of any kind.

There'll be, if that day come,
I'll wad a boddle,
Some fewer *whigmaleeries* in your noddle.
—BURNS : *The Brigs of Ayr.*

I met ane very fain, honest, fair-spoken, weel-put-on gentleman, or rather burgher, as I think, that was in the *whigmaleerie* man's back-shop.—SCOTT : *Fortunes of Nigel.*

The etymology of this word, which is peculiar to Scotland, is not to be found in any of the current languages of Europe. It is probably from the Gaelic *uige,* a jewel, a precious stone ; from whence *uigheam,* adornment, decoration ; *uigheach,* abounding in precious stones ; and *uigheamaich,* to adorn. These words are the roots of the obsolete English word *owche,* a jewel, used by Shakspeare, Beaumont and Fletcher ; and which also occurs in the authorised version of the Bible :—

Your brooches, pearls, and *owches.*
Henry IV., Part II.

Pearls, bracelets, rings, or *owches,*
Or what she can desire.
—BEAUMONT AND FLETCHER.

The last two syllables of *whigmaleerie* are traceable to *leor* or *leoir,* sufficient, plenty. The quotation from the "Fortunes of Nigel" refers to the jewels in George Heriot's shop. The connection of ideas between the fanciful articles in a jeweller's shop and the fancies or conceits of a capricious mind is sufficiently obvious.

Jamieson notices a game called *whigmaleeries,* "formerly played at drinking-clubs in Angus, at which the losing player was obliged to drink off a glass. Perhaps," he adds, "the game was so denominated out of contempt for the severe austerity attributed to the Whigs!"

"This etymology," says Dr. Adolphus Wagner, "is very doubtful and difficult." Confused by the word *Whig*, and unaware of the Gaelic *uige*, and believing in the drinking bouts alluded to by Jamieson, he endeavours to account for the final syllable, *eerie*, by citing from Ben Jonson, "a leer horse," a led horse, as applicable to a drunkard being led in the train of another! The Gaelic derivation makes an end of the absurdities both of Jamieson and the erudite foreign critic.

Whilie, a little while; pronounced *fylie* in Aberdeenshire. A wee *whilie*, a very little while; *whiles*, at times.

On the Bishop (Skinner) making his appearance, the honest man (a crofter) in the gladness of his heart stepped briskly forward to welcome his pastor, but in his haste stepped upon the rim of the iron riddle, which rebounded with great force against one of his shins. The accident made him suddenly pull up, and instead of completing the reception, he stood vigorously rubbing the injured limb, and, not daring in such a venerable presence to give vent to the customary strong ejaculations, kept twisting his face into all sorts of grimaces. As was natural, the Bishop went forward, uttering the usual formulas of condolence and sympathy, the patient meanwhile continuing his rubbings and his silent but expressive contortions. At last his wife, Janet, came to the rescue, and clapping the Bishop coaxingly on the back, said, "Noo, Bishop, just gang ben to the house, and we'll follow when he's had time to curse a *fylie*; and then, I'se warrant, he'll be weel eneuch."—DEAN RAMSAY.

Whyles she sank, and *whyles* she swam,
    Binnorie, O Binnorie!
Until she cam to the miller's dam,
    By the bonnie mill-dam o' Binnorie.
            —*Border Minstrelsy: The Cruel Sister.*

Whillie-lu, a threnody, a lament, a prolonged strain of melancholy music; but, according to Jamieson, "a dull or flat air." He derives the word from the Icelandic *hvella*, to sound; and *lu*, lassitude. It seems, however, to be a corruption of *waly!* an exclamation of sorrow; as in the beautiful ballad—

O waly! waly! up the bank,
    And waly! waly! down the brae;

which, conjoined with the Gaelic *luaidh* (*dh* silent), a beloved object, makes *whillie-lu*, or *waly lu*. The final syllable *lu* enters into the composition of the English *lullaby*, a cradle-song, from *lu-lu!* beloved one, and *baigh*, sleep, which thus signifies "Sleep, beloved one!" or "Sleep, darling!"

Whillie - wa', to procrastinate; apparently from *while away* the time.

Whillie-whallie, sometimes abbreviated into *whillie-wha'*. This word in all its variations signifies any thing or person connected with cheaters, cajolers, or false pretenders. Jamieson has *whilly* or *whully*, to cheat, to gull; *whillie-whallie*, to coax, to wheedle; *whillie-wha*, one not to be depended upon; *whillie-*

wa, or *whillie-whal*, one who deals in ambiguous promises. In a South Sea song which appears in Allan Ramsay's "Tea-Table Miscellany" occur the lines—

> If ye gang near the South Sea House,
> The *whilly-whas* will grip your gear!

The etymology of all these words is uncertain. The English *wheedle* has been suggested, but does not meet the necessities, while *wheedle* itself requires explanation. *Whillie-whallie*, which appears to be the original form of the word, is probably the Gaelic *uilleadh*, oily, and, metaphorically, specious, as in the English phrase, an *oily* hypocrite, applied to a man with a smooth or specious tongue, which he uses to cajole and deceive, and *balaoch*, in the aspirated form, *bhalaoch*, a fellow. From thence *whillie-whallie*, a specious, cajoling, hypocritical person.

Burns, in "The Whistle," speaks of one of the personages of the ballad as—

> Craigdarroch began with a tongue
> 　　*smooth as oil*,
> Desiring Glenriddel to yield up the
> 　　spoil.

Whilper or **whulper**, any individual or thing of unusual size; akin to the English *whopper* and *whopping*, of which it may possibly be a corruption.

The late Rev. Rowland Hill, preaching a charity sermon in Wapping, appealed to the congregation to contribute liberally. His text was, "Charity covereth a multitude of sins." "I preach," he said, "to

great sinners, to mighty sinners,—ay, and to *whapping* sinners!"—JOE MILLER'S *Jest Book.*

What a *whilper* of a trout I hae gotten! —JAMIESON.

Whinge, to whine; from the Teutonic *winseln*, to whimper.

> If ony Whiggish *whingin'* sot
> 　To blame poor Matthew dare, man,
> May dool and sorrow be his lot,
> 　For Matthew was a rare man.
> —BURNS: *Elegy on Captain Matthew Henderson.*

Whinger, a knife worn on the person, and serviceable as a sword or dagger in a sudden broil or emergency. Jamieson derives it from the Icelandic *hwin*, fununculus, and *gird*, actio; and queries whether it may not mean an escape for secret deeds. The Gaelic *uinich* signifies haste, and *geur*, sharp, whence *uin geur* or *uinich geur*, a sharp weapon for haste. The word is sometimes written *whin-yard*, and is so used in the English poem of "Hudibras," and explained by the commentators as a *hanger* or hanging sword. It is, of course, open to doubt whether *whinger* is not the same as *hanger*, but the Gaelic derivation seems preferable, as expressive of a definite idea, while *hanger* admits of a multiplicity of meanings.

> And *whingers* now in friendship bare,
> The social meal to part and share,
> Had found a bloody sheath.
> —SCOTT: *Lay of the Last Minstrel.*

Mony tyne the half-mark *whinger* for the halfpennie *whang*. [Many lose the sixpenny knife for sake of the halfpenny slice.]—FERGUSON'S *Scots Proverbs.*

Jocteleg was another name for a *whinger*, which, though susceptible of a Gaelic interpretation (see *ante*), perhaps only signified a hunting-knife or dagger, from the Flemish *jacht*, the chase or hunt, and *dolk*, a dagger, pronounced in two syllables, *dol-ok*, a hunting-knife or dagger, a *jacht-dolok* or *jocteleg*. But whether the Gaelic or the Flemish origin of the word be correct, it is clear that Jamieson's derivation from the imaginary cutler, *Jacques de Liege*, is untenable.

Whinner, to dry up, like vegetation in a long-protracted drought. The derivation is uncertain ; probably a corruption of the English *winnow*.

A *whinnerin'* drouth. The word is applied to anything so much dried up, in consequence of extreme drought, as to rustle to the touch. The corn's a *whinnerin'*.—JAMIESON.

Whinner, to snort like a horse, to *whinney ;* French *hennir*, to neigh.

An' goblins *whinnered* through the air Wi' *whorled chaps* (distorted faces or jaws).
—GEORGE BEATTIE : *John o' Arnha'*.

Whipper-snapper, a contemptuous term for a little, presumptuous person, who gives himself airs of importance and talks too much. Jamieson says it "might be deduced from the Icelandic *hwipp*, saltus, celer cursus, and *snapa*, captare escam, as originally denoting one who manifested the greatest alacrity in snatching at a morsel ! " The true derivation seems to be from the Flemish *wippen*, to move about rapidly and restlessly, and *snapper*, to prate, to gabble, to be unnecessarily loquacious.

Whippert, hasty, irascible, impatient ; *whippert-like*, inclining to be ill-tempered without adequate provocation. Jamieson thinks the root of *whippert* is either the Icelandic *whopa*, lightness, inconstancy, or the English *whip*. He does not cite the Flemish *wip*, to shake in the balance, and *wippen*, to move lightly and rapidly as the scales do on the slightest excess of weight over the even balance. Thus *wippert-like* would signify one easily provoked to lose the balance of his temper.

He also cites *whipper tooties*, as silly scruples about doing anything, and derives it from the French *apres tout*, after all. This derivation is worse than puerile. The first word is evidently from the Flemish root ; the second, *tooties*, is not so easily to be accounted for.

Whish, whist, silence, or to keep silence ; whence the name of the well-known game at cards, formerly called quadrille.

Haud your *whish* (*i.e.*, keep silence, or hold your tongue).—SCOTT : *Rob Roy.*

Whisky, whusky, a well-known alcoholic drink, of which the name is derived from the Gaelic *uisge*, water. The liquor is sometimes called in the Highlands *uisge beatha*, the water of life; in Irish Gaelic written *uisque baugh*. The French pay the same complement to brandy, when they call it *eau de vie*.

Whisky tackets, pimples produced on the face by the excessive use of whisky or other spirituous liquors; from *tacket*, a small nail.

Whistle binkie, a musician, harper, fiddler, or piper who played at penny weddings or other social gatherings, and trusted for his remuneration to the generosity of the company. A *whistle* is a somewhat irrevelant name for a pipe, or for music generally, and *binkie* is a bench, a bunker, or seat. It has been supposed that these two words were the etymological roots of the phrase, but this derivation is open to doubt. *Uasal*, the Gaelic for gentle or noble, and *binkie*, a bunker, a seat, was the seat reserved at the weddings of the peasantry for the chief or landlord, who graced the ceremony by his presence when any of his tenants were married, and the place of honour thus appropriated to him was called the *uasal* (corrupted into *whistle*) *binkie*, and the epithet was thence transferred to the hired musician who stepped into it after the laird's departure. The late David Robertson of Glasgow published, in 1847 and 1853, a collection of Scottish songs by then living Scottish poets under this title, of which the contents proved what was previously known, that the genius of Scotsmen, even among the humblest classes, is pre-eminently lyrical, and produces many effusions of great poetical beauty.

Whistle kirk, a term of contempt applied by bigoted Calvinists and Puritans, who object to all music in churches except the human voice, to Episcopalian and other Protestant churches who make use of organs. That noble instrument is a far greater incentive to devotional feeling than the untrained singing, which is often little better than howling or braying of a miscellaneous congregation of old and young people who know nothing of music and have never been taught to sing in unison. A *whistle-kirk* minister is a contemptuous epithet for an Episcopalian clergyman.

Whitter, to move quickly, to talk quickly, to drink quickly a hearty draught. The etymology is uncertain, but is possibly allied to the English *whet*, the Dutch and Flemish *wetten*, the German *wetzen*, to sharpen.

> *Whitterin'* down the stair.
> —JAMIESON.

Syne we'll sit down and tak' our *whitter*
  To cheer our heart,
And faith we'll be acquainted better
  Before we part.
    —BURNS : *Epistle to Lapraik.*

Whittle, a clasp-knife ; to *whittle*, to chip or carve a stick.

A Sheffield *thwittle* bare he in his hose.
    —CHAUCER : *The Reeve's Tale.*

Gudeman, quoth he, put up your *whittle*,
I'm no designed to try its mettle.
    —BURNS : *Death and Doctor Hornbook.*

The word is common in the United States, and was scarcely understood in England until its introduction into humorous literature by Judge Haliburton of Nova Scotia, in the inimitable "Sam Slick, the Clockmaker." According to a ballad quoted by Mr. Bartlett, in his Dictionary of Americanisms, the "Yankie or New Englander will *whittle* or cut his way through the world by some 'cute device or other, in spite of difficulties."

Dexterity with the pocket-knife is part of a Nantucket education. I am inclined to think the propensity is national. Americans must and will *whittle*." — N. P. WILLIS.

Whommle, to turn over clumsily and suddenly, and with a loud noise ; transposition of *whelm.*

Coming to the fire with the said pan and water therein, and casting the water therefrom, and *whommeling* the pan upon the fire, with the pronouncing of these fearful words, " Bones to the fire and soul to the devil !" which accomplished the cure. — *Trial of Alison Nisbet for Witchcraft,* 1632.

Whommle means something different from *whelm*. *Whelm* means to cover over, to immerse ; neither does *whommle* mean to turn over clumsily and suddenly with a loud noise. Not one of these ideas is conveyed by the word itself ; it means literally and really nothing more than to turn upside down.—R. DRENNAN.

Whully, to wheedle, to endeavour, to circumvent by fair words and flattery ; in modern English slang to *carny*. *Wully-wha-ing*, insincere flattery.

My life precious ! exclaimed Meg Dods, nane o' your *wully-wha-ing*, Mr. Bindloose. Diel ane wad miss the auld girning ale wife, Mr. Bindloose, unless it were here and there a poor body, and may be the auld house tyke that wadna be sae weel guided, puir fallow.—SCOTT : *St. Ronan's Well.*

Whulte, a blow or hurt from a fall ; Gaelic *buailte* (aspirated *bhuailte* or *vuailte*), preterite of *buail*, to strike a blow.

Whuppie, a term of angry contumely applied to a girl or woman, signifying that she deserves whipping.

Whurlie - burlie. This Scottish word seems to be the original of the English *hurly - burly*, and signifies rapid circular motion ; from *whorl*, a small wheel; *whirl*, to spin round ; *world*, the earth that rotates or whirls in space around the sun.

Whyles, sometimes, occasionally, now and then.

How best o' chiels are *whyles* in want,
While coofs in countless thousands rant.
    —BURNS : *Epistle to Davie, a Brother Poet.*

Whyles crooning o'er some auld Scotch
sonnet.
       —*Tam o' Shanter.*

I took his body on my back,
And *whiles* I gaed, and *whiles* I sat.
       —*Lament of the Border Widow.*

A lady, visiting the poor, in the West
Port, Edinburgh, not far from the church
established by Dr. Chalmers, asked a poor
woman if she ever attended divine service
there. She replied, " Ou ay ! there's a
man ca'd Chalmers preaches there, and I
whiles gang in to hear him, just to encour-
age him—puir body ! "—Dean Ramsay.

Whylock, or a *wee while*, a little while.

Wi' a blush, as she keepit lookin' roun'
an' roun' for a *whyleock.*—*Noctes Ambrosianæ.*

Widdie, angry contention ; *wid-diefu'*, cross-grained, ill-tem-pered, half-crazy, cantankerous, angry without cause.

The miller was strappin', the miller was
ruddy,
A heart like a lord. and a hue like a lady ;
The laird was a *widdiefu'*, bleerit knurl,—
She's left the gude fellow and taken the
churl.
       —Burns : *Meg o' the Mill.*

Misled by the meaning of *wid-die*, the rope, or gallows, Jamie-son says that, properly *widdie-fu'*, or *widdie-fow*, signifies one who deserves to fill a halter. But as a man may be peevish, morose, irascible, contentious, and unreasonable without de-serving the gallows, the etymo-logy is not satisfactory. The true root seems to be the Flemish *woede*, the German *wuth*, the old English *wode*, the Scottish *wud*—all signifying mad, crazy, unreasonable.

Widdle, to turn, to wheel, to wriggle ; and metaphorically, to struggle ; akin to the English *twiddle*, to turn the thumbs round each other in idle move-ment. *Widdle* is from the Gae-lic *cuidhil*, a wheel.

Hale be your heart, hale be your fiddle,
Lang may your elbuck jink and diddle
To cheer you through the weary *widdle*
       O' worldly cares.
       —Burns : *Epistle to Davie.*

Widdy (sometimes written *woodie* and *wuddie*), the gallows.

The water will nae wrang the *widdy.*

[The English have another ver-sion of this proverb—

He who's born to be hanged will never
be drowned.]

It's nae laughing to girn in a *widdy.*

It's ill speaking o' the *widdy* in the
house o' a man who was hangit.
       —Allan Ramsay's *Scots Proverbs.*

The French have a similar pro-verb—" Il ne faut pas parler de corde dans la maison d'un pendu."

He'll wintle in a *widdie* yet [he'll wriggle in a rope yet, *i.e.*, he'll be hanged].—
Jamieson : *Scots Proverb.*

Her Joe had been a Highland laddie,
But weary fa' the waefu' *woodie.*
       —Burns : *The Jolly Beggars.*

On Donald Caird the doom was stern,
Craig to tether, leg to airn,
But Donald Caird wi' muckle study
Caught the gift to cheat the *wuddie.*
Rings o' airn an' bolts o' steel
Fell like ice frae hand and heel,
Watch the sheep in fauld and glen,
Donald Caird's come again.
       —Sir Walter Scott.

In very primitive times in Scotland the ropes used for hanging those who had offended the chief, or who had rendered themselves amenable to the death penalty, were formed of twisted willow *withes*—whence *withy*, or *widdy*, afterwards came to signify a rope, or, by extension of meaning, the gallows.

Wight, wicht, wichtly, wichty, wichtness. *Wight* remains an English word in mock heroic composition, and means a man, a fellow; originally, a strong or brave man, a sturdy fellow. The Dutch and Flemish *wicht* means a child or a little fellow. *Wight*, in the epithet "Wallace *wight*," given in Scottish poetry and tradition to the great national hero, means "brave Wallace," and was a kind of title of nobility bestowed on him for his prowess, and the patriotic use he made of it.

A *wight* man never wanted a weapon.
—ALLAN RAMSAY.

Wilie-wa', to cajole, to flatter, possibly from *wile away*; from *wile*, to trick, to beguile.

Willie. This suffix answers in meaning to the Latin *volens*, or *volent* in the English words benevolent and malevolent. The Scotch renders the former word by *guid - willie*, or *well - willie ;* from the Flemish *goed willig ;* and the latter by *ill-willie*, in which *ill* is substituted for the Flemish *quad*, or bad. On the same principle of formation, *ill-deedie* signifies nefarious, and *ill-tricky* mischievous, both of which might well become English if they found favour with authors of acknowledged authority.

Willie-winkie, a term of somewhat contemptuous endearment to a diminutive and not over intelligent child. The Jacobites of 1688 to 1715 long applied it to William III., when they did not call him the "Dutchman," "the Hogan Mugan," "Willie the Wag," or "Willie Wanbeard." "The Last Will and Testament of *Willie winkie*," is the title of a once popular Jacobite song.

Wilshoch, wulshoch, changeable of opinion or purpose, a bashful wooer. Jamieson derives the first syllable from the English *will*, and the second from the Anglo - Saxon *seoc aeger*, sick from the indulgence of one's own will. It seems rather to be from the Gaelic *uile*, all, totally; and *seog* (shog), to swing from side to side — whence, metaphorically, one who is continually at variance with his former opinion, and sways from side to side.

Wilt, to shrivel, or begin to decay, as a leaf or flower in the extreme heat or cold—not exactly *withered* in the English sense of the word, inasmuch as a *wilted* leaf may revive, but a withered one cannot. This old Scottish word has been revived in America, where it is in common use. The late Artemus Ward punned upon it, when he said to his lady love, "*Wilt* thou? and she *wilted.*"

Miss Amy pinned a flower to her breast, and when she died, she held the *wilted* fragments in her hand. — JUDD'S *Margaret.*

Wilt, though not admitted into the English dictionaries, is in local use in many northern and eastern counties, and is often pronounced *wilk*, or *wilken*, which seems to have been the original form; from the German, Dutch, and Flemish *welken*, to decay, to droop. Spenser used *welk*, in speaking of the sunset, to describe the fading light of the day.

When ruddy Phoebus 'gins to *welk* in west.—*Faerie Queene.*

Wimple, to flow gently like a brook, to meander, to purl.

Among the bonnie winding banks, Where Doon rins *wimplin'* clear. —BURNS: *Hallowe'en.*

Win, this word in English signifies to gain, to make a profit, to acquire; but in the Scottish language it has many other and more extended meanings, such as to reach, to attain, to arrive, to get at. It enters into the composition of a great number of compound words and phrases, such as—to *win above*, to surmount; to *win about*, to circumvent; to *win awa*, to escape, and,

poetically, to die, or escape from life; to *win forret*, to advance, to get on; to *win owre*, to get over, to cajole; to *win past*, to overtake, or get by; to *win free*, to get loose; to *win hame*, to get home; to *win aff*, to get off, or away, to be acquitted on a trial; to *win ben*, to be admitted to the house; to *win up*, to arise, or get up.

Win and tine, a man able to *win and tine*, is a man of substance and energy, able to win and able to lose without hurting himself, and to whom winnings and losings are alike of little consequence.

Winnock, a window corner; abridged from window-*nook*. *Winnock-bunker*, a seat, ledge, or bench at the window.

A *winnock-bunker* in the east, Where sat Auld Nick in shape o' beast ; A towsie tyke, black, grim, and large, To gie them music was his charge. —BURNS : *Tam o'Shanter.*

Winsome. This pleasant Scottish word is gradually making good its claim to a place in recognised English. The etymology is undecided whether it be from *win*, to gain, or the Teutonic *wonne*, joy, pleasure, or delight.

I gat your letter, *winsome* Willie. —BURNS.

She is a *winsome* wee thing, She is a bonnie wee thing, This sweet wee wife o' mine. —BURNS.

Wintle, a corruption of *windle*, to gyrate, to turn round in the wind; also, to reel, to stagger, to walk unsteadily; also, to wriggle, to writhe, to struggle.

Thieves of every rank and station,
From him that wears the star and garter,
To him that *wintles* in a halter.
—BURNS : *To J. Rankine.*

He'll *wintle* in a widdie yet.
—JAMIESON.

Winze, an oath, a curse, an imprecation, an evil wish; from the Flemish *wensch*, a wish, which, conjoined with the prefix *ver*, became *verwenschen*, to curse, to wish evil.

He taks a swirlie auld moss-oak
For some black gruesome carline,
And loot a *winze*, and drew a stroke.
—BURNS : *Hallowe'en.*

Wirry-cow, a bugbear, a goblin, or frightful object, a ghost; the devil; also a scarecrow.

Draggled sae 'mang muck and stanes,
They looked like *wirry-cows*.
—ALLAN RAMSAY.

The word was used by Scott, in " Guy Mannering," and is derived by Jamieson from the English " worry," and " to cow." *Wirry*, however, seems to be a corruption of the Gaelic *uruisg*, which, according to Armstrong's Gaelic Dictionary, signified a " brownie," or goblin, who was supposed to haunt lonely dells, lakes, and waterfalls, and who could only be seen by those who had the " second sight." Ruddiman thought that the *uruisg* was called a "brownie" in the Lowlands, on account of the brown colour of the long hair which covered his body when he appeared to human eyes ; but it is more probable that " brownie " was derived from the Gaelic *bròn*, sorrow or calamity. The attributes ascribed to the *uruisg* are similar to those of the " lubber fiend " of Milton.

The final syllable of wirry-*cow* was sometimes written and pronounced *carl*, a fellow. According to Jamieson, *cow*, or *kow*, signified a hobgoblin, and to " play the *kow*," was to act the part of a goblin, to frighten fools and children.

Wisp, to currycomb a horse, or rub it with a *wisp* of straw.

A short horse is sune *wispit* (*i.e.*, a little job is soon done).—*Old Proverb.*

Wissel, to exchange. *Wissler*, a money-changer ; from the Flemish *wissel*, and *geld wisselaar*, a money-changer ; the German *wechsel*. To *wissel* words, is to exchange words ; usually employed in an angry sense, as in the English phrase, to " bandy words with one," the irritation preceding a quarrel.

Withershins, backwards, against the course of the sun. To pass the bottle *withershins*, or the wrong way, at table, is considered a breach of social etiquette. The word seems to be derived from the Teutonic *wider*, contrary, and *sonne*, the sun ;

or perhaps from *wider*, and *sinn*, sense ; whence it would signify, in a " contrary sense." The word *wider*, corrupted in the Scotch into *wither*, enters into the composition of many German words, such as *wider-spruch*, contradiction ; *wider-sinn*, nonsense ; *wider-stand*, resistance.

The ancient Druids called a movement contrary to the course of the sun, *car-tual.* On this subject, apropos of the word *withershins*, a curious note appears in Armstrong's Gaelic Dictionary. "The Druids," he says, " on certain occasions moved three times round the stone circles, which formed their temples. In performing this ceremony, *car-deise*, they kept the circle on the right, and consequently moved from east to west. This was called the prosperous course ; but the *car-tual*, or moving with the circle on the left, was deemed fatal or unprosperous, as being " contrary to the course of the sun."

The said Alison past thrice *withershins* about the bed, muttering out certain charms in unknown words. — *Trial of Alison Nisbet for Witchcraft*, 1632.

To be whipped round a circle *withershins*, or *car-tual*, would thus be considered peculiarly degrading, and probably, as the meaning of Gaelic words was perverted by the Saxon-speaking people, was the origin of the phrase, "to be whipped at the cart's tail."—*Gaelic Etymology of the Languages of Western Europe.*

Witter, to struggle, to fight, to strive in enmity ; from the Teu-

tonic *wider*, against, contrary to ; *wider-sacher*, an antagonist ; *wider-sprechen*, to contradict ; Flemish *weder-partij*, an adversary, an opposing party.

To struggle in whatever way,—often for a subsistence ; as, "I'm *witterin* awa'." A *witterin body* is one who is struggling with poverty or difficulty.—JAMIESON.

Wittering, a proof.

And that was to be a *wittering* true,
That maiden she had gane.
—*Border Minstrelsy: The Broomfield Hill.*

Witterly, knowingly, wittingly ; to do a thing *witterly*, to act on good information, or with full knowledge ; to *witter*, to inform, and also to prognosticate.

Wod or **wud**, stark mad, raging mad ; old English *wode*, *wuth*, and *wouth ;* Dutch and Flemish *woode ;* German *wuth.*

Ye haud a stick in the *wod* man's e'e, *i.e.*, you hold a stick in the mad man's eyes, or you continue to provoke one already enraged.—JAMIESON.

When neebors anger at a plea,
And just as *wud* as *wud* can be,
How easy can the barley bree
Cement the quarrel.
—BURNS : *Scotch Drink.*

The wife was *wud*, and out o' her wit,
She couldna gang, nor could she sit ;
But aye she cursed and banned.
—*The Gaberlunzie Man.*

Won, to dwell, to reside, to inhabit. *Woning*, a dwelling-place. From the German *wohnen*, and *wohnung ;* Dutch and Flemish *wonen*, to dwell ; *wonen-huis*, a dwelling-house, a lodging.

There's auld Rab Morris that *wons* in
   the glen,
The king o' guid fellows, and wale o'
   auld men.
                          —BURNS.

Wonner, wonder; applied in contempt to any odd, decrepit, or
despicable creature.

Our whipper-in, wee, blastit *wonner.*
        —BURNS : *The Twa Dogs.*

Wont to be, a phrase applied to
any ancient or obsolete custom
or observance, a thing that used
to be or was *wont to be* in olden
time.

Mony *wont-to be's,* nae doubt,
An' customs we ken nought about.
—JAMIESON : *The Piper o' Peebles.*

Wooer-bab. It was formerly the
custom among the young men
and lads of the rural population
in the Highlands and Lowlands
of Scotland to wear bows of ribbons of flaunting colours in their
garters on high days and holi-
days, when they expected to
meet the lasses, and to dance or
flirt with them.

The lasses' feet are cleanly neat,
   Mair braw than when they're fine,
Their faces blythe fu' sweetly kythe,
   Hearts leal an' warm an' kind ;
The lads sae trig wi' *wooer-babs*
   Weel knotted on their garten,
Some unco blate, and some wi' gabs
Gar lasses' hearts gang startin'.
        —BURNS : *Hallowe'en.*

"*Bab,*" says Dr. Adolphus
Wagner, the German editor of
Burns, "seems akin to the English *bob,* something that hangs
so as to play loose, and is a
tassel or knot of ribbons, or the
loose ends of such a knot." The
English word *bob,* in this sense,
is a corruption of the Gaelic
bab, a fringe ; and *babag,* a little
fringe. Perhaps the English
phrase, "tag, rag, and *bobtail,*"
is from the same source, and
bobtail may signify the ragged
fringe of a frayed outer garment, *bobbing* or dangling loose
in the wind.

Wool or **oo'**. English ; from the
German and Flemish *woll ;* in
Scottish parlance, *oo'*. *A' oo'*,
all wool ; *a' ae oo',* all one wool ;
ay, a' ae oo', yes, all one wool.
There is a popular proverb which
formerly ran—

        Much cry and little *oo'*,

to which some humorist added—

As the Deil said when he shear'd the sow.

   The addendum was at once
adopted by the people, though
some strict philologists remain of the opinion that the
first line is complete in itself,
and that " cry " does not signify
the noise or uproar of the animal, but is a corruption either
of the Gaelic *graidh,* or *graigh*
(*gry*), a flock, a herd, or *cruidh,*
which has the same meaning,
and signifies a large flock that
yields but little wool. However this may be, the idea in
the lengthened proverb has a
grotesque humour about it,
which insures its popularity.

Wooster, a wooer, a lover, a
sweetheart.

Wooster-tryste, a lonely meeting.

> At kirk she was the auld folks' love,
> At dance she was the laddies' e'en,
> She was the blythest o' the blythe,
> At *wooster-trystes* on Hallowe'en.
> —ALLAN CUNNINGHAM : CROMEK'S
> *Remains of Nithsdale and Gal-*
> *loway Song.*

Word. " To get the *word* of,"
i.e., to get the character, or the
repute, of being so and so.
" She gets the *word* o' being a
licht-headed quean," *i.e.*, the
character of being a light-
headed or frivolous woman.

Worl, wurl, wroul, wirr. All
these words of a common origin
express the idea of smallness,
or dwarfishness, combined with
perversity, disagreeableness, and
ill-nature. Jamieson has *wurlie*,
contemptibly small in size; a
wurlie body, an ill-grown person ; *wurlin*, a child or beast
that is unthriven ; *wurr*, to snarl
like a dog ; *wirr*, a peevish and
crabbed dwarf ; *wurr*, to be
habitually complaining or snarling ; and a *wurlie* rung, a knotted stick. He suggests that
wirr and *wurr* are corruptions of
were-wolf, the man-wolf of popular superstition—one afflicted
with the disease called lycan-
thropy, in which the unhappy
victim imagines himself to be a
wolf, and imitates the howlings
of that animal. The true etymology is uncertain. Perhaps
all these words are derivable
from the Teutonic *quer*, oblique,
athwart, perverse—the origin of
the English *queer, quirk,* and

quirky. Jamieson has also *wurp*,
a fretful, peevish person ; and
wurpit, afflicted with fretfulness.
These latter seem akin to the
Gaelic *uipear*, a clown, a churl,
a bungler ; and *uipearach*, ill-
tempered, churlish.

Worry, to vex, to torment. In
some parts of Scotland it signifies to strangle, to choke, or
to be suffocated. *Worry carl*, a
troublesome fellow, or ill-
natured churl, who vexes both
himself and others. Possibly
from the Gaelic *uaire*, stormy.
(See WIRRY-COW, *ante.*)

Wow ! an exclamation of surprise
or wonder, without etymology.
as exclamations usually are.

> A fine fat fodgel wight,
> Of stature short, but genius bright,
>   That's he ! mark weel !
> And *wow !* he has an unco slight
>   O' cauk and keel !
>   —BURNS : *On Captain Grose.*

> And *wow !* but my heart dances boundin
>   and licht,
> And my bosom beats blythesome and
>   cheery.
>   —JAMES BALLANTINE : *The Gloamin'*
>   *Hour.*

Wowf, partially deranged. The
Scottish language is particularly
rich in words expressive of the
various shades of madness and
insanity ; such as *wud*, raging,
or stark staring mad ; *daft*,
slightly deranged ; *gyte, cranky,*
subject to abberrations of intellect on particular points ; *doited*,
stupidly deranged—all which
words are in addition to, and

not in supercession of the English words, *mad, idiotic, lunatic, crazy,* &c.

It is very odd how Allan, who, between ourselves, is a little *wowf,* seems at times to have more sense than all of us put together.—SCOTT: *Tales of My Landlord.*

Wrack, to break in pieces, to *wreck.* In English the phrase "*wrack* and ruin" is more often used than "*wreck* and ruin;" from the same source as *wreak,* to act, do, or perform a deed of anger; to *wreck* spite or vengeance. It is possibly of the same origin as the Teutonic *werken,* the English *work,* employed in the sense of destroying rather than of creating or constructing.

Oh, roaring Clyde, ye roar o'er loud,
  Your stream is wondrous strong;
Make me your *wrack* as I come back,
  But spare me as I gang.
—JOHNSON'S *Musical Museum: Willie and May Margaret.*

Wraith, an apparition in his own likeness that becomes visible to a person about to die; a water-spirit.

He held him for some fleeting *wraith,*
And not a man of blood or breath.
              —SIR WALTER SCOTT.

By this the storm grew loud apace,
  The *water-wraith* was shrieking,
And in the scowl of heaven each face
  Grew dark as they were speaking.
              —THOMAS CAMPBELL.

The etymology of this word is uncertain. Some suppose it to be derived from *wrath,* or a wrathful spirit, summoning to doom. Jamieson is of opinion that it is from the same root as *weird,* fate or destiny, or the Anglo-Saxon *weard* or *ward,* a guardian, a keeper, and thence a fairy, a guardian angel. This derivation is scarcely tenable; that from *breith,* doom or judgment, aspirated as *bhreith,* is more probable, as the apparition of the *wraith* is always supposed to forebode the doom of the person who sees it.

Wrang, English *wrong.* The etymology of this word has been much disputed; but it seems to be from *wring,* to twist, and *wrung,* twisted or distorted from the right line. *Wrang* in Scottish parlance sometimes signifies deranged—out of the right line of reason. "He's a' *wrang,*" *i.e.,* he is demented. *Wrang-wise* is a wrong manner; the opposite of the English *right-wise* or righteous.

Writer, an attorney. *Writer to the Signet,* a solicitor licensed to conduct cases in the superior courts.

Wroul, an ill-formed or diminutive child; a name originally applied to one who was supposed to have been changed in its cradle by malicious fairies; a *changeling.* Jamieson refers to *wer-wolf,* a man supposed to be transformed into a wolf, called by the French a *loup-garou,* but this is evidently not the true derivation, which is more probably from the Dutch and Flemish *ruil*, to exchange.

Wud-scud, a wild scamper, a panic, called by the Americans a *stampede ;* from *wud*, mad, and *scud*, to run precipitately and in confusion. The word is sometimes applied to an over-restive or over-frolicsome boy or girl, whom it is difficult to keep quiet.

Wudspur, a Scottish synonym for the English *Hotspur*, wild, reckless, one who rides in hot haste ; from the Flemish *woete*, German *wuth*, old English *wode* and *spur*. It is difficult to decide which of the two words was the original epithet, and whether *wood-spur* in Scottish parlance was, or was not, anterior in usage to the *Hotspur* of the great poet.

> There was a wild gallant among us a',
> His name was Watty wi' the *wudspur*.
> —*Border Minstrelsy : Ballad of Jamie Telfer.*

Wyg to wa'. "A thing," says Jamieson, "is said to gang frae *wyg to wa*', when it is moved backwards and forwards from the one wall of a house to the other." He suggests that *wyg* is but another name for wall, and that the phrase signifies really "from wall to wall." It is more probable that *wyg* is but a misspelling of the Gaelic *uig*, a corner.

Wyte, to blame, to reproach The etymology is derived by Jamieson from the Anglo-Saxon *witan*, to know, and the Gothic *wita*, to impute. But the root of the word is the Flemish *wyten*, to blame, to reproach.

> Ane does the skaith, and
> Another gets the *wyte*.
> —ALLAN RAMSAY'S *Scots Proverbs.*

> Many *wyte* their wives
> For their ain thriftless lives.
> *Idem.*

> Alas ! that every man has reason
> To *wyte* his countrymen wi' treason.
> —BURNS : *Scotch Drink.*

"Dame ! deem warily ! Ye watna wha *wytes* yoursel."—*Old Proverb.* (A warning to a censorious or tattling woman to beware of scandal, lest she herself should be scandalised.)

This was an English word in the time of Chaucer, but has long been obsolete except in Scotland.

Wyter, one who blames ; an accuser.

Wyteworthy, blameable, blameworthy.

Y

Yald, sprightly, active, nimble, alert ; *yald-cuted* (erroneously spelled *yaul-cuted* in Jamieson), nimble-footed ; from *yald*, nimble, and *cute*, an ankle.

Being *yald* and stout, he wheel'd about,
And clove his head in twain.
—Hogg's *Mountain Bard.*

Yammer, yaumer, to lament, to complain ; from the Flemish *jammer*, lamentation ; *jammern*, to complain or lament ; *jammervoll*, lamentable.

Fareweel to the bodies that *yammer* and mourn.
—Herd's *Collection of Scottish Songs,*
    Bide ye Yet.

We winna, shauna, *yaumerin'* yirn
Though Fortune's freaks we dree.
    —*Whistle Binkie.*

In Lancashire and the North of England *yammer* is used in another sense, that of yearning or desiring ardently.

I *yammer'd* to hear now how things turned out.
—Tim Bobbin : *Lancashire Dialect.*

And the worm *yammers* for us in the ground.
    —Waugh's *Lancashire Songs.*

Yankee, an inhabitant of Massachusetts, Rhode Island, Vermont, Connecticut, New Hampshire, and Maine, the six New England States of the American Union. The etymology of the Scottish word has not been ascertained. *Jank* (pronounced *yank*) in Dutch and Flemish, signifies to cry out lustily, and *junger*, in German, is a young man, the English *younker ;* but neither of these words can account for *yankie*, either in the Scottish or American sense. Danish and Swedish afford no clue. In provincial English, *yanks* are a species of leather gaiters worn by agricultural labourers, which, according to Halliwell, were once called "Bow Yankies." But this cannot be accepted as the origin, unless on the supposition that at the time of the emigration of the first colonists to America, the term signified not only leather gaiters, but those who wore them. This epithet is often erroneously applied in England to all Americans, though it is repudiated by the people of the Middle, Southern, and Western States. It is supposed to be a mispronunciation of *English* by the aboriginal Indian tribes, on the first colonisation of the Continent. Much controversy has arisen on the subject, which still remains undecided. No one, however, has hitherto remarked that the Scottish vernacular supplies the words *yank*, *yanking*, which signify a smart

T

stroke ; *yanker,* an incessant speaker, and also a great falsehood ; *yanking,* active, pushing, speculative, enterprising. It is not insisted that this is the correct etymology, but if it be only a coincidence it merits consideration. No true New Englander would dissent from it for any other than philological reasons, in which it is certainly vulnerable, though on moral grounds it is all but unassailable.

Yap, yappish, sometimes written *yaup*, hungry, eager, brisk covetous.

> Right *yap* she yoked to the ready feast,
> And lay and ate a full half-hour at least.
> —Ross's *Helenore.*

This word is probably derived from the Gaelic *gab* or *gob*, the mouth—whence by extension of meaning, an open mouth, craving to be filled. The English word *gape*, to yawn, or open the mouth wide, is from the same root. The eminent tragedian, Philip Kemble, always pronounced *gape* as *gahp*, not *gaipe*, and the late W. C. Macready followed his example. Jamieson travels very far north to find the derivation in the Icelandic *gypa*, vorax.

> Although her wame was toom and she grown *yap.*
> —Ross's *Helenore.*

> Though bairns may pu' when *yap* or drouthy
> A neep or bean to taste their mouthy.
> .   .   .   .   .   .
> But a' the neeps and a' the beans,
> The hips, the haws, the slaes, the geens,

> That e'er were pu'd by hungry weans
>   Could ne'er be missed,
> By lairds like you, wi' ample means
>   In bank and kist.
> —JAMES BALLANTINE : *To the Laird of Blackford Hill.*

> Now hell's black table-cloth was spread,
> The infernal grace was duly said ;
> *Yap* stood the hungry fiends a' owre it,
> Their grim jaws aching to devour it.
> —*Jacobite Songs and Ballads : Cumberland's Descent into Hell.*

At that moment *yap* as ever.—*Noctes Ambrosianæ.*

Yare, a word still used by sailors, but obsolete in literature, signifying ready, alert, heedful, or in a state of readiness ; used by Shakspeare and the writers of his time.

> Our ship is tight and *yare.*
> —*Tempest,* act v. scene 1.

If you have occasion to use me for your own turn, you shall find me *yare.*—*Measure for Measure,* act iv. scene 2.

Be *yare* in thy preparations, for thy assailant is quick, skilful, and deadly.—SHAKSPEARE : *Twelfth Night.*

Nares derives it from the Saxon *gearwe,* paratus ; but the real root seems to be the Celtic *aire,* heed, attention, alertness, readiness for action or duty ; as in the modern Gaelic phrase, "Thoir an *aire,*" pay attention, be on the alert ; be *yare !* allied to the French *gare !* and the English *beware !*

Yark, to smite suddenly, forcibly, and aimlessly ; possibly a corruption of *jerk.*

> He swat an' *yarkit* wi' his hammer,
> The sparks flew frae the steel like glamour.
> —BEATTIE : *John o' Arnha'.*

Yatter (a corruption of the English *chatter*), to talk idly and incessantly; also, to complain querulously, and without reason. " She's a weary *yatter*," *i.e.*, she's a tedious and wearisome gossip. *Yatter* also signifies a confused mass or heap, and is synonymous with *hatter*. (See *ante*, p. 841.)

Yaud or "far yaud!" an interjection or call by a shepherd to his dog, to direct his attention to sheep that have strayed, and that are far in the distance. *Yaud*, in this sense, as cited by Jamieson, seems to be a mispronunciation or misprint of *yont!* or *yonder*.

Yeld, or **yell**, barren, unfruitful. In Galloway, according to Jamieson, *yald* signifies *niggardly*. The etymology is uncertain, though supposed to be a corruption of *geld*, to castrate, to render unproductive.

A *yeld* soil, flinty or barren soil. A cow, although with calf, is said to gang *yeld* when the milk dries up. A *yeld* nurse is a dry nurse. Applied metaphorically to broth without flesh meat in it (soupe-maigre).—JAMIESON.

A *yeld* sow was never good to grices [*i.e.*, a barren sow was never good to little pigs, or, a barren stepmother to the children of her husband by a previous wife.]—ALLAN RAMSAY's *Scots Proverbs*.

Thence country wives, in toil and pain,
May plunge and plunge the kirn in vain,
For oh, your yellow treasure's ta'en .
     By witching skill,
And dawtit, twal-pint Hawkie's gaen
     As *yell's* the bull.
          —BURNS : *Address to the Deil.*

Yerk, a smart blow; *yerker*, a very smart and knock down blow; supposed to be a corruption of *jerk*, with which, however, it is not synonymous.

There's news, news, gallant news,
There's gallant news o' tartan trews,
    An' red Clanranald's men, Joe ;
There has been blinking on the bent,
    An' flashing on the fell, Joe,
The redcoat sparks hae got the *jerks*,
    But carle daurna tell, Joe.
—*Jacobite Relics : Clanranald's Men.*

Yestreen, last night, or *yesterday* evening. *Yester*, both in English and Scotch, was used as a prefix to signify time past ; as *yester*-year, *yester*-month, *yester*-week; but in English its use has in modern times been restricted to day and night ; and, by a strange surplusage of words, to yesterday night instead of *yester* night, and yesterday morning instead of *yester* morn. In Scotland, its use is more extended, and *yestereen* or *yestreen*, *yesternoon*, *yesternight*, are employed alike in poetic style and in everyday conversation. The word is from the German *gestern* (*g* pronounced as *y*) and the Flemish *gistern*.

I saw the new moon late *yestreen*,
    Wi' the auld moon in her arm,
And if we gang to sea, master,
    I fear we'll come to harm.
          —SIR PATRICK SPENS : *Border Minstrelsy.*

I gaed a waefu' gate *yestreen*,
    A gate I fear I'll sairly rue,
I gat my death frae twa sweet e'en,
    Twa sparklin' e'en o' bonnie blue.
          —BURNS.

The derivation of the Teutonic *gestern* and *gistern* is probably from the Gaelic *aosda*, aged or old; so that *yesterday*, in contradiction to *this* day, or the new day, would signify the old day, the day that is past. Latin *hesternus.*

Yethar, a willow-wythe; also, a blow with a switch; probably a corruption of *wyther*, a stroke with a wythe.

Yevey, greedy, voracious, clamorous for food. Of doubtful etymology, though possibly from the Gaelic *eibh* (*ēv*), to clamour.

Yill, ale or beer.

> A cogie o' *yill*
> And a pickle oatmeal,
> An' a dainty wee drappie o' whisky—
> An' hey for the cogie,
> An' hey for the *yill*,
> Gin ye steer a' thegither, they'll do unco weel.
> —*A Cogie o' Yill*, 1787.

Yird-fast or **earth-fast**, a stone well sunken in the earth, or a tree fast rooted in the ground.

The axe he bears it hacks and tears,
'Tis formed of an *earth-fast* flint;
No armour of knight, though ever so wight,
Can bear its deadly dint.
—*Minstrelsy of the Scottish Border:*
LEYDEN —*The Count of Keeldar.*

A *yird-fast* or insulated stone, enclosed in a bed of earth, is supposed to possess peculiar properties. Its blow is reckoned uncommonly severe.—SIR WALTER SCOTT.

Yirr, the growl of a dog, English *gurr*. *Gurl*, growl; *gern*, to grin or snarl with ill-nature or anger.

Yoak, to look, to look at; possibly from the German *aug*, the Flemish *oog*, the Latin *oculus*, the eye; the English *ogle*, to look at.

Yoak your *orlitch* [horloge]. Look at your watch [or clock].—JAMIESON.

Yon. The use of *yon* and *thon*, in the sense of *that*, is much more common in Scotland than in England; as in the phrase, "Do ye ken *yon* man?" do you know that man. It is also used for yonder; as, *yon* hill, for yonder hill. It is sometimes pronounced and written *thon ;* as in the following anecdote of a wilful child, narrated by Dean Ramsay:—

When he found every one getting soup and himself omitted, he demanded soup, and said, "If I dinna get it, I'll tell *thon*." Soup was given him. At last, when it came to wine, his mother stood firm and positively refused. He then became more vociferous than ever about telling *thon ;* and as he was again refused, he again declared, "Now, I'll tell *thon*," and roared out, "Ma new breeks were made out o' the auld curtains!"

Yorlin, a small bird, more commonly known in England as the "yellow hammer." Scottish and English boys have a traditional prejudice against this bird, for some imaginary reason, or no reason at all. It sometimes reads in the old rhyme:—

> Yellow, yellow *yorling*,
> You are the devil's darling.

Yorne, prepared, made ready; part participle of *yare* ready, or to make ready.

To Norroway, to Norroway,
  To Norroway o'er the faern,
The king's daughter o' Norroway,
  'Tis we maun bring her hame ;
Ye'll eat and drink, my merry men a',
  An' see ye be weel *yorne,*
For blaw it weet, or blaw it sleet,
  Our gude ship sails the morn.

Mr. Robert Chambers, in his Collection of Scots Ballads, 1829, prints *thorne* instead of *yorne,* without note or comment, or apparent knowledge of the unmeaning word.

Youk or **yeuk**, to itch ; *yowky,* itchy. From the Teutonic *jucken,* pronounced *yucken.*

Your neck's *youkin'* for a St. Johnstone ribbon. — ALLAN RAMSAY'S *Scots Proverbs.*

(A taunt, implying that a man's career and character is such as to merit hanging, and that he is nearly ready for it. St. Johnstone, now Perth, was the assize city. A ribbon signified the rope.)

How daddie Burke the plea was cookin',
If Warren Hastings' neck was *yeukin.*
  —BURNS : *To a Gentleman who Promised him a Newspaper.*

Thy auld darned elbow *yeuks* with joy.
  —BURNS : *To Colonel de Peyster.*

A parishioner in an Ayrshire village, meeting the minister, who had just returned after long absence on account of ill health, congratulated him on his convalescence, and added, anticipatory of the pleasure he would have in hearing him preach again— " Eh, sir ! I'm unco *yuckie* to hear a blaud o' your gab."—DEAN RAMSAY.

Youllie, a name formerly given to the police in Edinburgh by idle boys or bad characters. " A

low term," says Jamieson, "probably formed from the *yowling* or calling out." Was it not rather formed from the Gaelic *uallach,* proud, haughty, arrogant, and given to the police derisively by the blackguards of the streets when, as they thought, they were interfered with unnecessarily, or ordered to move on ? Or it may be from *yoly,* the French *jo'i,* pretty or handsome, used contemptuously, as in the phrase, "my fine fellow."

Yowe, a ewe, a female sheep, a lamb ; *yowie,* a eye lamb.

Ca' the *yowes* to the knowes [hills],
Ca' them where the heather grows,
Ca' them where the burnie rowes,
  My bonnie dearie.
                    —BURNS.

An' neist my *yowie,* silly thing,
Gude keep her frae a tether string.
  —BURNS : *Poor Mailie.*

Yowf, to strike hard and suddenly, as the ball is struck at the favourite Scottish game of golf. The common pronunciation of *golf* is *gowf,* and *yowf* is probably, as Jamieson alleges, a corruption of that word.

But had we met wi' Cumberland
On Athol's braes or yonder strand,
The blood o' a' his savage band
  Had dyed the German Sea, man.

An' cousin Geordie up the gate
We wad hae *yowf'd* frae Charlie's seat,
And sent him hame to bide in state,
  In's native Germanie, man.
—*Jacobite Minstrelsy : Bauldie Travers' Lament for Culloden.*

Yowff, to bark in a suppressed or feeble manner ; said of a dog who is not very earnest in his displeasure.

Ye puir creature you! what needs ye *yowff* when the big dog barks?—*Laird of Logan.*

Yowl, to howl, or whine as a dog; sometimes written *gowl;* from the Gaelic *guil,* or *gul,* to lament.

And darkness covered a' the ha',
  Where they sat at their meat,
The gray dogs *yowling* left their food,
  And crept to Henrie's feet.
    —*Border Minstrelsy : King Henry.*

Yule. *Yule* was a Druidical festival in honour of the sun, celebrated at the winter solstice, in ages long anterior to the Christian era.

Yule, about the etymology of which there has been much controversy, was probably named in honour of the sun—the source of all heat and life upon this globe; from *uile,* all, the whole, whence, by extension of meaning, the whole year, ending at what we now call Christmas, and which in early times signified completion, the full turn of the wheel of the year. The Gaelic *cuidhil,* a wheel, has also

been suggested as the true root of the word; while *iul,* guidance, knowledge, has found favour with other etymologists, because on that day the assembled Druids, in their groves or in their stone circles, laid down rules for the guidance of the people during the coming year. *Iul oidche,* or the guide of night, was a name applied by Ossian to the Polar star. The French *noel,* and old English *nowell,* names for Christmas or *Yule,* are from the Gaelic *naomh,* holy, and *là,* a day. Jamieson, in citing the northern appellation for Odin as *iul-fader,* is in error in translating it as the father of *Yule,* or Christmas, instead of "All-Father," or father of all, which was an epithet applied to the sun as the Father of Light and Life.

Langer lasts year than *yule.*—ALLAN RAMSAY's *Scots Proverbs.*

Duncan Gray cam' here to woo
On blythe *yule* night when we were fu'.
    —BURNS : *Duncan Gray.*

Yurn, coagulate, churn, curdle.

And syne he set the milk ower het,
  And sorrow a spark of it wad *yurne.*
    —*The Wife of Auchtermuchty.*